"A Defense Weapon Known to Be of Value"

"A Defense Weapon Known to Be of Value"

Servicewomen of the Korean War Era

Linda Witt, Judith Bellafaire, Britta Granrud, and Mary Jo Binker

University Press of New England
HANOVER AND LONDON

IN ASSOCIATION WITH THE MILITARY WOMEN'S PRESS
OF THE WOMEN IN MILITARY SERVICE FOR AMERICA
MEMORIAL FOUNDATION, ARLINGTON, VIRGINIA

Published by University Press of New England.
One Court Street, Lebanon, NH 03766
In association with the Military Women's Press of the Women In Military Service For
America Memorial Foundation
www.upne.com
© 2005 by Women in Military Service For America Memorial Foundation, Inc.
Printed in the United States of America

5 4 3 2 1

Library of Congress Cataloging-in-Publication Data
A defense weapon known to be of value : servicewomen of the Korean War era /
Linda Witt, Judith Bellafaire, Britta Granrud, and Mary Jo Binker.—1st ed.
     p.   cm.
"Published in association with the Military Women's Press of the Women in
Military Service For America Memorial Foundation, Arlington, Virginia."
Includes bibliographical references and index.
ISBN 1–58465–471–6 (cloth : alk. paper) — ISBN 1–58465–472–4 (pbk. : alk. paper)
1. Korean War, 1950–1953—Women. [1. United States—Armed Forces—Women—
History. 2. Women and the military—United States—History.] I. Witt, Linda.
DS921.5.W64D44 2005
951.904'2'0820973—dc22   2005004389

CONTENTS

PREFACE   vii

Introduction   I

Chapter 1:   Women's Place—and the Servicewoman's Place—
             in Post–World War II America   13

Chapter 2:   Servicewomen's Integration: "Prayerful Assumption"
             versus "Prevailing Ambivalence"   31

Chapter 3:   Recruiting and Retaining "America's Finest Women"   65

Chapter 4:   Fitting Servicewomen In: Finding "Proper
             Employment for Sisters and Girlfriends"   88

Chapter 5:   A "Woman Imperative"?—Military Necessity Erodes
             Old Barriers   117

Chapter 6:   "Needed in Cadre"—Providing Support Around
             the World   141

Chapter 7:   The Nurses in Korea—Under Fire and on the Move   169

Chapter 8:   Recurring Issues Relating to Military Women   220

Conclusion: "The Old Dividing Line"   244

NOTES   255

INDEX   299

On cloudless days, words slide with the sun across the walls of the Women's Memorial at the ceremonial entrance to Arlington National Cemetery. Etched on the glass ceiling above—an actual, not just symbolic, glass ceiling—each phrase celebrates the contributions of women who served in or alongside the nation's military since before the American Revolution. The quotes also include a plea, written by a World War II Army nurse who served in the China-Burma-India Theater and left colleagues behind— buried in a camellia grove. "Let the generations know that women in uniform also guaranteed their freedom," she wrote. "That our resolve was just as great as the brave men who stood among us. And with victory our hearts were just as full and beat just as fast—that the tears fell just as hard for those we left behind."

This book is our attempt to let generations know of yet another era's military women: those who served in what has been called "the forgotten war," Korea, and the other uniformed women who helped support that war and the burgeoning Cold War in places as far-flung as the Pacific atoll of Kwajalein, the many bases in still-occupied postwar Germany and Japan, and lonely, isolated postings such as Great Falls, Montana. We also honor, as does the memorial itself, "those who also served"—in the Red Cross, the United Service Organization (USO), and other nongovernmental organizations that sent women overseas in support of U.S. military personnel.

This is our third effort to provide scholars a hundred years from now with a picture of who America's pioneering patriot women were and how our nation saw fit to utilize their skills. It follows *In Defense of a Nation: Servicewomen in the Second World War,* which the Women In Military Service For America Memorial Foundation, Inc., published in 1997 to coincide with the dedication of the Women's Memorial, and *An Officer and a Lady: The World War II Letters of Lt. Col. Betty Bandel, Women's Army Corps* (Sylvia J. Bugbee, editor), which the University Press of New England and the foundation's Military Women's Press copublished in 2004. There are other projects in the UPNE/MWP pipeline and, to paraphrase Humphrey Bogart's last words in *Casablanca,* we hope this is the beginning of a beautiful friendship.

This book has been a team effort. It began as a vast research project undertaken by the foundation's chief historian, Dr. Judith Bellafaire, who methodically pulled together the official records regarding the reestablishment of units of military women after World War II's temporary organizations passed out of existence and those relating to servicewomen during the Korean War era. Foundation Senior Fellow Linda Witt, a journalist and primary author of *Running as a Woman: Gender and Power in American Politics* (Free Press, 1994) took on the task of finding the story—and the book— hidden in the unit reports and reams of legislative debates, using Dr. Bellafaire's research and first drafts as a starting point and the unique resources of the Women's Memorial Foundation, its archival collections, and its Register of nearly a quarter-million military women. Dr. Bellafaire's early work is particularly evident in the riveting battle-by-battle story of nurses in theater in chapter 7. Britta Granrud, the foundation's curator of collections, brought amazing insight and resources to the project with her finds of diaries, scrapbooks, caches of servicewomen's letters home, old recruiting brochures, yellowed newspaper clippings, and her sense honed over many years (she was a military brat) of how the military works and how military women fit in—all of which vastly informed the book's analysis.

When the team realized the degree to which official records—and official policy—did not match the lives of the women who served, the foundation's president, Wilma L. Vaught, Brigadier General, U.S. Air Force (Ret.), generously stretched already thin resources to let us hire, part-time, historian Mary Jo Binker. Currently an assistant editor with the Eleanor Roosevelt Papers Project at George Washington University, Ms. Binker created our oral history project and conducted extensive interviews with many of the less well known military women mentioned in the text. Parts of those oral histories appear in this book, set off from the text as vignettes. They provide a kind of reality check to official policies and pronouncements that only first-person memories can. Unfortunately, although the book and its argument were enriched by Mary Jo's research, we could use only a small portion of the stories the women told. Fortunately, the audiotapes, notes, and in some cases full transcripts of those first-person stories are available in the foundation's archives.

Two other Women's Memorial Foundation staffers contributed to the project. Historian Lee Ann Ghajar made us sensitive to a grave omission: while the official record often was at odds with servicewomen's experiences, there was little or no record at all of the unique and very different experiences of African American servicewomen. We had not found much on black servicewomen; she did, in old "race" newspapers and magazines, manuscript collections, and the archives of black leaders' papers. Our newest staffer, Kathleen M. Scott, whose master's thesis and a documentary she produced for the Smithsonian Armed Forces Collection focused on the pathbreaking first woman general, the Army's Chief Nurse Anna Mae Mc-Cabe (Hays), contributed the vignette on General Hays. Ms. Scott is the new full-time director of the Memorial Foundation's Oral History Project.

Jeanne M. Holm, Women's Army Auxiliary Corps (WAAC), 1942. Courtesy Jeanne M. Holm.

The cornerstone for the entire project was an equally remarkable veteran, Major General Jeanne M. Holm, U.S. Air Force (Ret.), a noted military historian who started her career as a Women's Army Auxiliary Corps (WAAC) truck driver in World War II and rose to become the first two-star woman in the U.S. military. (The WAAC preceded the 1943 founding of the Women's Army Corps or WAC.) Time and again in this book we have referred to her published writings; she also pops up continually as a major actor on the stage as military women became a recognized asset in the defense of the nation. In one era she's a captain, then a major, then the "first woman" in this military school or that role, then director of Women in the Air Force, and on and on up the ranks until 1967 we see her standing beside President Lyndon Johnson as he signs the legislation that authorizes women generals. Now in her eighties, she is too big a personality—she once remarked that she has skied every winter since she learned how except the year she had her hip replacement—and too ubiquitous and central to the progress of U.S. military women to this day for us to sum up her career in a short vignette or even in this book. She rightly deserves a major biography that would examine both the woman and how she changed the military and her times. We cannot do that here.

General Holm's influence on this project is much greater than even the footnotes can possibly acknowledge. Although she read drafts of the book in various stages and made suggestions for where an additional fact or opinion might be found, she pointedly avoided trying to shape this book to her style or viewpoint. The authors are obviously younger than she by twenty to nearly fifty years and products of both the Women's Liberation Movement and university gender studies programs. Without pulling rank, General Holm

President Lyndon B. Johnson signs Public Law 90–130 opening promotions for women to general and flag ranks and removing the two percent limit on the numbers of women in each service branch, 8 November 1967. Left to right: Colonel Ethel R. Kovach, chief, AFNC; Colonel Frances Ballentine, chief, AFMSC; Captain Ruth Moeller, chief, NMSC; Colonel Mary L. Hamrick, chief, AMSC; Colonel Jeanne M. Holm, director of Women in the Air Force; Captain Veronica Bulshefski, chief, NNC; Captain Rita Lenihan, assistant to the chief of naval personnel (women); Colonel Anna Mae McCabe Hays, chief, ANC; Colonel Elizabeth P. Hoisington, director, WAC; Colonel Barbara J. Bishop, director, Women Marines (behind Captain Lenihan); and Vice President Hubert H. Humphrey. Veronica Bulshefski Collection, Gift of Elizabeth Linski, Women's Memorial Collection.

helped us see that while military women in the 1950s may have been limited by their times, they were not victims of those times so much as they were coauthors. Just one example: we wrote a line about retention problems, noting that Uncle Sam simply did not know how to stop young military women from getting married and having babies. Her wry penciled-in remark, "And why would he want to?" made us aware how little we were thinking outside our own time's conceptual boxes.

General Vaught and Brigadier General Connie Slewitzke, U.S. Army Nurse Corps (Ret.), a Vietnam veteran and a former chief nurse of the ANC, were also valuable resources. Both not only read multiple versions of the book and answered innumerable, occasionally arcane, questions, but also provided the kind of context that could only be provided by women who understand by experience the difference between ordinary institutions and the military's unique mission in society. General Slewitzke conducted several oral histories for the book, and also helped unravel the peculiar mystery of whether the Army actually tried to ban MASH nurses from the battle zone simply because they were women. Short answer: they tried, they failed (see chapter 5). She located material that only someone who knew the personalities (and, figuratively, where the bodies were buried) might think to look.

This book—and each of the ongoing projects of the Military Women's Press for UPNE—has another guardian angel: Colonel Lorry Fenner, a historian, a Ph.D., a former Supreme Court Fellow, and most recently a staff member of the 9/11 Commission. She has called upon her networks of military women and scholars more than once to aid us. For this book, she put us in touch with Dr. John Shy, professor emeritus of history at the University of Michigan, whose four-page review of the "finished" manuscript gave us new insights into the meanings of material we had inadequately analyzed (though he kindly did not say this) and resulted in one long meandering chapter becoming two more tightly focused chapters. Thank you both.

Readers will meet many stellar military women in these pages; we hope that readers who are also Korean War veterans will renew old acquaintances. To aid those reunions—and because the military itself flip-flopped throughout this era on whether married women could join the services or get married during their contracted time of duty—we endeavored to refer to a uniformed woman by the name under which she was serving at the time, and include her later married name in parentheses. Because some women (even some married women) were able despite cultural and institutional barriers to make careers in the military, they moved up in rank and we tried to note their individual career paths as the narrative of this complex era's history played out. Lieutenant Mary Jones (Smith) might have become Colonel or even General Mary Jones Smith before her career was over. To further compound the changing name and rank issue, the endnotes regarding Women's Memorial Foundation Collection's oral histories or artifacts citing a specific collection are cataloged in our database by name of the donor, be it the servicewoman or her heirs. In that case we use all relevant names with no parentheses to ease a search of the many records we store both on computer (some abbreviated material is accessible by computer in the Register at the memorial itself) and physically in the archives. Some historical material is also available via www.womensmemorial.org.

A mere thank you seems insufficient for those listed above, as it does for several friends of the foundation who aided research, and friends among the foundation staff who came to our rescue many a time with morale building and/or other support. We thank independent historian Joanne McFadden for providing us with expert guidance on the location of Korean War–era Army and Navy medical unit records at the National Archives, former Army captain and foundation staffer Marlene Reckling Murty for long hours at the National Archives delving into those same records, Jackie Radebaugh for her research at the Library of Congress on topics ranging from 1950s fashion through congressional politics and economic indicators, and Commander Frances Omori, U.S. Navy, for sharing her interviews with Navy nurses who served aboard hospital ships and at Yokosuka Naval Hospital during the Korean War. Foundation Executive Director Jan Shaw; tech gurus Sanjeev Sharma and Marie Farrar; Director of Support Services Barbara Bavera, Lieutenant Colonel, U.S. Air Force (Ret.); and former Assistant Curator of Collections Peter Strong all deserve particular thanks.

By far, our greatest gratitude is to the women who have served America and are serving today. If you are one of these, the Register and archives at the Women's Memorial Foundation—just as Uncle Sam once did—wants you. And if the servicewoman was your sister, wife, aunt, mother, grandmother, or friend, we need *you* to help make sure her story is recorded for generations to come. The history of patriot women didn't end with the Korean War. In some ways it has barely begun.

"A Defense Weapon Known to Be of Value"

Introduction

Any national defense weapon known to be of value should be developed
and kept in good working order and not allowed to rust or to be abolished.
—Captain Joy Bright Hancock during the post–World War II debates
   on permanently adding women to the military [1]

There is a pseudo gallantry which discourages using women for war duty . . .
the bane of existence of women in the services during World War II. It took
the shape of "protecting" [women]. . . . It led recruiters across the length
and breadth of the land to think they had to "glamorize" the services as
playgrounds for "cute" girls.
—Mildred McAfee Horton, World War II director of Navy women
   (WAVES) [2]

L ESS THAN FIVE YEARS after World War II the United
    States found itself once again confronted by a war for
which it was unprepared. Once again a downsized military establishment
rushed to call up, draft, and recruit the needed manpower. And once again
when it came up short, the services asked American women to leave their
homes, jobs, and families to serve their country.

This book traces those women from the days immediately after World
War II, when U.S. service personnel were being demobilized in droves,
through the dawning of the Cold War and the Korean War.[3] Those few short
years, 1945 through 1953, saw pivotal changes in women's status in the U.S.
Armed Forces. They went from being almost a historical footnote in the immediate postwar period—a source of labor and skills the nation's military

took for granted—to winning a permanent place in each branch of the armed services.

Nurses, who had gained a permanent place a half century earlier with the establishment of the Army and Navy nurse corps (1901 and 1908 respectively), finally achieved equal rank, and with it, equal pay. Servicewomen made progress on the job front despite early setbacks and constant attempts to reclassify as "male only" some of the military occupational specialties (MOSs) that women had excelled at during World War II. Navy women, banned from all overseas assignments during World War II, began seeing the world, if only in small numbers (and, by congressional fiat, never aboard any naval vessel but hospital or transport ships and aircraft). At the same time other gender barriers began to fall in the medical professions.

African American servicewomen, subject to quotas and segregation during World War II, made progress, too. Black women, who during World War II had been enlisted and commissioned in significant numbers only by the Army, became officers and enlisted personnel in the Navy and Air Force and were among the first members of their race to integrate the Marines. By the end of the Korean War, they began to be fully integrated throughout the services.

Servicewomen's gains did not come without struggle, and there were many setbacks along the way. Recruiting women had been a constant challenge for the military even during World War II, and it continued to be difficult. No branch of the service came anywhere near filling its womanpower needs during the Korean War.

Retaining the women who did enlist became an even more complex problem because of the postwar social pressure on women to marry and start families, and what can be seen in retrospect as the military's own paternalism and fear of upsetting Mr. and Mrs. America's "prevailing ambivalence"[4] (a Joint Chiefs of Staff's phrase) regarding the role of women. Even General Dwight D. Eisenhower, who went to bat to make women a permanent fixture in the armed services, was quoted as saying during the hearings on the Women's Armed Services Integration Act: "Ordinarily the enlisted [woman] will come in, and, after an enlistment or two they will ordinarily—and thank heaven—get married."[5]

In World War II, the military (with the exception of the nurse corps) allowed married women to join if they did not have minor children, but a woman who married while in service was allowed to request a discharge. Two months after the Korean War began, when it became obvious that recruiting was falling far short of goals, leniency on the marriage issue ended and married servicewomen were told they could not be spared. Of course, as pregnancy still meant automatic discharge for women, married women who were determined to leave the service simply started their families. Uncomfortable with the high pregnancy rate, the Department of Defense (DOD) in September 1951 reluctantly reinstated the earlier policy for enlisted brides of discharge if requested, but brides who were officers did not win back that easy out until after the war was over in 1953. Fathers were not subject to the draft, but by early 1952, DOD was cracking down on men who were using unborn children to obtain deferments. "The military required a doctor's certificate that conception occurred before a man was called for service. Apparently, a not insignificant number of men had gotten women pregnant to avoid the draft."[6]

At the beginning of World War II, nurses who married had been discharged—sometimes *dishonorably* if their commanding officer so decreed. As that war's nurse shortages grew, the Army became more lenient but the Navy did not allow its nurses to marry until January 1945. Although none of the nurse corps would commission married women during the Korean War, nurses were permitted to marry but with this penalty: they almost automatically were transferred to the Reserve, a less competitive career status. Obviously, the military did not want to be blamed for breaking up families, and was conceding that, where his wife was concerned, a husband outranked Uncle Sam. But the military also seemed to be saying that if women were serious about their nursing careers they would not get married.

Time and time again during this period, some negative attitude about women would prove to be a barrier to servicewomen, whether it was servicemen's attitudes about them, the military's concerns about finding "proper employment for girlfriends and daughters," women military leaders' own fears of seeming too ambitious, or civilian advisers' reluctant conclusions that although American women might be amenable to being registered, perhaps even drafted, American men would never stand for it. The War for Public Opinion was fought on many fronts and with unique stealth weapons: designer uniforms, good grooming classes, even inveigling women college professors, celebrities, and publishers to lend their high status and propriety to the cause of servicewomen. This latter thrust lead to the Defense Advisory Committee on Women in the Services (DACOWITS), and was one of the era's success stories that continues to this day.

Post–World War II Americans were marrying and producing babies at a furious rate, but the era's reputation for peaceful domesticity was a facade. Americans faced a series of domestic challenges that tore at the unity that had characterized the American home front during the war: labor strikes that came with the end of wartime bans, runaway consumer prices, and housing shortages that left a reported one hundred thousand veterans homeless in Chicago alone.[7] President Harry S. Truman captured the mood of the immediate postwar period perfectly: "Everybody wants something at the expense of everybody else and nobody thinks much of the other fellow."[8]

The Cold War—and the frightening possibility of total nuclear annihilation—was in full swing well before the hot war, Korea, began. On 9 February 1946, the Soviet Union's Joseph Stalin publicly declared that communism and capitalism were incompatible, and that another world war was inevitable—and most probably in the 1950s. Less than a month after Stalin's remarks, on 5 March, Winston Churchill made his famous "Iron Curtain" speech.[9]

Here at home, the Civil Rights Movement took on new urgency. African American veterans had served in segregated units and recognized the gap between what they had fought for and what they were being allowed. During World War II the Double V campaign launched by the *Pittsburgh Courier* defined the Civil Rights Movement, linking the battle for victory abroad to the fight against racial discrimination on the home front.[10] As blacks agitated against discrimination and segregation, whites responded with violence. In the first six months of 1946 alone, more than fifteen African Americans, many of them veterans, were killed in separate instances in the Deep South. Another one hundred–plus blacks were arrested in Columbia, Tennessee, following an altercation between a white store clerk and an African American woman and her son. Conditions in the North were almost as difficult. During the war, blacks and whites had clashed over jobs and housing as African Americans from the South, lured by promises of work and a better life, continued their decades-long migration to such cities as Detroit and Chicago. The end of the war just exacerbated the tensions.[11]

If civil rights was a cauldron beginning to boil, the unrest that would become the Women's Liberation Movement was at best lukewarm. It would be a quarter century or more or more before "Help Wanted—Women" and "Help Wanted—Men" classifieds would disappear from the back of the daily newspaper, even longer before the idea of gender as a leading job qualification would be discredited in civilian life, much less the military.

As World War II was ending in 1945, the preamble to the United Nations Charter declared "faith . . . in the equal rights of men and women," and the United Nations Commission on the Status of Women was established in June 1946, thanks in some part to Eleanor Roosevelt. Modeling on the U.N.

language, California Democrat Helen Gahagan Douglas introduced a bill in the House of Representatives in early 1947 to eliminate unfair discrimination based on sex and empower the president to establish a similar commission on the status of women. Meanwhile, the equal rights amendment (ERA) was making its slow, and ultimately (or still) unsuccessful, way through legislatures, but was eyed suspiciously by those (including some wary progressives) who felt women still needed legal protection.[12]

It is no surprise then that the ERA debate became entwined with the issue of military women's status. Tennessee Democrat Estes Kefauver worried that equal rights for women would mean women, too, would be subject to the draft, which would cause "such confusion I don't see how we could have any armed services. . . . there would be no way of establishing which parent would stay home and take care of the children if war came." Maine Republican Margaret Chase Smith, a champion of both the ERA and military women, maintained that equal citizenship required equal responsibilities, and declared, "It is time to stop thinking of women as second-class citizens."[13] Unlike as with the fight for civil rights, however, there was no long-standing sense of terrible injustice concerning the inequality of women in society as a whole, much less in what was one of the most masculine of domains, the military. Remarkably, although the fledgling women's components of the services did not come through the era unscathed, they did survive and carved out a permanent place for women in the defense of the nation.

The story begins in the days just after World War II until the fight for the Women's Armed Services Integration Act was finally won in 1948, the span of time covered in chapter 1. To forestall a repeat of history, a few farsighted military leaders began working toward establishing permanent women's military organizations to replace the temporary wartime WACs, WAVES, and Women Marines.[14] Although the Army and Navy nurse corps were a half century old, the establishment in 1948 of permanent women's military line organizations in the armed forces was a hard-fought, two-year battle. These efforts were won, in part, because the emerging Cold War made continuation of the draft inevitable, and politicians in Washington were nervous about voting to draft the nation's young men while ignoring the pool of potential volunteers its young women constituted.

In their half-hearted passage of the bill, Congress reflected postwar attitudes of the American public toward women and women's work. In the three years since the war ended, Rosie the Riveter had been told to lay down her tools; if she did not return to the kitchen, she at least was supposed to go back to more traditionally female employment. Uniformed women were supposed to be happy to join her. Though it was not explicitly stated, white middle-class women were expected to be happy housewives reincarnate, while African American and other minority women, who were far more likely to have been employed outside the home before the war, were stripped of their high-wage jobs in industry and expected to resume low-wage service jobs. Inexplicably, given very recent experience, many of the same jobs at which women in industry and in uniform had been considered superior to men during the war were summarily redefined as "men's work" for which women had suddenly become unsuited. It was a return to prewar Depression-era attitudes when a working woman could be castigated for displacing a breadwinning man, a family's "natural" head. In response to the times, when Congress finally passed the Women's Armed Services Integration Act in June 1948, it limited both the size of the women's services and servicewomen's career opportunities as well as any authority they might wield over men.[15]

The two years between the enactment of the integration act and the start of the Korean War, the subject of chapter 2, were critical to the development of the roles women would play in the future military. The tiny cadres of women officers and noncommissioned officers (NCOs) who had remained in the service at the end of World War II were faced with establishing methods of operation, recruiting women, organizing training programs, planning and developing field programs and, all the time, running a giant public relations campaign about military women. By the end of their first two years of operation, the idea that women should be a permanent part of the armed forces was firmly established and planning for future growth was under way; nonetheless, the women's services were far from ready for rapid mobilization. When the Korean War broke out on 25 June 1950, the women's service components were so tiny, so new, and so restricted that they were unable to mobilize the large number of women that the armed forces suddenly realized was needed.

The Department of Defense began planning a rapid buildup of male and female personnel, militarywide efforts that are explored in chapter 3. The services called up reservists of both sexes (the first time that women were included) and stepped up recruiting and the draft.[16] When it very quickly became apparent that more women were needed than were being recruited, a few senior military women spoke out about the possibility of drafting women.

Indeed, drafting women was not a new idea. In his 1945 State of the Union address, President Franklin D. Roosevelt had suggested drafting nurses. The

Senate concurred, but before the more conservative House of Representatives could act, victory in Europe eased the nurse shortage and the idea was dropped.[17] During the Korean War, men were being conscripted, but the United States was counting on women to step up and volunteer, even though recruiting women had been difficult even during the patriotic years of fighting Hitler. Rumors about servicewomen's morals, which circulated in 1943 and 1944, and the disparagement of women in uniform (some of it barely cloaked suggestions of lesbianism) prevented many women from enlisting then and during the Korean War era.

The services also faced a more difficult recruiting environment for Korea, a war less broadly supported than World War II. Tired of war in general, the American public never came to see the Korean "conflict" as a true national emergency; in fact, the conflict was only upgraded to the status of a "war" in 1958, four years after the cease-fire, partially as a result of pressure from veterans.[18] To attract women recruits, DOD launched a nationwide recruiting campaign complete with a flood of "glamorizing" newspaper stories and media events. It tried lowering qualifications and age limits. But, as its civilian advisory committee, DACOWITS, and the service branches soon discovered, the problems inherent in recruiting and retaining servicewomen could not be fixed with publicity campaigns and photo opportunities. The majority of the target group, young American women, treated military service in much the same way they treated the civilian jobs they gravitated to in the early 1950s: temporary stops along the road to marriage and motherhood, which seemed inevitabilities given the messages society was sending them. Lowering age limits and qualifications simply resulted in servicewomen who didn't fill the bill, either in performance or, what was increasingly a concern, looks. By the end of the war, DOD had virtually thrown in the towel; the women's service directors called off the national recruiting campaign because they were so concerned about the deteriorating quality of recruits.

Chapter 4 deals with the individual women's service components' unique personalities and problems during the Korean War, as well as their struggles simply to fit in. The organizations, as well as individual military women from the highest ranking on down, bent over backward not to offend men by seeming too pushy or presumptive. In 1949, when the Air Force selected a woman officer to attend the U.S. Armed Forces Staff College, she turned down the career-enhancing and path-breaking assignment. Much later, in 1952, a memorandum to the Office of the Secretary of Defense attempted to explain the situation; because the woman officer understood that another service (the Navy) opposed its women officers attending this school, she elected not to attend.[19] During this same time period, the women service directors themselves all worked against congressional legislation that would have given them higher rank than colonel. They were afraid of appearing "grasping." [20] Ever sensitive to the resentments of male military members and to public perception, military women attempted to walk the fine line demanded of them. They strove to be competent but did not want to be perceived as ambitious; they wanted to be dependable, but they avoided looking aggressive.

Throughout this time period, what the military branches did *not* do to recruit and retain servicewomen is just as telling as what they did. There was no great call for women to do their patriotic duty, as there had been in World Wars I and II. Despite the fact that the military arguably offered women, especially officers, somewhat better career opportunities than did the civilian workplace, civilian women advisers repeatedly noted the lack of career opportunity and challenge for women. The services' own retention surveys found the same thing. Other civilian women remarked on the many capable women officers of stellar character who had been kept for years at junior rank, when men of similar quality would have long been promoted. Still, the services continued to limit women's responsibilities and begrudge—or completely deny—them command authority over men. By the time the Korean War started, the post–World War II ethos that a woman's place was in the home subject to her husband's authority was dogma to many Americans.

A large proportion of women left before their initial enlistment period was up. To turn this around, the services did everything they could think of (or everything that seemed thinkable given the times) to make women in the ranks happier. First, they conducted surveys to pinpoint the problems. Then they tried a series of quick fixes. They provided women with lighter meals in the dining halls. The Army and Marines hired the best and most expensive couturiers to design new uniforms, while the Navy and the new Air Force relied on in-house designs. When it was suggested that servicemen did not appreciate military women, the DOD at DACOWITS's recommendation required the male recruits to attend lectures that explained why servicewomen were valued members of the armed forces.[21] But again, what the services would not do is as telling as what they did. Although they flip-flopped on the marriage issue, they would not for another two decades rethink the total ban on military motherhood, not withstanding a challenge to the ban by one veteran Women's Army Corps reservist, a specialist on Korean affairs, who took her battle to remain in the service to Congress and the press.

Even nursing and the women's medical specialty corps, accepted by most Americans and most military men as womanly professions (despite the growing numbers of male nurses, physical and occupational therapists, and other specialists) were not immune from career strangulation in the military. For example, in the middle of the war, the Navy took a group of prominent nurse educators on a tour of the hospital ship USS *Haven* stationed off the coast of Korea. Struggling with a nurse shortage, the Navy hoped that the visitors would be impressed enough to recommend the Navy Nurse Corps as a career to their students. One visitor, Hazel Baird Macquin, dean of the University of Utah College of Nursing, noted that the very efficient and extremely well liked chief nurse aboard the *Haven* was a mere lieutenant, despite ten years in the service. "I would doubt that many men officers of similar personal quality would have remained lieutenants so long." [22]

That male nurses and other nondoctor male specialists would not be satisfied with such limited career possibilities (nor, as it turned out, would Congress feel it proper to limit men in the same ways) combined with the desperate shortages of military medical personnel to loosen some of the rigid gender barriers. The idea of men in the nurse corps was suggested; a few women doctors were given regular commissions with career track parity; and one desperate women's medical specialist corps director quietly began arranging for male physical therapists to receive commissions, even though Congress had earlier refused to authorize such a step. The quiet but important erosion of rock-hard attitudes about gender in the medical area, the subject of chapter 5, was in reality not anything new for military women, but a repeat of how women had won, defended, and expanded their role in the defense of the nation from the Revolution on—by being the skilled personnel available to fill a critical manpower need. What would be new was (1) men arguing *they* were the true victims of gender bias, and (2) the attempts to roll back history and remove nurses from the combat theater altogether.

In 1952, the Army experimented with a Mobile Army Surgical Hospital (MASH) in Korea that functioned with male medical technicians instead of nurses. When the doctors at the experimental MASH complained that the male medics made too many mistakes because of insufficient training, the Army was forced to bring back the nurses.[23] That the experiment was conducted at all, after a half century's experience with Army and Navy nurses and more than a century's before that of civilian women's valor as nurses in previous wars, demonstrates how rigidly women's roles were once again being defined after World War II.[24]

But the Dean Macquin episode does illustrate perfectly the situation in which all American servicewomen during the Korean War era were caught. The military had decided that women were suited only for a specific, narrow group of jobs, that is, "women's work," and few women at the time would have disagreed. One Air Force chief of staff even groused that servicewomen "ought to be more feminine and stick to secretarial work instead of trying to be mechanics, truck drivers and grease monkeys."[25] Whatever women's work was deemed to entail, it had little to do with men's work and should not involve supervisory or command authority over men. Yet without upward mobility, many of the talented women the military needed to retain would go elsewhere, despite the military's arguably being the only employer from which women could expect equal pay for equal work, even if their opportunities and benefits were less than those of similarly situated men.

That the resulting talent drain was occurring at a time when military women were desperately needed was especially sad; as chapter 6 will show, individual women enlisted and officers were proving their value every day at postings throughout the world. Just one example among those women was Sergeant Alice O'Connor of the 8032nd WAC Battalion in Japan, assigned to the 8034th Signal Service where she handled telephone communications on the night shift. On the night of 18 November 1952, an emergency developed that required O'Connor to establish rapid and clear communications between Yokota and air rescue units in Korea. Her knowledge and capable handling of the situation resulted in a letter of appreciation from the commanding officer of the 98th Bombardment Wing.[26] Many servicewomen played similar vital, if seldom celebrated, roles.

The cardinal role, of course, was that of the military women actually serving in theater of war, the nurses. When military men and woman of the Korean War era speak of Korea as "the nurses' war," they refer neither to an actual war nor to images of nurses like those in the movie and television series M*A*S*H (which arguably stereotyped and trivialized all of the medical personnel, but particularly the nurses). While a memorable antiwar statement, M*A*S*H was set in the fairly static second and third years of the war, not its horrific first months. Army, Navy, and Air Force nurses and a handful of women medical specialists performed magnificently in dangerous and harsh conditions close to the front lines, often too close for official comfort.[27] Their achievement, the subject of chapter 7, could rightly be a book unto itself and proved once again the ability of military women to carry out their duties while in harm's way.

Despite the nurses' performance, throughout the war the armed forces refused to send other servicewomen into Korea even when commanders there specifically requested them. Yet, as chapter 8 will show, civilian women with the Red Cross, the USO, and even DOD were assigned to the Korean Theater during hostilities. Famed war correspondent Marguerite Higgins's stories from the front were the stuff of daily headlines, and *Life* photographer Margaret Bourke-White "risk(ed) her life . . . (beyond) current battle lines to cover the guerrilla war, overcoming objections of many officials who thought it was no place for a lady."[28] Women combatants were among the United Nations troops, including Turkish fighter pilot Major Sabiha Gokcen, and what the *New York Times* called "little Korean WACs" trained as infantry marksmen, at least one of whom was killed.[29]

What today might be labeled the military's paternalism regarding women was also the mind-set of an entire society. That mind-set added to the failure of the wartime recruiting effort and the low retention rate for servicewomen created a vicious cause-and-effect loop. The number of servicewomen remained far below authorized levels throughout the dawning of the Cold War and the Korean War period, and the continued smallness of the women's services resulted in their inability to accomplish their mission. Their raison d'être had been to be the nucleus around which rapid mobilization could take place. Small numbers of peacetime servicewomen working in a large variety of jobs would be ready to train the larger numbers needed during war. But the small size of the women's services prior to and during the Korean War caused the services to limit women's training and assignments. That meant that there were no women mechanics, truck drivers, grease monkeys, or whatever other nontraditional MOS had been re-designated "men only" available to train others to fill men's noncombat positions. The nucleus concept's failure in turn hurt the credibility of the women's services and haunted them for years, reinforcing the rock-solid belief of many in society and the male military that women belonged in the home, or at the very least that the military should be a male domain.

Traditionalists insisted that the services had failed in their attempts to recruit and retain women because women were simply unsuited to military life. They were by nature too sensitive, needed too much privacy, were too emotional, and thus too difficult to train. Further, women tended to fall in love, get married and pregnant, and couldn't be counted on to serve out their enlistments. Moreover, their emotional nature made it hard on male supervisors in the field. In short, women soldiers were more trouble than they were worth. Indeed, several years after the Korean War, some military leaders would seriously consider eliminating servicewomen. On top of all this, servicemen who believed such stereotypes brought negative expectations and remarks to their dealings with servicewomen, making an already challenging work environment more difficult, especially during the Korean War.

The U.S. military was the ultimate loser. Low expectations, negative attitudes and the lack of meaningful opportunity stopped many young women from enlisting and drove out many of the servicewomen who might otherwise have stayed. How many Alice O'Connors were not given the opportunity to put their skills to use for the nation during the Korean War?

In retrospect, it is easy to see that the armed forces attempted to establish a permanent place for women at an inauspicious time. During the 1950s, "the institution of marriage had a power and inevitability . . . that it has never had since. You simply didn't ask yourself if you wanted marriage and children; the only relevant questions were when, and how many?"[30] Given the American public's social values during the years after World War II, it may be astonishing that the very idea of a military that included women, other than nurses, managed to survive. That servicewomen did manage to carve out a place for their gender within the nation's armed forces says a great deal about the performance, dedication, and abilities of those unsung heroines who served their country during these exceptionally domesticated years. That was the Korean "war" won by servicewomen.

CHAPTER 1

Women's Place—and the Servicewoman's Place— in Post–World War II America

It would be tragic if, in another emergency, a new generation had to start from scratch; had to duplicate effort; make the same mistakes. . . . It would be foolhardy to wait for another war to find out how and where women could best be used for national defense. To write "finis" to women's contributions . . . would be turning back time.
—Colonel Mary Hallaren, Director, Women's Army Corps[1]

When [the Women's Army Auxiliary Corps] was first proposed in the beginning of [World War II], like most old soldiers, I was violently against it. . . . [However] every phase of the record they compiled during the war convinced me of the error of my first reaction. . . . I assure you that I look upon [legislation to permanently add women to the United States military] as a "must."
—General Dwight D. Eisenhower, testifying before the House Armed Services Committee, 18 February 1948[2]

W HEN WORLD WAR II ENDED in August 1945, the United States celebrated the Allied victory, immediately began a massive demobilization, and tried to turn back time. Its armed forces, which had expanded to record levels during the war, rapidly demobilized. Troops scattered around the world wanted nothing more than to go home, and their waiting families wanted the G.I. Joes and Janes home from war as quickly as possible so that life could return to "normal."

The nation understood that some servicemen, as well as many of the Army and Navy nurses and medical personnel, would have to remain in the military. The United States now had to field large armies of occupation in the defeated countries, and the armed forces had always needed to maintain a small contingent of men in arms for defense purposes even during peacetime. And for some returning soldiers, a long stint of medical treatment and rehabilitation would be necessary before they would be able to go home, and that meant nurses would still be needed. The general public, however, expected the military to disband all other women in uniform. In fact, it was the law. The legislation that had created the Women's Army Corps (WAC), the Navy Women's Reserve (WAVES), the Marine Corps Women's Reserve, and the Coast Guard Women's Reserves (SPAR) specifically authorized these separate women's branches only for the duration of the war plus six months, after which they were expected to self-destruct.

The American people recognized World War II as an emergency of such desperate scope that extraordinary steps were necessary to win it. The employment of women in nontraditional jobs in industry and the large-scale enrollment of women in the armed forces were two extraordinary steps that the country had accepted as necessary during that war. On factory floors and on military posts, American women proved themselves capable of successfully performing a wide variety of jobs that would have been unthinkable before the war. Civilian women built military planes; others flew them cross-country and towed targets for male antiaircraft artillery gunners. The girl-next-door worked on the line in factories and learned to repair and drive two-and-a-half-ton military trucks. The military trained women to pack parachutes, repair turret guns, make terrain maps, decode top-secret military messages, and handle aircraft traffic control. Servicewomen also requisitioned supplies, worked switchboards, made training films, routed mail, wrote propaganda, and taught student pilots how to fly military aircraft. In offices, classrooms, hospitals, and laboratories, military women had proven themselves so essential that, by war's end, their commanders wondered how the United States Armed Forces had ever gotten along without them.

In the midst of the rapid postwar demobilization, military leaders realized that they could ill afford to lose all uniformed women, but their legislative authority to keep women other than the nurses was running out. In addition to fielding armies of occupation in Germany, Austria, and Japan, and staffing the medical facilities caring for the tens of thousands of war casualties, the U.S. defense establishment also had to maintain a force capable of defending the nation against the emerging communist threat, a threat that seemed to be growing stronger year by year. During the first years after the war, the Soviet Union consolidated its hold on Eastern Europe by turning the countries of East Germany, Poland, Romania, and eventually Czechoslovakia and Hungary into satellites, and ringing down what Winston Churchill so chillingly named the "Iron Curtain" between these nations and the rest of Europe. Meanwhile, the army of communist revolutionary Mao Tse-tung began winning control of large sections of China away from the Nationalist government of Chiang Kai-shek. As the communists appeared to be taking over large sections of the world at a rapid rate, the U.S. military, in the throes of budget cuts and downsizing, looked for ways to do more with less. Skilled, efficient servicewomen working in offices behind desks would free men to fight and perhaps help avoid a continuation of the wartime draft, an action that was sure to be unpopular with peace finally at hand. If another war broke out, small cadres of women already in uniform could train the larger numbers that would then be needed, substantially reducing the time required for total mobilization.

Consequently, not all non-nurse servicewomen were released from service after the war. In order to justify retaining these women, almost immediately after the war both Army Chief of Staff General Dwight D. Eisenhower and the Chief of Navy Personnel Vice Admiral Louis E. Denfeld, ordered their staffs to craft legislation that would permit permanent—albeit small—numbers of women in their service branches.[3] The generals and admirals were extremely aware that such legislation would be controversial. Many Americans and their elected representatives appeared to expect women to return happily to domesticity now that the national emergency was over and the men were back as the family breadwinners. Millions of Rosie the Riveters were fired from their factory jobs so that returning male veterans could go back to work. During the first nine months after V-E Day, the number of women employed dropped from nineteen and a half million to fifteen and a half million.[4] Charlcia Neuman, a wartime riveter, took it in stride. "I was laid off in September of 1945. I just got a slip of paper saying that I wouldn't be needed again. Most of us went at the same time. . . . the idea was for the women to go back home. The women understood that. And the men had been promised their jobs when they came back."[5] This was as it should be, many Americans believed; the American family needed a mother at home and a father at work.[6]

In the booming postwar economy, young men and women were encouraged to get married, start families, and create homes. "Never had husband, home and children been more sentimentalized," author Caroline Bird noted in her landmark 1968 history of modern American women, *Born Female: The High Cost of Keeping Women Down.* "Magazines kept printing figures proving it didn't pay a wife to work. Aggressive women were losers, they said, because the only right that mattered was the right to be loved."[7]

The average age of a woman at marriage dropped from 21.5 in 1940 to 20.5 in 1947, 20.3 in 1950, and 20.2 by 1955. The average age of a woman at the birth of her first child dropped significantly as well, and birth rates leaped from 20.4 per 1,000 to 24.1 per 1,000 during the five years between 1945 and 1950.[8] So eager were women to marry that fewer bothered with college and women's educational levels declined dramatically. In 1940, female students constituted 40 percent of the student body at institutions of higher education in the United States. By 1950, the number was down to 30 percent. Divorce rates, after the wartime marriage mistake phenomenon worked itself out of the system, also declined. Rarely had so many women defined themselves so exclusively as "mother."[9]

The amount of time women spent doing housework actually increased between 1945 and 1955, in spite of new labor-saving appliances and convenience foods. Women could be found guilty by an amorphous jury of peers if they didn't cook elaborate meals and "decorate" their homes to express their family's individuality. Men also were pressured to conform. Those who remained unmarried too long ran the risk of harming their corporate careers or being judged juvenile, irresponsible or, worse, deviant. There was a great deal of concern about men who could not make their wives "behave."[10]

Jobs were plentiful in the postwar economy, but a single woman was not expected to work for more than a few short years—at entry-level positions only—before meeting the right man and settling down. Instead of preparing for professional careers, most young women worked at any job that would bring in money: secretary, sales clerk, bookkeeper, waitress. As a result, fewer women became managers, accountants, lawyers, doctors, professors, or architects. In 1950, for example, a record 11 percent of the students graduated from medical school were women; by 1960 this figure had dropped to 7 percent. The apparent reason for the drop? The first group had begun their education during World War II; the second were teens and young women of the 1950s, when the cult of domesticity was at its peak. The same thing happened in other professions: law, science, engineering, journalism, and academia.[11] Men even began edging into professional jobs (jobs where seniority and experience were rewarded) that had been the traditional preserve of women, becoming librarians, social workers, and elementary school teachers.[12]

A white, middle-class, married woman was not expected to work outside the home; if she did, her employer expected her to leave when she started having children. (While the same societal pressures existed for minority women, larger percentages of them were in the job market both before and after the war.) Despite these expectations, the proportion of all working mothers with preschool children kept rising during the fifteen years after World War II. In 1950, some 14 percent worked, twice the percentage of 1940, and by 1960, some 20 percent were working. The biggest increase in women workers was in older women who worked to put their children through college or to finance other family needs. Women's jobs, however, were on the lower end of the wage scale, unskilled jobs in the service industry or on the factory floor. They were jobs that could be picked up and dropped according to the needs of the family rather than careers. Indeed, the label "Career Woman" became almost a slur after World War II.[13]

Although by 1950 the number of women who were employed was as high as it had been at the end of World War II, their jobs paid less and offered far less status and prestige.[14] Kay Baker's experience in the job market was typical of many women. The only postwar job the former shipyard worker thought she might be able to get was in a grocery. "I thought there wouldn't be any soldier boys lining up to be grocery clerks," Baker said, "so that's what I decided to be."[15] The average woman worker made 66 cents to her male counterpart's one dollar of wages in 1945, but only 53 cents to his dollar by 1950.[16]

In fact then, society's rhetoric about what women should have been doing—staying home and raising children—was far from what was actually happening, and the sheer numbers of women in the job marketplace caused concern in some quarters. In a May 1950 article, "Women: They're Grabbing Off a Greater Share of Jobs in Office and Factory," *Wall Street Journal* writer Stephen Galpin sounded an alarm. The number of women workers had risen by 24 percent within the past decade, he reported, while the number of male workers had risen only 7.7 percent. Recalling the "tearful ballad of the early 1900s that cried 'Heaven Will Protect the Working Girl,'" Galpin grumbled:

Perhaps it should read "Heaven Must Protect the Working Male," for women are taking over. They have been elbowing their way into factory and office at three times the rate men have in the past decade. Especially married women. The number of wives who have forsaken washboard for typewriter has soared 90 percent in that period. According to Department of Commerce figures, in one in every five families both spouses worked or looked for work as opposed to one in every nine a decade ago.[17]

Although postwar wages were generally higher, "Retail employers and others who want to cut labor costs can pay women less than men. They can pay married women less than single ones too, because they usually have a husband bringing in money," the writer noted. Family dynamics had changed during the war years and afterward. People were living longer, and some women worked to help support aging parents. Children were going to school longer, more were going on to college and universities; some women worked to help pay this cost. Many businesses still preferred that the women on their payroll be unmarried, and some, such as IBM and Metropolitan Life Insurance Company, refused to hire married women. A spokesman for Metropolitan Life put a paternalistic spin on the policy, explaining, "If they come to us single and get married and want to stay, we'll keep them." Naturally, if the woman got pregnant, she would be expected to quit her job. However, a new trend was developing that disturbed Galpin: young married women continued to work until family responsibilities kept them at home; once the children had left the house, however, they were electing to return to work.

Painting the picture even more starkly, Galpin noted that women were less likely to be unemployed than men, and asked, "In what fields are women scoring their gains at men's expense?" Women held 59 percent of the clerical jobs in the country compared to 53 percent in 1940; he answered, and they had increased their share of factory jobs as well, from 26 percent to 28 percent. The number of women proprietors and executives had risen from 12 percent to 14 percent. His final observation: "Men have made gains in one direction anyway—women's share of domestic service jobs dropped from 94 percent to 92 percent." [18]

It is important to remember that the majority of the jobs Galpin was talking about were not professional positions, and most had little chance for advancement. (The "proprietors" the article referred to could well have been the owners of small shops, and it is unclear what was meant by the term "executive.") While the number of women holding such jobs as secretary, factory hand, waitress, sales clerk, and bank teller grew, the number of women who were lawyers, college professors, doctors, scientists, and engineers actually declined throughout this period.[19]

Galpin's commentary reflected the concerns that many Americans felt about women in the workforce. Although they acknowledged that some women needed to work outside the home, in an ideal world, wives and mothers would find their highest calling in the home. Other historians have found a dichotomy between what Americans thought a woman should do and what individual women did do to aid the family coffers. Many men, for example, saw nothing wrong with their wives working so that the family could afford a better vacation or a bigger car. Women who worked to "help the family finances" did not believe that they were harming their families or acting unfeminine, as long as their job did not become too important.[20]

Galpin's piece inspired at least one letter to the editor. Florence L. C. Kitchelt, chairman of the Connecticut Committee for the Equal Rights Amendment, responded: "May I suggest that it is Victorian to discuss women as a caste, or sect, in our society. Women, like men, first and foremost are human beings. To them, as for other humans, all doors and opportunities should be open."[21] But Kitchelt's view placed her in a distinct minority in 1950. Given Americans' ambivalence about women's role in the workforce, it is not surprising they were even more bothered by the idea of women in the military. This attitude, clearly understood by both military leaders and members of Congress, was the primary barrier to the service's attempts to secure legislation making women a permanent fixture in the military establishment.

Nonetheless, the armed services had begun maneuvering to retain women as early as February 1946 when, at the direction of Chief of Staff General Dwight D. Eisenhower, the Army drafted legislation to establish a women's corps in the regular and Reserve of the peacetime Army.[22] That same month, the Navy transferred Commander Joy Bright Hancock, a veteran of both World War I and II's temporary "yeomanettes" and WAVES, to the Bureau of Naval Personnel with orders to begin drafting legislation for permanently including women in the Navy.[23]

Hancock recalled encountering a great deal of negative feeling regarding women in the Navy:

> Looking back on those months of work and the many conferences in which I was involved, I recall . . . [an] apathy that appeared to me to be a lack of cooperation and it finally brought me to a point where I began conferences by saying "I have been instructed by the Chief of Naval Personnel to prepare these plans concerning the possible use of the services of women in the Navy on a permanent basis. If you care to work from an absolutely negative recommendation, I will be glad to append your views to my report to the Chief." Such an approach was the measure of my desperation.[24]

Hearings on the Navy bill before the House Committee on Naval Affairs in May 1946 did not go well. Because the bill involved women, the Navy sent women officers to testify in favor of it, which made some committee members wonder why they were hearing only from women. Didn't the Navy's senior male officers support the bill, they asked? The testimony of WAVE Director Captain Jean Palmer, who did not believe that women should serve in the Navy on a permanent basis, also damaged the bill's chances. Palmer was following orders by testifying at the hearing. Although she did state that she believed that women should have the right to serve in both the regular and Reserve of the Navy on a permanent basis, when she was asked point-blank whether she personally approved of women serving in the Navy on a permanent basis, she felt compelled to admit her misgivings.[25]

Palmer's attitude reflected the concerns of several, although not all, of the World War II women's service directors. In their experience, servicemen's acceptance of military women during the war had been at best marginal, and usually grudging, regardless of what the military's top brass thought. They also worried that servicewomen would find it impossible, even heartbreaking, to overcome those attitudes now that the nation was no longer at war. Nonetheless, the retired World War II directors did not want to spoil the chances of those women who felt differently and wanted to remain in the service. Finally, they feared that their personal opposition might be construed as a condemnation of servicewomen's wartime record. Thus they chose not to testify.[26] It was unfortunate that Palmer, still on active duty and subject to orders, was compelled to testify, and that she had not told her superiors of her true feelings.[27]

The proposal was not helped by Georgia Representative Carl Vinson's statement: "The Navy is a fighting military organization, and trying to put women into the regular Navy would be a nice way for women to get killed."[28] Vinson wanted to establish a permanent women's Reserve, whose members would be at the beck and call of the military, subject to unlimited active duty when the service branches needed them—a "happy solution," he believed.[29] Maine Representative Margaret Chase Smith felt very differently and was exasperated by the men's arguments. "They either need these women or they do not!"[30] she exclaimed during the hearings. A woman in the Reserve on a permanent basis would be subject to being recalled at any time. Her civilian life and career would be subject to constant disruption, yet she could not build a military career, she explained. Smith was persuasive, and in the end the committee took no action on the recommendation.[31]

The Army's proposed bill was introduced to Congress two months later, in July 1946, as the Women's Army Corps Integration Act; by the time Congress voted to adjourn in August at the height of the election campaigns, however, no action had been taken.[32] During the interim, the services obtained authorization for small numbers of women to remain in uniform.[33]

Captain Edith Sullivan, stationed at Fort Lewis, Washington, kept her parents informed of the legislation's ups and downs. "They are very busy these days setting up criteria for selecting WAC officers for the regular Army," the Chazy, New York, WAC wrote in August 1946. "We are being tested, rated by the men. . . . At one time I would have considered it very favorably, but now [it] is a different matter. . . . The WAC, in general, has been knocked around by legislation that has killed most of the desires any of us have had toward staying in permanently. . . . Too bad the country doesn't know a good thing when it has it."

Captain Edith Sullivan (Moss), Women's Army Corps, 1947.
Edith Sullivan Moss Collection, Gift of Marcia J. Moss, Women's Memorial Collection.

Two months later her concern had grown more acute. "Right now the status of the WAC is hanging in the balance. We don't know what will happen to us in the next few months but some definite action will have to be taken by Congress and very soon. If they do decide to have a regular Army WAC they will have to reenlist hundreds of old WACs or start training again for there aren't enough of us left to even make a large enough nucleus on which to build. The greatest interest on the part of the girls has been lost and I'm afraid the project if approved and started would prove a failure."

By August 1947, Sullivan, now stationed at Camp Stoneman, California, was more sanguine. After spending an evening with Lieutenant Colonel Geraldine Pratt May, she wrote they "spent the evening discussing the future plans for the WAC as Regular Army. It will be good to have the legislation all passed and to be sure. We've lived on expectations so long."[34]

The Congress that came back to the debate about women's place in the military in 1947 was the famous "Do Nothing Congress"—so named by Harry S. Truman. Republicans swept the 1946 elections, carrying both houses of Congress for the first time since the Depression, and—with 246 seats in the House and 51 in the Senate—had little reason to do what the Democratic president wanted. Republicans, long out of power, felt the 1946 election bode well for their future. They had, they thought, found a winning campaign message: blaming the Democrats for the rise of international communism. Or, as the GOP's National Committee chair, Tennessee Congressman B. Carroll Reese, told the press, the 1946 election was a choice between "Communism and Republicanism."[35]

In April 1947, Congress finally broke with precedent and created permanent regular and reserve status for two special groups of military women: Army and Navy nurses and Army medical specialists. Before World War II, Army nurses had held "relative rank," which carried less authority and pay and fewer privileges than comparable male officers, while Navy nurses existed in a uniformed limbo with no rank at all, neither officer nor enlisted and did not achieve even relative rank until 3 July 1942.[36] During the war, both groups of nurses were granted full military rank, but only on a temporary basis. Because military nurses had performed outstandingly during the war, there was little opposition to the bill. Army and Navy nurses viewed the 1947 act as a long overdue step forward.

Meanwhile, the Army and Navy each reintroduced their proposed legislation to establish a permanent place for other servicewomen. The two bills were combined into one, the Women's Armed Services Integration Act of 1947. This time the service branches sent in the big guns to testify on behalf of it, including General Dwight D. Eisenhower, chief of staff of the Army, and Fleet Admiral Chester Nimitz, chief of naval operations. Eisenhower told the committee that women's service was a matter of military necessity: "I want to emphasize the urgency of action by *this* Congress. Due to the critical shortage of trained infantrymen we have recently permitted all combat men presently holding military desk jobs to be reassigned to the Infantry. We need replacements for these soldiers: the WACs are the most logical source of replacement."[37]

Navy Women's Director Captain Joy Bright Hancock echoed Eisenhower's sentiments. "It would appear to me that any national defense weapon known to be of value should be developed and kept in good working order and not allowed to rust or to be abolished."[38] WAC Director Colonel Mary Hallaren was also persuasive, perhaps because she chose strategically to frame her argument within a domestic context. "When the house is on fire we don't talk about a woman's place in the home. And we don't send her a gilt-edged invitation to help put the fire out. In the future, we shall be concerned with her utilization, where she can best fit into the plan for fire prevention and control, with her equipment, what she needs for her own protection, what she needs to do the job, with her training, how by the quickest most expeditious method she can learn the job that needs to be done."[39]

In late May 1942, Massachusetts schoolteacher Mary Agnes Hallaren's mother propped a newspaper article up against her daughter's morning coffee cup. The article announced the last day to apply for the Women's Army Auxiliary Corps (WAAC) officer training program. That morning Hallaren went to the local recruiting office and filled out an application. On it, she listed fifteen years' teaching experience and stated that she had used her summer vacations indulging her passion for travel on walking tours of the United States, Canada, South America, Europe, and parts of the Far East.[40]

Hallaren was accepted into the first WAAC officer class and appointed its executive officer. After the WAAC became the Women's Army Corps or WAC, she commanded the first WAC battalion sent to London in mid-July 1943, consisting of 557 enlisted women and 19 officers assigned to the Eighth Air Force. Then a captain, Hallaren was appointed WAC Staff Adviser for the area. Within two years, Major Hallaren found herself WAC Staff Director for the entire European Theater of Operations, which placed her in charge of nine thousand WACs in England, France, Germany, Austria, and Belgium. As she had literally walked through England, France, Germany, and Italy, Hallaren was undaunted.[41]

Colonel Mary A. Hallaren, director of the Women's Army Corps, 1953. U.S. Army photo, Virginia K. Straszewski Collection, Women's Memorial Collection.

The wartime legislation creating the women's military services anticipated that women would be needed only for the duration of the war plus six months. After the war, realizing the military could ill afford to lose all women in uniform, service leaders obtained a series of extensions from Congress while they studied the feasibility of keeping a token force of women. In June 1946, Lieutenant Colonel Hallaren was recalled from Europe to become WAC deputy director. Ten months later she became director.[42]

Colonel Hallaren firmly believed that young women should serve their country just as men did. She supported the idea of a national service program that would require all young people to give their country at least one year's ser-vice in the military or a civilian service.[43]

According to the 1948 Women's Armed Services Integration Act, there could be only one full colonel in each of the women's service components. When Colonel Hallaren's tour of duty as WAC director came to an end, she had to decide whether to retire or remain in the WAC and accept a demotion. In January 1953, again a lieutenant colonel, Hallaren returned to Headquarters, European Command, in Frankfurt, Germany. From 1957 until her retirement in 1960, she served as an operations officer in the Office of the Assistant Secre-tary of Defense for Personnel and Reserve Affairs.[44]

Impressed, the Senate committee and full Senate approved the bill in mid-July and forwarded it to the House for action. There the bill stalled when the House Armed Services Subcommittee, chaired by New York Republican Walter G. Andrews with Georgia Democrat Vinson as the ranking minority member, voted to postpone further hearings until January 1948.[45] Both Andrews and Vinson were determinedly opposed to women in the regular service branches.[46]

All the while there was an even bigger battle going on. The entire defense establishment would be reorganized by the National Security Act that Truman sent to the hill in February. The Army and Army Air Forces wanted all services unified under a single defense department headed by a civilian secretary; the Navy was adamantly opposed because the Army was so much larger that the Navy felt it would dominate all future debates and funding. The Navy was also jockeying to control all aircraft required for naval operations, including those based on land. The Army Air Forces in particular were opposed to ceding what it saw as its mission to the Navy. Both wanted control over aircraft capable of delivering nuclear weapons, which most observers saw as the future of warfare. Meanwhile, the Army was also attempting to downsize the Marine Corps' historic mission and take over the land phases of amphibious operations.[47]

When Congress passed the final bill in late July 1947, it failed to act on the Women's Armed Services Integration Act; it did, however, unify the services under a civilian secretary of defense, who was head of the newly created National Military Establishment. It institutionalized the Joint Chiefs of Staff, an ad hoc group that had been meeting informally since World War II, as an official entity of almost autonomous peers. The National Security Act also established the United States Air Force as a stand-alone service, but only vaguely defined the services' "roles and missions," and rivalries continued to simmer just below the boiling point well into 1948. Navy Chief James V. Forrestal became the new secretary of defense, and within fifteen months had recommended changes that reined in the Joint Chiefs, gathered authority into the secretary of defense's office by creating a cabinet-level Department of Defense to which the Joint Chiefs were answerable, and defined more clearly each service's mission. But the personal costs to him were high. He suffered a nervous breakdown early in 1949 and committed suicide, a tragedy some blamed on the intensity of infighting among the services and service chiefs in a world that was growing more dangerous by the day.[48]

When hearings on the servicewomen's integration resumed in 1948, the Army and Navy sent in reinforcements to argue for it. The Marine Corps joined the Navy in asking for permanent regular, as opposed to exclusively reserve, Women Marines, and the Air Force arranged to have its proposal for the utilization of women incorporated into the bill.[49] An act to grant small numbers of women a permanent place in the military undoubtedly was an easy place for the services to cooperate, when each service's leaders felt they were battling the others for survival.

The revised bill, the Women's Armed Services Integration Act of 1948, went to the Senate and House Armed Services Committees in January. Once again, the debate was contentious. War was a special circumstance; the idea of the peacetime military utilizing women was a hard sell. Only a tiny group of women would be affected if no bill were passed, and arguments in favor of the bill were largely pragmatic, not based on righting any great societal wrong against women. Conservative congressmen could continue to demagogue against the idea knowing full well their reactionary views reflected majority opinion and would never cost them votes. The most influential among these, Andrews and Vinson, continued to insist that women at most be allowed reserve status; that is, to be called upon only in the event of a national emergency. Publicly, they stated that women should not be admitted into the regular forces until their peacetime reserve service could be "studied and observed," a classic legislative dodge that is equivalent to burying an issue.[50]

Once again, in 1948, the highest-ranking military leaders in the country testified in favor of the act. Eisenhower admitted, "When this project [the Women's Army Auxiliary Corps] was first proposed in the beginning of [World War II], like most old soldiers, I was violently against it. I thought a tremendous number of difficulties would occur. . . . [However] every phase of the record they compiled during the war convinced me of the error of my first reaction. In tasks for which they are particularly suited, WACs are more valuable than men, and fewer of them are required to perform a given amount of work. . . . In the event of another war . . . It is my conviction that everybody in this country would serve under some form of call to duty. . . . I assure you that I look upon this measure as a 'must.'" [51]

Fleet Admiral Chester W. Nimitz, chief of naval operations, admitted he, too, had needed convincing. "I was one of the doubters in the early days, and I was definitely reluctant to see this (women's) program started. However, after it (the WAVES) started and after I saw it work, I became a convert."[52] The list of other military leaders who urged Congress to approve the bill included Forrestal, Army Chief of Staff General Omar N. Bradley, and Navy Chief of Staff Admiral Louis E. Denfeld. But doubts remained strong, and the House committee, rebuffing testimony from the country's most prestigious military leaders, voted in April to allow women only reserve status. Observers were shocked.[53] "The blow left us speechless," said Captain Joy Bright Hancock. "I had been seated alongside my boss, Admiral Sprague. We looked at one another in absolute astonishment, so convinced had we been that our presentations had met with approval."[54]

Joy Bright, born in 1898, was one of three sisters in a stimulating Wildwood, New Jersey, family. Their father was a state legislator and their mother was an active suffragist. Suffrage leaders Carrie Chapman Catt and Jane Addams were frequent visitors and role models for the sisters, the eldest of whom became a lawyer, the second a teacher, and the third—Joy—a military pioneer.[55]

When the Navy broke ground by enlisting women in World War I, Joy Bright became a yeoman (F) first class (the "F" was for female). She rose quickly to the rank of chief yeoman, serving as a courier at the Camden shipyard and later at the Naval Air Station at Cape May, where she remained as a civilian employee at war's end. Her first marriage, to naval aviator Charles Little, ended several months after the wedding when he was killed in the explosion of his experimental airship.

The young widow returned to work at the Navy's Bureau of Aeronautics in Washington and, in 1923, took a job at the Naval Air Station in Lakehurst, New Jersey, where she fell in love with another aviator, Lieutenant Commander Lewis Hancock. Fifteen months after they married, his plane crashed in a violent storm and she was widowed a second time.

To recover and to conquer her fear of aircraft, Joy Bright Little Hancock learned how to fly; she quickly discovered, however, she was more interested in the mechanics of how aircraft flew than in flying them. When she learned to assemble and disassemble engines she realized women could do these jobs as well as men. Rejoining the U.S. Bureau of Naval Aeronautics in 1930, she wrote and edited magazine articles and, in 1938, wrote her first book, *Airplanes in Action.*

When World War II started, the Army established a corps of uniformed women to supplement military manpower, but the more conservative Navy balked. The Bureau of Aeronautics, more used to innovative thinking, assigned Hancock to look at how the Royal Canadian Air Force was using women in noncombat positions. Hancock wrote a glowing report and, although many commanders were reluctant, the Navy established Women Accepted for Volunteer Emergency Service or WAVES. Hancock

Commander Joy Bright Hancock, U.S. Navy Women's Reserve (WAVES), World War II. U.S. Navy photo, Gift of Ada B. Jones, Women's Memorial Collection.

joined as a lieutenant. WAVES Lieutenant Commander Mildred McAfee, an academic, found Hancock's knowledge of the Navy and how it worked invaluable.[56]

Hancock persuaded McAfee to allow WAVES to take specialist training at then all-male aviation schools. Although some Navy pilots initially protested the idea of women servicing their planes' engines, Hancock pointed out that civilian women were building the very same engines. Some three thousand WAVES eventually earned their aviation machinist mate rating and women officers taught advanced navigation classes to aviators. WAVES also staffed control towers and repaired intricate navigational instruments. Hancock then turned her attention to getting WAVES overseas billets. In late 1944, Congress allowed WAVES to be assigned to Hawaii, Alaska, and the Caribbean. Eventually four thousand WAVES served in Hawaii, freeing men for frontline combat duties.

When the war ended, Hancock began lobbying for WAVES to remain in the Navy on a permanent basis. She became director of the Navy Women's Reserve in 1946, and testified in favor of the Women's Armed Services Integration Act in Congress in 1946 and again in 1947 and 1948, until the act making women a permanent part of the United States Armed Forces finally became law.[57]

Eventually, the bill's supporters learned that behind the scenes, the House committee had convened closed sessions at which members heard off-the-record testimony presented by unnamed members of the Navy

Department. These unnamed "experts" claimed that the vast majority of Navy men did not want women aboard ships, and pointed out that if women did not serve aboard ships, their mere presence in the Navy onshore would disrupt men's ship-to-shore assignment rotations and damage morale. Afterward, California Representative Leroy Johnson remarked he had found it suspicious that only senior military leaders were testifying in favor of the bill. What about the "many, many" midlevel officers in the military? he asked. He assumed these men opposed women regulars.[58]

Michigan Representative Paul W. Shafer wondered aloud if granting women officers regular status would be fair to men. Many male officers with combat records, he reminded his fellow members of the House, had not been accepted into the regular Army after the war. Committee chair Andrews echoed Shafer's argument, asking incredulously, "You would dish out regular commissions to women in spite of the fact that these young men, who fought for their country during the war, were denied these commissions?" And there were those with a different argument: Representative Edward H. Reese contended that civil service women could do almost all of the jobs performed by military women, so there was really little need for women in uniform.[59]

There does not appear to have been a party alignment in the House on this issue. Both Andrews, for example, and Margaret Chase Smith were Republicans, and they were diametrically opposed on the issue. Vinson, on the other hand, was a Democrat.

Because the Senate had already voted to approve the Women's Armed Services Integration Act as written (with women as regulars and Reserves of the Army, Navy, Marine Corps, and Air Force), a joint committee was appointed to resolve the discrepancies between the House and Senate versions of the bill. Twenty days after it first rejected the Women's Integration Act, the House Armed Services Committee voted a second time to reject the Senate's version of the bill, offering instead its own version, with women serving in a reserve capacity only.[60]

As the fine-tuning of the Women's Armed Services Integration Act continued, a steadily worsening international situation during the first half of 1948 began to affect the thinking of many representatives. During that time, the Soviet Union consolidated its hold on Eastern Europe, gaining complete political control of Czechoslovakia. In May, war broke out between Arab and Israeli armies immediately after the proclamation of the state of Israel. Beginning in March, the Soviet Union began to restrict rail and highway traffic into the divided city of Berlin, located in the Soviet zone of Occupied Germany, and by June had totally blocked access to Berlin. Because the United States did not want to invade the Soviet zone and start World War III, the U.S. Air Force began a massive yearlong airlift to supply Berliners with food and fuel.

The deteriorating situation in Europe and the Army's inability to recruit enough volunteer men led President Truman to ask Congress for a peacetime draft. At the same time that the draft and the Women's Armed Services Integration Act were wending their way through Congress, an alternative solution to the manpower crisis was being pushed. Universal Military Training (UMT) would conscript all young men between eighteen and twenty for six months to a year of military training and then National Guard service. It struck the conservative newly Republican Congress as too comprehensive and expensive, and especially too New Deal–ish, the sort of social program they were trying to end. Reluctant to vote for a draft and suspicious of UMT, politicians began to waver on the issue of military women. They did not want their constituents to think that they had turned down a potential source of volunteers when they were voting to send unwilling boys to war. Grudgingly they began to switch sides. "Let the draft fill up the shortages that only men can fill," California Representative Harry Sheppard said. "But let us not take a man away from farm, home or school . . . to be a telephone operator. There are and always will be . . . jobs women can do better."[61]

The integration act, which became law on 12 June 1948, permitted women in both the regulars and Reserves of each of the services. It also attempted, however, to alleviate many of the other concerns expressed by members of Congress during the hearings. In an attitude that paralleled the business world's view of women executives and managers, representatives were disturbed at the idea of women officers ordering men about. They feared that "the military order and discipline necessary for success could never be sustained if male soldiers were faced with taking orders from 'Lady' generals, admirals and colonels." To allay these fears, the highest rank for a woman would be colonel or, if she were in the Navy, captain, and there could be just one such high-ranking woman in each service or nurse corps. The "women's director" would hold that rank on a temporary basis for the duration of her assignment, and then resign or step down a rank. Furthermore, the bill included language giving the service secretaries the prerogative of prescribing "the military authority which female persons . . . may exercise and the kind of military duty to which they may be assigned."[62]

The law also implied that women soldiers were not to be combatants. This was not controversial. No one in the military or in Congress had considered allowing women to serve in positions that would subject them to combat; the culture of the day could not conceive of it. Delineating women's noncombat positions in the Navy, Marines, and Air Force was simple: women were prohibited from serving aboard combat ships or aircraft. Because the Army could not come up with a clear-enough definition of combat, the law gave the secretary of the Army the responsibility of deciding how Army women might serve, as long as he took into account "the intent of Congress."[63]

As the combat restriction limited women's military usefulness, it is no surprise that legislators capped their numbers, although the combat restriction doesn't appear to have been the direct cause of the cap. The law established a limit on the number of women (they could not exceed 2 percent of the regular parent service, though there was no cap in the Reserves) and restricted both their command authority and promotion potential.[64] The net effect of these limitations would severely hamper the ability of the services to attract intelligent, skilled women. When the new war broke out only two years later, the newly established women's services found themselves incapable of responding in the way the Department of Defense, Congress, and their parent services suddenly expected them to.[65]

As a result of the laws granting women permanent status in the military, when the Korean War began the nation did not have to start entirely from scratch to define women's place in the national defense. Nevertheless, as Colonel Mary Hallaren had warned, much of the effort and many of the mistakes that had been made in World War II would be repeated.

Servicewomen's Integration: "Prayerful Assumption" versus "Prevailing Ambivalence"

We are proceeding on the prayerful assumption that [during the next war] the right kind of women are going to volunteer and in the proper numbers. Such optimism is not justified by past experience. The hard won lessons of the last war prove that we will need women.
—Congresswoman Frances P. Bolton, June 1949[1]

[In the event of mobilization, we plan to] utilize the greatest number of women possible, recognizing at the same time the prevailing ambivalence about the utilization of women's skills.
—Joint Chiefs of Staff policy statement, February 1950[2]

WITH THE ENACTMENT of the Army-Navy Nurse Act in 1947 followed by the Women's Armed Services Integration Act in 1948, military women finally gained permanent status in the officer and enlisted ranks of the Regular and Reserve of the Army, Navy, Marine Corps, and the newly established Air Force. Their transition to this new status would take place at a time when the military itself was in the throes of a major reorganization, compounded by a growing threat of another war. Manpower was once again being mobilized with the restoration of an all-male draft and the Joint Chiefs of Staff directed the services to use military womanpower to the maximum extent practicable.

Within days of the passage of the 1948 Integration Act, all the services swore in small numbers of women World War II veterans, many of whom had remained on active duty. They were to form the nuclei of women other than nurses and medical specialists, the female enlisted and line officers for each service. As mandated by the law, the number of women serving in the Women's Army Corps (WAC), Navy Women's Reserve (commonly referred to as WAVES, Women Accepted for Volunteer Emergency Service, the name of their World War II predecessor), Marine Corps Women's Reserve, and the Women in the Air Force (which became known as WAF) remained tiny.

Each service made a public ceremony of swearing in the first women. Master Sergeant Anne Peregrim remembered that she and five other Women Marines working at nearby offices in the Navy Annex were sworn into the service on the birthday of the Marine Corps, 10 November. "It was a solemn occasion, and we were all on our best behavior because the director of Women Marines was with us. That night, however, we all attended the Marine Corps Ball, and that was our celebration."[3]

The 1948 Integration Act strictly limited the number of non-nurse women in each of the regular services, although there were no restrictions on the number of women in each Reserve. Each service was given a maximum number of regular officers, warrant officers, and enlisted women it might commission or enlist during the two-year period between June 1948 and June 1950. After that date, the number of women regulars was limited to 2 percent of each service.

The Women's Army Corps (WAC), limited to 7,500 enlisted women, counted 6,551 by June 1950. The WAC also was limited to 500 officers and appears to have been at or near strength on the eve of the Korean War; the actual number is unclear because the documents enumerating women Army officers lump WAC officers with nurses and medical specialists. The Navy Women's Reserve was limited to 500 officers and 6,000 enlisted. The actual number remained much smaller than authorized, however; by June 1950, just before the outbreak of the Korean War, the WAVES had 490 regular officers but just 2,800 active duty regular enlisted.[4]

The number of Women Marines was by far the smallest; as of mid-1950, it had only 65 regular officers and 496 regular enlisted on active duty. The Women's Marine Corps Reserve, meant to supplement the regular component, consisted of 15 platoons, each with two officers and 50 enlisted, in major cities across the country and 18 officers and 41 enlisted women on active duty in the Reserve.[5]

The WAF (pronounced to rhyme with "staff") were predominantly women who had served as WACs in the Army Air Corps during World War II. By the end of June 1948, the Air Force had 168 women officers and 1,433 enlisted women, far below the 300 officers, 40 warrant officers and 4,000 enlisted allowed by law. As a result, over the next two years, the Air Force would devote many resources to recruiting and training. By June 1950, the WAF, with 3,800 enlisted women, 200 regular officers, and 90 reserve officers on active duty, was still under strength.[6]

Growth in all the services was so slow that, by the beginning of the Korean War, there were only about twenty-two thousand women on active duty, one-third of those in the health professions. The roughly fifteen thousand women in the line (i.e., not in the nurse corps or the medical specialist corps) actually constituted less than 1 percent of America's total military force, or less than half the legally permissible strength.[7]

With the passage of the Integration Act, the service branches were free to set up the official frameworks necessary to enlist, train, commission, place, and maintain regular and reserve servicewomen in jobs where they were needed across the United States and overseas. Because the Coast Guard at that time only became a part of the Navy during war, the Integration Act did not apply to it. It was not until November 1949, spurred by a congressional appropriation, that the Coast Guard reactivated the Women's Volunteer Reserve (called SPARs during World War II) and invited former women officers to apply for new reserve commissions. In March 1950, its Volunteer Reserve opened to enlisted women. Although in theory the Coast Guard then had in place the framework necessary to utilize its women veterans during the Korean War, the Coast Guard recalled fewer than thirty women to active duty during the war.

> When the Korean War started in June 1950, former Coast Guard SPARs Pearl Faurie and Betty Splaine were civilians working in Washington, D.C., but both missed their days in uniform.
>
> During the war, Faurie had worked at Coast Guard Headquarters; when she received a letter from the commandant asking her to return to duty, "I decided . . . to take a chance on the Coast Guard." "I really was 'taking a chance,' because the Coast Guard told me that they could only guarantee my job for five months, until they obtained the necessary authorization from Congress to retain women on extended active duty. But I figured that headquarters would probably get the authorization because of the [Korean] war. Also, I liked the retirement benefits and health coverage that came with military service. I was a single woman, and my civilian job didn't offer any comparable benefits."
>
> Faurie returned to duty at Coast Guard Headquarters in January 1951. Because the Coast Guard did not yet have the authorization to place women on active duty, they moved Faurie and other female reservists to an office building

Pearl Faurie, center, with four other U.S. Coast Guard women who also were on active duty from 1952 to 1954. Clockwise from top left: Ruth V. Perry, Faurie, Irene Fullam, Ruth Rohan (Lewis), and Carol Stillwell Scott. U.S. Coast Guard photo, Betty Splaine Collection, Women's Memorial Collection.

in the nearby Clarendon neighborhood of Arlington, Virginia, where they would be less visible. "They really wanted to hide us. They even told us not to wear our uniforms to work!"

As chief yeoman, Faurie supervised six other enlisted women, all with the rank of yeomen first class, in the Reserve Training Unit Program, typing lesson plans and office correspondence. She remained on active duty in the Coast Guard, became the first woman E-9 (master chief) in the Coast Guard in 1964, and retired a master chief yeoman.[8]

SPAR Betty Splaine had returned to her hometown of Boston and her civil service job at the Veterans' Administration when the Coast Guard demobilized the SPARs in 1946. When the VA job was moved to Philadelphia she decided instead to move to Washington, D.C., to work for the law firm headed by her

Chief Yeoman Betty Splaine models the U.S. Coast Guard service uniform for Armed Forces Day, Philadelphia, Pennsylvania, 1952. U.S. Marine Corps photo.

former Coast Guard boss. She wanted to get back into the Coast Guard, but they had no women on active duty at that time. In 1949, however, she was able to join a Coast Guard VP Squadron, a reserve port security unit. The personnel of this unit were not on active duty; they were reservists with civilian day jobs who met twice a week in the evenings as a unit to keep their military skills current. She was in charge of personnel records and attendance rosters.

The Coast Guard did not call Splaine back to active duty until 1953, but thereafter she remained on active duty until 1970, and retired as a chief warrant officer 4.[9]

An important early question with which the services grappled was just what "integrating" women would mean. The WAC and the Army and Navy Nurse Corps (ANC and NNC), for example, already were separate and distinct organizations with separate chains of command responsible for training, assigning, supervising, promoting, and disciplining personnel; the Air Force Nurse Corps (AFNC) and Medical Specialist Corps, formed in 1949, followed that example and was separate. The Navy and Marine Corps stuck to the organizational philosophies and policies each had developed during World War II: on the job, Navy and Marine women reported to regular unit commanders; in their barracks, they were supervised by women officers and NCOs. The newly formed Air Force decided to integrate enlisted women and line officers as much as possible into its existing personnel structure. Although it had the same World War II precedents as the Army, it felt more freedom to improvise and define itself as separate from the Army.

From the outset, Air Force leaders decided that the WAF should be integrated fully throughout the force, rather than set apart in separate women's units as had been done in the Army. Although full integration was the Air Force's theoretical goal, the degree to which women should or could actually be integrated into an overwhelmingly male organization rapidly became problematic.[10] The majority of male Air Force officers vigorously advocated the total integration of women into the units to which they were assigned to work; they wanted to eliminate WAF officer supervision of enlisted women as well. On the other hand, these same male officers assumed that as a matter of course Air Force women would be trained and housed separately.[11]

The prevailing attitude concerning women in the late 1940s was that women needed guidance and protection. Director of Women in the Air Force Colonel Geraldine Pratt May and her officers insisted that some kind of formalized structure of supervision and control was essential so that the women's problems did not get lost. In the end, a compromise developed that was similar to Navy and Marine Corps' operating procedures. Unit commanders supervised the women on the job but the women were attached to a WAF squadron with its own commander for off-duty supervision.[12]

Nonetheless, WAF officers were more nearly integrated into the Air Force than were their Navy and Marine Corps counterparts. Two important innovations: officer candidate school was coeducational (the first for the military); and there was just one officer promotion list, not separate lists as in the other services. "The WAF was to be a small, elite group of women—the best—which in the eyes of most Air Force leaders meant being superior to the WAVES. Comparing the WAF to the WAVES became almost an obsession with Air Force leaders," according to Major General Jeanne M. Holm. Not coincidentally, when WAF Director Geraldine Pratt May was replaced in 1951, her successor was a former WAVE officer.[13]

Some DOD-wide policies affecting servicewomen required legislation. For example, Congress needed to act if the dependent spouses of women veterans were to receive benefits, although the wives of male veterans had been receiving benefits for years. The process started in January 1950 when the House Veterans' Committee approved a bill to make the term "dependent spouse of a veteran" applicable to both men and women. In April the bill was approved by the full House and sent to the Senate. Male dependents, however, had to prove that they were totally dependent on their military spouse to receive benefits, a process that for wives was automatic.[14] There were other inequities as well that persisted for years. For example, military quarters could not be assigned to a servicewoman married to a civilian, nor could her husband shop at the post exchange or commissary store.[15]

In 1948, while the services were making plans for women, President Truman embarked upon two other controversial policies that affected the armed forces. First, he called on Congress to reduce military spending, which forced the services to cut strength levels[16] and resulted in inadequate supplies, worn-out or obsolete equipment, and abbreviated basic training. The service branches competed for the limited money available, a situation that led to significant interservice rivalry, tension, and hostility, especially among the service chiefs. While the nurse corps were seriously affected by the belt-tightening, the other women's service components had not yet even begun to approach their 2 percent limit.[17]

The second challenge came on 26 July 1948, when Truman issued Executive Order No. 9981, mandating an end to racial discrimination and segregation in the armed forces. To facilitate the order, Truman named an executive committee headed by former U.S. Solicitor General Charles O. Fahy to prepare and submit a plan for desegregating the military. Fahy was well known, having led the Roosevelt administration's battles against Supreme Court challenges of various New Deal social programs. Fahy did not rush his committee's deliberations; it was clearly a sensitive topic, and almost two years elapsed before the committee submitted its final report. In the interim, in 1949, the Air Force desegregated all units quickly and without fanfare. At best, the Army, Navy, and Marine Corps moved more slowly.[18]

During these early postwar years, the United States took on the lion's share of international responsibilities, setting a pattern that would continue. As the relationship between the Soviet Union and the West steadily deteriorated, the United States became the world's principal defender against international communism. U.S. military strategists and planners believed that Europe was the most vulnerable target of communist aggression. The Soviet blockade of Berlin in 1948 and the resulting Berlin Airlift reinforced this idea.

At the end of World War II, Germany had been divided into four zones, each occupied by one of the wartime allies, the United States, Great Britain, France, and the Soviet Union. The city of Berlin was also divided and controlled by the four Allied Powers but was inside the Soviet zone. When the Soviet Union blocked off all rail lines and roads into the city of Berlin in mid-June 1948, the United States sent additional B-29 and C-54 aircraft to Europe and began supplying the city with food and fuel via a giant airlift. The airlift continued for a year, although as winter set in, the demand for fuel increased and the number of planes flying in and out of the city had to be increased as well. Finally the Soviets, realizing that the United States would indeed supply the city indefinitely, backed down and reopened the rails and roadways.

One direct result of the Berlin Airlift was the creation in 1949 of the North Atlantic Treaty Organization (NATO) by the United States and its European allies. NATO's treaty bound member nations to consider an armed attack against one of them an attack against them all, and demonstrated the strength and determination of the United States and its allies to stand against the communist threat on the European continent.

The Soviet detonation of a nuclear bomb in August 1949, years ahead of what the United States had believed possible, was a profound shock to the West. Truman was also concerned about the fall of China to communist forces under Mao Tse-tung. By early 1950, the increasingly unstable international environment gave the president a change of heart about budget tightening. Accordingly, he instructed the secretaries of defense and state to study defense preparedness and funding. Their recommendation for increases in defense spending was awaiting consideration by the National Security Council when the North Koreans invaded South Korea in June 1950.[19]

Military life in the early years of the Cold War was fraught with tension both at home and abroad, although the situations could sometimes feel surreal. WAF Airman Second Class Joan DeAngelo (Fogelstrom) of Philadelphia, Pennsylvania, assigned as an aircraft control and warning specialist stationed in Great Falls, Montana, was part of a team that monitored flights over the U.S.-Canadian border. She recalls great concern over the presumed Soviet threat via Alaska, but admits she and her colleagues "never really saw anything suspicious."[20]

In Europe, the Soviet threat was even more serious. Because of its proximity to the communist Yugoslavian border, the hospital in Trieste, Italy, where Army nurse Captain Dorothy Looby (Manfredi) of Artesian, South Dakota,

Airman First Class Joan DeAngelo (Fogelstrom), U.S. Air Force, 1953. Courtesy Joan DeAngelo Fogelstrom.

Army nurse Dorothy Looby (Manfredi)'s hospital unit participates in field training exercises, Germany, 1951. Dorothy Looby Manfredi Collection, Women's Memorial Collection.

worked was a self-contained unit, almost a bunker. Looby and her fellow medical personnel could work, eat, and sleep without ever venturing outside. Her next assignment, a military hospital in Regensburg, Germany, was even closer to the communists—only about thirty miles from the East German border. Emergency field medicine procedures, in preparation for an attack, became a priority there.[21]

Living and working so close to a flash point meant that contact with a would-be enemy was an ever-present possibility for all servicewomen stationed in Europe. Nonetheless, the divided city of Berlin, deep in the Soviet sector, was a popular destination for U.S. troops on leave. Army Major Irene Michels (Sorrough) of New York, stationed in Heidelburg from 1949 to 1952, recalls that American military personnel traveling to Berlin by train had to be in uniform at all times and have their papers ready for the Russian guards when the train reached their sector.[22] Those who went to Berlin via car ran a different gauntlet. According to Army Major Irene Van Houten (Munster), the road leading to the city was lined with guard shacks at one-mile intervals. Inside each was a Russian soldier with a rifle "who always demanded a cigarette to let us by."[23]

Irene Michels (Sorrough), Women's Army Auxiliary Corps (WAAC), World War II. Women's Memorial Register.

Despite increasing international tensions, young women who joined the Army, Navy, Marine Corps, and Air Force in the years after World War II became members of small, tightly knit organizations that functioned in some ways almost like sororities. New recruits were carefully guided through their initial training and were frequently mentored during their early assignments. The longer a woman was in the service, the more of her peers she knew, and the greater the chance that she would be working with friends or acquaintances regardless of where she was assigned.

For example, the first exposure to service life that WAC officer candidates and enlisted recruits experienced was basic training at Fort Lee, Virginia, thirteen weeks for enlisted and six months for officer candidates. Regular Army officers had to be college graduates, but women with two years of college could be commissioned as reserve officers and, beginning in May 1950, women without previous military experience could enlist in the Reserve.[24]

Basic training oriented WACs to the Army and their place in it and included 385 hours in thirty-three different subjects such as military courtesy, drill, the care of uniforms and equipment, and Army administration.[25] Not all of the subjects taught were military in nature, however. WACs referred to certain aspects of basic training as "Hallaren's School for Young Ladies" (Colonel Mary Hallaren was then director of the Corps). One woman likened the "personal development" portion of WAC basic training to "the training any girl could get from her mother—if her mother was the dean of women at a good college, a fashion and beauty editor of a national magazine, and a trained teacher of art, applied psychology, and comparative cultures." Trainees, for example, learned how to use their voices properly, how to pack a suitcase, and "techniques of good grooming."[26]

The two-story barracks, where women lived sixteen to twenty to a squad, were a surprise to at least one visiting reporter from *Cosmopolitan* magazine. "Since Army regulations say nothing about the color of latrines, bulletin boards, scrub brushes, wash buckets, and tin cans for cigarette ashes," she told her readers, "these were painted a feminine pastel pink. The latrine was decked out with pink mirror frames, pink shelves over the sinks, pink toilet doors, and pink elephants bounding across the drab pine walls."[27]

An important part of basic training was learning how to wear the Army uniform properly, and this meant obtaining the right fit. One surprised newspaper reporter wrote, "In the Women's Army Corps there are nine sizes between 14SS (Short, Slender) and 14LF (Long, Full). There are 40 sizes of slacks, skirts and suits, and 23 sizes of jackets, overcoats, raincoats and summer dresses. Even with this range, alterations are frequently made to improve (a woman's) appearance at inspection." Recruits were each given $35 to buy their own, but officially approved, underwear at the post exchange. Because appearance was so important, all women were required to wear girdles for dress parade.[28]

Another aspect of WAC basic training, and one that elicited much commentary from newspaper reporters, the public, and the recruits themselves, was the class in weapons familiarization. The trainees studied the .45 automatic pistol, the M-1 .30 caliber carbine, the M-2 .22 rifle, and the M-1 .30 caliber rifle, but firing weapons on the rifle range was optional. The majority of women elected to try, and many did "surprisingly well," according to their instructors.[29]

Overseas weapons training was taken more seriously particularly in places closer to the front lines such as Tokyo where Army Private Muriel Scharrer (Wimmer) of Brooklyn, New York, worked as a medical technician. Although the women could absent themselves from the rifle range if they chose, no one did. "It reflected poorly on your company."

Muriel Scharrer (Wimmer) and other WACs wait outside their quarters at the Mitsubishi Building before heading to the rifle range, Tokyo, Japan, 1952. Muriel Scharrer Wimmer Collection, Women's Memorial Collection.

Toward the end of their training, WACs spent a week on bivouac, living in a field camp and wearing fatigues and helmet liners. They washed in their steel helmets, marched, studied mapmaking, crawled through an obstacle course (although without the machine-gun fire whistling overhead that their male counterparts experienced), and pitched the tents in which they slept. The vast majority of women Army recruits got through the rigors of basic training. In two and a half years, the WAC Training Center returned only 125 out of 9,000 women to civilian life.[30] The Army's WAC Officer Candidate School lasted twenty weeks and the soon-to-be second lieutenants covered many of the same subjects plus classes in military law, food service, personnel management, leadership and morale, recruiting, and unit management.[31]

The Navy trained its women officer candidates and enlisted women at different locales. Officer candidates spent five months at Newport, Rhode Island, while enlisted women received ten weeks of recruit training at Great Lakes Naval Training Center in North Chicago, Illinois, and then went on to specialist schools or field assignments.[32]

Officer candidates studied Navy tradition, history, customs, organization, administration, and correspondence; according to historians Jean Ebbert and Marie Beth Hall, however, the most significant thing about the program was the "unremitting emphasis on ladylike behavior. Trainees were issued a handbook that closed with these words: 'Remember always that you are a lady, a woman whose habits, manners, and sentiments are characteristic of the highest degree of refinement.'"[33] The Navy also emphasized ladylike deportment in the enlisted women's training. Female chief petty officers were in charge—and they were "all career Navy," emphasized Navy Personnelman Third Class Gloria Minich (Finucane) of West Chester, Pennsylvania. They were "very efficient women who could push us—but very proper," she said. "There were tremendous guidelines and ethical situations . . . formats that we had to follow, dress codes, etc. We were really watched over like some private girls' school."[34]

In the summer of 1950, a Reserve Officer Candidate Program for women started at the Great Lakes Training Center.[35] The reserve course condensed the Regular Navy's sixty-four days of basic into fourteen. Enlisted reservists trained in their naval district. Reserve recruits living in the 3rd Naval District, for example, trained at St. Albans Naval Hospital on Long Island, New York.[36]

Women once again wearing uniforms and saluting were such novelties in the domesticity-oriented postwar years, that just five days before the Korean War exploded into the headlines, the *New York Times* ran a feature story on the phenomenon of women Navy reservists training to become seaman apprentices. One recruit, Alice Lauer of Brooklyn, New York, boasted she had received two weeks of military leave with pay from her job at the telephone company in order to take basic training. Her obligation was one weekend each month on drill with the Reserve at the Floyd Bennett Air Station in Brooklyn. The other women in training with her at St. Albans also were office workers in civilian life. Dorothy Powers of Poughkeepsie, New York, said the uniform she wore on leave the previous Saturday night had inspired the theater owner to give her better seats. Another recruit said that she had noticed that store clerks were more courteous when she was in uniform.[37]

Meanwhile, the Marine Corps wasted no time in gearing up. In January 1949, for the first time since World War II, the Marine Corps had begun training women enlistees at the 3rd Recruit Training Battalion at Parris Island, South Carolina. The six-week course included Marine Corps history, mission, and organization, the mission of Women Marines and close order drill supervised by male drill instructors. Graduates were sent either to a specialist school or directly into the field. Most went to personnel administration school. Because of the small number of Women Marines on active duty and the Corps' desire to assign women in large units for ease of administration, there were very few opportunities for Women Marines to serve overseas and even stateside assignments were limited. The vast majority of women regulars served at Marine Headquarters in Washington, D.C., and at the bases in Parris Island and Quantico, Virginia.

The first class of women officers began in April 1949 at Quantico, under the direction of Captain Elsie E. Hill. Officer candidates could attend WOTC for six weeks during the summers of their junior and senior years of college, and become second lieutenants in the Marine Corps Reserve upon completion and reaching twenty-one years of age. Qualified enlisted women could attend the second-year course. A handful of honors graduates were selected to go on to the eight-week basic indoctrination course and receive regular commissions. Thirty-four women were recommended for commissions, seven as regular officers, at the first graduation on 9 September 1949.[38]

Marine Women's Reserve platoons, formed around the country, included both World War II veterans and some women who were completely new to the military. These platoons conducted weekly two-hour training sessions for which privates received $2.50 pay for each evening "drill" and officers as much as $7.67.[39] Because Marine women reservists met regularly, the Marine Corps was the only service that managed to keep its rosters of women reservists up-to-date, a fact that would reflect well on them when the Korean War broke out. It was a promising start, but in May 1950, just a month before the invasion, the Marine Corps suspended recruit training for the Regular Corps for lack of recruits. The training staff was reassigned and boot camp for women was not reestablished until after the start of the Korean War.[40]

The Air Force began training new women recruits at Lackland Air Force Base, San Antonio, Texas, in October 1948. Although Lackland was where all Air Force recruits were trained, enlisted men and women trained separately. The Air Force had considered coeducational training, but women enlisted had higher mental and educational levels and required less training (eleven weeks as opposed to thirteen) than did male volunteers. Basic training for males also involved bodybuilding, which it was agreed was "hardly appropriate for the ladies."[41]

Many of the women recruits had been store clerks or secretaries in civilian life, and, according to one newspaper account, had enlisted for reasons that ranged from wanting the money to continue their education or simply feeling they were in a rut. After basic training the women were assigned to advanced technical training in such areas as weather observation (Chanute Field, Illinois), radio operation and radar mechanics (Keesler AFB, Mississippi), photography and supply schools (Lowry AFB, Colorado), or the school of aviation medicine (Randolph Field, Texas).[42]

As an expression of the Air Force philosophy that women be integrated throughout the force, the Air Force began training new women officers with male officer candidates at Lackland in January 1949. The women received the same instruction as men except for physical training and field exercises. When men participated in field exercises, the women studied the administration of enlisted women, as the majority of them would serve as squadron commanders in charge of enlisted women during the early years of their careers.[43]

Although the military had discovered during World War II that enlisted women were capable of performing many more jobs than had originally been assumed, and the Joint Chiefs were committed to greater utilization of women, opportunities for any but traditional job assignments declined significantly after World War II. The main reason for this was simple: the restoration of the all-male draft. The military no longer faced reasons powerful enough to override cultural inhibitions against turning women into truck drivers and airplane mechanics, and the variety of jobs open to them declined steadily during the late 1940s and throughout the 1950s. Not even another war would be enough to expand enlisted women's opportunities in an era when society so rigidly relegated women to the home or to secretarial pools.

During World War II, there had been 408 military occupation specialties (MOS) considered suitable for Army women; by the end of the war, WACs served in 274 of them.[44] Now, there were fewer MOS and fewer still that were open to enlisted WACs: approximately one hundred, or about one-third of all Army jobs. These included clerk typist; draftsman; cook; cryptographer; machine accountant; pharmacy clerk; dental, X-ray, pharmacy, and laboratory technician; driver; supply specialist; finance clerk; signal message clerk; band member; high speed radio operator; stenographer; photographer; and postal operator. An individual's work preferences were considered when assignments were made. Slightly more than one-half of the women wound up in personnel and administration. The second largest group of enlisted women was assigned to the medical area. Very few escaped what would become known in a later era as "female ghettoes."[45]

> Military women who did avoid the female ghettoes were more often officers and quite often veterans who had remained in the military after World War II. Women's Army Corps Major Irene Van Houten (Munster) twice served on General Dwight D. Eisenhower's staff in Germany, once during the immediate postwar period and again in the early 1950s when Ike returned to Germany as

Supreme Commander of the Allied Powers in Europe. During her second tour of duty she served as assistant supply officer. When Eisenhower moved SHAPE headquarters to Versailles, Van Houten (Munster) was responsible for setting up the catonment.[46]

WAC Captain Esther Pulis (Corcoran) accompanied her boss, Brigadier General Robert McClure, to several assignments including the Army's Informational Control Division in postwar Germany and what became the Army's Psychological Warfare Division. A World War II veteran, Pulis originally enlisted in the WAC in 1943 as a new widow, after learning that Japanese friends, made when she and her late businessman husband lived in Japan, had been interned at POW camps in the Philippines. She was quickly spotted as officer material and recommended for Officer Candidate School (OCS).

In 1951, Pulis was named one of the first ten female lieutenant colonels, at the time the highest rank a woman could hold unless she was appointed WAC director. She remarried in May 1952 and left the WAC in October of that year.[47]

Major Irene Van Houten (Munster), Women's Army Corps (WAC). Women's Memorial Register.

WAC Lieutenant Colonel Esther Pulis (Corcoran), assistant executive officer of the Psychological Warfare Division, right, with WAC Private First Class Jimmie Nesom, the Pentagon, Washington, D.C., 20 August 1951. U.S. Army photo.

In 1948, enlisted women could in theory be trained for and assigned to thirty-one different Navy ratings or job areas similar to those of their World War II counterparts. Navy women worked at shore establishments as clerks, communications specialists, storekeepers, and medical technicians. The Navy realized, however, that women, in order to be a part of a team or to effectively replace men reassigned aboard ship, might have to know more than their permitted jobs. As a Bureau of Naval Personnel publication explained: "The Navy is still going to be made up of men—98 percent of it or more. If women recruits are to be able to fit into their own small niches, assuming their proper positions as working members of a very large outfit where there are many jobs which are beyond them physically, then it is necessary for them to recognize the ratings held by men only and to understand something of the basic responsibilities of those ratings." Inferred in this bureaucratese, explain Navy historians Ebbert and Hall, was an understanding that unlike the Yeomen (F) of World War I and the WAVES of World War II, some of the Navy's new generation of women might serve an entire career—but only in "small niches" and "proper positions."[48]

By 1950, the number of Navy ratings available to enlisted women had begun to decline. That year, 104 women specialists were transferred from three aviation ratings to other, more traditional (read "more feminine") career fields. The Navy's argument for limiting the ratings open to women was that women constituted such a small percent of the Navy, it would be more efficient to administer them if they were clustered in just a few job categories.[49]

Still, some Navy enlisted women held unique, nontraditional jobs during this period. Mary Redfern became the first regular enlisted woman to make an authorized parachute jump and graduate from the parachute rigger school. Although hundreds of Navy women had qualified as parachute riggers during World War II, these women had not been required—or allowed—to jump themselves. Redfern jumped with her class in January 1950, landing well within the keyhole of the jump circle. Speaking to reporters after the jump, she admitted she had been a bit nervous as the plane approached the drop zone, but when it came time to jump, she was in such a hurry that she did not have time to be frightened. She lost a ripcord as the chute snapped open. The same thing happened to one of the male students. According to tradition, both new riggers had to treat their fellow graduates to a round of drinks.[50]

Although Air Force enlisted women were not allowed to become jump qualified, there were more military jobs opened to them than to Navy women. Throughout this early period, the Air Force was discovering new ways to utilize enlisted women at the urging of WAF Director Geraldine Pratt May, who believed that the majority of Air Force jobs could be performed by women.[51]

WAF Corporal Dorothy Crawford (Ulrey) of Charleston, South Carolina, who enlisted in March 1951, was one of the first six WAF to go through teletype maintenance school. Five of the women, including Ulrey, passed and were as-

Dorothy Crawford (Ulrey), standing third from right, was a member of Class 06141-B, Teletype Mechanics School, Francis E. Warren AFB, Wyoming, September 1951. Courtesy Dorothy Crawford Ulrey.

signed to various bases. (The sixth woman stayed behind to repeat the course.) From teletype maintenance Ulrey moved on to radio maintenance while serving in Germany.[52]

WAF Staff Sergeant Joan Eastwood (Neuswanger) of Chicago, Illinois, who enlisted in October 1950, also worked with teletype equipment before the Air Force sent her to cryptography school. She encoded and decoded messages at two Air Force bases before being assigned to the Pentagon's communications center. Later, she volunteered to go overseas and was sent to Germany.[53]

Crawford and Eastwood were assigned their specialties. WAF Corporal Corinne Gogue (Cook) of San Diego, California, who enlisted in 1948, chose hers. Long fascinated by the weather, she asked to be sent to weather school.[54]

Air Force Staff Sergeant Joan Eastwood (Neuswanger) and a German civilian in front of the Old Heidelberg Bridge that stretches across the Neckar River, Germany, December 1952. Courtesy Joan Eastwood Neuswanger.

New Air Force privates, left to right, Geraldean Moore, Bettyjean Kinniebrue, Eleanor Jackson, and Corinne Gogue (Cook) are issued their service uniforms for basic training, Lackland AFB, San Antonio, Texas, February 1949. U.S. Air Force Photo.

After basic training, enlisted WAF were sent to schools for the 124 specialties open to women, and by June 1950; a total of 299 women had been trained as clerk typists, 211 as weather observers, 195 as supply technicians, 145 as radio operators, 125 as tabulation machine operators, 118 as teletype operators, and 106 as radio mechanics.[55]

During May's tenure as WAF director, between 1948 and 1951, the Air Force trained a much higher percentage of women in radar, radio, and wire maintenance than the Army Air Forces had during the World War II era. It also trained more women in intelligence, photography, and weather and flight operations than during World War II. Nonetheless, the percentage of women assigned to teach flying techniques to male pilots and gunners dropped substantially. Arguably, this reflected the same societal pressures that were driving other services' cutbacks on women's opportunities, as well as the concerns Congress had expressed in the debate surrounding the Women's Armed Services Integration Act that women not command men. The Air Force had no rules against women teaching men. At the same time, however, the Air Force's concern for creating the most elite women's service cut the percentage of women assigned to food service, transportation, medical services, and personnel administration.[56]

By June 1950, the Air Force had thirty-six WAF squadrons in the field and was planning to activate additional squadrons. Although many of these were small, with strengths ranging from nineteen to 107, the Air Force had plans to enlarge them significantly.[57] Having no way to know that war was imminent, May had reason to believe that her plans for the WAF were on course. Integration seemed to be working well, and May was particularly pleased that the Air Force was finding more ways to utilize and assign women. Although the director knew that some Air Force brass harbored lingering questions about whether women should even be in uniform, she could not foresee that a new war emergency would so quickly give these doubters the issue they needed to attack the viability of the WAF program.

In the midst of rapid growth between 1948 and 1950, the women military leaders were also struggling to follow the guidelines for racial integration established by each service following the president's executive order in July 1948. Through mid-1950, the Women's Army Corps stuck to the 10 percent quota for African Americans it had established during World War II. The WAC Training Center had five training companies for enlisted women (companies A, B, C, D and E) and black recruits were always sent to Company B, 1st Battalion, which was staffed with black officers and cadre. Every aspect of basic training—schedules, rules, and methods of doing things—was supposedly equal for blacks and whites, but black enlisted WACs were trained separately, housed separately, and dined separately. Although the Army's Officer Candidate School for women was integrated, as were specialist schools for women, on Army posts housing, dining, and entertainment facilities still were segregated.[58]

When Mary Teague (Smith) considered joining the service, the Army appeared to be the most welcoming. The former WAC lieutenant recalled, "When I enlisted in November 1948, Navy recruiters told me that they were not enlisting blacks. The Air Force told me that they had filled their quota. So I ended up in the first black (WAC) basic training company for women after World War II." After basic training, Smith attended racially integrated WAC Leadership School and WAC Officer Candidate School, was commissioned a second lieutenant, and then was assigned to a segregated basic training platoon and rotated through assignments as mess officer, supply officer, and executive officer.[59]

Even after segregation in the armed forces officially ended, racial incidents still occurred among troops stationed overseas. WAF Sergeant Ernestine Johnson (Thomas) of Warren, Ohio, who served in Japan during the early 1950s, recalls

Air Force Staff Sergeant Ernestine Johnson (Thomas) and an unidentified friend on a rooftop overlooking Tokyo, Japan. Courtesy Ernestine Johnson Thomas.

that Air Force personnel stationed in Toyko in the early 1950s were integrated but the Army personnel were not. According to Thomas, [General Douglas] MacArthur, the Supreme Allied Commander, "sent MPs up to Tokyo to investigate what the black WAFs stationed there were doing." MPs also harassed her male Army African American friends.[60]

Army Lieutenant Colonel Lucy Bond who had purposely delayed enlisting until the armed forces were officially desegregated, nevertheless experienced discrimination as a private first class when she was forbidden to sit with the troops she was escorting on a train from New Jersey to Washington, D.C. "It was frustrating," she recalls, "but there was nothing I could do about it."[61]

When the long-awaited Fahy report was finally issued in January 1950, it produced a plan for the immediate racial integration of the entire armed forces. The Army then issued a new directive entitled "Utilization of Negro Manpower in the Army," and by the middle of that year, WAC training and field units, as well as billets and mess facilities, were being desegregated.[62] Fort Lee had been totally desegregated by the time Smith left to be a WAC detachment commander at Fort Lewis, Washington, where, she discovered, integration was not yet complete. At Fort Lewis, she commanded a completely black detachment, and commanders refused to assign white women to her unit.

"Then I noticed that the white women were getting promoted faster than the women in my unit," said Teague. "I complained to the WAC staff advisor at 6th Army Headquarters at the Presidio, and she conducted a staff assistant visit. Although she told me that she reported discrepancies forward through the chain of command, nothing was done about it. Then I was assigned to Japan. I will always believe that they reassigned me to get rid of a troublemaker."[63]

Marine Corps Private First Class Annie Graham visits Marine Corps Private First Class Ann Lamb at the Post Supply Office, Henderson Hall, Arlington, Virginia, 24 March 1950. National Archives (127-N-313656).

It was a full year after Truman's order before Ann Estelle Lamb of New York City and Annie E. Graham of Detroit, Michigan, became the first African American Women Marines, making their platoon, Platoon 7, the first racially integrated unit in the entire Marine Corps in summer 1949. (Lamb was sent to personnel administration school after boot camp, where she graduated first in her class.) In 1950, "attracted to the Marines by an advertisement in a magazine that promised to train women for administrative duties, while offering opportunities for travel, adventure, and education,"[64] Chicagoan Annie L. Grimes became the third black woman to enlist in the Marines, and went on to make the Marine Corps her career. (In 1968, she became a warrant officer, and in 1970, the first black woman officer to retire after a full twenty-year career.)[65]

The Air Force had phased out race-segregated training at Lackland in 1949, but training flights (Air Force terminology for basic training units) were still segregated when Corinne Gogue (Cook) enlisted in December 1948. She was placed in the 3743rd (Colored) WAF Training Squadron. "There were only seventeen of us in the 3743rd compared to the 33-trainee strength of the white flights," she recalled, boasting, "On graduation day we competed with over ten thousand men trainees in the first 'All Basic Training Parade,' and our group came in third."[66] (After basic, the Air Force sent Gogue to weather school at Chanute AFB in Illinois, then to Wright-Patterson AFB, near Dayton, Ohio.)[67]

By the time Ernestine Johnson (Thomas), also an African American, "wound up in the Air Force by chance" in 1949, racial segregation was ending. "One afternoon a friend and I were out on a walk, and just happened to pass the recruiting station in Warren, Ohio. On an impulse, I went inside. . . . By the time I walked out of that building, I had signed up to join the Army. Originally the Navy had appealed to me because of the good-looking uniform, but they told me that I was too young to join the Navy." When Johnson traveled to Canton, Ohio, to take more tests and be sworn into the Army, recruiters took a look at her scores and asked her to enlist in the Air Force instead. Johnson was thrilled to join the "more glamorous" Air Force. At Lackland, Johnson discovered that the last all-black flight of WAFs had just been formed, and she was placed in the next WAF flight, the only African American among 150 women. "The woman who was my roommate in basic training became my close friend for life," she recalled.[68]

Perhaps the most obvious outward change regarding women that the Army, Navy, Marine Corps, and Air Force made between World War II and the years just before the Korean War broke out was the sudden concern for fashion each service evinced. Each service ordered that new uniforms be designed to reflect "the spirit of the modern day servicewoman," as opposed to her World War II counterpart. This largely public relations gesture ultimately created more problems than it solved. It was as if the military thought fashion the only way to recruit young women. However, as Major General Jeanne M. Holm, has pointed out, "In the immediate postwar period in all of the services, men's uniforms got a lot of attention and for essentially the same reasons—morale, public image, and recruiting. . . . When the Air Force became a separate service in 1947, its fashion-conscious leaders could hardly wait to get rid of their old World War II Army 'OD' (olive drab) duds."[69]

The Army at least could justify the change as an attempted morale booster based on solid information. A survey of WACs in late 1948 and early 1949 indicted many WACs found the old uniform both unattractive and uncomfortable. The Army picked designer Hattie Carnegie, famous for her suits, to design new uniforms. The Army also carefully put together a committee of highly visible women in the fashion industry to advise Carnegie, including Dorothy Shaver, president of Lord & Taylor; Edna Woolman Chase, editor-in-chief of *Vogue* magazine; and Carmel Snow, editor of *Harper's Bazaar*. In February 1950, at a major press event at the Fort Jay Officer's Club at Governors Island, New York, the National Research Council Advisory Committee to the Quartermaster General on Women's Clothing unveiled the new uniforms for women: WACs, Army Nurse Corps (ANC), and Women's Medical Specialist Corps (WMSC). Reporters at the event praised the "feminine, flattering" appearance of the taupe-colored uniforms, which had Carnegie's trademark "nipped-in waist, rounded hips, and an angled hat."[70]

Army women were not so ecstatic over their new uniform. Then Captain Mildred Inez Bailey (later to become director of the WAC and a brigadier

WACs model the new Hattie Carnegie–designed uniforms. U.S. Army Photo, Virginia K. Straszewski Collection, Women's Memorial Collection.

general) was serving in Europe at the time the new uniform was issued and regarded it less than fondly: "Most of us preferred the old uniform over the new. The old uniform looked just like the men's, and we were disconcerted to discover that our new uniforms were very different from those of our male counterparts. They were a different color, a 'taupe' shade, and the hat looked crooked perched over one eye."[71]

When the Air Force in 1947 adopted its distinctive new blue uniform with a similar summer uniform in a khaki shade called "silver tan," it apparently had given no thought to a uniform for women. But with the creation of the WAF in 1948, and the AFNC and AFWMSC the following year, there was an urgent need to come up with compatible uniforms for women.

Rather than hire a famous designer, the Air Force designed its own uniform. As the senior woman, WAF Director Geraldine Pratt May was very involved, selecting the blue shade herself. The winter uniform and shirt (with tabs rather than a necktie) were the same blue as the new men's uniforms, but the cut and design were patterned after uniforms worn by airline flight attendants. By the fashion standards of the time, it was very smart and contemporary. "The girls are much happier now that we don't have to wear neckties," May said, referring to the old Army uniform.[72] Other uniform items were less successful. The summer uniform in particular, a light blue two-piece, cotton-cord dress, that fit poorly and was difficult to maintain, was a near disaster.

When Airman Second Class Joan DeAngelo (Fogelstrom) arrived for basic training at Lackland Air Force Base in San Antonio, Texas, she and her fellow enlistees were issued Army clothing for everyday wear during basic training. "They had just switched over from the Army [the Army Air Forces became the Air Force in 1947] . . . so we . . . had khaki and the regular safari helmet and wrap-around seersucker dresses."[73]

WAF Corporal Dorothy Crawford (Ulrey) recalled that the seersucker was so "ancient" that the uniforms had be "washed, starched and ironed every day" to make them presentable. Crawford and her squadron mates eventually traded their seersucker dresses for men's fatigues, which they modified by moving the zippers from the front to the side of the pants.[74]

Off-duty, an Air Force squadron mate of Dorothy Crawford (Ulrey) irons the dreaded seersucker uniform in the barracks at Lackland AFB, San Antonio, Texas, Spring 1951. Courtesy Dorothy Crawford Ulrey.

When the Air Force decided to design its own new uniforms, WAF Technical Sergeant Mary Russ (Veres) of Roebling, New Jersey, field-tested parts of the proposed uniform. The suggested raincoat was a case in point. When she wore it in the rain, "the [coat] dye ran and ruined my dress." She had better luck with the sample hats. "When the review board asked me why I liked the hat I wore I told them I liked it because it had 'The Air Force Forward' Look." The board later chose that hat to accompany the dress uniform.[75]

The Navy also changed the color of its uniform, going to a midnight blue color for all Navy women, officers and enlisted, the same color as that worn by Navy men.[76]

In the fall of 1950, the commandant of the Marine Corps also decided to throw out the green World War II Women's Marine dress uniform, despite its being quite popular among the women. The Marine Corps asked another society couturier, Mainbocher, at the time among the most expensive of the world's fashion designers, to create a new blue uniform for Women Marines. The Chicago-born stylist (born Main Bocher) stated he was less than delighted with the assignment, as he had designed the famous WAVES uniform for the Navy during World War II but had never been paid the agreed-upon one dollar for his services. Once involved, however, he designed a complete new set of uniforms. Women Marines responded positively, and the Marine Corps made a point of presenting Mainbocher with a framed dollar bill.[77]

During 1948 and 1949, the Army also surveyed WAC enlisted trainees regarding their impressions of Army life, including food, medical care, training, job assignments, and social life. The results indicated most women were happy with their job assignments, and even found Army food to be "adequate and attractive" and medical care to be "adequate." The majority reported they enjoyed a good social life. Alarmingly, however, the majority of the respondents said they would not recommend joining up to a friend. Even worse, more than two-thirds of the women planned to leave the Army after their initial enlistment.[78]

Concerned about losing the servicewomen it had battled Congress for the authorization to permanently merge into its forces, the Army undertook to make servicewomen feel more a part of the team. In February 1950, it selected the first WAC "Outstanding Soldiers of the Month." The program, instituted the previous year, had already seen several contingents of much-ballyhooed male "Soldiers of the Month." The criteria were neatness, military bearing, courtesy, attitude, and leadership. The first WAC honorees were Sergeant Veva R. Halouska, "a dental technician with gleaming white teeth," stationed at Murphy General Hospital in Waltham, Massachusetts; Sergeant Concetta Nenni, of the Postal Adjutant's section at Fort Jay, New York; Private Audrey McCulloch, who worked at the Personnel Center in Fort Dix, New Jersey; and Private 1st Class Nettie Ellington, a stenographer at Fort Monmouth, New Jersey. They received a free weekend in New York City, courtesy of the Army.[79]

Army Special Services reserved rooms for the women at the Hotel Astor and supplied them with a guide for the weekend, Private 1st Class Marie Bankowski. A *New York Times* article reported that the weekend was patterned after those awarded the eight male "Soldiers of the Month" groups sponsored by the Army, but certain activities were changed.[80] The women were first treated to a Fifth Avenue beauty salon visit and then to lunch. Afterward, they toured Central Park in a hansom cab, and visited the Empire State Building and Statue of Liberty. That evening, they saw the ice show at Rockefeller Center, rather than the chic nightclubs where the servicemen had been feted—reportedly because the club owners did not want unescorted servicewomen on their premises.[81]

The WAC "Soldiers of the Month," received as much publicity as the Army could muster, but such efforts did little to reduce the high WAC attrition rate. More than half of the enlisted WACs were leaving the Army after their initial enlistment period was up. In response, the Army designed a second survey specifically for those enlisted women who indicated that they planned to leave. Their responses indicated that women were leaving the Army for a variety of reasons. Many wanted to get married and follow their husbands. Some wanted more autonomy; others wanted to live closer to home. Some felt that their job opportunities would be better outside the service.[82] Although the survey's format did not encourage women to explain why they as individuals were unhappy in the service, most young women appeared to want the same thing society expected of them: a home and family. Few aspired to any type of career, in the service or otherwise. Here was a battle the Army could not win. Nor could the other services.

The military's very emphasis on femininity (as expressed by the WAC Basic Training and the Navy Women Officer's Handbook), attractive new uniforms, makeup and etiquette lessons (not to mention girdles) represented an attempt to tailor women's military service to traditional American values. The Marine Corps was exceptionally concerned about the image its servicewomen presented and put considerable pressure on Women Marines to project an impeccable, elite image at all times. Each had it drilled into her that each represented all Women Marines at every hour of every day, and that by her deportment and actions she could prove a credit to the Marine Corps. In early 1950, Colonel Katherine Towle, director of the Women Marines, wrote to Captain Helen Wilson, commander of the Philadelphia platoon, "I think you were wise to put a stop to post-drill activities such as drinking in bars while in uniform. The very fact that a woman is in uniform makes her liable to criticism even though she may be behaving herself in every respect." She went on to say that Women Marines could do a great deal to prevent even unfair criticism. Criticism could be countered only by impeccable deportment, Towle believed.[83]

Official public appearances were seen as an opportunity to present the proper image. Although, owing to supply problems, few Women Marine reservists possessed complete uniforms, they felt themselves under considerable pressure to present the proper spit-shined image at public drills and parades. Concerned because her reservists had not yet been issued official brown oxfords, the officer in charge of the St. Louis, Missouri, platoon, Captain Nita Bob Warner, requisitioned a case of cordovan shoe dye and instructed her reservists to dye their civilian shoes. To her satisfaction, her platoon presented a finished look at the St. Louis Armed Forces Day Parade on 20 May 1950.[84]

Throughout this period, while the military worked simply to weave women into each of the services, the long-established Army and Navy Nurse Corps were having different problems, not the least of which were the Truman-ordered budget cuts. The size of the nursing corps historically had been tied to the size of the parent service. As the service branches shrank in 1948 and 1949 due to budget cuts, the authorized size of the nursing corps shrank with them. This had less impact than might be expected because the ANC was well below authorized strength during this period. During 1948, 1949, and the first half of 1950, the Army and Navy were closing unneeded hospitals in the name of cost cutting. Because the number of nurses authorized was tied to the number of hospital beds—one nurse for each ten beds with a 10 percent override for nurses performing nonhospital functions—closing hospitals might have meant nurse cutbacks had the ANC not already been understaffed.[85]

Many nurses, through no fault of their own, had not passed muster after the 1947 Army-Navy Nurse Act was enacted. With the exception of 671 Army nurses whose service predated World War II, veteran Army nurses were now required to apply for the 2,558 authorized commissions in the Regular ANC. This included those women who held relative rank[86] as well as those with commissions in the Reserve. There was a tough application process, which included strict age requirements, as well as a physical, technical proficiency requirements, and psychological exams. The ANC also had stricter marital requirements than the WAC; nurses who wanted to join the Regular Army could not be married. Finally, a board of five officers reviewed each applicant's nursing school records, professional references, and efficiency reports. Only 1,565 of 2,725 nurses who applied for the Regular Army were accepted. Nurses who could not qualify for Regular Army could apply for the Reserve, however, and the ANC made up the difference between the authorized strength and the shortfall of regular nurses by placing reserve nurses on active duty.[87] According to the official Army Nurse Corps history, in 1947 the Army was not so much interested in authorized strength as it was in acquiring only the best nurses.[88] The country was not at war, the extreme wartime nurse shortage was over, and administrators believed they had plenty of time to build.

In a move that further added to the shortage of Army nurses, in mid-1949, the ANC transferred twelve hundred regular and reserve nurses to the newly established Air Force Nurse Corps (AFNC). Regular Army nurses now totaled less than 40 percent of authorization, and retirements and resignations were exceeding new appointments. Chief of the ANC Colonel

Mary G. Phillips said the shortage was "a reflection of the overall shortage of nurses in civilian hospitals throughout the country."[89]

Certainly, the newly established Air Force Nurse Corps had difficulty recruiting nurses. By June 1950, the end of its first year in operation, it was 876 nurses short of its authorized strength.[90] The first AFNC chief, Captain Verena Zeller (Pettoruto Seberg), never had enough nurses to meet demands at the fifty-seven medical installations in the "zone of the interior" and the eighteen overseas facilities where they were needed.[91]

The Navy Nurse Corps (NNC) consisted of about 1,500 regular and 450 reserve nurses assigned to twenty-six naval hospitals and sixty-seven station hospitals and dispensaries in the United States and on the Aleutian Islands off Alaska; on Guam, Saipan, Samoa, and Midway; in China, and other Caribbean and the Atlantic stations. In addition, Navy nurses worked in three hospital corps schools, two hospital ships, eight Military Sea Transport Service (MSTS) ships and naval air transport planes.[92] MSTS, formerly under the Army, was placed under Navy jurisdiction in 1947, and Navy nurses replaced Army nurses on those vessels. Although the number of nurses on active duty never hit authorized strength between 1947 and 1950, the Navy Nurse Corps managed to fill all necessary authorized billets on ship and shore by placing nurses from the Reserve on active duty for assignments of one year.

The three nurse corps competed for newly graduated nurses with civilian hospitals, doctor's offices and clinics, the numbers of which were burgeoning during this time period as both the economy and the number of babies were booming. The World War II Cadet Nurse Corps nurses, many of whom graduated during the first three years after the war, were under no legal obligation (although some felt a moral obligation) to join the service. Only a limited number of young graduate nurses were interested, and recruiters sometimes felt the interservice rivalry to be intense. The Army was well aware that while the ANC traditionally promoted second lieutenants after three years, the AFNC made first lieutenants of them in just eighteen months. Young nurses looking at issues of rank and money obviously were more attracted to the Air Force, and by 1950 the issue became a morale problem for the ANC.[93]

Although the three nurse corps all faced a general shortage of nurses, shortages in some specialties were even more critical. Because the Army had so few nurse anesthetists, they had the least choice in assignments. When an opening for an anesthetist appeared, it was necessary to send someone to that spot, regardless of whether she wanted to go or not. Once assigned, nurse anesthetists frequently worked longer hours because there were fewer of them to handle the work. Not surprisingly, the Corps found it difficult to recruit and retain nurse anesthetists.[94]

When Captain Dorothy Looby (Manfredi) was assigned to the 7th Station Hospital in Trieste, Italy, in 1948, she was pleased and excited to serve in Europe. Excitement turned to trepidation when she learned that the anesthetist had gotten sick and she was to serve in his stead. "They gave me a book," she said, and "told me to have it read and be ready to go to work tomorrow morning! Well, I did a great deal of praying during operations, but everything always worked out alright." As the sole remaining anesthetist at the hospital, Looby was on 24-hour call every day except for infrequent single days off."[95]

Army nurse Captain Dorothy Looby (Manfredi), center front, and other 7th Station Hospital personnel sing Christmas carols, Trieste, Italy, 1948. Dorothy Looby Manfredi Collection, Women's Memorial Collection.

With hindsight, it is easy to see that the nursing services were in serious trouble in June 1950. Military cutbacks had required the Army and Navy to shut down scores of hospitals. The ANC lost twelve hundred nurses to the year-old AFNC. There was a nationwide, not just militarywide, shortage of nurses and critical shortages in nursing specialties. The nurse corps directors were attempting to find solutions. They had no way of knowing that they were out of time.

The situation with women medical specialists was equally dire. The Army Women's Medical Specialist Corps (WMSC) and the Air Force Women's Medical Specialist Corps (AFWMSC), established in 1947 and 1949 respectively, included dietitians, and physical and occupational therapists whose services were spread thin in military hospitals around the world. Throughout the first years of their existence, neither came near reaching their staffing goals.[96]

The greatest shortage was occupational therapists, but shortages existed in all areas; there were simply not enough trained women to meet needs. Under the supervision of Colonel Miriam E. Perry, the AFWMSC, which had been started with eighty-nine officers transferred from the Army, did grow to 139 officers during its first year; however, in addition to establishing new administrative procedures, training programs, and regulations, Perry and the chief of the Army Women's Medical Specialist Corps, Colonel Emma Vogel, were forced to spend inordinate amounts of time and effort on recruiting.[97]

Despite such incentives as full pay, a commission from day one, and opportunities for advanced education at civilian universities, both corps faced hurdles. As was the case with Army nurses, many veteran Army dietitians and therapists who had wanted to stay in the service after the war had been arbitrarily discharged. Moreover, the military did not have a reputation for providing women medical professionals with career longevity or opportunity for advancement. More important, only a limited number of young women were receiving the professional training that would make them eligible for the WMSCs. College programs for these medical specialties were fairly new and, as we have seen, fewer women were opting to go to college. College women who planned to marry joined civilian institutions that did not require overseas service or make the special demands the military often had to make of its personnel.

At the same time, the service branches were fine-tuning the job descriptions of medical specialists. In 1947, an Army regulation abolished the position of mess officer in Army hospitals, and assigned the responsibility for food service to the chief dietitian of the hospital and the mess administrator. The mess administrator became responsible for the procurement of food and property and the administration of the hospital fund; the dietitian was responsible for food selection and preparation. In 1948, the Army again reorganized the hospital food service program, and the chief dietitian was redesignated as the chief of the food services division in each hospital responsible for all activities related to food.[98] The Air Force dietitians' role similarly went from supervising special diets to managing all food service activities, making their duties and responsibilities more commensurate with their training and eliminating many non–food service functions such as bookkeeping and patient welfare.[99]

The shortages created another problem. Army and Air Force physical therapists on their first field assignment often were given responsibilities for which they simply were unready. In some military hospitals, new second lieutenants might be placed in charge of an entire physical therapy department and expected to supervise enlisted personnel and civilians. While many fledgling officers rose admirably to the challenge, others were overwhelmed with the responsibilities. When the practice of assigning second lieutenants as department heads came under fire, the directors explained they had no option. In many small Army and Air Force hospitals there was only one authorization for a physical therapist, and there just were not enough seasoned officers to send to all the small military hospitals in the United States.[100] The corps still had responsibilities at hospitals in the United States, Alaska, Japan, the Philippines, England, France, Germany, and Africa. (As of mid-1950, some forty-five Army medical specialists and a lesser number of Air Force medical specialists were assigned overseas.)[101]

The Navy did not establish a women's medical specialist corps; rather, throughout the first two and a half years of the Korean War, it continued its World War II practice of using specially trained Navy nurses, WAVE technicians, and civilians as dietitians and therapists. It established a Women's Medical Specialist section of the Medical Service Corps only after the increasing wartime demand for these professional services became too great to continue on as before.[102]

On the eve of the Korean War, in mid-June 1950, women military leaders had barely finished the reorganizations, policy-making, and consolidations necessary to establish women as permanent, if under-strength, elements within each of the armed services. Looking into the future, these women military leaders anticipated slow but steady growth until they achieved maximum authorized strength of women. They hoped that the problems they faced (the small number of Regulars in some service branches, the high attrition rate, and the scarcity of servicewomen in certain specialties) would eventually be alleviated as young women were attracted by the educational and career opportunities.

This hope was misplaced, for several intertwined reasons. First, because the numbers of women remained small, well below 2 percent of the parent service, women were destined never to be a significant manpower source, and subsequently were treated as insignificant by service leaders. Their small numbers also kept servicewomen from being able to fulfill their original mission, which was to serve as a mobilization base for expansion in the event of a national emergency; this further damaged their credibility with the men, who tended to regard them as little more than a secretarial pool. Finally, the 2 percent limit had another negative result: service planners limited job assignments for which women could be trained and assigned. They justified these limitations by claiming that it was more efficient to train larger numbers to fill a smaller number of jobs.

Partially as a result of this situation, the education and career opportunities offered to women by the services were also inferior to those offered to men, yet even with those extras, the armed forces were unable to recruit enough men, forcing the nation to resort to an unprecedented peacetime draft. The degree to which the continued draft created a negative social environment that hurt all service personnel could not have helped the services' women directors, who felt it was imperative for servicewomen to be held in high esteem.

The bottom line was that the armed forces continued to assign women to traditional women's jobs, all the while assuming that they could continue to be able to count on women to serve voluntarily when needed. But as history would show, until the services provided their female members with greater opportunities to reach their potential, they would continue to have difficulty obtaining and keeping the numbers of women they needed.

Studies conducted by DOD between 1948 and 1950 indicated that military planners were well aware that the country would have a shortage of "manpower" if a national emergency occurred "within the next 10 years." Because of the low birth rate during the Great Depression of the 1930s, the cohort upon which the military could draw—the number of "prime military age" individuals—would be unusually small during the ten-year period between 1950 and 1960, especially when compared to the cohort available at the beginning of World War II. Accepting women into the military, the director of the National Security Resources Board Manpower Office proclaimed, was preferable to using "older or handicapped people" to fill the military manpower gap.[103]

In short, although the military realized that if a war occurred before the baby boom generation came of age for military service, the nation's armed forces would need to utilize womanpower, its leaders could not, for whatever reasons—the zeitgeist, lack of flexibility, and, finally, the press of war—take the necessary steps to do so. Interestingly, in June 1949, just one year before the start of the Korean War, Ohio Representative Frances P. Bolton had made all these arguments publicly. In her article "Women Should Be Drafted," in the *American Magazine,* she wrote that in the event of another war, *man*power alone would not suffice. Nor would the country be able to rely on volunteers to supply the needs of the armed forces.

"We came close to the limits of our manpower in the last war," she said. The war department had tried to recruit one million volunteers for the Women's Army Corps during the last war and got only one hundred and fifty thousand. "Yet we are proceeding on the prayerful assumption that (during the next war) the right kind of women are going to volunteer and in the proper numbers. Such optimism is not justified by past experience. The hard won lessons of the last war prove that we will need women and that there is only one way to get them—by a general registration and selective service." [104]

In February 1950, the Joint Chiefs of Staff issued a policy statement that said in part that in the event of a future mobilization, DOD planned to "utilize the greatest number of women possible, *recognizing at the same time the physical differences between women and men and the prevailing ambivalence about the utilization of women's skills*" (emphasis added). Although this statement implicitly recognized the value of women to the military, it revealed the military's powerful conflicts about the utilization of women. This policy statement did little to diminish differences of opinion in what the role of women should be in the event of a national emergency, and had little if any impact on ways the service branches were training and assigning women.[105]

Literally just days before the outbreak of the Korean War, 21–22 June 1950, the idea of drafting women came up again. The Personnel Policy Board initiated a public meeting to discuss the status of women in the military "following two years of full integration of women into the armed forces," according to the statement of Secretary of Defense Louis Johnson with which the chairman opened the sessions:

> As the allotted period draws to a close, I am inviting a few outstanding women leaders to review the progress and plans for the utilization of womanpower in the department of defense. . . . We are mindful that while the present force, both military and civilian, is relatively small, the ground must be well laid for a wise and very much extended utilization of this important source of personnel in case of national emergency.[106]

The conferees responded by pressing DOD to have plans in place to "register" women, by which they meant gather the names, addresses, and skills of eligible women for a list that the government could use to contact them in the event of national emergency. They understood that registering women would make it easier to draft them if the need arose. Conferees disputed several DOD representatives who argued that the American people would never approve implementation of such a plan. Ironically, after some discussion, the group concluded that women might accept such a registration, but American men would not. As Towle, director of the Women Marines, said, "I do not think there is any question of the women accepting it. I think that it is the fathers and the brothers and the friends of the girls whom you have to convince."[107]

And while the women directors claimed recruiting was going well, they did have to acknowledge that the rates of attrition were high. Several of the conferees wondered aloud if among the reasons why procurement was difficult and attrition high were the limits placed on military women's career advancement and the limited opportunities to achieve higher rank. Here, however, the directors of the women's service branches disagreed. WAC Director Hallaren even told the conferees that she felt higher rank for women would be premature: "There was a bill introduced a couple of months ago in Congress to raise the rank of the chiefs of the women's services to brigadier general," she confessed. "When we heard about it, we tried to stop the bill from going in. . . . We have been under way for just two years . . . but if the bill passed we would have a strong feeling among the men that we were just grasping for more constantly."

Towle agreed, and explained that the time had not yet come to lift the ceiling on women's ranks: "I think the public has not yet actually accepted women in the regular peacetime military establishments." She added pessimistically, "I do not think they are willing to accept them. . . . It was different in wartime—people accepted us as part of a wartime emergency, as an exigency of war. We are often subjected to not too complimentary remarks on the part of civilian men and women . . . because of the fact that we are in uniform." [108]

The conferees, however, were not convinced. Dr. Margaret Craighill, who had served as a World War II Army physician, questioned, "Why not have larger numbers [of nurses] in the colonel rank? I think that is the thing that is very discouraging to women in the services, the fact that they can only go so far." Mary Lord, who had been the chairman of the Civilian Advisory Board of the Women's Army Corps during the war, agreed, and added, "Isn't it Congress as much as anything? It was hard to get the public just behind this small nucleus. We had to work awfully hard to get support because we know that Congress will go along with something they think the public is behind."

Towle continued, "Women have had a hard enough time, up to the present, getting the men, as well as the public generally, to accept them in the regular establishment even in the rank of colonel. I think all of us who have had the rank of colonel, or captain, will bear me out in this. That there has been the feeling that women should not have even that much rank."

In the end, the conferees agreed that the American public needed to be educated about the need for women in the service and that "education must begin with our men."[109]

Three days later the nation was again at war.

CHAPTER 3

Recruiting and Retaining "America's Finest Women"

If this country is to have the proper respect for its women, the women have
to take a share of the responsibility.
—Assistant Secretary for Defense Anna M. Rosenberg[1]

The Girls Get Ready to Serve
—March 1951 *Collier's Magazine* article[2]

Recruitment is slow in all women's services, apparently for two reasons:
there has not been enough public awareness of the career opportunities . . . [and] "the unknown" . . . still troubles some mothers and fathers,
who . . . have not been encouraging their daughters (to join).
—"The WACs (Age 10) Take the Salute," *New York Times Magazine*,
11 May 1952[3]

WHEN THE ARMY OF COMMUNIST NORTH KOREA
crossed the 38th Parallel and invaded South Korea on
25 June 1950, a stunned United Nations Security Council quickly appointed
the president of the United States as its executive agent to restore peace in
Korea. Just two days later, on 27 June, President Truman ordered U.S. air
and sea forces into action in support of South Korea. That same day, Congress approved a one-year extension of the Selective Service Act, and incorporated a provision authorizing the president to mobilize all service reservists, including—for the first time—women. On 30 June, day five of the
war, the president ordered U.S. ground forces from Japan into combat in
Korea.[4]

The Eighth Army had four under-strength divisions widely scattered throughout Occupied Japan—the 7th, 24th, and 25th Infantry Divisions, and the 1st Cavalry Division—any of which the commander, Lieutenant General Walton H. Walker, could rush into South Korea. Each division had an average strength of about 13,000 men, far below their authorized strength of 18,900. The 24th and 25th Divisions, located in the south of Japan, were the closest and went in first.[5] Before dawn on 1 July, "Task Force Smith," commanded by Lieutenant Colonel Charles B. Smith, started for Korea with orders to stop the enemy where it found them. Several hours later, his 400-man task force (composed of elements of the 21st Infantry Regiment of the 24th Infantry Division) reached Pusan airfield. On 5 July, Task Force Smith met the North Koreans twenty-two miles south of Seoul in the hills near Osan, and was defeated. The Americans lacked heavy anti-tank equipment to repel the enemy.

Colonel Edwin Overholt, the physician assigned to Task Force Smith, described the scene: "The North Koreans quickly overran us because our weapons were useless against their (Russian-made) tanks. I set up an aid station at the rear of our force. I had the medics place the most severely wounded on stretchers, and sent all those wounded who were ambulatory away as fast as they could walk. Unfortunately, by the time I realized that our position was being overrun, I didn't have enough men to carry all the wounded off. . . . When the North Koreans reached the litter patients and the chaplain who had remained with them, they shot them."[6]

All told, about 150 of Smith's men were either killed or captured.[7] Other elements of the 24th, the 25th, and the 1st Cavalry Divisions were sent from Japan into Korea, but they too were unable to stop the enemy advance; like Task Force Smith, they were outnumbered and outgunned.[8]

War correspondent Marguerite Higgins, described one such early encounter between troops of the 34th Infantry Regiment and a unit of North Koreans in Russian-made T-34 tanks:

> The 50-odd youngsters of the bazooka team gazed at the tanks as if they were watching a newsreel. Slowly, small groups of them left their foxholes, creeping through the wheat field towards the tank. The first swoosh from a bazooka flared out . . . . the aim was good and it looked like a direct hit. But it apparently didn't look good to Lt. Payne. "Damn," he said. "These kids are scared. They have to get closer to do any damage."
>
> The tank answered the bazooka with a belch of flame. We could see enemy soldiers jump from the tank and machine guns chattering at the

approaching bazooka teams. Through my field glasses I saw a blonde American head poke up through the grass. He was trying to adjust his aim . . . a flash from the tank flicked the ground horribly close and then I saw him fall. . . . bazookas were still sounding off.

We felt certain that the tanks, which were like sitting ducks, would be demolished in a matter of minutes . . . but time passed, and after an hour we saw the bazooka boys coming back to us across the fields.

"What happened?' I asked.

"These bazookas don't do any good against heavy tanks," a sergeant said bitterly. "They just bounce right off."[9]

Higgins's report was doubly revealing. It not only described the catastrophic problems American troops were facing; it also proved at least one American woman was at the front with the troops facing the same enemy fire and was demonstrably capable of doing her job, just as American nurses had proved they could in war after war.

When it became apparent that U.S. troops and Republic of Korea (ROK) troops alone could not successfully defend South Korea, the United Nations sent a multinational task force spearheaded by the United States. Army General Douglas MacArthur was designated the commander in chief of U.N. Forces, with headquarters in Tokyo. Ultimately, the U.N. task force would include personnel from France, Belgium, Turkey, the Netherlands, Puerto Rico, South Korea, Greece, Ethiopia, the Philippines, and Sweden.[10]

Because the United States still had significant military strength deployed in the armies of occupation in Germany, Austria, and Japan, sending troops to Korea required a rapid buildup. The armed forces called up reservists, stepped up recruitment, and used Congress's extension of the 1948 Selective Service Act to increase the draft calls. The Joint Chiefs of Staff (JCS) sought and obtained an increase in the Army's authorized strength from 834,000 to 1,061,000, an augmentation of more than 25 percent. The Air Force call-up of reservists resulted in an expansion of 10,268; the Navy authorization added 9,235.[11]

Mobilization of the reserves got under way less than a month into the war. Initially, the services put out calls for reservists willing to volunteer to return to active duty. But the need for reservists quickly exceeded the number of volunteers, and in early August male reservists were involuntarily recalled. By September, the service branches began involuntarily recalling women.[12]

The recall caused some reservists considerable distress, men and women alike. Major Alba Martinelli Thompson of Plymouth, Massachusetts, who was herself recalled to active duty during the summers of 1951 and 1952, remembers other men and women who were recalled. "It was a heartbreaker," she said. "Some were newly married. Some had started businesses. They didn't want to go."[13] Margaret Larson, a World War II Navy nurse, who had used the G.I. Bill to further her education, was working at the Menninger Clinic in Topeka, Kansas. She was shocked and dismayed when she opened her recall letter. "I just couldn't believe that the Navy still had a grip on me!" she said. She tried to get the orders rescinded by asking the clinic to write the Navy that she held an essential position, but that effort failed and she was ordered to report to the Oak Knoll Naval Hospital at Oakland, California.[14]

Army physical therapist and World War II veteran Florence Trask, a 1925 graduate of Walter Reed Army Hospital, was luckier. She lived with and was supporting her two aged parents. When Trask asked the Army for a deferment, explaining that both her parents were in poor health, she said she was told to put them into a nursing home. Unwilling to do that, Trask contacted Mildred Elson, the executive director of the Physical Therapists Association in Washington, D.C., who complained to the chief of the physical therapy branch of the Army Women's Medical Specialist Corps. Lieutenant Colonel Edna Lura responded that the WMSC director's office had little influence in the matter, but within the week, Lura managed to get Trask's orders revoked.[15]

One reason it was so difficult for women reservists to obtain deferments was that the services were discovering that the number of women they had counted as duty ready in event of emergency was far smaller than they had thought. A large proportion of women in the Reserve had exceeded the age limit for service, or had gotten married and started families since joining and were ineligible for active service. Unmarried women reservists, therefore, were in great demand.[16]

Despite the hardships of the call-up, the American people initially backed Truman's decision to involve U.S. troops in the defense of South Korea. "The lessons of World War II" taught that when totalitarian countries attacked small democracies, appeasement was the wrong response. It became known as the "domino theory." If communists were allowed to get away with overrunning South Korea, they could be expected to do the same thing to another developing nation three or four years down the road, and then another and another.[17]

As the military situation deteriorated, public support for the war and the draft, already fragile, dropped from 75 percent in June to 50 percent by year's

Army nurses Second Lieutenant Betty E. Williams, First Lieutenant Mary I. Couch, Second Lieutenant Donna E. Tolman, and Captain Alice E. Werner and "patient" Corporal Harold Collins ride the Army Nurse Corps float in the Armistice Day Parade, Oakland, California, 13 November 1951. U.S. Army Photo, Phyllis Edholm Carper Collection, Women's Memorial Collection.

end and continued to slide at an alarming rate. Meanwhile military manpower requirements continued to escalate, rapidly tapping out the supply of reservists and forcing stepped-up draft calls. It was time for the DOD to get more serious about womanpower. "Despite the recent pronouncements by service leaders about making maximum use of military women," recalled Major General Jeanne M. Holm, "once the all-male draft was back in business they seemed to lose interest."[18]

U.N. troops suffered defeat after defeat in the first few weeks of the war and withdrew southward down the peninsula. Finally, in late August, U.N. forces established and held a line north of the port of Pusan; MacArthur then proposed sending an amphibious force up the coast to attack the port of Inchon, far behind enemy lines. The plan, launched in mid-September, succeeded beyond all hopes. U.N. troops hit the North Koreans from behind, cut off their supply lines, sent them scrambling back up the peninsula, then pushed rapidly northward beyond the 38th Parallel almost to the border of China.[19]

The American public breathed a sigh of relief. Korea was beginning to look like a replay of World War II. A dictator had attacked while democracy slept, only to go down in ignominious defeat once the sleeping giant was aroused. MacArthur spoke complacently of "bringing the boys home by Christmas," and the public cheered him as a great warrior, fully expecting that this World War II hero could pull off what he promised, as he had when he told U.S. troops trapped behind enemy lines in the Philippines, "I shall return." [20] Back in Washington, however, President Truman was not so optimistic and in November, asked Congress for yet another draft law to replace the one that would expire in June 1951. Although many in Congress were unhappy about the draft and questioned whether it would still be necessary by then, they granted Truman's request.

Truman was prescient. In mid-November, intelligence reports indicated that Chinese Communists were poised to enter the war. At first only small numbers of Chinese soldiers were sighted; the day after Thanksgiving, however, the Chinese Army launched a massive surprise attack. U.N. troops once again retreated southward back past the 38th Parallel all the way to Seoul. By Christmas, U.N. troops were clustered on the southern tip of the Korean peninsula. It was now obvious to everyone that the war would drag on well into the new year. Recruitment was down, so the draft was stepped up.

Early in 1951, influential military women began to advocate drafting women. Among the most prominent draft proponents were WAC Director Colonel Mary Hallaren and former WAVES Director Captain Mildred McAfee Horton. Writing in a February 1951 *Ladies' Home Journal* article, "Why Not Draft Women?" Horton argued that it would be better for the nation to draw from sixteen million young men and women than attempt to find the necessary numbers from eight million men, many of whom were "fathers or boys in the midst of their educational training. I like the idea of the services being staffed by people who do not resent being there, even if some of them are women," she said.[21] Former Coast Guard Women's Reserve Director Captain Dorothy Stratton also weighed in, urging at least a compulsory registration of women. But even these women acknowledged that draft-weary American society was far from ready for such a step. The idea went no further than a few memos, several speeches, and some eye-catching headlines.[22]

Instead, DOD stepped up recruitment of women. Although banned from being actual combatants on the battlefields, women could free up thousands of men to fight. There had been an initial, patriotic flurry of women enlisting in the first days and weeks of the war and, because the numbers of women had been relatively small to begin with, the "surge" looked fairly impressive to government analysts. Indeed, the WAC did grow from 6,551 enlisted women in June 1950 to 10,883 in June 1951. The number of Navy enlisted women nearly doubled, from 2,746 to 5,268; as did the WAF, from 3,782 to 7,514 enlistees. In the same span, the number of Women Marines jumped nearly fourfold, from approximately 530 enlisted women to slightly over two thousand. But even during the first months of the war, there were warning signs that not "enough" women were joining up.[23]

The shortage of nurses became especially critical, as they were essential to care for battlefield casualties in the war zone as well as to staff hospital ships offshore and other medical facilities in the Far East. The *New York Times* in November reported the "acute shortage" of military nurses. The three corps combined had just 7,462 nurses on active duty, and anticipated needing at least 5,088 more nurses within the next six months. The Army had 3,700 nurses, and needed double that number by June 1951; the Navy had 2,250 nurses on active duty and wanted 2,650; and the Air Force had 1,512 nurses and expected needing 2,400 by the following June.[24] While military nurses were deploying to Korea, the Army, Air Force, and Marines banned other military women from assignments in-country, even to non-combat units, and the Navy, by law, could not assign them to most ships.

Assistant Secretary of Defense for Manpower and Personnel Anna M. Rosenberg believed that the growth in servicewomen's numbers in a single year showed significant potential. World War II had convinced her that womanpower was the most productive way to ease a manpower shortage. She fully planned on utilizing women to the maximum extent possible during a national emergency.[25]

Rosenberg, the first woman to hold the position of assistant secretary of defense, had been recommended for her post by the new defense secretary himself, former Army General George C. Marshall, and W. Stuart Symington, chairman of the National Security Resources Board and future secretary of the Air Force. Rosenberg's professional background was in labor relations and mediation. President Roosevelt had sent her to Europe during World War II as his personal representative in the planning for eventual demobilization where she met and impressed Eisenhower as well as Generals Bedell Smith, George C. Patton, and Walton Walker. After Roosevelt's death, Rosenberg had continued working on military issues for President Truman.[26]

Although Anna Rosenberg was well known in political and defense circles, she was surprised when newly appointed Secretary of Defense and former U.S. Army Chief of Staff George C. Marshall asked her to become assistant secretary of defense in 1951. "I asked whether he didn't think the fact that I was a woman would be a disadvantage," she wrote later. "He seemed slightly taken aback by the question and then said he did not. . . . Months later he confided,

Assistant Secretary of Defense Anna Rosenberg appears with the directors of the women's services at a television station to discuss plans for a DACOWITS meeting, 16 September 1951. Left to right: Colonel Mary A. Hallaren, WAC; Colonel Mary Jo Shelly, WAF; Mrs. Rosenberg; Colonel Katherine Towle, Women Marines; Captain Joy Bright Hancock, Navy; and Colonel Mary G. Phillips, ANC. National Archives (111-SC-378754-S).

'You know, I never thought about whether a man would have been more suitable. . . . All I was looking for was somebody to do the job.'"

Rosenberg's new job involved coordinating the efforts of seventeen different defense agencies that dealt with civilian and military personnel and developing strategic targets and goals for recruiting and combat training. Her job was made more difficult by a hostile political climate. Congress had already twice rejected legislation calling for Universal Military Training (UMT) before Rosenberg was appointed. Marshall believed strongly that UMT might prevent World War III by demonstrating to enemies that the nation was both resolved and prepared, and he thought Rosenberg was the one person who could sell the idea to Congress. Rosenberg failed and her subsequent proposals for recruiting more women, lowering the draft age, and integrating the service branches to promote efficiency also failed.

Still, Rosenberg did have some successes, among them lifting of the 2 percent ceiling on women in the services and the establishment of the Defense Advisory Committee on Women in the Services (DACOWITS). She was also able to win passage of the Veterans Readjustment Assistance Act of 1952, the Korean War G.I. Bill.

She stumbled, though, when she promised that soldiers serving in Korea could rotate out after one year, a position that commanders believed would jeopardize the military mission. The 1952 Republican victory making retired General Dwight D. Eisenhower president further weakened her politically, and Rosenberg resigned in 1953.[27]

Swayed by what appeared to be statistically significant growth in strength of the women's programs during the first year of the war, Rosenberg projected that the armed forces could use—and more important, recruit—72,000 more military women, bringing the total to 112,000. Optimistically she asked Congress to remove the 2 percent ceiling. Congress complied, suspending the ceiling until 31 July 1954.[28] With no ceiling, the Army planned to go to 4 percent women, the Navy and Marines to 7 percent, and the Air Force to 10 percent.[29]

Each service began to concentrate on trying to make military service more appealing. The Women's Army Corps added recruiters and established a shorter two-year enlistment. All the services added female recruiters, bought advertising time on radio and television, and printed promotional literature and posters.[30]

A March 1951 *Collier's Magazine* article, "The Girls Get Ready To Serve," was typical of the press coverage given military women during the war's first year. It quoted Colonel Geraldine Pratt May, director of women in the Air Force, who said, "Thirteen percent of all jobs in the Air Force today are administrative. Women can't do all those jobs, but they can do a large share of them, and a lot of others. We want a chance to do the jobs we can do and that need to be done."[31]

Air Force women who held especially glamorous or exciting jobs frequently appeared in press releases and publications geared toward sparking the interest of young women considering joining the Air Force. During the spring of 1951, when news from the front was particularly discouraging, Corporal Dolores Troy and Private First Class Dorothy Hylton traveled from Westover Air Force Base to New York City to do a series of newspaper and radio interviews. Troy, a "25-year old blonde from Nebraska," had been "a fashion assistant in a Denver department store before joining the WAF 16 months previously" gushed the *New York Times*. Hylton, a "25-year old brunette from Virginia," had been "a telephone operator before enlisting in August," and her brother was a paratrooper in Korea. The two WAF were assigned to the 1600 Air Traffic Squadron Air Transport Service, and described their experiences on the job as flight attendants serving a variety of passengers, including "amputees from the Korean War," and "mothers and babies en route from the U.S. to join husbands and fathers in Germany."

These young servicewomen were appealing role models for young women considering the military.[32]

The *Saturday Evening Post* called WAF Third Class Elizabeth Alden (Roe) of Braintree, Massachusetts, the "Flying WAF" in a story on the life of WAF MATS flight attendants—one of the most coveted enlisted jobs for Air Force women.

But Alden's fame expanded considerably that September when the C-47 on which she was serving made a forced landing in Newfoundland while on a routine flight from Germany to Westover Air Force Base in Massachusetts in 1952. "We lost one of our engines completely," she said. "Two others were cutting out . . . so we had the use of only one good engine."

As the plane lost altitude, Alden, one of two attendants on board, had to calm passengers and brief them on ditching procedures. "Staff Sergeant Benjamin appeared hatchet in hand . . . to jettison 14,000 pounds of cargo. When they dropped the latrine I was caring for a hysterical passenger, consequently I was not an eyewitness. . . . I did, however, have a first

Airman Elizabeth Alden (Roe), U.S. Air Force, 1951. Women's Memorial Register.

class view of the passengers' reactions when the pressure in the cabin was forced to decompress. There was an explosion and a sensation of pressure on the head and ears. . . . Throughout, Lieutenant Anders kept the jettisoning progressing. . . . First the latrine, and second, much to our deep regret, the body of a United States airman in a tightly bound casket. We all felt in our own hearts that this would be God's wish, so as Staff Sergeant Benjamin . . . said 'So-long, Pal' . . . [w]e all felt these were not words from the scripture but words substituting for the thought in 37 hearts. The first class mail was next. . . . We flew for three hours with the cargo doors batting the wind as it tore the padding from the tail of the plane." All passengers' personal baggage was tossed, including Alden's diary of five years.

Several Navy tankers and submarines tracked the C-47's progress and a Coast Guard Air Sea Rescue team was sent out to locate the ailing aircraft. When the plane touched down, the passengers "exploded with a round of applause and thanks" for Alden and the crew.[33]

In April 1951, nearly ten months into the war, Rosenberg announced DOD's plans for revamped Reserves to cut down on the time required to get units ready for action. The plan created a Ready Reserve, a Standby Reserve, and a Retired Reserve. It envisioned personnel serving three years in the ready reserve before being transferred to the Standby Reserve. In an emergency, the Ready Reserve would be the first to go, and the Standby Reserve would be called up only after all those in the Ready Reserve had been activated. Retired reservists who volunteered would be called last.[34]

Unfortunately, the bad news from the Korean front hurt all recruiting efforts. By the spring of 1951, the American people were already tired of the war. They were dismayed by the high casualty rates among the half-frozen Marines who staggered out of the Chosin Reservoir carrying their wounded and dead and those sustained by the 23rd Infantry, who had been surrounded at Chipyong-ni, and their embattled rescuers of the 1st Cavalry. Truman's decision to sack the revered MacArthur in April added to the discouraging news.[35]

As the war settled down to a stalemate near the 38th Parallel during the summer of 1951, it was difficult for many Americans to believe that the fighting was accomplishing little other than a continuation of the draft and growing casualties. In many minds, the Korean Conflict or "police action"—Truman's phrase—did not even qualify as a war. In contrast to their dress regulations in World War II, service personnel were required to wear civilian clothes when not on duty; as a result, during the Korean Conflict the public did not see many men and women in uniform to remind them of the fighting there.[36] This new rule hit servicewomen harder than it did servicemen. During World War II, almost everyone knew personally someone who was in the service, and both men and women in military uniform were everywhere, on the streets, on buses, in restaurants, in newspapers, and on movie screens. During the Korean War, a serviceman in uniform was a rarity and a servicewoman even rarer. World War II's 400,000-plus women in military uniform had gained a degree of acceptance that no longer held, as Navy nurse Lieutenant Nancy Crosby and a colleague discovered in San Francisco in late 1951 while preparing to leave for Korea on the hospital ship USS *Haven*. Crosby noticed that she and her friend attracted a disproportionate number of stares and attention while in public in uniform and confided to her diary, "The stares are rude, all this attention is not laudatory and makes me very uncomfortable."[37]

But recruiters, aware of the rising need for more women, pressed on. "Operation Independence" held 4 July 1951, at the Fresno County, California, fairground kicked off a giant recruiting effort in the western states, which netted the Army slightly more than two hundred enlistees, and the Air Force some three hundred. Among these were eleven WAF who, after being sworn in, boarded a C-47 aircraft for the flight to Lackland Air Force Base.[38]

Despite the publicity drive, it was becoming obvious to DOD analysts and planners by the second half of 1951 that there simply were not enough servicewomen to meet the need. Military medical installations in particular were inundated with work. In August 1951, DOD considered issuing a directive requiring the Army and the Air Force to use at least 25 percent enlisted women at each stateside medical installation and mandating that 10 percent of Navy enlisted hospital corpsmen be women. When the proposed requirement was tentatively presented to the services, the Armed Forces Medical Policy Council enthusiastically approved it. By January 1952, however, all the service branches had rejected the plan, complaining they could not do it because there were too few enlisted women to meet requirements. Rosenberg agreed and the proposed requirement was dropped.[39]

Ensign Sarah Jim Cook, U.S. Navy Nurse Corps. Courtesy Sarah Jim Cook.

Travel, adventure, and patriotism were powerful spurs to women's enlistment in the 1950s. Family example helped, too. Two of Lieutenant (jg) Sarah Jim Cook's uncles and her older brother Tom served in World War II and her two other brothers, Eddie and Raymond, donned uniforms for Korea. Yet when the red-haired Fort Worth, Texas, native joined the Navy Nurse Corps in 1951 it surprised both the family and her—"It still does"—that with an R.N. behind her name she became an officer and outranked them all.[40] The sister of WAF Staff Sergeant Joan Eastwood (Neuswanger)[41] had been a World War II WAVE. WAF Staff Sergeant Ernestine Johnson (Thomas)'s father had served with General John "Black Jack" Pershing during World War I,[42] while WAF Airman Second Class Joan DeAngelo (Fogelstrom)'s godmother had been a Navy Yeoman (F).[43]

Sergeant Mildred Stumpe (Kennedy), U.S. Marine Corps, 1952. Women's Memorial Register.

Technical Sergeant Mary Russ (Veres), U.S. Air Force.
Courtesy Mary Russ Veres.

Marine Sergeant Mildred Stumpe (Kennedy)'s older brothers, all of whom had served in the armed forces "thought that the military discipline would be good" for their "spoiled" younger sister.[44]

Some women joined up because their friends were doing so or because they met a servicewoman (or -man) who inspired them. WAF Technical Sergeant Mary Russ (Veres) enlisted in the Air Force because she admired an Army woman she befriended while working as a civilian employee at Fort Dix, New Jersey. "I just thought she was a lovely girl," she recalls, "and I thought 'I could be as nice' as she is."[45] A male Army recruiter she met while working at a Holyoke, Massachusetts, dry cleaning establishment encouraged Airman Second Class Jacquelyn Tomasik (Anderson) to enlist. "He would come in every day," she said, "leave one (uniform), carry one out, and wear one. The more he talked to me, the more interesting it sounded."[46]

Marine Corps Staff Sergeant Jacqueline Gates (Reichert), left, with Marine Corps Corporals Sara Duke and Regina Bigelow.
Women's Memorial Register.

Other women were just waiting to grow up. Marine Staff Sergeant Jacqueline Gates (Reichert) wanted to join during World War II but was too young. Korea gave her another chance and she enlisted just before she turned twenty-seven.[47] Marine Staff Sergeant Anna Yachwan, who would tell her Ukrainian father "I'm an American-American" when he spoke to her in Ukrainian, had wanted to be a Marine since she was a little girl; she achieved her dream at thirty.[48] Private First Class Jerry Robb, by contrast, was so young (barely eighteen) that her mother had to sign her Marine enlistment papers.[49]

Staff Sergeant Anna Yachwan, U.S. Marine Corps, October 1950. Women's Memorial Register.

Reactions to the women's decisions to join were also varied. When Army Second Lieutenant Jean Ertwine (Disterdick) was commissioned, her father, a career soldier, arranged to swear his daughter in.[50] The father of Captain Janice Feagin (Britton) encouraged her to join the Air Force Nurse Corps, saying, "Your country needs you."[51] Other parents were not so supportive. Air Force Second Lieutenant Dorothy Russian (Horne) waited until after she had joined to break the news because she knew her parents would be upset at the thought of her "going so far away."[52] Other parents worried about their daughters' reputations or the harsh realities of what they might experience during wartime. The father of First Lieutenant Muriel Raymond (Batcheller) didn't think she should join because servicewomen's "reputations weren't that good."[53] Yet most friends and family members who were initially opposed eventually took pride in their service. WAF Tech Sergeant Russ's parents, Rumanian immigrants, cried when she enlisted because "they thought I would do what they did and never come back." But later, her father boasted to his friends, "My daughter is in the United States Air Force of America!"[54]

First Lieutenant Muriel Raymond (Batcheller), U.S. Army Nurse Corps. Women's Memorial Register.

DOD was becoming increasingly concerned. At Rosenberg's suggestion, Secretary of Defense George Marshall formed a committee of fifty prominent civilian women to advise and assist in recruiting. Called the Defense Advisory Committee on Women in the Services (DACOWITS), it comprised the four former wartime women's directors, plus well-known women academics, doctors, politicians, and philanthropists. The first DACOWITS was led by Mary Pillsbury Lord, who had chaired a similar Army committee,[55] and included Vassar College President Sarah Gibson Blanding, renowned radio news commentator Hazel Markel, and actress Helen Hayes.[56]

At the first meeting, 18 September 1951, WAC Director Hallaren admitted, "requisitions for women have been coming into headquarters faster than we can fill them, requisitions to fill new vacancies in the expanding services, requisitions for (non-nurse or medical specialist) women to replace men shipped overseas." Moreover, the gap between the actual num-

At Bolling AFB, Washington, D.C., members of the Defense Advisory Committee on Women in the Services (DACOWITS) deplane after an inspection tour of Langley AFB, Virginia. Left to right, front row: Marietta Moody Brooks; Dr. Lillian Moller Gilbreth; Mrs. Gilford Mayes; Elizabeth Taylor; Dean Myrtle Austin; Lena Ebeling; Colonel Verena Zeller (Pettoruto Seberg), chief, AFNC; and Colonel Mary Jo Shelly, director, WAF. Left to right, second row: India Edwards, Unknown, and Edith R. Stern. National Archives (111-SC-378760-S).

bers of women and the strength objectives established at the start of the recruitment campaign was growing, not shrinking. Current WAC strength was 12,250; the Army wanted 32,000 women. Air Force women numbered 8,200; the Air Force hoped for 30,000 in all. The Navy boasted 6,300 women but wanted 11,000, while the Marines had 2,250 women and wanted 3,000 in all. "In other words," Hallaren said, "we have a total of 29,000 women on duty and a need to recruit more than 70,000. Remember, every woman volunteer means one less male draftee."[57]

Hallaren asked DACOWITS to help the service branches reassure parents that their daughters would be well supervised and protected in the service, just as if they were living in a college dormitory. Young women also needed to be reminded of the career opportunities available in the service. Most important, Hallaren emphasized, "the prestige of military women needs to be reinforced in the public mind." She urged committee members to do this through speaking in public, on radio, through magazine articles and in speeches to business and professional groups, civic organizations, and church groups.[58]

DACOWITS members took up Hallaren's challenge. Those affiliated with colleges invited service recruiters to their campuses. The journalists, broadcasters, and publishers among the group devoted space and airtime to feature the exciting lives of servicewomen. In print and over the air, service recruiters described how the training and skills acquired in the military could benefit women throughout their lives.

That same September, now fifteen months into the war, Rosenberg wrote the service secretaries announcing a November start date for a nationwide enlistment drive to add 78,000 servicewomen by the end of the following year. She optimistically asked the services for estimates of how many recruits they could train per month, not whether they would be able to do it. Rosenberg wanted to avoid another situation similar to that at Lackland Air Force Base in January and February 1951, when the Air Force could neither adequately house nor outfit all its new female recruits.[59] Air Force clothing contractors had had difficulty making their delivery schedules, and many of the uniforms that were delivered were of such poor quality that they could not be issued. Of 5,100 women's uniforms delivered to Lackland AFB in 1951, only 1,200 were salvageable, and each of those had to be altered before it could be worn. Many recruits had not received complete and adequately fitting uniforms by the time they left Lackland and reported to specialist school.[60] Although the Air Force managed to avoid a discussion of this debacle in the newspapers, it was well aware that the scarcity of properly fitting uniforms was adversely affecting morale among women.

Within days, the *New York Times* reported the new recruiting drive.[61] Two days later, the *Washington Star,* covering the "Women in the Defense Decade" conference, quoted former WAVE Director Horton once again touting the idea of drafting women. Ohio Representative Frances Bolton, long a supporter of drafting women, was again quoted. "Let's revise the old saying that woman's place is in the home. Let's realize that today woman's place includes the saving of the home."[62] Mirroring a similar conference of civilian women nearly a year and a half earlier, the majority of conferees did not believe that the public would agree to drafting their daughters, and the discussion evolved into one about the feasibility of national registration of women.[63]

The proposed DOD recruitment campaign drew unwanted attention from Congress to the issues surrounding women in the armed forces. In November, Rosenberg personally answered two letters from concerned senators. Texas's Lyndon Baines Johnson inquired about numbers: how many women were serving? Minnesota's Hubert H. Humphrey wanted information on the cost of servicewomen compared to civilian women employees. The first answer was easy; Rosenberg was only too familiar with the numbers. The second was more complicated: Rosenberg had to admit that female military personnel cost "slightly more" than their civilian counterparts; nevertheless, she argued "some positions by their nature must be filled by military personnel and females are needed to replace combat qualified personnel due to a manpower shortage."[64]

The DOD kicked off its recruitment campaign as planned in November 1951. It included traveling teams of women in uniform and an advertising campaign with slogans like "Share Service for Freedom" and "America's Finest Women Stand Beside Her Finest Men." Lieutenant Helen Mannion (Doyle), an Air Force nurse assigned to the recruiting campaign was on the 1951 road show "through Texas, Oklahoma, and New Mexico . . . promoting women in the military. The state Federation of Business and Professional Women's Clubs sponsored our visits,"[65] she recalled. Teams were assigned to every part of the United States. Some DACOWITS members served as coordinators in their areas of the country; in each city, a centrally located recruitment station was staffed by all nine women's components.[66]

The typical way local newspapers covered the recruitment campaign was to profile one of the recruiters, a tactic the military encouraged so that readers could identify with her and feel comfortable that military women were just like "the girl next door." The Corpus Christi, Texas, and Montgomery,

Alabama, newspaper articles on Mannion, who had been a World War II Cadet nurse before joining the Air Force, described her training at Brooklyn Hospital and talked of her mother's Army Nurse Corps experience.[67]

The *New York Herald Tribune* ran an article, "The Typical Day of an Air Force Nurse," profiling Mannion on the job at Kelly Air Force Base in San Antonio. "Everyday and sometimes late at night," said the article, "big Air Force hospital planes arrive with wounded from Korea. Flight nurses Captain Madeline Barneycastle and Lieutenant Mannion help the patients off the C-97 evacuation plane. First come the 'walking wounded,' patients on crutches, using canes, or with bandages over their eyes. Then the litter patients are unloaded." Readers of the article learned that Barneycastle and Mannion felt needed and professionally fulfilled.[68]

Fluffy feature stories to the contrary, military nursing in the first few months of the Korean War—even stateside—was no picnic. Second Lieutenant (later First Lieutenant) Dorothy Russian (Horne) of Windber, Pennsylvania, who was stationed at the newly reopened Lackland Air Force Base hospital recalled that the facility, which had been shuttered in 1949 due to budget cuts, was "short of everything—there weren't even enough wash basins." The Air Force was also short of nurses, so short that new recruit Russian and her colleagues went right to work without benefit of military training. Her job was dispensing pain medication to patients, most of who had battle-related wounds or infectious disease. But others were shell-shocked, and those were among the most difficult to care for, she soon learned.[69]

Second Lieutenant Dorothy Russian (Horne), U.S. Air Force Nurse Corps. Women's Memorial Register.

The Ponca City, Oklahoma, newspaper profiled Captain Lillian Dunlap, later to become chief of the Army Nurse Corps and a brigadier general. A San Antonio native, Dunlap had served in the Army Nurse Corps during World War II in New Guinea, the Admiralty Islands, and the Philippines. The article added that Navy nurse Lieutenant Eugenia Moseley of the recruiting team had also served in the Philippine Islands during World War II and suggested that young nurses considering military service could look forward to serving under nurses of this caliber.[70]

That fall, the 543rd Women's Air Force Band from Lackland Air Force Base joined the University of Texas Longhorn Band and Baylor University's Golden Wave Band in a half-time performance dedicated to servicewomen in all branches. Officially introducing Texans to "National Recruiting Week for Women in the Armed Services," the bands marched in formations representing each of the service branches. Marietta Moody Brooks of Austin, one of two Texan DACOWITS members, was escorted onto the field by representatives of the Unified Recruiting Team and presented with a bouquet of roses.[71] In Binghamton, New York, the local newspaper proudly announced that seventy-nine local women had enlisted since the war started,[72] and similar stories appeared in hometown newspapers all over the country.

That same November, however, newspapers carried a story that the military wasn't so happy with "caustic and increasing congressional criticism" of recruiting costs and the fact that young people simply were not interested in military service. The draft would have to continue as long as the war dragged on, and DOD announced that the number of men to be drafted for the Army and Marine Corps would be increased through the remainder of the year.[73]

The military's need for both manpower and womanpower was immediate and undeniable, but the American public was still ambivalent about women in the military, as evidenced by a letter from a constituent to Maine's Senator Margaret Chase Smith, long a champion of servicewomen. The writer refused to allow his daughter to join the WAC because of his experiences at Camp Gruber, Oklahoma, during World War II, where, he said, "WACs were used like prostitutes by the officers—and those women who refused their advances were shipped off to Alaska." The letter was forwarded through Rosenberg's office to Hallaren, whose representative said that the WAC did not remember such rumors about Camp Gruber (although they certainly had to combat rumors like it at other installations during World War II), and suggested this father was simply remembering specious "jealous enlisted men's gossip" about WACs during the early days of that war.[74]

Each of the service branches had increased the numbers of young women it sent out as recruiters. In April 1952, Marine Sergeant Ila Carter Holzbauer did "not feel at all comfortable with the idea of a recruiting assignment" in Omaha even though Nebraska was her home state. "[I] was the only Woman Marine in town. Then I found out that my predecessor had been relieved of duty because of poor judgment and the undesirable image that she had projected. This made me even more nervous. I knew that my primary responsibility was to present a good image of Women Marines, even when people criticized the idea of women in the Marine Corps and insulted me. I just decided to do the best job I could."

Holzbauer traveled a great deal to county fairs, spoke at community gatherings and school events, and did radio and newspaper interviews. With time, she became more confident, and although assigned a quota, was "never pressured to achieve it." Indeed, her summary of her three years as a recruiter is a telling commentary on the dilemma facing the military during that era: "I was very careful to recruit only those women whom I thought would reflect well on the Marine Corps."[75]

By this time, only DACOWITS's second meeting, it was apparent that the recruitment campaign was a failure. Despite six months of intensive recruiting, only 8,532 new servicewomen had been added to the nine female components of the armed forces—less than one-tenth the number hoped for by 1 July 1952, nine months earlier. More troubling, the service branches were having trouble retaining women. DOD itself had contributed to the exodus with a July 1951 decision to allow women once again to leave the service at marriage. Prior to the Korean War, servicewomen could request discharge if they got married; DOD ended this practice in August 1950. The policy reversal resulted in large numbers of new brides leaving the military during a time when the recruitment drive was at its peak.[76]

> Discharge was a routine matter for most military brides, but not so for Airman Second Class Dorothy Crawford (Ulrey), who married an American civilian while serving in postwar Germany. "The Air Force did not want to give me a discharge until I had my passport and the (American) Consulate didn't want to give me a passport until I had a discharge." They went "back and forth for awhile," says Crawford, until the issue could be resolved and Crawford could obtain both a military discharge and an American passport.[77]

Dorothy Crawford and Hugh Ulrey cut wedding cake at their reception, Skyhook Service Club, Wiesbaden AFB, Germany, 28 February 1954.
Courtesy Dorothy Crawford Ulrey.

DACOWITS remained upbeat, emphasizing that overall the services were doing a good job housing, feeding, and placing women in good assignments. "For girls who can't afford college, it's the next best thing," said Dr. K. Frances Scott, a professor at Smith College.[78]

DACOWITS brainstormed on ways to make military service more appealing to young women, although, in retrospect, the majority of their wartime recommendations can be seen as mere Band-Aids on a gaping wound. They suggested, for example, that a special program to stimulate nurse recruitment and proposed improved orientation for the youngest (ages eighteen to twenty) servicewomen. Continued concerns about appearance prompted recommendations that salad bars be placed in mess halls, that servicewomen receive more guidance in food selection, and that DOD and cosmetic manufacturers work together to recommend cosmetics for servicewomen. Two significant initiatives that the committee had recommended at its first meeting and recommended again were a special six-week training class for servicewomen recruiters and improved indoctrination of male recruits on the role of women in the military and why they serve. It is interesting to note the beginning at this meeting of a DACOWITS tradition: it repeats—and repeats—recommendations until the military acts upon them. DOD moved to institute the majority of the committee's recommendations.[79]

One of the committee's recommendations was paralleled in a report by the Attitude Research Branch of the Office of Armed Forces Information and Education. "The Servicewoman as a Public Relations Agent for Her Service" found that the best recruiters were young and had been in the service less than six months, but would, as a group, benefit from additional training in recruiting.[80] It also found that women who joined the service to obtain education and training were happy, but those who had joined to go into a specific line of work or to "do something useful for their country" were often disappointed.[81]

Another report by the same office, "Attitudes of Enlisted Women in the Regular Service to Re-Enlistment," addressed the retention problem. The report looked at the reasons women enlisted in the service: 38 percent to learn a skill, 19 percent to travel, 18 percent to serve their country, 10 percent to get away from home, and 15 percent for other reasons. The most frequent reasons for not reenlisting had been seen before: dissatisfaction with the job, promotion opportunities or pay, desire for more civilian education or training, unhappiness about the lack of acceptance of women by the services themselves and/or concern about the reputation of servicewomen and, as always, marriage. Only one in four enlisted women intended to reenlist, the report said. Older women and those with responsibility and authority were more likely to reenlist, while others in less challenging jobs often decided, not surprisingly, that they would find more interesting work as civilians.[82] It was confirmation of countless earlier studies that the services apparently failed to address adequately.

By June 1952, much to the Army's chagrin, it actually had fewer servicewomen than it had before the Unified Recruiting Campaign. And it was not alone; none of the other service branches had met its recruiting goals regarding women. It became painfully clear that many qualified American women were indifferent to the notion of military service and some elements of the population, particularly parents and male friends, were downright hostile. While the campaign lent some prestige to military women, it also revived old accusations of immorality and the attribution of masculine traits to military women.[83]

By 1952, Rosenberg appeared willing to try anything that would have aided recruiting and retention of servicewomen; when she heard a civilian idea that dovetailed with the Defense Department's efforts to recruit more women, she jumped. The president of a Washington, D.C., stamp club, Louis Tosti, had embarked on a letter-writing campaign calling for a commemorative stamp featuring military women. Initially, the post office rejected Tosti's suggestion; when the idea came to Rosenberg's attention, however, she wrote President Truman, "I feel that the national recognition accorded by the issuance of such a stamp at this time would be of great value." He agreed, and within a month, the post office announced that a stamp honoring servicewomen would be released later that year.[84]

On 11 September 1952, the U.S. Postal Service issued the deep blue, three-cent commemorative stamp emblazoned with the words "Women In Our Armed Services" and the faces of four uniformed women representing the Army, Navy, Marine Corps, and Air Force. President Truman presided over the first-day-of-issue ceremony at the White House, and the Department of Defense introduced the stamp to the American public at a series of recruitment rallies.[85]

These rallies came at the height of the 1952 presidential election campaigns, which revolved almost solely around the issue of the Korean War. The Republican candidate, former general Dwight D. Eisenhower, promised the American people that if he were elected, his first priority would be to find a way to extricate the country from the war in Korea. Further, he promised to go to Korea himself, study the situation firsthand, and devise an honorable peace. Disgusted with the stalemated war and the communists' refusal to cooperate in the ongoing peace talks, Americans overwhelmingly put their trust in the World War II leader, electing him over Democrat Adlai Stevenson by a vast majority. Eisenhower made good on his promise and jump-started the peace talks.[86]

The Department of Defense's high-profile recruitment campaign continued to lag through Eisenhower's election and inauguration. Recruiters, unable to meet inflated quotas, began sacrificing quality to gain quantity, accepting women who scored in the lowest percentiles of the military entrance exams. The women's directors, upset at the quality of women recruits being added to the force, called a halt to the recruiting drive in 1953. They felt it was essential to maintain the prestige of military women to encourage acceptance by servicemen and the nation. Further, they justifiably feared that lowering the quality of servicewomen would quickly undermine military women's hard-won reputation for quality and efficiency. The directors were well aware of all the biases servicewomen faced, especially the traditional cultural bias that required a woman to be twice as qualified as a man to do the same job.[87] "The Korean War experience reinforced the lesson that should have been taken from World War II: the mobilization of large numbers of women through volunteer means is not possible," Major General Jeanne M. Holm wrote in her 1992 book, *Women in the Military: An Unfinished Revolution.* In a later memo she put an asterisk next to the word "volunteer" and added the note that volunteer is "the operative word."[88]

Fitting Servicewomen In: Finding "Proper Employment for Sisters and Girlfriends"

The main thing . . . was to fit us into the mass and do it as easily as possible as far as the men were concerned; very carefully and slowly . . . as a real positive [re]source.
—Director of Women in the Air Force Colonel Geraldine Pratt May[1]

In authorizing job assignments for women, particular care is taken to see that the job does not involve a type of duty that violates our concept of proper employment for sisters and girlfriends. In the military transport field, for example, women do not drive heavy trucks.
—A 1951 Army pamphlet's twice-repeated promise, meant to ease soldiers' concerns about serving with women[2]

THE UNITED STATES MILITARY had just begun the task of carving out a permanent niche in the services for women other than nurses when it suddenly found itself fighting another foreign war. Much as the war itself surged and retreated up and down the Korean Peninsula, the effort to integrate women would be a constant push-pull. As in World War II, the military, accustomed to dealing with male draftees, faced an entirely different set of challenges when it came to women in their ranks. Each service struggled with prevailing social perceptions of what women wanted, what it would take to entice them to volunteer for a tour of duty in the wartime military, and what roles would be "proper" for the "nice girls" they hoped to recruit. By the end of the war, some opportunities for women had expanded, often despite the military's initial plans. There had been small but significant advances: many officers chose the military because there were opportunities to manage, many enlisted women learned technical skills, and integration of African American women began to be a reality. However, most servicewomen—white and black alike—were still ghettoized in what the civilian world later came to call "pink-collar" jobs; the overriding concern of both the public and the services was that female soldiers first be feminine.

During the first months of the Korean War, the armed forces took action to retain as many personnel as possible by calling up the Reserves and extending all enlistments. As previously noted for the first time—and quite remarkably given the public's attitudes toward women in uniform—women were included in the call-up. One by one, however, the Reserves discovered their lists were out of date: women had moved, married, and begun families. The military was loath to separate spouses and had rules banning mothers. Both issues—marriage and motherhood—would prove to be conundrums.

"When I left active duty in 1946, I thought I was out of the Navy," recalled Lieutenant (jg) (later Commander) Florence Scholljegerdes of Waseca, Minnesota. Not so. "Nobody had ever told me I had to resign my commission." When the newly recalled nurse reported to San Diego in January 1951, among her fellow Navy nurses were two women who had reported with their children in tow. They were "allowed to resign." Scholljegerdes ultimately served three more years, much of it with the Military Sea Transport Service (MSTS PAC) as part of a team that traveled with troops and military dependents.[3]

Lieutenant Florence M. Scholljegerdes, U.S. Navy Nurse Corps.
Women's Memorial Register.

All the services stepped up recruiting, and a surge of patriotism created a rapid growth spurt for the women's services; nonetheless as public support for the war waned, so did enlistments. And just as the number of women entering the military began to decline, attrition began to rise. During the war's second year, attrition doubled and only half as many women signed up. By the third year of the war, the size of the women's services had begun a slow and steady decline, which continued apace regardless of all of the services' efforts. As the 1950s progressed, fewer and fewer women opted to give military service a try, and only a limited number of women (or men, for that matter) joined the service hoping for a military career. Nor was that the issue for the military. What it wanted was for enlisted at least to finish out their enlistment contracts and possibly enlist for another term.[4]

A month after the war started, the service branches stopped automatically letting go married women who requested a discharge; a year later, however, as the number of brides who got pregnant in order to get out of the service skyrocketed, DOD backflipped and reinstated the old, more permissive policy. Attrition soared even further.[5]

Marriage and motherhood seemed to be issues on which the military could not win, no matter what it tried to do. In January 1951 a former Women's Army Corps (WAC) major and mother made the cover of *Parade* magazine, a national newspaper Sunday supplement, and headlines such as this one from the *Brooklyn Eagle:* "Ex-Wac, Fired as Mom, Tells U.S. Facts of Life." Alba Martinelli Thompson had been discharged from the Army Reserve as a result of pregnancy and, with her infantry colonel husband, fought the discharge, challenging the military regulation that stipulated female reservists with children under eighteen be discharged. The major had six years of active duty to her credit, including pre-war service in Korea—in 1948 she had served as an assistant chief adviser to the Korean Government—and she argued the Army was foolish to discharge her and thus lose her expert knowledge, especially during war.

New mother and WAC Major Alba Martinelli Thompson and the reason she was discharged from the service, her two-month son, Loren B. Thompson, Jr., spend a Sunday afternoon in an Orange, New Jersey, park, December 1951. Courtesy Alba Martinelli Thompson.

"Army 'Shortsighted': WAC Reservist Blasts 'Motherhood' Discharge," trumpeted the *Long Island* (New York) *Star Journal,* which also reported, "A pert young lady soldier—discharged from the reserves because of motherhood—had the Defense Department on the spot today." On the spot or not, all that Assistant Secretary of Defense Anna Rosenberg could tell Thompson was that DOD and all the service branches were in firm agreement on banning mothers with children under eighteen from serving, a decision that inspired the *New York Daily News* to declare: "Army Knows Best, Mother Gives Up Rank."[6]

Thompson's case was supported by both senators from New York, her home state, as well as Senator Margaret Chase Smith of Maine, and she was invited to testify before the Senate Armed Services Committee. Several months later, New York newspapers reported Thompson's "victory." "The Senate last night passed a bill forbidding the dismissal of a woman from the armed forces reserves just because she becomes a mother. Automatic dismissal is the present rule." The news reports were too rosy; although the Senate action was promising, the bill apparently never had a chance of passage in the more conservative House.[7] Furthermore, the Women's Armed Services Integration Act of 1948 had given the service secretaries the authority to terminate the regular commission or enlistment of any servicewoman "under circumstances and in accordance with regulations proscribed by the President."[8] On 27 April 1951, President Truman, in Executive Order 10240, defined motherhood (by birth or adoption of a minor child) as one of those circumstances.[9]

In its drive for unencumbered women, the Army had appealed to its enlisted reservists to return voluntarily for active duty for one year or until the emergency ended. Since 1948, members of the Women's Army Corps had been allowed to join the Organized Reserve Corps (renamed the United States Army Reserve or USAR in 1952), and by 1950 there were 4,281 WAC reservists. The Army would have liked 20,000 such women in waiting, but outdated records made it difficult to count on even the 4,281 women classified as reservists, because many had neglected to report relocations, marriages, and, especially, the birth of children. By June 1951, already a year into the war and after the records had been screened and updated and ineligible women had been discharged, the roster of available WAC reservists numbered just 2,524 women.

The initial call-up for volunteer enlisted reservists (both men and women) was for mechanics, radio operators, X-ray technicians, translators, and stenographers. Within a few weeks, however, such picking and choosing went out the window, and volunteers with any military occupational specialty (MOS) were accepted. But there were not enough volunteers, so the Army began involuntarily recalling reservists to active duty, beginning with enlisted male reservists. After some men complained to their congressional representatives they were being "unfairly" recalled for neglecting to drill with their units in the past, the Army stopped its involuntary recall before enlisted women were recalled.

At the same time enlisted reservists were being recalled, officers in the Reserve with any MOS were asked to return voluntarily. When the call for volunteers did not bring in enough officers, the Army was forced to call up selected officers (including women) for nonvolunteer active duty for a period not to exceed twenty-one months. Single women without children or dependents were recalled first, and then, as the last choice, married women who did not have children or dependents. Obviously, women with children under eighteen could not serve and were not recalled. During the first year of the Korean War, 67 WAC officers and 1,526 enlisted reservists volunteered to return to active duty, and 175 WAC officers were recalled.[10]

Although the Army did not want mothers, its need for womanpower compelled the WAC to boost the age limits for women seeking commissions in the Reserve to between twenty-eight and thirty-nine years of age. Previously, only college graduate women under twenty-seven had been eligible, and only as second lieutenants. Now older women could apply for commissions as first lieutenants or captains, their rank depending on years of education and experience.[11]

By September 1950, as it became obvious that massive infusions of American troops would be needed, the Army put its hopes in continuing the male-only draft. To get the new troops where they were needed as quickly as possible, the Army cut basic training for both men and women to just eight weeks; it had been sixteen weeks for men and thirteen for women. During the same time, the WAC more than doubled the number of its recruiters, streamlined its application procedures, offered new recruits a shorter, two-year enlistment period, and bought advertising time on radio and television. WAC Director Colonel Mary Hallaren had hoped for a joint male-female recruiting campaign, but the Army's recruiting theme for 1951 was "The Mark of a Man." Although the WAC didn't reach the Army's goal of 17,000 women by June 1951, the total WAC strength did jump to 11,932, a 60 percent increase from June 1950. But the unpopularity of the war, the eventual start of truce talks, public apathy, and the service branches' competition for recruits—all began severely cutting into WAC recruiting numbers. WAC recruiters also found themselves competing directly with Air Force recruiters, often in the same room, and knew that many prospective recruits saw the Air Force as more elite and exciting, as well as more open to promoting women.[12]

On the more positive side, the Army's ongoing need to fill critical jobs created some new career opportunities for women. In one case, it attempted to deal with the shortage of nurses in 1950 by training WACs as medical technicians at Walter Reed Army Hospital.[13] By the end of the war, the medical technician MOS was one of the fastest-growing WAC jobs. A 1951 study found WACs could handle more than 80 percent of hospital jobs and alleviate both the nurse shortage and gaps left as male medical technicians were sent to Korea.[14] In another case, two WACs, Captain Mary G. MacDonald and Captain Mercedes M. Ordstrom, members of the first class of WACs to graduate from the Military Police School at Camp Gordon, Georgia, were assigned to the faculty.[15] Then, in early 1952, the Army began sending enlisted WACs to the language school in Monterey, California. WAC officers had attended the school, graduated in the top tier of their class, and gone on to teach at the school, so the Army opened the doors to thirty enlisted women per year for the one-year course.[16]

In her public speeches, Hallaren cautioned that the women were not "replacing" men but "complementing" them. She stressed that Army women worked in the same fields that were dominated by civilian women: fields such as administration and communications, in other words, traditional, female-identified occupations.[17] Apparently, the phrase "replacing men," which was highly acceptable during World War II, was no longer viewed as favorable. Indeed, the prevailing social climate was such that even in the midst of the war in Korea, the Army felt the need to explain the presence of WACs to incoming soldiers. The 1951 Army pamphlet 20–138, "Leave It To The WAC" read: "If men in the Army—particularly new soldiers—understand the WAC's important role, the job of these enlisted women is made easier and more pleasant. . . . Women can do and are doing many important jobs in the Army—jobs that bear directly on the personal welfare of every soldier. Assigning women to jobs they can do, so that men in turn can concentrate on jobs that require men is simply a case of using manpower to the best advantage."

The Army repeated one statement twice, once in boldface type: "Each thousand new WACs means close to another battalion that can be made available for combat forces." It then reassured soldiers "In authorizing job assignments for women, particular care is taken to see that the job does not involve a type of duty that violates our concept of proper employment for sisters and girlfriends. In the military transport field, for example, women do not drive heavy trucks, and as military police they are used only in actions involving women." They were also assured that before the Army assigned WACs to a particular job, it first ascertained that women could do the job as economically as men and that they could be trained just as easily. At the time of the pamphlet's publication, WACs worked in eighteen of the

Army's thirty-one career fields; of 491 job specialties, 146 were open to women.[18]

There was other progress. For example, the WAC detachment at the 3rd Armored Division, Fort Knox, Kentucky, was activated 31 October 1950, to relieve soldiers of administrative duties, provide instructors for Fort Knox's clerk-typist school, and be a parent unit for WAC students attending coeducational clerk-typist classes. Because at this time WACs could not number more than 2 percent of the Army, many clerk-typists were male, and in the interest of efficiency, the Army elected to train them alongside the WACs. By March 1952, what was obvious in the classroom—that women could do the job as well as men—was tested in the division and the battalion assigned 136 enlisted WACs.[19]

During the war, 20 percent of the WAC served overseas, and new detachments shipped out every month—everywhere except the Korean Theater, although that theater requested WACs in late 1951 and again in late 1952.[20] The majority of the WAC detachments were stationed at Army posts across the United States and the outbreak of war meant that every WAC was needed. WAC Sergeant Dorothy J. Vanden Oever (Barron), a blood bank technician at San Francisco's Letterman Army Hospital who was responsible for keeping the blood supply updated, stayed put despite twice receiving orders to Germany and once to Japan. Vanden Oever had wanted to go overseas, but each time she was able to wangle an overseas posting she was told her critical MOS at Letterman meant she could not go.[21]

Although the Army and the Marine Corps sent higher numbers of male personnel to the Korean Theater and thus had the greatest need for women to fill stateside vacancies, the Navy also needed them. It suddenly became responsible for transporting—across seven thousand miles of ocean—all the food, ammunition, and other supplies needed by U.N. troops. The Navy also maintained a vital network of communications stations on tiny islands across the Pacific, and when the United States went to war, those stations expanded. As a result, as in World Wars I and II, the Navy again began using women (still unofficially called WAVES) to replace sailors assigned aboard ship and overseas.[22] Captain Joy Bright Hancock, director of the women's division, was against using the World War II acronym because women were now full-fledged members of the Navy, not Women Accepted for Voluntary Emergency Service, the temporary organization in World War II.[23] The nickname continued in popular use well into the early 1970s, partly because Hancock's successor, Captain Louise Wilde, who had a strong public relations background, nurtured the positive public opinion of the WAVES, an opinion the other service branches envied.[24]

Like the Army, the Navy also recalled reservists and stepped up recruitment and training. When the war broke out there were just 3,239 women in the Navy. In October, the Navy began doubling the recruit quota from 160 women every six weeks to 160 every three weeks, then, in March 1951, to 88 women per week and in September to 132. Although the Navy was aiming for ten thousand women, it had reached only nine thousand by the end of the war.[25] The Navy also cut basic training from ten weeks to nine and moved women's recruit training from Great Lakes Naval Station in Illinois to larger facilities at Bainbridge, Maryland. Beginning in the third month of the war, the Navy began recalling enlisted women reservists with critical ratings. Just as the other service branches had, the Navy found itself discharging reservists who had married and become mothers.[26]

When the Navy, in line with other services, also dropped, then reinstated, the discharge-upon-marriage policy for its women, attrition skyrocketed; for the first time, attrition for women was higher than that of men. Nonetheless, throughout the 1950s in all of the services, male draftees would have a higher dropout rate—even though nearly 80 percent of enlisted women left the service before their first enlistment was up.[27]

By December 1950, some 172 female officers in the Reserve had voluntarily returned to active duty, so there was no need for an officer recall. The Navy also commissioned 60 regular officers and 180 reserve officers each year, and shortened training at Newport, Rhode Island, from five to four months. Beginning in September 1952, officers were commissioned into the Navy Reserve as a convenient shortcut around regulation. Reserve officers could immediately apply for regular status, but regular commissions required individual congressional approval. The Navy also began offering prospective reserve officer candidates the chance to do their training during the summers of their junior and senior years of college.[28]

Growth created problems. The rapid growth in the number of very young women coming on active duty created a parallel need for more female petty officers to recruit and supervise enlisted in communication centers and hospitals. There were too few experienced petty officers available for administering enlisted women's barracks, and seamen fresh from recruit school often proved too green for the task. To fix the problem, two four-week leadership schools opened in February 1953, at San Diego, California, and Bainbridge, Maryland.[29]

Opportunities for overseas service expanded for Navy women during the Korean War. During World War II, the only "overseas" billets to which Navy women could be assigned had been in Hawaii and Alaska, then territories. After the war, however, even those opportunities were withdrawn, and Navy women's overseas assignments were limited to a small number of bases in Europe that had quarters for women. The issue of proper facilities has been a recurring theme in military women's struggle to gain acceptance and equal treatment; as had happened in the past, as the need for women's services overseas increased during the Korean War, the Navy found acceptable quarters for them. In the fall of 1950, Lieutenant Florence Coyne was ordered to Navy Weather Central in Kodiak, Alaska, and Lieutenant Anita Crews was ordered to the Military Sea Transportation Service (MSTS), Mid-Pacific, Honolulu. By February 1951, Coyne had been joined in Kodiak by Lieutenant Dorothy J. Joyce, who was assigned to the naval air station.[30] Navy women were also assigned to Supreme Headquarters Allied Powers Europe (SHAPE) in France and to bases in Italy, England, and the Philippines. In 1953, a minimum of two women per MSTS ship were assigned as hospital corpsmen to care for traveling dependents.[31]

As a result of the war, the pace of activity for women in the Reserve stepped up. The World War II veterans of Submarine Battalion 3–7 at the Navy Shipyard in Brooklyn, all of whom had civilian jobs, soon were putting in one evening each week handling the paperwork for a reserve battalion of three hundred enlisted sailors and seventy-five officers. Their commander, Lieutenant Commander Kay Wilson, who had organized the group in 1949, worked during the day for the national board of the Young Women's Christian Association, but had commanded all women's barracks in the 3rd Naval District during World War II. In 1949, the reserve unit numbered twenty-four, but some were recalled to active duty in 1950, with the unexpected consequence that the few who remained with the unit were promoted frequently. World War II gunnery instructor Marvel Purvis, an editorial secretary in postwar civilian life, jumped from a second class petty officer to lieutenant (jg) as a result of her reserve activity during the Korean War.[32]

Korean War–era women could only be assigned to 36 out of 62 job ratings in 1952, down only slightly from 37 of 61 ratings in 1948, but still fewer nontraditional job ratings than World War II WAVES could take on. They could still be hospital corpsmen. They tracked and directed air traffic and maintained flight schedules. They worked as storekeepers, radiomen, communications specialists, and disbursing clerks. They also packed parachutes, collected weather information, and served as yeomen (clerks) in a variety of administrative jobs. For the seven aviation ratings that remained open to women, airmen could go from boot camp directly to an eight-week course that familiarized them in electronics, structural mechanics, machinery, storekeeping, parachute rigging, aerography (meteorology), and control tower operation at facilities such as the U.S. Naval Air Technical Training Center in Memphis, Tennessee.[33] Job opportunities aboard the noncombat Navy vessels transporting personnel and dependents was a breakthrough, because it put women in jobs aboard ships without contravening the 1948 Integration Act.

A small number of Navy women held jobs that required them to qualify with and carry a weapon. In the fall of 1950, Ensign Debbie Belka became paymaster of the naval air station at Lakehurst, New Jersey, and was responsible for disbursing—in cash—the wages of three thousand personnel. She carried a .45 caliber automatic pistol in her belt when she made her rounds on payday. Although not the only female paymaster in the Navy, no other was responsible for an installation the size of Lakehurst.[34] Reserve Lieutenant (jg) D'Anne Aultman (Evans), custodian of registered publications at the naval supply center in Oakland, California, was required to wear a .38 caliber pistol when picking up top-secret material or when taking coding machines to be repaired.[35]

As the Marine Corps began gearing up for the Korean War, its actions seemed to bode well for women; the results, however, would prove to be mixed. There were only 46 Women Marine officers (28 regular and 18 reserve) on active duty when the war broke out, along with 537 enlisted women (496 regular and 41 reserve), and the Corps immediately began a six-month recall of veteran enlisted reserve women. The Corps cast a wide net, seeking experience in more than the usual female-identified administrative assignments. The job categories included fire control instrument repair, operational communications, motor transport, photography, training and training aids, air traffic control, aviation operations, and intelligence.[36]

Not all women in organized reserve units were World War II veterans, however. Many were just learning Marine Corps ways and had yet to complete basic training. Only those reservists who had ninety days' active duty experience were recalled, yet when the dust had settled, more than 98 percent of the Reserve had been mobilized: 287 enlisted veterans and 298 new enlisted who were ordered to Parris Island, South Carolina, for boot camp. Unlike the low recall rate of the other services, only twelve of the women had to be rejected or deferred because the Marine Corps alone had formed reserve units after the 1948 Women's Armed Services Integration Act. By

January 1951, all available enlisted in the Reserve had been trained and as-signed. The only glitch: the Corps chose not to recall women reserve officers so that male officers could be rotated stateside. This made the male officers happy, but created a morale problem among enlisted women reservists who could not understand why their officers were not recalled with them.[37]

Many entire Women Marine Reserve platoons were ordered to active duty when the Korean War started. The Chicago platoon, attached to the 9th Infantry Battalion, was ordered to San Francisco in July 1950. Twelve of its sixteen members were World War II veterans.[38] The year-old Philadelphia platoon, made up primarily of women who were secretaries in civilian life, was the second reserve platoon ordered to report in July 1950, soon followed by Boston's. In 1952, the Corps organized another Boston platoon of fifty re-servists, all trained in classification procedures, and attached it to the 2nd Infantry Battalion. The Corps filled the platoon via a direct mail campaign to single women voters. When it reached allotted strength, a sister platoon specializing in disbursing was established in nearby Worcester.[39]

As the Marine Corps also stepped up recruiting, it found women's moti-vations for joining up varied greatly; many had very personal and patriotic reasons. Connie Musemeci enlisted in the Marines because her Marine brother had been listed as missing after the Chosin Reservoir disaster. Maria Matta of Puerto Rico paid her own way to the United States to enlist in the Marine Corps to honor her brother, who had died during World War II. Ellen Juhre's father, a Marine veteran who was wounded at Okinawa, told his daughter that she would not be able to make it through Marine boot camp; she enlisted to prove him wrong.[40]

As the other services found, the pressure for more recruits created a quality versus quantity dilemma as requirements for raw recruits soon were eased. The age limit was dropped from twenty to eighteen, and the re-quirement for a high school diploma was modified to the ability to pass an equivalency exam. Colonel Katherine Towle, director of the Women Marines, opposed lower standards, but she was pressured to conform by the other services and DOD. As a result, women recruits during the Korean War were generally younger and less skilled than their World War II counterparts had been. To compensate for the differences in this cohort, the Marine Corps was the one service to actually extend women's boot camp, upping it from six weeks to eight weeks in 1952.[41]

The Korean War also significantly changed and shortened—from six to four weeks—Women Marine officers' basic training. The 1948 Women's Armed Services Integration Act had envisioned women serving fully in both the Regular and Reserve of each service, but before the Korean War broke out, only a few new officers had been offered regular commissions and allowed to remain on active duty. In 1951, however, the entire officer graduating class was ordered to active duty for twenty-four months. Intended as a temporary emergency measure, it continued, and changed only to lengthen the required service, changing the nature of the Women Marines from a mostly reserve force to a true nucleus of trained women. In other words, the war emergency forced the Corps to comply more fully with the 1948 Integration Act.[42]

Although it had been only five years since World War II, male Marines appeared to have no institutional memory of Women Marines. Returning to posts where they had once been accepted as a matter of course, Women Marines found themselves a phenomenon. Captain Helen Wilson was the first woman assigned to duty at the Marine Corps air station at Cherry Point, North Carolina, since the last days of World War II, but there were no longer quarters for Marine women; she bunked with the Navy nurses. At her entry conference, the commanding general pointed out to her that male Marines were unaccustomed to seeing Women Marines on a daily basis, which might lead to problems for the women. Wilson was stunned when the general then informed her that he would hold her "personally responsible if anything happened" to any of the two hundred women who would be under her command. He suggested that she establish a policy that no Women Marines could leave the base except in pairs. Fortunately, nothing untoward happened.[43]

Platoons of Women Marines were assigned to duty, with mixed results, at several other Marine posts that similarly had not seen Women Marines since the last days of World War II, including California's El Toro Air Station, Camp Pendleton, and the Marine Corps Reserve Depot in San Diego. At Camp Pendleton, Women Marines were assigned the same barracks occupied by their predecessors during World War II, but now a guard was ordered posted. Because this required manpower, which was in short supply, the barracks was fenced and the gate locked each night when liberty expired. Despite women's complaints that it looked like a POW compound, the fence remained until the mid-1950s.[44] At El Toro, originally slated to receive only ninety Women Marines, women proved their value so totally that the commanding general identified 235 more positions where he could use them and the detachment eventually grew to two hundred and fifty.[45] Women Marines also returned to Hawaii during the Korean War, a small unit arriving at Pearl Harbor in October 1951, and another group assigned to the Marine Corps Air Station at Kanoehe Bay in 1953.[46] The women's units were attached to male units, and—breaking precedent—ate in male mess halls. The Corps sensibly opted to avoid establishing additional administrative units.[47]

Less sensible, in retrospect, was the shrinking of job opportunities for women. When the Korean War started, Women Marines were being utilized in twenty-one of forty-four occupational fields. Only small numbers of women were placed in nontraditional jobs, and they were exclusively veterans trained during World War II. During Korea, the Marines initially (in fact, throughout most of the war) refused to train women in nontraditional fields, even though the Corps was looking for but unable to find enough trained women for jobs in cartographic drafting, weapons repair, and motor transport. Of the 469 Marine Corps occupational specialties, enlisted women were allowed to fill eighty-six. A few went on for advanced training following boot camp: air traffic control at Olathe, Kansas; photography at Washington, D.C.; journalism at Great Lakes Naval Training Station in Illinois; public information at Fort Slocum, Georgia; naval justice in Newport, Rhode Island; and personnel administration at Parris Island. Some newly minted Women Marines were sent directly to recruiting assignments, and in January 1953, the Marine Corps did establish a four-week leadership school for women NCOs at Camp Lejeune.[48] However, 95 percent of Women Marines were concentrated in only six of the twenty-one occupational fields for which they were eligible—all administrative jobs in personnel, information, and supply.[49]

In 1951, the Marine Corps did place six women World War II veterans into motor transport positions. Although one of these, Sergeant Theresa Souza, at Camp Pendleton, recalled she had to prove that she could handle a truck and a jeep before she got the job, by the fall of 1952, five more women were sent to motor transport school for the intensive five-week course. Only two Women Marines, both veterans, worked in radio repair between 1950 and early 1953, but in March of that year, four more women received orders to attend a sixteen-week course at Fort Holabird, Maryland. During the war, although the Corps needed women in the weapons repair and security guard fields, few women—again only those veterans with previous training and experience—were placed.[50]

Towle and her staff understood that the Corps' refusal to train women to perform nontraditional jobs meant that they were ignoring the entire nucleus concept of the 1948 act. The phrase that best describes the Corps' circular illogic, however, had not yet been coined: "Catch-22." Until the Marine Corps experienced a pressing need for, say, radio repair personnel, and could not meet that need with men, it would not consider training women. That meant that when the need suddenly presented itself, servicewomen wouldn't be there to train others.[51]

In a May 1951 study, less than a year into the war, the procedures analysis office evaluated which jobs were fitting for Women Marines and came up with twenty-seven occupational fields, an increase of six from previous regulations. Still listed as unsuitable: infantry, antiaircraft and field artillery, utilities, construction and equipment, tank and amphibian tractor, weapons repair, ammunition and explosive ordnance disposal, supply service, steward, guided missiles, chemical warfare and radiological defense, security and guard, aircraft maintenance and repair, aviation ordnance, and pilot.[52]

Although the division of aviation had suggested that a greater percentage of women be assigned to aviation specialties, and had especially recommended the addition of occupational field 64, aircraft maintenance and repair, it was overruled. Also considered and ruled out was the use of women as instructors at the communications-electronics school, because of their lack of combat experience and because they would have to supervise men.[53]

Towle accepted the study's general conclusions, but took exception to the statement "situations in which women supervise mixed gender groups or men should be minimized." She commented dryly that "the commissions of women officers are identical in wording to those of their male counterparts, charging them not only with the duties and responsibilities of their grade and position, but also assuring them of comparable military authority." The Marine Corps, however, continued to avoid giving Women Marines authority over men.[54]

The number of Women Marines quadrupled between the start of the war in June 1950 and the end of the war in July 1953, when they numbered 2,787. Immediately after war, the number of Women Marines, like the numbers of women in the other services, dropped rapidly, finally stabilizing at figures that were only slightly higher than prewar levels.[55] Nonetheless, the Korean War—as had World Wars I and II before it—did expand opportunities for women in the Marine Corps by increasing the number of regular women officers, growing the tiny women's component, and by affirming the lessons of earlier history that women could also do the jobs of a few good men.

Astonishingly, even as it was having to reinvent the wheel, the Corps was already primed to re-forget. In April 1952, fifty-seven Women Marines took the three-hour examination to qualify as warrant officers, and two, Lillian

Hartley and Ruth Wood, became the first women warrant officers in the Marine Corps. Chief Warrant Officer Wood remembered, "We took the same exam the men did, at the same time. It included questions on whether to dig a one-man or two-man foxhole in a given situation, and when to retreat from an airstrip and on whose authority. A couple of years later (after the war was over), the Corps decided to test some other women, and they called me when they couldn't find a copy of the 'women's exam.' They were astonished when I told them that we had taken the men's exam." Did the Corps dust off the Korean War–era test and use it for women? No, Wood said, "They proceeded to devise a second exam for women candidates." [56]

Theoretically, the brand-new Air Force should have been the place where the military could break new ground. Created from the old Army Air Forces, it had scant separate institutional memory to lose. It also had some incentive to put aside the old and embrace the new. Instead, it was the service in which the stereotypes about women and what they could or should be interfered most with their successful performance. The Air Force had been in existence as a separate service only three years and its women's program just two when the Korean War started. At that point it had only 303 women officers, most of whom were World War II WAC veterans, and 3,782 enlisted women.[57] Colonel Geraldine Pratt May, the director of women, believed her personnel should be integrated throughout the force as much as possible, and pushed the envelope on what women were permitted to do. May believed that as long as a woman was qualified for the job and did it well, she should be allowed to do it. Unfortunately, May could only influence, not direct, overall Air Force policy toward women. Her authority was limited and the perceived needs of commanders in the field often clashed with her philosophy. During the war emergency, it became increasingly difficult for May to maintain the integrity of the women's program against pressures from local commanders and some Air Force leaders who were opposed to women's integration.[58]

After the war began, the Air Force, like the Army, extended all enlistments and began aggressively recruiting. A month into the war, it raised the recruitment ceilings for enlisted women from 175 to 350 per month, and then raised it again in September to five hundred. By November, however, the Air Force was facing problems supplying and training all its new female recruits, so it backed off to two-hundred fifty per month. In December, the Air Force took in no new enlisted women because it was out of uniforms.[59]

Meanwhile, the coeducational officer candidate school tentatively upped its two annual classes of 25 women to four classes of 15 each, adding just 10 officers. Then, in 1951, the number jumped to 40 per class, up from 60 new officers a year to 160. In April 1951, the Air Force began fast-tracking active duty WAF officers by appointing qualified women as second and first lieutenants, first to the Reserve, then straight to active duty bypassing the traditional congressional review.[60] They also assigned 33 additional women officers and 378 enlisted women to recruiting duty.[61]

Unlike men, WAF recruits did not train with weapons (and men did not receive administrative training) and there was such an emphasis on good grooming that Air Force recruiting brochures went into great detail on the subject. Prior to the war, women's basic training was eleven weeks compared to the thirteen weeks men received. In August 1950, the training of both was reduced to forty days. When the Air Force decided that forty-day training wasn't enough, it was nudged up to a full eight weeks.[62]

In October 1950, Air Force Chief of Staff General Hoyt Vandenberg asked well-known pilot Jacqueline Cochran to serve as a "special consultant" to him on "matters pertaining to Women in the Air Force" to "determine whether our current programs for women form a sound basis for expansion in wartime." He then instructed the office of the deputy chief of staff for personnel to provide Cochran "with such assistance as she may require." [63] It was the beginning of a storm.

Vandenberg's reasons for appointing Cochran remain a mystery. Was he unhappy with the WAF program, and if so, why? It is known that Vandenberg and Cochran were close friends and that he valued her opinion. Interviews with former WAF director Colonel Geraldine Pratt May indicate that she had been well aware at the time that both Vandenberg and Secretary of the Air Force Stuart Symington, would have "preferred . . . someone else" in her job.[64]

Jacqueline Cochran had been the director of the Women Airforce Service Pilots (WASP) during World War II. Flamboyant, glamorous, and an exceptionally skilled pilot, Cochran was described as the type of woman who could "sweep into (an) Air Force base at the controls of her own C-47 with a perfect three-point landing, toss her fur coat to the nearest colonel to hold, talk over old times with the commanding general, meet a few military women, and be off again—all in the space of an hour." [65] Significantly, Cochran counted as her personal friends a large number of highly influential military officers and politicians. She and her husband, industrialist and financier Floyd Odlum, routinely had as house guests Vandenberg, his wife and son, and Air Force secretary Symington. In 1948, she made another close friend and admirer, soon-to-be senator Lyndon Baines Johnson of Texas.[66]

In her autobiography, Jacqueline Cochran claimed, "'Van' Vandenberg, then chief of staff, was dissatisfied with the standards of the WAF and asked me if I would become the director, even if only for one year. I had to refuse for many reasons. He then asked me, as a special consultant, to check the various bases where WAF were stationed and to make recommendations."[67]

Cochran's 6 December 1950, report rocked the WAF. "My findings indicate that there has been a lack of careful, aggressive supervision over the entire program," Cochran wrote. "I have seen nowhere much indication that there is a good, sound, overall plan for the future, quick expansion and utilization of the WAF. . . . I met and talked with approximately 30 OCS trainees and was certainly not impressed, either with their physical appearance or grooming. In fact, three or four women in this group seemed out of balance weight for height. The data I have shows that this is not the case, which only emphasizes the point that balance must also take into account bone structure and bodily profile in order to get a smart looking group." [68]

The report included twenty specific recommendations pertaining to recruiting, physical and mental standards, training, utilization, clothing, housing, a reserve program and—ominously for May—reorganizing the office of the director. Among other things, Cochran suggested that stricter height and weight requirements (comparable to those for the Navy) be established, that no further recruiting should be done until adequate uniforms were available, and that Air Force women be trained at civilian secretarial schools. Time and again in her report Cochran stressed unsatisfactory appearance. "I have seen several hundred of the WAF at Lackland (near San Antonio, Texas)," she said, "and they are the most tattered, bedraggled persons I have ever seen in the services. Some of them were in cotton, with raincoats for a degree of warmth; some were in cast-off Army woolens, and without overcoats. The fatigue uniforms . . . were of at least six different varieties and were exceedingly poor in appearance and unattractive. These WAF are certainly anything but a credit to the Air Force in the present non-uniform clothing they are forced to wear."[69]

According to Cochran, prior to submitting her report to Vandenberg, she had informally discussed her twenty recommendations with "most of the top Air Force officers who had worked with WAFs in their commands," all of whom had approved.[70] But her report was received very differently at Air Force headquarters. Headquarters set up a committee of six officers, four male colonels and two WAF lieutenant colonels, Kathleen McClure and Emma Jane Riley, to study Cochran's report. The committee went over Cochran's recommendations and, one by one, discounted them. The committee noted that several recommendations, such as revised height/weight standards and improved uniform procurement, were already in process. Other recommendations either went against regulations or had to be rejected because they were impractical.[71]

Regardless of what the committee thought, it appeared that Vandenberg agreed with Cochran's views on the appearance of Air Force women. An exceptionally good-looking man—Vandenberg was often called "handsome" and "dashing," and was compared to aviation's romantic hero Charles Lindbergh[72]—he seems to have placed significant value on physical appearance, equating it with success or at the very least public support. On 21 December, a message went out to Air Force commanders saying the chief of staff of the Air Force had observed that the appearance of some women was "not up to the required standards of the USAF." The chief of staff, said the memo, was specifically concerned with "a lack of grooming, neatness and the improper wearing of the uniform. The chief of staff desires that all commanders take proper action to insure that all members of the WAF reflect credit upon themselves, their uniform and the United States Air Force."[73]

Meanwhile, Cochran's report was leaked to the press, and columnist Drew Pearson probably had the gist of it correct when he reported, "Cochran's confidential report stated that the Air Force should pay more attention to shapely figures in recruiting women," adding that "General Vandenberg agrees that the Navy seems to be getting all the better looking females and that the WAF could go in for taller women. The chief of the Air Force also suggested that WAF ought to be more feminine and stick to secretarial work instead of trying to be mechanics, truck drivers and grease monkeys."[74] Left unsaid was that women excelled at all of the above occupations during World War II, and at one point the nation had been grateful that they had.

Cochran said rather defensively in her autobiography that she had indeed emphasized the need to take into account body shape in her report, "I recommended that consideration should be given in selection of applicants to *proper distribution of weight* as well as to weight in relationship to height."[75] She went on to say that the reason these words had caused such a furor was that they had been taken from her report out of context.

Garbled and isolated parts of my report were allowed to leak in a way which gave a completely wrong impression. It was made to appear from these stories that I wanted to make the WAF a glamorous, kid glove, lily-fingered organization, composed mostly of beautiful girls who would act as companions to the top brass. . . . It was made to appear that my statement that weight should be properly distributed as well as being in proportion to height should be read with a lifting of the eyebrows. . . . Presumably there were some who thought or were being made to think the Air Force should fill its quota of WAFs by catering to the pot-bellied and bowlegged of our American womanhood.[76]

Early in 1951, the deputy chief of staff for personnel, Major General R. E. Nugent, discussed the Cochran report and the committee's findings with Vandenberg. Nugent took a middle ground, agreeing with some of Cochran's suggestions while supporting some of the committee's findings. According to Nugent, the conversation led the two men to a discussion of the overall "integration" concept.

> We agreed that the extent to which this concept had been carried out was faulty in that women cannot, and should not, be treated in the same way as male officers and airmen. It was decided to reorient the WAF program with this fact in mind, and to approach the WAF more as a separate personnel component of the Air Force instead of being individually integrated into the Air Force personnel structure. I informed General Vandenberg at that time of Colonel May's unalterable opposition to this change. Both General Vandenberg and I, however, felt that such a change would raise the quality of the WAF, would encourage improved relations between the male members and female members of the Air Force, and would attract more desirable women to the WAF.[77]

If Vandenberg had decided that the WAF should be an elite group of highly trained, "desirable," and polished executive secretaries, Geraldine Pratt May was not the "desirable" woman to direct such an organization. Within four months, May left her job "for personal reasons." Reports in the press indicated that more than one woman had her eyes on May's job. Jacqueline Cochran was rumored to be interested, and (almost comically, given the Air Force's interest in fashionable women) so was Fleur Cowles, editor-in-chief of a much-heralded, recently defunct fashion magazine named *Flair*.[78]

When Geraldine Pratt (May) graduated from the University of California at Berkeley in 1915, she planned a career in social work and happily accepted a job with the California immigration and housing commission. Several jobs and a dozen years later, Pratt married and left the workforce. Widowed by World War II, she applied to the newly created Women's Army Auxiliary Corps (WAAC), and at age forty-seven—two years over the official age limit—joined 440 other carefully selected women in the first officer candidate class of the WAAC, the predecessor to the Women's Army Corps (WAC). Soon assigned to headquarters of the Air Transport Command (ATC) of the Army Air Forces (AAF) as WAC staff adviser, she ultimately became responsible for six thousand Army women. In an interview long after her retirement, May said she'd enjoyed that job because her boss was a former head of personnel at Macy's, and he "knew what women could do." ATC officers were not "staid old Army types," but had been aviators before the war, and she added, were more open-minded about women's potential.[79]

Lieutenant Colonel Geraldine Pratt May, first director of women in the U.S. Air Force, 1948. U.S. Air Force photo.

At war's end, May, by then a major, was on terminal leave when she heard from WAC Deputy Director Lieutenant Colonel Mary Hallaren, a fellow member of that first WAAC officer class. Hallaren suggested that May return to WAC headquarters. The Army Air Forces would soon become a separate service and May was the logical choice to head up the Women in the Air Force (WAF). In June 1948, at fifty-five, May became the new Air Force's director of women.[80]

May described herself as "not the pushy kind and so not too aggressive"; her friends described her as gentle and low-key. She avoided confrontation, but would not compromise on matters of principle. Throughout her tenure as director of women, she fought for greater opportunity for WAF, and counted among her accomplishments the institution of gender-integrated officer candidate training early in the Air Force's history.[81]

Cochran herself said "General Vandenberg felt the start had to be made by putting in a new head of the WAF, because Colonel Geraldine May was nearing the end of her term of duty. Again I was asked to take over but again I refused. Colonel May resigned. Colonel May considered that I was her undoing, which was farthest from the fact. . . . But I did not want that job. . . . I wouldn't have taken it if a full general's rank had been thrown in." [82]

In May's final report, 11 June 1951, she avoided discussing both Cochran's recommendations and the integration issue. Instead, she blamed her difficulties since June 1950 on recruiting lags and the negative fallout from uniform and housing shortages, the latter of which, she emphasized, were Air Force–wide. The decision to give Air Force women a new uniform to match the men's new uniforms, May reported, could not have come at a worse time. Contractors were slow in producing and delivering the new uniforms, women were forced to wear incomplete and ill-fitting uniforms, and morale plummeted. "Sloppily" dressed women gave Air Force leaders the impression that they were poorly trained and administered.[83] May clearly understood how much of her problem stemmed from Air Force men's notions of what Air Force women should look like and be allowed to do, but she elected to write her final report as if women's full integration into the Air Force was a given and not in question. This gave her successor a mandate to carry out the integration concept unless specifically directed not to.

The war was barely a year old when May's successor, Colonel Mary Jo Shelly, was appointed to the job of director. One of the first twelve lieutenants to have been commissioned in the WAVES in 1942, Shelly left the Navy after World War II and worked as the assistant to the president of Bennington College in Vermont. She had a master's degree in education from Columbia University, and had taught there for six years.[84] An experienced administrator, she also had definite ideas on the training of young women. Air Force leaders, who had always admired the Navy WAVES, now had reason to hope that the new director would instill a Navy-like demeanor in the WAF.

That propriety was a significant issue for Shelly is evident from a 1951 staff report by an officer who conducted an inspection visit of Lackland's WAF Basic Training Center. Male officers were not training the women properly, the officer reported. Newcomers were being trained in things that they would never be given opportunity to use: preparation for guard duty and flight emergency procedures. At the same time, the women were not being taught some of the things that they would need to know: how to wear their uniforms properly and how to be feminine in uniform. In short, they were treating the women like men. The fourteen hours of instruction on personal appearance and selection of civilian clothing women did receive taught them nothing about how to look and act feminine in a uniform. For WAF to look good and act feminine had become an obsession of the Air Force hierarchy.[85] The massive DOD united recruitment campaign got under way in late 1951; before long, Shelly realized that it was doomed to fail. Its failure would cause her a variety of problems. WAF strength had doubled from four thousand to eight thousand in the year between the start of the war and Shelly's appointment in June 1951. The Air Force goal, however, was to have 48,871 active duty women, and the DOD campaign set a goal of 49,871 by the end of 1952—a more than sixfold increase. Monthly recruitment targets were tripled, the number of recruiters increased, and an even more aggressive publicity barrage launched.[86]

Unfortunately, the Air Force had counted their recruits before it signed them and had established too many new squadrons. With only forty to fifty women each, these squadrons were too small to be administered efficiently, a problem compounded by the fact that officer recruiting had failed to bring in enough women officers to administer them. When the recruiting fell short, the new squadrons were in place and had to be supervised by an officer, and very few officers were given the opportunity to do anything other than supervise enlisted women.[87] Further, many of the newest officers had been assigned directly overseas and veteran officers felt stuck in squadrons, unable to move on to new, career-building assignments.[88]

In 1952, Shelly began consolidating squadrons to achieve a smaller number of larger squadrons (minimum 120 women per squadron), thus freeing some officers.[89] But this created a new problem: some male Air Force officers felt women officers should only be allowed to supervise women and should not compete with men for other jobs. As long as women officers were sufficiently junior, there was no problem. Beyond squadron commander, however, male officers frequently resisted having high-grade female officers in assignments commensurate with the women's qualifications and experience. It became very difficult to place senior majors and lieutenant colonels in the field. Major commands frequently resisted the assignment of women field grade officers regardless of their qualifications, particularly if they were to supervise men. This attitude also caused problems in the assignment of women NCOs.[90]

One enlisted WAF in ten received an overseas assignment during these years. Posts included Wiesbaden and Erding Air Bases in Germany; Supreme Headquarters, Allied Powers Europe (SHAPE) near Paris; Hickam Air Base in Hawaii; and Nagoya Air Base in Japan. Throughout 1951, overseas opportunities for enlisted personnel increased significantly. Then, because recruiting could not even fill all the openings stateside, the Air Force abruptly halted overseas assignments in January 1952, a ban that proved bad for morale because so many women had enlisted precisely for the opportunity to go overseas. Shelly realized this, and asked that small numbers of overseas postings be resumed in May, before the reenlistment drive started in July.[91]

Director of Women in the Air Force Colonel Mary Jo Shelly, second from right, and the directors of the other four women's service branches, Washington, D.C., 20 November 1953. Left to right: Captain Joy Bright Hancock, Navy; Colonel Mary A. Hallaren, WAC; Lieutenant Commander Beatrice V. Ball, Coast Guard; Colonel Shelly; and Colonel Katherine A. Towle, Women Marines. U.S. Coast Guard photo.

Mary Josephine Shelly, the youngest of four children in a Grand Rapids, Michigan, family, planned from an early age to be a teacher. She graduated from the University of Oregon in 1926, earned a master's degree in education from Columbia, and went on in the 1930s to Bennington College in Vermont, where she cofounded its innovative School of Dance. One of her instructors was the pioneering modern dancer, Martha Graham.

Early in World War II, the Navy, spurred by the creation of the Women's Army Auxiliary Corps, called on the deans of leading women's colleges to handpick its first women officers and Shelly's name came up. In mid-1942, without undergoing basic or officer training, the college physical education administrator found herself one of the first twelve women commissioned in the WAVES (Women Accepted for Volunteer Emergency Service). She was promptly put to work in the area she knew best: training young women.[92]

After the war, Shelly returned to Bennington, believing she had left military life behind. During lunch at the Pentagon in 1951, however, Assistant Secretary of Defense Anna Rosenberg, Secretary of the Air Force Thomas Finletter, and Air Force Chief of Staff Hoyt Vandenberg prevailed upon her to take over the embattled Colonel Geraldine Pratt May's job, director of Women in the Air

Force (WAF). She was at first hesitant. "One hitch in the military was enough," she said. "Besides, I can't stand uniforms." Eventually she agreed, but only after obtaining the personal assurances of Finletter's and Vandenberg's complete support.

Shelly, then forty-nine, was well aware that she was stepping into a difficult situation. Many Air Force women were disillusioned by May's departure, and resented that a former Navy officer was replacing her. Shelly also understood that Air Force commanders and their staffs were unclear about what they wanted out of the WAF program. But shackled neither by aspirations for a military career nor emotional ties to the old Army Air Forces and its traditions, Shelly was able to sidestep many potential problems, impressing her new bosses with her pragmatism and impartiality.[93]

Shelly inherited the uniform and housing problems that had plagued May. Although uniforms were being distributed on schedule, the majority still could not be issued. Of 5,100 uniforms delivered to Lackland in 1951, only 1,200 were usuable because the manufacturer had not followed pattern specifications and even those all had to be altered.[94] Housing continued to remain inadequate. When the Air Force had surveyed the availability of base housing for women early in the war, many bases had reported ample potential housing. Much of this "potential housing," however, had been converted to family quarters, and Air Force women were being assigned substandard quarters. Shelly reminded Air Force leaders that women were, after all, volunteers, so recruitment would suffer if housing conditions remained poor.[95]

Shelly had further problems with the way women were being utilized. At some posts, civilian women workers were assigned the same office jobs as WAF, thus hurting morale. Civilian women working as secretaries, clerks, receptionists, and switchboard operators could wear attractive clothing and live less restricted lives than their military sisters, some of whom wondered why the Air Force insisted they needed women in uniform if they could get civilian women to do the same jobs.[96]

Shelly's worries that the aggressive DOD recruiting campaign would compromise the quality of Air Force recruits began to prove as true as it had for the Marine Corps. By December 1952, as recruiters pressed to make quotas, 29 percent of recruits showing up at Lackland lacked a high school diploma. Compounding (and related to) the quality problem, Shelly also was facing an attrition rate approaching 24 percent a year.[97]

In 1952 Shelly heard further grim news from a young captain in the planning and program section of her office, Jeanne M. Holm. Comparing recruit statistics to retention rates, Holm realized that the WAF was in danger of shrinking substantially each year until it disappeared.[98] Women were leaving the Air Force for a variety of reasons. Many left when they got married or became pregnant. Some left because they never should have been accepted into the service in the first place. Others left because they were disappointed in the Air Force. The latter were the women Shelly wanted to do something about.

After analyzing Holm's report, Shelly proposed to Secretary of the Air Force Thomas Finletter that the Air Force focus on achieving a smaller but more elite WAF in December 1952. He agreed, with one caveat: the public must come to hold Air Force women in as high esteem as they did Navy women.[99] With Finletter's approval, Shelly got enlistment quotas dropped and potential recruits' minimum score on the Armed Forces Qualification Test (AFQT) raised from 49 percent to 65 percent. She also decided to retest all enlistees when they arrived at Lackland to be certain they met minimum standards. Between February and June 1953, the toughened standards cut enlistments by half.[100] Facing reality, Shelly recommended a maximum of 12,000 women, less than one-quarter of DOD's original plans for 49,871 enlistees.[101]

By the middle of 1953, technical scores of enlisted women had risen and were higher than those of male airmen, indicating the benefits of raising the minimum AFQT score to 65. Women outperformed men as flight center tower operators, weather observers, and stenographers. Shelly's office even suggested that the Air Force's best interests would be served if women could become flight instructors for men training for combat, thereby releasing male personnel for other operational duties. This suggestion did not fly.

Enlisted Air Force women's assignments reflected the Air Force's willingness to utilize women in technical fields—as long as their ranks were low enough. The number working in administration actually dropped from 31.5 percent in 1951 to 26.7 percent by mid-1953, by which time more than twice as many women were in rapidly growing high-tech communications. By 1953, almost 40 percent worked in weather observation and forecasting, air traffic control and warning, radio and radar maintenance, or statistics. The remaining women worked in medical, dental, and supply fields.[102]

However, there were some glaring snags in the progress. In 1951, for example, the Air Force trained Joan DeAngelo (Fogelstrom) and five other women as aircraft control and warning specialists and assigned them to

Great Falls, Montana, where they coordinated radar identification with the Western Air Defense Command and Civil Air Patrol. But after a year, when the women were sent to Ramstein AFB in Germany, they became secretaries. They were told that they could not be control and warning operators because these jobs were "in very isolated areas . . . no place for women."[103] The Air Force clearly shortchanged itself, as it did again in the spring of 1952, when it assigned Lieutenant Marjory V. Foster to the 19th and 307th Bomb Wings on Okinawa. Foster was an experienced pilot, having flown P-39, B-25, T-6, and T-17 aircraft as a WASP during World War II before joining the Air Force in 1949. Aircraft from the 19th and 307th Bomb Wings made regular runs from Okinawa to Korea, bombing strategic targets and providing close support to frontline U.N. ground troops. Because she was a woman, Foster was grounded and placed in charge of casualty reports and officer personnel records.[104]

Although the Air Force had managed to reestablish the quality of women recruits, the entire WAF program was still shrinking. Recruiting and retention continued to be problems. Recruiters blamed American fathers, many of whom were convinced that no young man in uniform, and certainly none of those out of uniform, would respect a woman wearing one, and women under twenty-one had to obtain a parent's consent to join the service.[105] Fathers were simply reflecting society's overall lack of acceptance of military women. Young women were expected to become the nurturers of the next generation, and military training was seen as contributing very little toward this goal.

Shelly was convinced that military training benefited young women and that much of the retention/attrition problem could be solved by taking special care with new, very young trainees who were away from home for the first time and whose expectations of the service may have been formed by overzealous recruiters or too-glamorous brochures. Many young recruits were disappointed with poor looking uniforms, the near-total lack of overseas postings, early assignments at isolated Air Force bases and mundane jobs that did not seem particularly important or "essential" to the war effort or their own careers. Trainers and supervisors had to provide close supervision, frequent encouragement and strong guidance to prevent high numbers from leaving the service.[106]

Shelly knew that of every four or five hard-won recruits, only one who got through her first enlistment would stay on for a second term. Given the prevailing social climate with its emphasis on marriage and family, there was little Shelly could do about it. She was counting on the quality of the

one remaining woman to compensate for the expense of training the original five.[107]

By mid-1953 and the end of the Korean War, WAF strength was 11,776,
and enlistments were down to 150 per month. Still, there was reason to be
optimistic. The vast majority of the women enlisted for a three-year tour of
duty, and 52 percent said they intended to reenlist at the end of their first
term. Statistics, however, told a disturbingly different story. In July 1952, exactly 815 women entered the program and 230 left. In August, 713 women
entered and 333 women left; in October, 666 entered the program while 351
left. By January 1953, the 354 gains were nearly wiped out by the 342 losses.
In March of that year, they fell below replacement level: 257 gains versus
346 losses. By May, with 120 gains and 338 losses, the downward spiral indicated that the women's program might eventually disappear, as Holm's
research had predicted.[108]

Six months after the war was officially over, in December 1953, Shelly
would drastically downsize her estimate of the future strength of women in
the Air Force. Given selective recruiting, which the Air Force believed was
essential, and the seemingly unavoidable high attrition rate, she predicted
that by 1956, the Air Force could expect a total of only six thousand women.
Shelly rationalized that a small force was not necessarily a bad thing, and
recommended that women be consolidated within a few select commands,
so that they could be efficiently administered.[109]

Regardless of its growing pains during the war years and regardless of
the individual attitudes of some of its brass, the Air Force only once, much
later in the 1950s, considered phasing out women. The services had all publicly committed themselves to servicewomen as a permanent part of the
force and, despite problems, the need for women remained obvious. No one
service could comfortably go it alone and eliminate them. The Air Force's
own studies demonstrated that women performed certain jobs particularly
well, and that women were more likely than men to stay with a job, even
when it became boring. The Air Force particularly valued women in communication and supply. By mid-1953, the major Air Force commands were
even quarreling over which of them should get the limited number of
women available, in stark contrast to their earlier resistance. The Strategic
Air Command (SAC) had built new housing for women and its commanders were incensed that under Shelly's plan they would not be assigned any.
Some bases to which women were not scheduled to be posted insisted that
they had to have them because they were located in an isolated area where
it was difficult to hire civilians. If, by the end of the Korean War, the small

band of Air Force women had won a major battle, it was this: most Air Force leaders (certainly not all) still believed the WAF to be of value.[110]

The Coast Guard only becomes a part of the military in time of war; yet when the Korean War broke out, Coast Guard women reservists already were on duty. Chief Warrant Officer Betty Splaine had, at her first opportunity in 1949, reenlisted in the Reserve.[111] And soon after the war began, another former SPAR, Pearl Faurie, received a letter from the commandant asking her to leave her civilian job and return to duty. She was not being recalled—the Coast Guard did not yet have legal authorization for active duty women—so it reverted to the tactic it successfully used between World War II and its authorization for women in the Reserve. In January 1951 it simply moved Faurie and the six reservist yeoman first class she supervised from Coast Guard headquarters in Washington to an office building several miles away in Virginia. After five months, the Coast Guard received the authorization it needed, and the women came in from the cold.[112]

In retrospect, one can see that each of the fledgling women's organizations in the armed forces, as well as the nurse and medical specialist corps, were severely tested during the Korean and early Cold War period. At this distance, that is neither the surprise nor the disappointment it surely was then to the dedicated women directors who had fought so hard to make their organizations a permanent part of the nation's defense and then were unsuccessful in meeting recruiting targets. There were many reasons for this lack of success. The services had just begun to reorganize their women's components in response to the undeclared war against communist Eastern Europe when hostilities broke out in Asia. The America of the 1950s was less hospitable to the idea of military women than it had been during World War II, and the military itself was unclear about the role it wanted women to have. The military perhaps also forgot the difficulties it had had recruiting and fitting women in during World War II (it never met recruiting goals for either WACs or nurses) and focused solely on the fact that 400,000 women had volunteered. Moreover, the services offered military women limited jobs with limited promotion potential, limited supervisory and decision-making responsibility, and limited personal freedom. In trying to assure "proper employment for sisters and girlfriends," the military offered the young women they were desperate to recruit job opportunities that were more traditional and less exciting than those of their World War II big sisters and certainly not much better than those civilian employers were offering.

If asked, military leaders might have responded that women had always volunteered in the past. This time a national emergency coincided with massive emphasis on domesticity, putting patriotism and motherhood at odds. And while the armed forces attempted to accommodate that pressure by releasing servicewomen from their service obligations when they married and by prohibiting them from serving if they became mothers, they did not take the more innovative steps required to convince more of the few available career-minded women to serve.

CHAPTER 5

A "Woman Imperative"?—Military Necessity Erodes Old Barriers

Military nurses do some of the "hardest and dirtiest work in the world. . . . There is little of the "glamour" or "romance" about its deadly serious day-to-day routine of jobs that require an infinity of patience, endurance and good temper . . . (and) good, sound women who know their job and do it.
—Editorial, *New York Times*, 2 February 1952[1]

Nursing is supposed to be dedicated to the relief of suffering. Does the sex of the practitioner matter? Certainly, men nurses are more appropriate for an army—unless the fiction of a "woman's touch" or the presence of "mom" in times of trouble makes . . . a woman imperative.
—Morris Wolf, R.N., in a letter to the editor of the *New York Times*, calling for "rectification of this inequity." [2]

Babies . . . babies . . . and more babies. That's how the U.S. Force's only woman doctor cheerfully defines her job.
—Unnamed upstate New York newspaper, heralding the arrival of "modest, dark-haired with eyes to match" Captain Dorothy A. Elias at a nearby base.[3]

E VEN BEFORE THE KOREAN WAR STARTED, there were indications of incipient crisis in military medicine. As polio epidemics devastated the nation, military hospitals with their own polio victims to rehabilitate and World War II wounded still needing care found themselves competing with civilian hospitals and with the other services for the roughly 550 new physical therapists (PTs) who graduated each year. Many of these were off-limits to the military anyway: some women PTs were married and had children; others had gone to school on scholarships from the "March of Dimes" (National Foundation for Infantile Paralysis) that required they work in civilian hospitals. But there was an even bigger hurdle: one-half of the new graduates and one-third of the nation's existing 4,500 physical therapists were men.[4] Yet two months after the war began, when Ohio Representative Frances P. Bolton introduced a bill to delete the word "women" from the legislation establishing the Women's Medical Specialist Corps, Congress would have none of it. Her bill failed largely because the Army-Navy Nurse Act of 1947, under which the WMSC was established, placed limitations on grade and age at retirement that were specifically geared to women, limits that Congress felt would be inappropriate to place on male officers.[5]

Joining up came naturally to Army Second Lieutenant (later Air Force Captain) Jeanne Ertwine (Disterdick). The only child in a military family, she had lived on stateside military bases all her life—and the Army paid its physical therapists better than the civilian world.

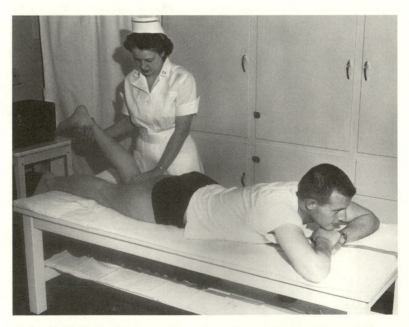

Air Force physical therapist Captain Jean Ertwine (Disterdick) works with a patient on exercises to increase the range of motion in the knee and hamstring flexibility.
Jean Ertwine Disterdick Collection, Women's Memorial Collection.

After basic training Ertwine was assigned to Brooke Army Hospital in San Antonio, Texas, where she worked with victims of the 1949 polio epidemic. The crippling and sometimes fatal disease often struck children and young adults; a half century later Ertwine still remembered two-year-old twins who died. "The first time I saw them, they were so sick I just left them alone. By the time I went back later that afternoon, the nurse told me they were gone."

After the Korean War broke out, the twenty-two-year-old began dividing her time between her already full load of polio patients and a steady new stream of wounded. "They were bringing in as many as one hundred . . . every couple of days." Her patients ranged in age from seventeen to thirty-six and one told her that "the (North) Koreans were shooting to maim rather than to kill so that the (U.S.) government would have to spend money to take care of them." Ertwine had little time to get to know individual patients, but she recalled one young man who had lost both legs. When she asked if he had told his parents yet, he replied, "I don't know how. . . . My father was in World War I and he lost both legs."[6]

Even before the war began, the Army Nurse Corps (ANC) knew it needed a hundred new nurses per month simply because of "those who drop out to get married."[7] The Navy Nurse Corps (NNC) was similarly handicapped and, although the Air Force Nurse Corps (AFNC) was just starting out, when the war began all three nurse corps were competing with one another for the same pool of unmarried, unfettered women. Again the operative word was women, though the number of male nurses was minuscule compared to that of male PTs.[8] Nonetheless, despite the growing need for nurses, male nurses were being drafted to serve as privates but could not volunteer and be commissioned in the Army Nurse Corps. Although in some cases male nurses who were drafted might be matched to a medical technician MOS, they were at least as likely to be "mal-assigned"; the military was also short on combat troops. In January 1951, a point at which nurse shortage was much discussed in the press, a *New York Times* editorial accused the services of discriminating against men by not commissioning them as nurses and insisted the DOD "give men nurses the professional standing to which they are entitled in the armed services."[9] A few months later, the *Times* printed a somewhat sarcastic letter to the editor from registered nurse Morris Wolf questioning whether the sex of the nurse caregiver mattered and insisting men nurses made more sense in an army.[10]

By war's end, the severity of the shortages in all the medical professions would begin to erode the resistance to gender-integrating the nurse corps and women's medical specialists corps. The changes were born out of military necessity, however, not from any long-term policy discussion, and certainly not from concern about the second-class status of women. The questions being raised were a beginning, but the erosion of old notions about women's roles and men's needs for superior ranking and recognition was glacially slow. One minor-seeming thing DOD did do was to make better use of its nurses. In June 1951, a DOD directive relieved them of the nonnursing responsibilities in housekeeping, food service, and clerical minutia that military nurses as women had traditionally been assigned.[11]

The ANC and NNC's shortfalls were compounded by outdated lists of nurses in the Reserve. Of the reserve nurses the Army had been counting on coming back into the fold, 40 percent had married and many had children. Moreover, there was another problem unique to the Army Nurse Corps: the fury of women scorned, nurses whom the Army had dropped from active duty against their wishes in postwar demobilization. When a large number of these World War II veterans were recalled, also against their wishes, they were understandably angry. They saw no reason why they should now give up civilian work to return to the organization they felt had treated them poorly.[12] At the same time, the NNC was having difficulty retaining what nurses remained because many still resented the Navy's less competitive pay and traditionally slower promotion schedules. For example, Navy nurses had not even received a commensurate pay raise in 1944 when both Army and Navy nurses had their relative rank temporarily upped to be on par with male officers—regular commission status that disappeared, like Cinderella's coach at the stroke of midnight, precisely six months after the war ended.[13]

In contrast to the newly created, nonmedical women's components of the service branches, the three nurse corps had one important factor in their favor: they did not need a case made for their very existence. Nurses were an obvious military necessity and had been viewed so since General George Washington's time. Indeed, when the Army Nurse Corps had been established in 1901 and the Navy Nurse Corps in 1908, women officially became a part of the United States military for the first time. Army and Navy nurses and members of the Army Women's Medical Specialist Corps won permanent status in 1947 with little congressional debate while the role of military women other than nurses was still a political football. There was the same cap on rank that the women's components would be saddled with: only one officer per unit permitted at the Army colonel or Navy captain level and limits on the number of nurses relative to the force as a whole. And there were interesting caveats in the section dealing with Navy nurses that addressed the special gender roles of women.

SEC. 205: Officers of the Navy Nurse Corps . . . shall exercise such military authority as may be prescribed from time to time by the Secretary of the Navy. . . . *Provided,* That they shall not be eligible for the exercise of command . . .

SEC. 208: (a) All provision of law relating to . . . male officers of the Navy . . . are hereby made applicable to officers of the Navy Nurse Corps: *Provided,* That . . . husbands of female officers appointed under the provisions of this Act shall not be considered dependents unless they are in fact dependent on their wives for their chief support, and the children of such officers shall not be considered dependent unless their father is dead or they are in fact dependent on their mother.[14]

The Army section of the law seemed to give ANC and WMSC women officers and their dependents the same status as male officers of the Regular Army and their dependents; in practice, ANC and WMSC officers found it extremely difficult to declare anyone a dependent, with the possible exception of elderly parents. The very mention of husbands in the Navy section of the law, when at the time neither the Army or Navy Nurse Corps were commissioning married women is interesting, but the mention of dependent children is nothing short of astonishing, as military motherhood would not even be permitted for more than a quarter-century. Clearly the Navy wanted to be certain it had its officers' gender parameters tightly drawn. Despite nurses having won permanent status a year before, 1948's Women's Armed Services Integration Act brought nonmedical women permanently into the military, the outbreak of the Korean War caught the medical units in vulnerable states and forced them to expand dramatically.

The ANC grew from 3,460 in July 1950 to 5,397 by July 1951, not nearly enough. The Army itself had grown threefold between the beginning of the war and November 1951, and desperately needed nurses.[15] Colonel Mary G. Phillips, the chief of the corps when the war in Korea started, retired on 30 September 1951, and when Colonel Ruby F. Bryant took over, her prime focus then and for the remainder of the war was recruiting. The same retention/recruitment conundrum that had plagued the WAC was apparent. Although the Army immediately relaxed its ban on nurses getting married, it commissioned just twelve hundred nurses in 1951—a number that would have barely balanced attrition even before the war. At the same time, another six hundred left the Corps for family reasons or to return to school. Meanwhile, the Korean War had produced ninety-five thousand wounded. Still, Bryant found she had to assign some nurses to full-time recruiting duty, to spread the word about how desperate the nurse shortage was.[16]

Born the daughter of a Virginia county sheriff in 1906, Ruby F. Bryant had always wanted to become a nurse. Instead, to please her parents, she taught in rural schools for four years before entering the Army School of Nursing, graduating in 1933. As a nurse at Fort Mills Station Hospital on Corregidor Island before World War II, she and six other Army nurses helped establish the facility within Malinta Tunnel that would function as a hospital during the fall of Bataan and the siege of Corregidor in 1941 and 1942. Bryant already had returned stateside by then and was being promoted rapidly. By 1947 she was chief nurse, Far East Command, Tokyo, supervising all Army nurses serving in Japan, Saipan, Iwo Jima, Korea, Guam, Okinawa, and the Philippine Islands. In 1948, she became chief nurse, Sixth U.S. Army Area (The Presidio, California). Then, in 1951, she was "elected" chief of the ANC by her fellow Army nurses in an unusual popular vote organized by her predecessor.

Colonel Ruby F. Bryant, chief of the Army Nurse Corps from 1951–1955. Army Nurse Corps Collection, Office of Medical History, Office of the Army Surgeon General.

As a colonel and chief nurse, Bryant increased the use of civilian nurses in Army hospitals and actively supported the commissioning of male nurses in the Army Nurse Corps Reserve, which finally became reality in 1955, two years after the Korean War ended.

When her term-limited four years as chief of the Army Nurse Corps ended in 1955, Bryant decided to remain in the Army rather than retire, which meant she had to go back to the rank and lesser pay of lieutenant colonel. She became chief nurse at Headquarters, U.S. Army Europe. In 1958, when Congress authorized three ANC colonels (but still no higher ranks), Bryant was again promoted to colonel, a rank she retained until her retirement in 1961 after twenty-seven years' service.[17]

The Army hoped to commission three thousand more nurses from its stepped-up recruitment drive and assigned extraordinary role models, battle-seasoned women just home from Korea, to get maximum publicity. One of them, Captain Ann Steele, recounted for audiences how, during the battle for Taejon, she had staffed a rescue train on a thirty-six-hour mission to evacuate more than one hundred soldiers from a clearing station in Kumchow, which fell to the Koreans just thirteen hours later.[18] Another, Captain Margaret Blake, told reporters that the First MASH was so close to the front lines that "we were part of the rear echelons. One time the hospital was reduced to two pints of blood, but we never ran out." Blake, a recipient of the Bronze Star, had been burned on her face and hands while on duty, but reassured newspaper readers "that the excellent on-the-spot-treatment available at the hospital prevented scars from forming."[19]

Carmela Filosa (Hix), a nurse at Queens Hospital in New York, was typical of those who answered the call. She joined the ANC Reserve in early 1951 and almost immediately was called to basic training, then to Fitzsimons General Hospital in Denver, Colorado. By year's end Filosa was in Korea. "We knew when we joined the Reserve that we would be called to active duty very quickly; and that chances were good we would end up overseas," she said. "You didn't join unless you were ready to go. The Army was desperate."[20]

Like the ANC, the NNC—increasingly understaffed as the war progressed—froze all active-duty assignments and recalled reservists. The corps director, Captain Winnie Gibson, a seasoned veteran who had been operating room supervisor and anesthetist at Pearl Harbor Naval Hospital on 7 December 1941, was ordered to call up at least 125 reservists each week until further notice.[21] She, like other directors, quickly discovered her personnel files were out of date and her staff spent months trying to straighten out the backlog. In several cases, they simply resorted to recalling their friends.[22]

Texan Winnie Gibson, born in 1902, was just three months into the job as director of the Navy Nurse Corps when the Korean War started in June 1950. On 19 September, the hospital ship *Benevolence* sank en route to Japan, killing one nurse.[23] Less than a month later, eleven Navy nurses were killed in a plane crash near Kwajalein Island in the Marshalls. The nurses were en route to assignments at the naval hospital at Yokosuka, Japan, which was being inundated with casualties from

Captain Winnie Gibson, director of the U.S. Navy Nurse Corps, 1950–1954. U.S. Navy Bureau of Medicine and Surgery Archives.

MacArthur's 15 September invasion of Inchon. As the personal items of the dead nurses washed ashore on Kwajalein bit by bit for weeks, each remnant was carefully boxed and sent on to Gibson's office, where she and her staff made sure the material reached the victims' families.[24]

Despite the fact that the NNC's personnel records were out of date and many reservists had married, by 1951 Gibson was managing to send the Navy so many nurses that it had to scramble to provide housing.[25] Growth came with one tiny victory. The jump in numbers caused a shortage of quarters, so nurses were allowed to live off-post and draw subsistence pay for the first time. Although World War II WAVES and their World War I predecessors, called Yeomen (F), had been allowed to live off base, this was the first time nurses were allowed such freedom.[26]

The NNC started the war with 1,510 regular and 440 reserve nurses on active duty on land, aboard ship, and as flight nurses, most at stateside Navy base hospitals and at Marine Corps bases on the Atlantic or Pacific coasts. By 1951, the number of nurses reached a peak of 3,238 (including 1,515 regular and 1,723 reserve nurses).

To bridge the gap between new nurses' civilian training and the Navy, the NNC established a single five-week indoctrination and training center at St. Albans Naval Hospital, similar to the Army's course for nurses at Fort Sam Houston, Texas. The class that every graduate seemed to remember was "Survival at Sea." Students, wearing their white duty uniforms, shoes and stockings, were told to jump into the hospital swimming pool from the high diving board, and once in the water take off shoes, stockings, and dress. The hard part was next: they had to swing the dress over their heads to inflate its sleeves, and knot the sleeves to trap the air in them. The inflated dress was supposed to substitute for water wings. Few women managed the feat. Most had trouble removing their shoes and stockings while treading water, and many just couldn't seem to swing a dress hard enough to capture air in the sleeves.[27]

The newness of the AFNC may have saved it from problems with its reservists having married, although many Air Force nurses were World War II Army nurse veterans. Recruiting was still a challenge. Colonel Verena M. Zeller (Pettoruto Seberg), chief of the corps, had 1,088 nurses on active duty, sixty-eight of whom already were in the Far East when the war started. Zeller (Pettoruto Seberg) remembered that one afternoon shortly after the start of the war, the head surgeon for the Military Air Transport Service (MATS), came to her office and announced, "I need one hundred

flight nurses . . . as of yesterday!" The shortage of trained flight nurses in
the combat theater meant that, when the fighting was intense, some nurses
were making up to three flights a day, or averaging three hundred flight
hours a month.[28] Zeller (Pettoruto Seberg) canvassed all Air Force nurses
still working at Army hospitals, asking for volunteers. Those who stepped
forward were assigned directly to flight nurse duty and—as the next best
thing to formal flight nurse training—paired with a seasoned flight nurse.[29]

Kansas native Verena Zeller (Pettoruto Seberg)
trained at Saint Francis Hospital in Topeka and
was a civilian nurse at a nearby Fort Riley Army
Hospital before being commissioned in 1936.
In 1939, she moved on to a plum Army Nurse
Corps assignment at Sternberg General Hospital in Manila. Two years later, just months before the Japanese attack on the Philippines,
Zeller (Pettoruto Seberg) was reassigned stateside, thereby escaping being taken prisoner by
the Japanese as eighty-six other American military nurses were. She spent the duration of
World War II at March Army Air Field, California. In 1946, offered the chance to take flight
nurse training she recalled being thrilled; instead of assigning her to flight training, however, the Army sent the now captain to New
York's Columbia University for postgraduate

Colonel Verena Zeller (Pettoruto
Seberg), first chief of the U.S.
Air Force Nurse Corps. U.S. Air
Force photo.

study. In January 1949, by now a major, Zeller (Pettoruto Seberg) was assigned
to the Air Surgeon's Office. When the corps was established in July of that year
she was appointed the chief nurse of the new Air Force Nurse Corps (AFNC)
and promoted to colonel.[30]

The AFNC also stepped up recruiting and, to accelerate deployment,
shortened the flight nurse course at the Randolph AFB School of Aviation
Medicine in Kentucky from nine to six weeks, and moved it to Gunter AFB
in Alabama. Gunter, closed after World War II, reopened in 1950 expressly
for the Air Force school, and began turning out sixty flight nurses every
seven weeks, graduating slightly more than four hundred Air Force, Navy,
and Canadian flight nurses in 1951, another 456 in 1952, and a final 61 in
1953, when the war was winding down.[31]

Four nurses went on full-time recruiting detail, and Zeller (Pettoruto Seberg) was grateful when Hollywood's *Flight Nurse,* starring Joan Leslie, gave her recruiters a leg up on the other nurse corps' recruiters. The AFNC appears to have been the choice of most qualified nursing graduates considering a military career, but Zeller (Pettoruto Seberg) still faced a nurse shortage.[32]

Recruiting medical specialists—dietitians, physical therapists, and occupational therapists—was one of the most difficult challenges of the war for each of the services. Only a limited number of schools were training them, graduates were in high demand, civilian jobs offered more personal freedom and fewer restrictions than military service, and, as noted earlier, a goodly percentage of them were male.

At the onset of the war, the strength of the Army Women's Medical Specialist Corps (AWMSC) was three hundred and forty: 149 regular and 191 reserve officers. During the first half of 1951, AWMSC recruiters invaded selected colleges, universities, and teaching hospitals around the country carrying fact sheets, brochures, and several "traveling exhibits" for career days and job fairs, hoping to recruit 2,467 dietitians, 146 OTs, and 179 PTs. The Army produced three one-minute public-service announcements for television that were sent to stations around the country with a letter from the Army Surgeon General requesting they be broadcast. After six months and already a full year into the war, the chief of the PT branch reported that of the 179 PTs sought, just six had volunteered.[33]

When the AWMSC also was forced to institute two recalls of reservists, it hit many of the same roadblocks the other women's organizations were hitting—plus one that was unique. The first involuntary recall in September 1950 included seventy dietitians, forty PTs, and thirty-five OTs, and, in certain parts of the country, put civilian and military needs in direct conflict. In March 1951, Mildred Elson, executive director, American Physical Therapy Association, complained to the Army about the unfairness of the recall to regions that did not have enough physical therapists for civilian needs. Maine had only twelve professional PTs, yet the Army had recalled two, while the nearby state of Massachusetts had two hundred such women, "and could easily spare two physical therapists." The recall was not a success. Only seventy-eight of 145 recall targets reported for active duty; the remainder (including the two PTs from Maine) were deferred.[34]

One of the seventy-eight reservists who did return to active duty was First Lieutenant Margaret Hartwig (Pithkethly), a physical therapist who had served in the South Pacific during World War II and joined the Reserve after the war. When the Korean War started, she had been working with handicapped children in the Flint, Michigan, school system. She was recalled and assigned to Percy Jones Army Hospital in nearby Battle Creek for two years. "I had to give up a job I enjoyed and rent out my house in Flint," Hartwig recalled. "Because I had seniority, I was allowed to live off base; they gave me a housing allowance. So I found an apartment, kept my car and traveled home to Flint on weekends. Like many of my colleagues, I made the best of it. There was no use grumbling; everyone was inconvenienced to a certain extent. We believed it was our duty to return and do what we could for the soldiers."[35]

In mid-1951, the AWMSC joined the servicewide recruitment drive, further shrinking the available medical staff as women were diverted to talk to civic groups, make radio and television appearances, and visit high schools and colleges. In February 1952, resignations were frozen and DOD tried calling up another 125 AWMSC reservists. This time, in an attempt to avoid some of the problems of the previous recall, Assistant Secretary of Defense Anna Rosenberg directed that the National Advisory Committee on the Selective Service System, which was used to draft doctors and dentists, also screen nurses and women specialists to make sure that no individual essential to the national health and safety would be obliged to leave her civilian job. This recall was even less successful than the first had been. As of June 1953, only twenty-three medical specialists had been recalled to active duty: nine dietitians, five PTs, and nine OTs.[36]

During this time, although the vast majority of AWMSC members were assigned stateside, small numbers of dietitians and PTs were sent to station hospitals in Europe and Japan; just five served in Korea. As facilities were established or expanded in Japan, dietitians were needed to help with the special nutrition requirements of soldiers with diseases such as hepatitis and encephalitis, and PTs were needed to treat injuries, as well as large numbers of frostbite patients. And at stateside military hospitals, additional OTs were needed to handle the mushrooming numbers of convalescents.[37]

In 1952, the AWMSC offered a shortened twelve-month tour of duty and, as the war was winding down in early 1953, won legislation enabling the Regular Army WMSC to bring in women as full first lieutenants, rather than lower-ranking second lieutenants.[38]

Emma Vogel had already decided she did not want to spend her life teaching music in small Minnesota towns when the United States entered World War I and the Army put out a call for physical therapists. The Army surgeon general

approved emergency courses in physical therapy (PT) at colleges across the country and the
thirty-year-old Vogel attended one of the first at
Oregon's Reed College. After finishing, she
helped train subsequent classes, then went
on to become the first civilian PT at a Pennsylvania Army hospital where she cared for
wounded from the 28th Division. Many years
later, Vogel boasted that physical therapy had
been an unrecognized science prior to World
War I; it was "the results it achieved in the after-
care of war injuries" that established the profession.

Colonel Emma E. Vogel, first
chief of the U.S. Army Women's
Medical Specialist Corps, April
1951. National Archives (111-SC-362220).

After the war Vogel, still a civilian, was assigned to Walter Reed Army Hospital where
she organized and supervised the first postwar
Army training course for PTs. In 1931, now Supervisor Vogel recommended that the Army es-
tablish a corps that included dietitians, physical therapists, and occupational
therapists. It took a dozen years and another war before the Army established
the Women's Medical Specialist Corps (AWMSC). In 1943 the Army militarized
its civilian physical therapists and Vogel was commissioned a major and made
the first director. A newspaper story reporting her appointment quoted her as
saying that physical therapists needed "a great inner well of human understanding," to enable them to inspire a patient "to withstand temporary dis-
couragement and setbacks before repeated practice . . . (makes) the patient
realize he is 'licking' his disability."[39]

Like the nurses, Vogel held "relative rank," which meant that although she
was addressed as "Major Vogel," she only received the pay and privileges of a
captain and no survivors' or dependents' benefits—a status that was partially
remedied by the 1947 legislation which provided full rank and benefits to military nurses and medical specialists. She received the Legion of Merit for her
wartime services and in 1947 became head of the new Women's Medical Specialist Corps and a colonel. She remained the corps' commander until she retired in 1951.[40]

During the first year and a half of the Korean War, the Navy made do
without a medical specialist unit. It used small numbers of specially trained
active duty nurses, as well as enlisted women trained as medical techni-

cians, and did not attempt to recall dietitians, physical, or occupational therapists. When a reservist was recalled, she was arbitrarily assigned the first critical vacancy and the Navy could not guarantee it could match these women to an assignment in their specialty. By 1952, however, the Navy's need for medical specialists was acute and in February it established its own women's medical specialist section (not a separate, self-directed unit) within its existing Medical Service Corps. This small section of fifty women medical specialists had commissioned slots for thirty dietitians, ten physical therapists and ten occupational therapists.[41]

Ensign Pauline Fauser's experience illustrates how desperate the Navy was for skilled personnel and how rapidly it deployed them once it had established its own women's medical specialist group. A physical therapist accepted in 1953, Fauser expected to receive orders to the indoctrination center at Newport, Rhode Island. Instead, a telephone call ordered her to Boston to be commissioned an ensign in the Reserve. Four days later she received orders to report immediately to the Philadelphia Naval Hospital. There was no time for basic training, she was told; amputees from Korea were en route to the Philadelphia hospital. Fauser finally received orders to report for basic training as the war wound down.[42]

The smallest corps of military women during the Korean War was the new Air Force Women's Medical Specialist Corps (AFWMSC). As of July 1951, the chief of the corps, Colonel Miriam E. Perry (Goll), had fewer than one hundred women on active duty and was staring at a projected need of three hundred twenty. Because the corps was so small, the vast majority of Air Force medical specialists ended up serving in the United States, although records indicate that one officer was sent to England in 1951, and at least two others, one physical therapist and one dietitian, were in Japan by then. Even filling home-front assignments presented a problem, as more than half of the officers were brand-new graduates, with little to no work experience. Working with minimal supervision and no other professional in their field to turn to for advice or camaraderie, young officers often felt overwhelmed on their initial assignments. But, as Perry (Goll) explained to one who complained, very few Air Force hospitals were authorized a second, much less a third, dietitian or therapist.[43]

Perry (Goll) personally conducted several recruiting trips across the country in an effort to obtain the necessary numbers of qualified and experienced personnel. PT Jean Ertwine (Disterdick) was working as an Army WMSC at Brooke Army Hospital in San Antonio when she heard Perry (Goll) speak about the Air Force's need for medical specialists. Ertwine volunteered to transfer to the Air Force, a plus for Perry (Goll) but a wash as far as the number of PTs available to the military.[44]

How desperate the Air Force was can be seen in one prescient step Perry (Goll) took: the AFWMSC broke ranks with the other services in 1951 and actually managed to have a small number of male physical therapists commissioned in the Air Force—not in the Women's Medical Specialist Corps per se, however, but in the Medical Service Corps, which covered pharmacists, X-ray technicians and other, more traditionally male, medical specialties. Perry (Goll) obviously did it because the AFWMSC was so understaffed, but the other women's specialist corps were equally hurting for staff and no evidence to date has appeared to indicate they were so bold. Notes by Mildred Elson, executive director of the American Physical Therapy Association (APTA), from a July 1951 meeting with Perry (Goll) indicated the service director had come to discuss the PT shortages. "Col. Perry also indicated that efforts will be made by them (the AFWMSC) to commission any male physical therapist . . . in the Medical Service Corps. . . . This is not to be discussed."[45] In a letter dated 11 December 1951, Perry (Goll) told Margaret Moore, educational consultant for the APTA, "Fully qualified male applicants will be considered for appointment in the Medical Service Corps. However, since the number which can be appointed is limited it was not considered advisable to make a formal public announcement re: these appointments. All inquiries are being answered on an individual basis."[46]

Once the Air Force had a male PT aboard, even on the Q.T., it was quick to assign him, as a letter less than a month later written by Elson to the Institute of Rehabilitation and Physical Medicine in New York City attests:

> a recent graduate in physical therapy, now commissioned in the Air
> Force, . . . is the sole physical therapist (at Lockborn AFB near Columbus,
> Ohio) and has been asked to set up the department, order equipment and
> supplies etc. He is naturally upset since he recognizes that he needs supervision and that he is not qualified to assume administrative responsibilities.
> This was called to the attention of Colonel Miriam Perry. . . . There seemed
> to be no concern professionally about the situations as far as the boy was
> concerned.[47]

After Perry (Goll) discovered the loophole enabling her to staff AFWMSC positions with male Medical Service Corps personnel, it appears that physical therapists and perhaps even occupational therapists and dietitians at Air Force hospitals could be officers of either sex. This presaged the eventual disestablishment of both the Army and Air Force's women-only medical specialist corps in 1955. Whether or not the Air Force's early, if ambivalent, commitment to gender integration allowed them to adopt this policy before other services would consider changing old ways is an interesting question.[48] How Perry (Goll) pulled it off, even quietly, given the earlier failure of the Bolton legislation to drop the word "women's" from the medical specialist corps authorization, is unknown. Also unknown is whether men's career tracks and benefits were held to women's lower standards. The only paper trail discovered to date consists of those letters and conversation quoted above.

Miriam Esther Perry (Goll), born in Lynn, Massachusetts, in 1909, was a graduate of Simmons College and Walter Reed General Hospital's school of dietetics. Then, in the early 1930s, Army dietitians and physical therapists were all civilians. She was head dietitian at the Army hospital in San Juan, Puerto Rico, when the United States entered World War II in December 1941.

As the Caribbean Defense Command moved to wartime footing with frequent drills and blackouts and German U-boats prowled the surrounding sea, supplies began to run short, making food planning difficult. Although the hospital had plenty of food, variety was sadly lacking and Perry (Goll) amazed herself by thinking longingly of "the lowly potato!" In the middle of the war, the Army commissioned its medical specialists, and Perry (Goll) and her staff proudly "donned our gold bars . . . and were called 'Lieutenant!'"[49]

In 1943, the new lieutenant was reassigned stateside, but now that she was formally in the Army, she had to take basic training, whereupon she was promoted to captain. After the war, by now Major Perry became the director of the Army's School of Dietetics at Brooke General Hospital at Fort Sam Houston, Texas. In 1949, after thirteen years with the Army as a civilian and officer, now Colonel Perry (Goll) was appointed the first director of the Air Force Women's Medical Specialist Corps.[50] Shortly after the Korean War, Perry (Goll) married Air Force Lieutenant Colonel Moxie F. Goll. She retired in 1956.[51]

Colonel Miriam Esther Perry (Goll), first chief of the Air Force Women's Medical Specialist Corps. Women's Memorial Register.

Physicians were also needed, and here the Navy appeared to lead the way. The reality, however, is a bit more complex. According to the historian and Air Force Colonel Lorry Fenner: "The inconsistencies in gendered divisions of labor became even more indefensible when the services began accepting female doctors. Male doctors, some trained with military funds, would not answer the call for volunteers in sufficient number, so a male doctor's draft was implemented. When this measure fell short, the Army and Air Force finally asked legislators to allow female physicians. . . . Even though they had told Congress they thought the public's 'unfavorable' attitudes toward female doctors had improved, military leaders assured the public that women would have to pass the same standards."[52]

Starting in October 1948 the Navy began commissioning women physicians who had completed internships at Navy hospitals; by the time the Korean War started, the Navy had two regular and three reserve women physicians on duty. One of these was Lieutenant Commander Bernice R. Walters, a 1936 graduate of Women's Medical College of Pennsylvania who had served in the Navy Reserve during World War II. When she reported to the hospital ship *Consolation* in March 1950, she became the Navy's first non-nurse female officer ordered to a regular tour of duty aboard a naval vessel.[53]

After the war started, the Navy established a medical intern program for women and commissioned the first seventeen physicians to complete the program as lieutenants (junior grade) in the Medical Corps U.S. Naval Reserve. They were ordered to twenty-four months' active duty at stateside Navy hospitals and dispensaries in the United States.[54]

The Navy was the only service still authorized to commission women doctors at the start of the Korean War; the Army's World War II authorization had expired in 1947, and the Air Force again was simply too new to have established a program. In July 1950, the Army and the Air Force together requested that Congress grant them the authority to commission female doctors and dentists. Here again was a potential change that ran head-on into the prejudices regarding women that were then common in the military and Congress. Navy women physicians did not have career tracks comparable to the Navy's male doctors, but were viewed as the equivalent of nurses and other women officers. Now the Army and Air Force were proposing to give women doctors and dentists the same career opportunities, benefits, and presumed command authority enjoyed by men. Congress wanted women physicians to be limited in the same fashion as were the other Navy women, separate and not equal to male officers. "No one suggested resolving the issue by putting women (line personnel, nurses and physicians) on equal footing with men as a matter of practicality and fairness."[55] Because the need for physicians was so great and because, once again, it was politically difficult to turn down a pool of ready volunteers when the draft was forcing many men into service, Congress capitulated and an Army–Air Force female physicians bill passed in August 1950, making physician reserve officers—male or female—eligible for the same opportunities for clinical practice and advancement, and throughout the Korean War the same pay allowances and retirement benefits.[56] "Through this debate, male nurses gained ammunition for their battle to enter the nurse corps."[57]

On paper the legislation was a major step forward; the number of women allowed to take the step, however, was minuscule, and then they were often assigned to roles where they were most likely to treat women and children, not men. And note again: these new women doctors and dentists were in the Reserve, not Regular Army and Air Force; as such they were still a little less equal. Not until June 1952 did Public Law 408 pass, including the Navy in with the Army and Air Force and extending equal privileges to both the reserve and regular elements of each service. Virtually the same language that had been in the Navy section of the 1947 nurse act—that husbands and children of female officers had to prove absolute dependency to receive benefits—was attached. It acknowledged at least that women were likely to have husbands and children, whether or not the military was willing to give women officers equivalent benefits regarding them.

In early 1951, the Army Medical Corps Reserve (AMCR) commissioned as majors Dr. Ruth E. Church and Dr. Theresa T. Woo, the first two of this new breed to volunteer and be accepted since the end of World War II. They were assigned to the preventive medicine division of the surgeon general's office, not to roles that would have them treating or commanding men. The Harvard and University of Michigan–educated Woo, who had come to the United States as a child from her native China, had served in the Army for two years during World War II. Church had no previous military experience, but had a Columbia University master's degree in public health and had graduated from the University of Wisconsin Medical School as a specialist in public health and preventive medicine. Within weeks, four other women doctors were serving along with them.[58]

First Lieutenant Fae M. Adams of San Jose, California, the first woman physician commissioned in the Regular Army, seems to have been an anomaly. For one thing, she was a veteran, having been a WAC physical therapist in the Southwest Pacific during World War II. She attended medical school on the G.I. Bill. In July 1952, Adams was commissioned as a medical reserve officer; in order to intern at a military hospital, however, she needed to be Regular Army. She applied and was accepted in 1953.[59] Assigned as a general duty medical officer at Camp Crowder, Missouri, a separation center where soldiers back from Korea were processed out, part of her job involved giving physical exams. "They [her male colleagues] said, 'Fae, you can do everything from the top of the head to the waist, and we'll take care of the rest,' and I said, 'Oop, no.'" She made her case for examining men, including some prisoners of war. "Some of the young men were surprised. . . . [The prisoners] were even more shocked. . . . But I managed. . . . There were four young doctors and (the others) were delighted to see me because we all had to rotate through general medical officer of the day routine (which included pulling night duty). . . . At that point we were all working so hard that it didn't make any difference what sex you were."[60]

The Army's first woman dentist, Dr. Helen E. Meyers, a 1941 Temple University graduate, commissioned in 1951, was still the Army's only woman dentist when she was sent to Trieste, Italy, early in 1952.[61]

The Air Force's first female physician, Dr. Dorothy Armstrong Elias, a Duke University–trained obstetrician-gynecologist, was sworn in March 1951 as a reserve captain.[62] Married to a fellow doctor at George Washington University Hospital in the nation's capital, she apparently was asked about (or felt compelled to explain) her long-distance marriage—"He's perfectly happy that I'm happy"—when interviewed by an upstate New York newspaper reporter. The lead into the reporter's story: "Babies . . . babies . . . and more babies! That's how the U.S. Air Force's only woman doctor cheerfully defines her job at Sampson. . . . In the 'down to brass tacks' talk of a medical man, the pert captain resignedly smiles off her woes with, 'I'm just another doctor, not a curio, a woman doctor, and I can't comprehend all the fuss.'"[63]

The fuss of course was that barriers were being broken, even if the women who were breaking them were being marginalized by some of their assignments and trivialized by the way in which the breakthroughs were being reported to the public. For example, when Navy enlisted women were trained as medical corpsmen and some were sent to the Military Sea Transportation Service to relieve nurses, the *New York Times* reported on the "sea duty debut of the comeliest sailors, the WAVES . . . (accorded) courtesies any admiral's lady could hope for,"[64] including a welcome of tea sandwiches and ice cream with the admiral and other officers. Male sailors had seldom, if ever, been treated so well, and probably neither had nurses who had long served aboard hospital and transport ships. Just getting non-nurse women on board, however, was a victory that opened doors to others. After enlisted women in the hospital corps did begin going to sea in Navy transports in 1953, Ensign (and later Captain) Katherine Keating, a pharmacist and the first woman commissioned to the Navy Medical Service Corps in 1950, petitioned to be sent to a hospital ship. She received orders to the USS *Haven* which, lacking a full complement of nurses, had an extra female berth, and became one of the first women officers to relieve a man at sea. Keating stood watch with men and had several collateral duties, including officer training and cryptography; when the *Haven* was chosen to host a prisoner of war exchange in 1953, she was delegated the official "disinterested witness" at the request of United Nations officials. "There I sat with General Mark Clark on the one side and the commander of the custodial force on the other. . . . It was a privilege to watch history being made." [65]

The uniformed Public Health Service (PHS) also became part of the military during wartime. The agency backfilled the positions of military health care professionals who accompanied troops to the theater of operations. Within the war zone, the PHS worked with the Red Cross and other civilian agencies to control communicable disease, and provide clean water, uncontaminated food, sanitary waste disposal, and immunizations among the civilian population, prisoners, and occupying troops.

Among the women on deck in the PHS when the Korean War broke out was Dr. Faye Abdellah, a Ph.D. nurse who had taught at Yale and joined the PHS in 1949 at the behest of its chief nurse Lucille Petry Leone, the first woman assistant surgeon general. Assigned to nursing education, she set out to update nurse

Faye G. Abdellah joined the U.S. Public Health Service in 1949 and retired as a rear admiral in 1989. Women's Memorial Register.

training and assess nurse resources in community hospitals, industrial plants, schools, and rural areas across fourteen states, a vital task during the Korean War's nationwide nurse shortage.[66]

Meanwhile, numerous PHS nurses throughout the country battled the recurrent polio epidemics and other contagious diseases. World War II Army nurse Margaret DeLawter, who had served in the Pacific Theater and then used the G.I. Bill to obtain more training, spent the Korean War as chief night nurse at the 350-bed PHS hospital in Seattle, Washington.[67]

While the military necessities created by the Korean War were opening some doors to medical women, in the theater of war itself, experiments were afoot that might have radically altered and deprofessionalized military nursing. Some Army commanders questioned whether, because they were women, nurses should be near the front. Given that World War I and II nurses had efficiently and courageously performed near the front, under fire, and even (in World War II) as prisoners of war, such restriction would have been a major step back.

During the Korean War, with very few exceptions, the armed forces allowed nurses (but almost no other military women) to serve in the combat theater; military leaders traditionally had accepted the presence of nurses in the combat theater because there was no other practical, efficient, or timely way to care for ill or wounded soldiers. Within days after American troops went into Korea, the Army sent in Mobile Army Surgical Hospital (MASH) units, which included nurses. During the first six months of the war, these units followed the troops as the battle line moved rapidly back and forth across Korea, several times putting Army nurses in harm's way, or at least too close to the front lines for the comfort of some commanders. After the first year, as the war and the hospitals settled down around the 38th Parallel, the Army had time to reconsider the nurses' exposure and consider the option of future deployments without them.

Individual unit reports indicate, however, that some field commanders had already begun to change procedures because of concern about the safety of their nurses. In November 1950, the commander of the 8063rd MASH pointed out that "for safety reasons" the unit's nurses had not been allowed to accompany the unit on its actual moves across country but had joined the unit later after the hospital was set up. He asked for an equal number of new enlisted men to take over the nurses' duties in setting up the hospital.[68] The annual report of the 8055th MASH, written in January 1951, reveals that the group had already tried substituting male corpsmen for nurses, out of concerns for the latter's safety, and found it unfeasible: "The question of having nurses in a field unit of this type has been raised and discussed. Nurses have their place in an organization of this nature and without them, operations would be definitely handicapped. Corpsmen are not a suitable replacement for nurses, as demonstrated by the experience of this unit. . . . This is especially true in surgery, where they are considered most essential."[69] During the same time frame, the commander of the 64th Field Hospital wrote, "Nurses have moved with the unit each time, and have been instrumental in setting up the hospital rapidly."[70]

In 1952, with the situation in Korea at a stalemate, the Army decided to experiment officially to see if there was a way, without women nurses, to provide soldiers with MASH quality medical care near the front. How this came about, and the degree to which it may have been agreed to by the Nurse Corps director, Colonel Ruby F. Bryant, and Lieutenant Colonel Alice M. Gritsavage, the chief nurse in the Far East Command, or been a top-down directive from male commanders, is unclear.

In a May 1952 newspaper interview, Gritsavage did suggest replacing female MASH nurses with male nurses. Note that she did not suggest training male corpsmen to replace the women nurses. There were no male ANC nurses to be sent in, however. There was notable ambivalence in Gritsavage's remarks headlined in the *New York Herald Tribune* (5 May 1952), "Men to Replace Nurses Upfront Urged by Korea Nurses' Leader," and in the *Washington Post* (10 May 1952) "Calls Army Nurses 'Hazard to Troops.'"

Calling the women "a distinct liability to themselves and the troops," Gritsavage went on to say, "In oriental warfare women nurses have no place at the battle front." She claimed "bitter experience proves the enemy ruthless and unprincipled."[71] It appears the bitter experience she mentions may have had to do with the specific ferocity of the Korean enemy toward U.N. combatants rather than experiences of American military nurses in Korea or previous wars. The most pertinent previous example would seem to disprove her statement: eighty-six Army and Navy nurses had been taken prisoner in the Pacific by the Japanese in World War II; though they suffered extreme conditions and malnourishment, none were raped or brutalized.[72]

Gritsavage, a World War II veteran who certainly had seen action in Africa, Italy, and France, admitted she didn't know a nurse "who isn't eager to serve in Korea. . . . and when they get there, they take the rugged living conditions and severe climate quite as well as the men." She also took care to laud the "bravery, skill and loyalty of our nurses on duty with the mobile Army surgical hospitals," but agreed that when hospitals had to be put up and taken down "all in a matter of hours" women nurses simply did not have the physical strength that male nurses might have and often required troop assistance, "which may handicap defense tactics."[73]

Gritsavage anticipated opposition to her recommendation to bring men into the ANC, which she said had the backing of the chief nurse, Colonel

Ruby Bryant. In particular, she expected more opposition from "outside than inside the Army" because the men might be accused of invading "a woman's field." She also pointed out that opening the doors to male nurses might ease the ANC's nurse shortage, which was then the subject of a massive PR campaign. "We had better start being realistic about this nursing problem before it is too late."[74]

A few months later, in September, the Army reactivated the 8225th MASH with a full complement of surgeons and a group of experienced medical corpsmen pulled from other MASH units—but only two nurses, both women, whose job it was to train the corpsmen. The plan was that when the 8225th moved north and became the U.S. Army hospital farthest north, as it was expected to do within a few months, the nurses would no longer be needed.[75]

In late September, First Lieutenant Melvin Horwitz became the first surgeon assigned to the experimental 8225th MASH. After just a month with the unit, Horwitz was concerned that the lack of nurses hampered the 8225th. On 29 October, Horwitz wrote to his wife:

> Last night, excitement was one patient who bit off the end of a thermometer and swallowed the bulb. Didn't hurt himself, but could have. He was just coming out of anesthesia. A corpsman who didn't know any better took an oral temperature. We keep asking for more nurses. I hope it won't be necessary for someone to die because of a mistake before they send them to us. The boys just haven't had the experience with patients.[76]

In a 24 November letter, Horwitz complained to his wife that the unit was expecting some visiting officers and reporters, and that his commander, a colonel and an Army physician, said to him, "When someone asks you whether this experimental MASH will work, you WILL tell them that it will work." Horwitz told his wife that he responded, "If I am asked for my opinion I will tell the truth, regardless of whether the truth is what the questioner wants to hear." According to Horwitz, his boss immediately backed down and asked only that he use "discretion" when he answered.[77]

The visitors, Major General George E. Armstrong, surgeon general of the Army, and Major General William E. Shambora, Far East Command surgeon, arrived at the 8225th MASH in early January 1953. Horwitz complained to his wife, "Why they are going to spend so much time here I don't know, but this MASH, sans [female] nurses, is one of their babies."[78] Horwitz soon learned why the Army was so eager to learn whether it could run a MASH without nurses; the 8225th, he wrote his wife, was scheduled to be part of another amphibious invasion, similar to the Inchon invasion two years before.[79]

The official unit reports of the 8225th MASH confirm Horwitz's story. In his report of December 1952 (before the visit of the surgeon general), the unit commander wrote, "On 23 September, one of the missions given this hospital was the training of special ward technicians to assume nursing responsibilities. An additional 13 operating room technicians were assigned for this purpose. The men were selected for this assignment after careful screening considering intelligence, former training and experience, aptitude, and willingness to accept responsibility. Two nurses were assigned to organize and conduct instruction." Problems began to develop early in the experiment. The commander explained, "The program was somewhat impeded by the rotation of approximately 50 percent of the personnel that started the program. . . . Because these men were not trained in nursing arts, an additional load had to be placed on the doctors." Regardless, the unit commander concluded, "The concept of operating this type of hospital without nurses appears to be basically sound. . . . It is believed that if this hospital were staffed by the necessary number of enlisted technicians trained in the requisite nursing procedures, that it could function effectively without female nurses."[80]

By 1 February 1953, however, even the commander of the 8225th MASH was expressing significantly different sentiments. "The training program progressed with many problems," he admitted, "among them being the lack of any basic nursing concepts among the men and the constantly rotating personnel. On occasion much of the nursing care of post-operative patients had to be assumed by the doctors, thus increasing their load. Formal classes had to be curtailed due to an influx of cases."[81] The reader must assume that at some time after the visit of the surgeon general and prior to the 23 February report, the commander decided that the nurseless MASH was a failure. On 23 February 1953, Horwitz wrote "We are being assigned five nurses. The experiment is over. They have decided that they cannot run a MASH without trained personnel."[82] The Army had its answer. It was not possible to provide soldiers with MASH care without nurses.

Did Army leaders learn the truth from disgruntled physicians during their January visit? Did they consider opening the nurse corps to male nurses? Did the fact the war was winding down take the urgency out of the situation and mean the ANC could stop worrying that the Army was going to reduce the nursing profession's critical importance by assigning lesser-trained medical technicians to take the nurses' places? Neither Horwitz's letters nor the reports of the 8225th provide an answer.

By the end of the war, however, opportunities for medical military women (and as the Air Force physical therapist situation indicates, some medical men) had expanded, often despite the military's initial plans and Congress' reluctance. The war went away before "serious discussions of women's place in politics, the economy, society, education and war mobilization took place, (and, by and large) popular representation of women continued to trivialize or sexualize their every activity."[83]

Although today's reader may cringe at the era's news coverage, it none-theless could be strikingly pro-women. In late June, just weeks before the Army launched its test of a nurseless 8225th MASH, the same *New York Herald Tribune* reporter who broke the May story that nurse corps brass were suggesting male nurses, followed up her scoop with a story datelined Korea and coincidentally featuring the 8225th MASH. She made it very clear the 8225th MASH's nurses not only had no qualms about serving there, but had some reservations with the greenhorn medical technicians they were constantly having to train.

Headlined "Nurses Prove They Can Take Korea in Stride," Dorothy Brandon wrote of the women's jerrybuilt social hangout—The Last Chance Club—their dances and occasional movies, and their attempts to maintain their femininity in such rough surroundings. She also extensively quoted the 8225th chief nurse, Captain Elizabeth M. Cate of Pennsylvania, on how difficult it was to break in the medical corpsmen, who rarely had previous training or experience:

> "This isn't as easy as it sounds," declared Capt. Cate. "Some of the men haven't the educational background or the emotional stability to become nursing aides—but they sure try hard. Many are boys off farms who have milked cows and driven tractors. . . . Teaching them everything from shaking down fever thermometers to assisting in operating tents is quite a challenge."

According to Brandon, the nurses of the 8225th MASH "who live . . . only minutes by helicopter from the front lines, accept the danger, discomforts and isolation of their all-tent unit with soldier-like understanding." "It's rough and rugged—so what?" she quoted Cate. "'The men from upfront never complain, so who are we to be jittery or homesick? Besides, we're too busy. . . . Anyway, everyone of us volunteered for this duty.'"[84]

CHAPTER 6

"Needed in Cadre"—Providing Support Around the World

The U.S. really is getting in deeper every day in Korea. . . . They've really begun to sit on leaves and passes. . . . I'm needed in cadre . . . just in case.
—WAC Sergeant First Class Juanita I. Mooney, in a letter home from Bremerhaven, Germany, 13 July 1950[1]

[The casualties] came in huge plane loads. . . . many of them still had the dirt from the battlefield on them.
—Navy nurse Geraldine Houp, on the impact of the Korean War at Hawaii's Tripler Hospital[2]

Excitement . . . [a] Russian MIG defected over the 38th parallel!
—Red Cross staffer Shirley Peck (Barnes), secretary to the 20th Air Force staff surgeon on Okinawa[3]

FIRST LIEUTENANT JANET GINGRICH (Preston)'s Women's Army Corps detachment was on its way to Tokyo in June 1950. Three days out from California, the forty-eight WACs heard the news: the North Koreans had attacked South Korea and the United States was again at war. Gingrich and her colleagues were shocked. Suddenly, what had seemed an exciting assignment took on an element of danger. When they arrived in Tokyo, they were billeted at what had been the main building of Mitsubishi and immediately went on war footing, working seven days a week for the first month until other service personnel arrived to share the workload.[4]

Stateside when the Korean War started, Army Sergeant Dawn E. Yetman (Youells Croshaw) received an overnight transfer to Fort Jackson, South Carolina, and spent "seven-day weeks and 24-hour days" testing draftees for Korea.[5] Navy Petty Officer Third Class Louise Gorski (Richardson), a radio communications specialist who had barely become acquainted with her assignment at Treasure Island off San Francisco when the war broke out, recalled that the small communications station "was suddenly thrown into mayhem with a non-stop influx of messages arriving on our office's lone teletype machine for every activity on the base. Operating with a peace-time skeleton crew and working very long hours, we were vastly relieved when a complement of officers, recalled reservists, new enlistees and sailors began arriving for duty in our office."[6]

Halfway around the globe that summer, Sergeant First Class Juanita Mooney, a WAC assigned to Company D, Unit 7888, Headquarters, European Command, at Bremerhaven, Germany, was closely following events. By 13 July the administrative NCO was already feeling the war's impact. "The U.S. really is getting in deeper every day in Korea," she wrote her mother in California. "They've really begun to sit on leaves and passes. Only a small number of women can be away from post at one time, and I'm needed in cadre . . . just in case. . . . Wonder how many incidents and massacres we will allow before dropping all our force on 'em?"[7]

The United States emerged from World War II the most powerful nation on earth, and Mooney's musing to her mother reflects the sense of omnipotence many Americans felt. However, as her cautious "just in case" suggests, it was becoming clear to American armed forces in Europe that war could come to them. A challenger to U.S. power had already made itself known: the Soviet Union. Even in the last days of the previous war, the former ally had moved decisively to cement its control of Eastern Europe, throwing up what Winston Churchill would chillingly label an "Iron Curtain." Behind this curtain were the Soviet satellites: Poland, Hungary, Romania, Czechoslovakia, and Albania. In 1948, when the Soviet Union had blockaded road and rail access into West Berlin, the United States and its allies responded with a massive, unprecedented eleven-month airlift of all the basic goods and supplies needed to sustain the city.

The remaining Allied Powers, stunned by the treachery of their former partner, had joined together with the United States to form an equally unprecedented coalition, the North Atlantic Treaty Organization (NATO). The nations who responded—Belgium, Canada, Denmark, France, Iceland,

Italy, Luxembourg, the Netherlands, Norway, Portugal, the United Kingdom, and the United States—pledged to consider "an armed attack against
one or more of the parties to be an armed attack against all."[8] The first line
in the sand in what would become known as the Cold War had now been
drawn.

Tensions escalated, fed by countless small incidents, including this one
gleaned from the Register of the Women's Memorial. Corporal Jacquelynn
Janikowski (Meakin), who joined the Women's Army Corps in 1949 and
volunteered for overseas duty, was one of about twenty WACs assigned to
the Army "code room" in Berlin. The women carried special "four power
passes" at all times. The "four powers" were the victor nations—the United
States, Great Britain, France, and the Soviet Union—who had divided Germany and its capital, Berlin, into four sectors, each occupied and controlled
by one of the Allies. But even a "four power" pass couldn't insulate an
American from Soviet harassment. Janikowski recalled a time when her
group of WACs, traveling by train from Berlin to Heidelberg, were "inspected" by a group of Russian soldiers who boarded the train during the
middle of the night:

> We were forced to stand in night clothes and bare feet in a freezing hallway,
> holding our orders, while Russian soldiers tore our belongings apart and cut
> open things like puffy slippers. It was most frightening and degrading. . . .
> We were not allowed to speak, even to each other. One crying girl had her
> dog tags lifted off her neck by a Russian's bayonet. He cut her in the process
> and she fainted. The floor was . . . puddles of melting snow, and the Rus-
> sians just left her lying in the freezing wet. We all expected the worst by that
> time, but finally we were allowed to proceed.[9]

By 1949, recalled WAC Major Irene Michels (Sorrough), stationed in Heidelberg handling monthly financial reports on programs such as *Stars and
Stripes* and officers' clubs, it became increasingly difficult to travel anywhere in or pass through the Soviet sector. U.S. military personnel were
cautioned to be in uniform at all times, and have their papers ready for
Soviet guards when the train reached the Russian sector.[10]

That same year, the Soviet Union also dropped its first atomic bomb.
Western scientists glumly predicted that the Soviets were on the verge of the
much more powerful hydrogen bomb, which inferred an ability to challenge U.S. military supremacy. Also in 1949, China fell to Communist

forces. Now there was yet another, frighteningly large, communist nation threatening the political freedom of smaller nations close to its borders. For Pauline Schmid and four other Navy nurses assigned to the First Marine Hospital in Tientsin, the fall of China was direct and personal. "There were Marine guards at the hospital gate 24 hours a day," she recalled. "We could hear Communist gunfire outside the city limits."[11]

With China now in the clutches of communist revolutionaries and Europe still struggling to rebuild, it appeared that only the United States had the strength and will to defend the free world from the spread of communism around the globe. Such was the mindset on 24 June 1950, when North Korea attacked South Korea. U.S. military strategists immediately placed the war looming in Korea into a global context. It clearly demanded a response, yet if the United States were to divert too much of its military force to the Far East, American strategists feared that the Soviet Union would use it as an opportunity to move into Western Europe. The Joint Chiefs of Staff were so certain of this imminent threat that, even while fighting in Korea, they convinced President Truman and Congress to expand troop strength in Europe by deploying four additional U.S. Army divisions and eleven more Air Wings to Western Europe the following year. The Joint Chiefs called General Dwight D. Eisenhower from retirement to serve in the newly created position of Supreme Allied Commander of NATO.[12] And, once again, as it had in World War II and, to a lesser extent in World War I, the military turned to the women of the nation to fill in for men now needed on the battlefronts.

But times had changed. Although the military was attempting to reinforce traditional job classifications for women, the new war, coinciding as it did with the birth of the Cold War, forced the military to expand opportunities for servicewomen. It also found itself forced to begin rethinking servicewomen's potential. A telling indication of this was a May 1952 *New York Times Magazine* story that pointed out "a dramatic difference" between Korean War–era women and World War II servicewomen. The latter, "like the civilian male Army, . . . were not necessarily looking for careers in the Army; they came in to meet a need."

> Today the Army is frankly a "field of employment" for women. It offers careers. It philosophizes that if the military wants capable, enthusiastic and ambitious young women as well as young men in the service, it must give them opportunities for progress in a particular career field.[13]

If reality, at least for "ambitious young women," fell short of the "philoso-phizing," it was perhaps more an expression of the 1950s and not entirely the military's fault.

Only a handful of servicewomen other than nurses actually served in Korea, but the onset of war made the job of every servicewoman everywhere more urgent because of the military's need to divert large numbers of men into the actual battle theater, Korea, and the potential one, Europe. The onset of war also extended enlistments and altered personal plans. WAC Lieu-tenant Colonel Irene Van Houten (Munster), a World War II veteran serving at the Pentagon, had to postpone wedding bells. When the war broke out in June, she and her future husband, Lieutenant Colonel Daniel Munster, "were trying to find the time to get married," she said. "Because the war broke out, it was impossible for him to get away and we had to wait until Au-gust."[14] Army nurse Muriel Raymond (Batcheller) not only got her one-year hitch extended to three; on return from her honeymoon, the first lieutenant received word that she was being shipped to Japan. Although she could have resigned under rules existent at the time, she opted not to. She did manage to avoid going to Japan, but was eventually sent to Germany. She reported that she was unable to bring along her new husband, although male officers at the same facility were permitted to have their families with them.[15]

While nurses of all service branches and Army women had the best chance of going overseas and a number of Navy women served in Europe, fewer non-nurse Air Force and Marine women went overseas. Nonetheless, opportunities expanded significantly by the end of the war. Volunteers from organizations such as the American Red Cross and Special Services also re-sponded to the challenge.

A picture of Army Special Services' Jeanne Hamby (Gang), serving coffee to soldiers somewhere near the Czech border in 1951, includes Hamby's nota-tion: "Russians very near; [they] like to move border signs to catch American GI's behind the wrong lines. Had to give a password to truck in, but with all that dust, have a feeling 'they' knew we were there." Told she was "too near-sighted" to join the Navy's WAVES during World War II, Hamby joined the Red Cross and found she was "too young" during that war for overseas assign-ment. The Piedmont, California, native served as a recreational staff aide in hospitals in her home state. When the Korean War broke out, she volunteered for the Army Special Services and was sent to Germany for two years, where her first assignment was at the 7th Army Headquarters' Pyramid Service Club.[16]

Army Special Services workers serve coffee to American GIs at the Pyramid Service Club on the Czech border, 1951. From left: Unknown, Jeanne Hamby (Gang), Ann Dougherty, Dee Squire, and Nancy Millar. Jeanne Hamby Gang Collection, Women's Memorial Collection.

Japan, where the United States already maintained a substantial army of occupation, seemed the obvious place from which to launch an American response to the North Korean invasion of South Korea, and there were American servicewomen already stationed in Japan when the war broke out. Both the Army and the Navy maintained large (although recently downsized) hospitals with hundreds of uniformed nurses assigned. There were WAC detachments in Tokyo and Yokohama, and with the war's start, the numbers of nurses and WACs expanded dramatically.

The Army had three commands in Japan—the Far East Command, Service Command and the Japan Logistical Command—and WACs worked in the headquarters of all three, helping the Army transport, supply, care for, and evacuate combat and combat support troops in the Far East Theater. WACs typed and filed paperwork, kept the lines of communication functioning smoothly, and worked as research analysts, draftsmen, mapmakers, and Multiplex operators (the latter prepared multicolored photomaps used by the United Nations Command).

Approximately one-quarter of the enlisted WACs were assigned to various hospitals and medical units in Tokyo. During the early days of the Korean War, as hospital medical staffs were plundered by transfers to Korea,

WACs did double duty, working daytime jobs as laboratory and pharmacy technicians, entertainment specialists, nursing assistants, in medical records or as education supervisors, and then helping out at night in whatever capacity was needed. The Army in Japan also urgently needed women with skills as telephone and teletype operators, cashiers, motor vehicle operators, mechanics, and medical corpsmen. As the war continued, WACs were also assigned as ward masters in Army hospitals, a supervisory role traditionally the province of male NCOs.[17]

Service in the Far East Theater, even outside Korea and the war zone, was not without risk. Japan is prone to earthquakes, and several occurred between mid-1950 and mid-1953. During the first half of the Korean War, the Japanese were also an occupied people and servicewomen experienced political unrest and the bitterness of the population. The ravages of World War II were still obvious, and much of the populace was extremely poor. Most U.S. servicewomen lived and worked on military installations and were well protected, and those living in urban areas were bused back and forth between their quarters and work. On 28 April 1952, when the United States and Japan signed a formal peace treaty ending the Occupation, some of the pent-up frustration of the Japanese people surfaced in demonstrations against U.S. forces. In most cases, servicewomen watched from the safety of their quarters and workstations, but at least one WAC was caught in an Army bus as it transported her from her work assignment to her billet. An unruly crowd attacked the bus, but MPs got the WAC and the bus driver away safely. In July, the Japanese Diet passed an antisubversive law, which quelled the anti-Western demonstrations.[18]

Conditions in Japan were equally chaotic for Red Cross workers immediately after the war broke out. Veteran Evelyn "Hopsie" Higgins of Little River, New Jersey, who arrived at Itazuki Air Force Base, a major entry/departure point for U.S. troops, wrote home to her family about seeing "men everywhere [carrying] full field packs—helmets, et cetera, ready to leave, but those returning from Korea were "in need of everything—shaving equipment, toothbrushes, towels, soap, toothpaste."

That Japan was not the war zone was of little comfort. "Many accidents keep happen-

Evelyn "Hopsie" Higgins, American Red Cross. Women's Memorial Register.

> ing. . . . One jet pilot got a bullet in the cockpit . . . it exploded—hurting both
> his hands. He flew back . . . with them bleeding." Closer to home, "one of our
> nicest pilots . . . was killed on the line accidentally . . . when a rocket went off
> by mistake."
>
> Many military dependents remained at Itazuki. Their presence added a
> surreal quality to life on the front lines of the aerial war. "The fighter pilots
> come home at night to kiss 'oaksan' [Japanese for wife] and the baby-san good
> night and get up the next morning and take off to bomb and strafe the North
> Koreans."[19]

Army First Lieutenant Janet Gingrich (Preston), who had been part of
that detachment of forty-eight WACs en route to Japan when the Korean
War broke out, was assigned to the mail section of the casualty reporting
office at MacArthur's headquarters. Her office rerouted letters addressed
to soldiers on casualty lists but no longer with their units. Gingrich's job
was to track the wounded down by calling each hospital to which they could
have been sent and then forwarding their mail. If an individual couldn't be
located—an indication he was missing in action or dead—his mail was
kept on file, rather than returned to the soldier's correspondent, until the
mail office received confirmation that MacArthur's office had notified the
next of kin.[20]

By mid-1951, the two original WAC detachments in Japan, those at Tokyo
and Yokohama, had increased to six, and by mid-June of 1953, near the end
of the war, there were nine. The women's experiences and living conditions
varied greatly with their place of assignment. For example, Private First
Class Muriel Scharrer (Wimmer), a WAC medical technician, and her detachment trained at the rifle range in Tokyo. The women could opt out if
they felt uncomfortable, but "it reflected poorly on your company, if you
skipped practice," she noted.[21] WACs of the 8064th Army unit in Yokohama trained regularly with gas masks and weapons, although the imminent peril that training suggests was offset by the fact that, for recreation,
many also joined the softball team.

The WAC barracks in Yokohama consisted of metal Quonset huts all in
a row, and contrasted greatly with the housing assigned to the WACs in
Tokyo who lived in the far more comfortable Mitsubishi building. Billeted
along with Air Force women, they enjoyed maid service and a dining room
boasting table linens, candlelight, and gourmet food. Although the women
of the 8064th slept in Quonsets on standard metal Army cots, they were
able to hire local women to clean the barracks and wash their clothes.[22]

Work never became merely routine. The up-and-down nature of the war sometimes flooded the wards with patients, and the international mix of the United Nations' troops meant the patients could be of widely varying backgrounds, Scharrer recalled:

> During "pushes" all the wards were overwhelmed with patients directly from the battlefields. Beds were placed in hallways because there was no space for them on the wards. We worked twelve-hour days, six days a week . . . generally under the direction of Army nurses.
>
> One of my favorite patients was an Ethiopian soldier . . . badly shot up, but . . . unfailingly patient and good humored. He remained on the ward for at least three months. We also had Turkish, Colombian, and Greek patients. . . . Sometimes we had difficulty communicating with them. Two of the Colombian soldiers were so young, no more than fourteen or fifteen! That shocked me. There was one American soldier named Roy whose leg was amputated on Christmas Eve. He was worried about what his wife and two little girls at home would think when they saw him.[23]

WACs working at the 8th Station Hospital took semiambulatory patients on picnics and sightseeing tours. Others ran the lending library, and took mobile book carts to the wards. WACs planned evening entertainment, including movies, drawing contests, and variety shows. WACs also staffed a PX on port-bound troop trains, while other WACs on the train ran bingo games, card tournaments, and "community sings."[24]

In September 1950, the 8225th WAC Detachment, Tokyo, "adopted" the 27th Regiment of the 25th Division, which was already on duty in Korea, and acted as pen pals for soldiers who had no other correspondents. When Christmas came, other WAC companies treated local orphanages to holiday parties, complete with a visit from Santa Claus for the children. Many WACs volunteered at hospitals, and others taught night courses at local schools for the GIs.[25]

The first squadron of forty-eight Air Force women arrived in Tokyo in September 1950 three months after the Korean War started and took over jobs ranging from control tower operators at Haneda Air Base to cryptographic operators in headquarters to finance clerks in the new Kaijo building.[26]

WAF Private First Class (later Staff Sergeant) Ernestine Johnson (Thomas) of Warren, Ohio, volunteered for overseas duty as soon as the Korean War broke out and received orders for Japan. When she and two WAF friends reported in at San Francisco, they were mistakenly told that because they were all under twenty-one, they could not be assigned overseas. One of the young women's parents had called Washington to complain about their daughter's assignment. They knew the paperwork was already in the works changing the age limitation, Johnson said, so the young women took matters into their own hands, and sneaked their duffels onto the transport with the rest of the contingent's. A place aboard was found for them.

Johnson recalls she was one of perhaps four African Americans in her group of fifty WAF, who flew first to Hawaii and then on to Japan, where they were billeted at the Mitsubishi building. Johnson's first assignment there was as a clerk typist in the intelligence section in Air Force Head-quarters, transcribing reports from downed pilots who had been engaged in evasion and escape. When a young male airman she outranked was recom-mended for promotion ahead of her, she complained to the master sergeant in charge, but said she was told, "That's tough." Again taking matters into her own hands, she searched for and found a job as administrative assistant in a new department that handled procurement and contracting. "I under-stand I was the talk of the whole headquarters," she said. "The men were livid. They said, 'Who does she think she is that she can go and apply for positions and get interviews?'"

Johnson persisted and won both the job and the promotion to corporal. She said she protested because "I felt the government had spent too much money training me and I wasn't going to let the (situation) go like that." Al-though the atmosphere in her new office was much better than her old one, Johnson still encountered difficulties she blames more on gender than on race. One colonel "didn't like me at all. He just thought I had too much au-thority." The contracting group researched suppliers based in the Far East, and negotiated contracts to supply American forces. In her new position, Johnson supervised both airmen and Japanese personnel.[27] When General MacArthur was fired by President Truman, Johnson was one of the by-standers who made a special effort to go watch his plane take off, because, she said, she had heard that MacArthur refused to have black soldiers as-signed to his headquarters.[28]

In October 1952, a WAF detachment was assigned to the Japan Air De-fense Force in Nagoya. The women filled vacancies with the 601st Air Base Wing and Headquarters caused by normal rotation of male airmen to the states. Most WAF served in supply units, communications, and other ad-ministrative sections. When women filled the remaining vacancies, the WAF squadrons were brought up to full strength for the first time since the war began.[29]

In 1952, Air Force press releases boasted that three WAF control tower operators were assigned to Haneda Air Base: Staff Sergeant Margaret O'Neil, Airman First Class Margaret Stanford, and Airman First Class Doris Brown. O'Neil had been a member of the Air Force since 1949 and a fully qualified control tower operator for more than two years. Stanford and Brown received their assignments to Haneda after working one-year stints in the states.[30]

The Red Cross had more than three thousand volunteer workers at U.S. Army hospitals in Japan during the Korean War. Many were the wives of military personnel stationed in Japan; others had husbands in Korea. Red Cross workers tried to meet every plane, hospital train, and hospital ship arriving in Japan from the war front. Volunteers made 627,000 surgical dressings, bandages, wound packs that were flown to frontline aid stations, and thousands of kit bags for soldiers evacuated from the front lines.[31]

Yokohama had the greatest concentration of African Americans including Air Force and Army nurses, Air Force women, and an estimated one hundred Women's Army Corps members. When Red Cross worker Sylvia Rock arrived in Tokyo in October 1950, she was surprised, she told the *Baltimore Afro-American,* by "a huge metropolis every bit as large and mechanized as New

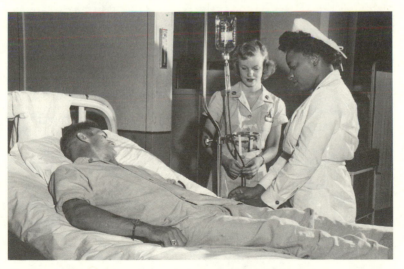

Army Captain Mary E. Brown, surgical ward chief nurse, and WAC Private First Class Vivian Lowe, surgical technician, treat French soldier Sergeant Jules Tellier, 155th Station Hospital, Yokohama, Japan, 1951. Army Nurse Corps Collection, Office of Medical History, Office of the Army Surgeon General.

York." Her living quarters—a hotel for women—took up almost an entire block and the women who lived there ate in a dining room with table linens, candlelight, and gourmet food. "I was amazed to suddenly find myself in possession of a maid. I confess, at first I didn't know how to react to this state of affairs. . . . I was embarrassed to have another human being doing the things for me that I was perfectly capable of doing for myself."

Rock recalled only eighteen other African American Red Cross workers at the time (although that number jumped to fifty within a year) and decided she was probably the first "brown" woman in Red Cross uniform most Japanese had seen. "When I walked down the street, I would be surrounded by crowds of people who would gingerly touch me to feel my skin, my hair, and my clothes. People turned around while driving to watch me on the street. I have never felt so conspicuous in all my life." Visiting a segregated club in Yokohama, "it seemed as though I were back in Harlem. 'After Hours' was the most popular song; 'The Huckka Buck' was the most popular dance, and 'The Bebop' was heard in all the dance halls." She noticed, however, that "most of the Japanese girls there had colored American soldiers. . . . Our boys did not seem to be impressed by the sight of a colored American girl."[32]

The 121st Evacuation Hospital had two large recreation rooms, usually staffed by three Red Cross workers, where Ping-Pong tables, card and writing tables, a piano, record players, and musical instruments were available. On twice daily ward rounds, they provided cigarettes and items such as shaving gear, toothbrushes, soap, and reading materials. The Red Cross personnel also wrote letters home, taking dictation from patients unable to write, and wrapped and mailed packages. Volunteers and staff at the 121st threw parties for patients whenever the occasion called—Valentine's Day, George Washington's birthday, Christmas—and baked thirty dozen "homemade" cookies twice a month.[33]

The Red Cross staff at the 172nd Hospital ran a shopping service for the patients. Other units provided small crafts that patients could do at their bedsides. In larger hospitals, such as the 8164th Army Hospital in Kyoto, Red Cross workers ran hobby shops where patients could build model planes, or do leather- or woodworking. Weekly entertainment programs brought local performers and educators to the patients.[34]

The 382nd Hospital's Red Cross established an exceptionally popular program by which patients could send tape recordings home to their families. Fathers recorded bedtime stories for their children and love songs for their wives. The Red Cross at the 382nd also sponsored a lively discussion group with provocative topics such as this question one Monday evening in May 1951: "Does Dagwood represent the typical American husband?" Reportedly, few patients could resist leaping into the fray with many and varied opinions, some of which came from personal experience, others from personal observation. At the end of the evening, the patients agreed that Dagwood was far too "henpecked" to represent the typical American husband.[35]

Japan and Korea were not the only Far East postings for servicewomen during the Korean War. Many of the Pacific islands critical in World War II remained strategic outposts for U.S. military, among them Okinawa, Guam, and Midway Island. A WAC detachment of about three hundred women arrived on Okinawa in April 1951 to support the hospital, which was part of the evacuation chain for battle casualties from Korea. The WACs worked as secretaries and cryptographers as well as in security and the motor pool. Sergeant Jerrie Hall, a medical secretary, enjoyed her time there, referring to the island as "tropical loveliness at its best." Bus dispatcher Sergeant Olive Bisard liked her job, but grumbled that "all my friends blame me whenever an Army bus is late."[36] Sergeant Martha Halyak (Fogle), an X-ray technician who arrived on the island in October 1951, recalled the humidity and lack of air conditioning in summer. The women slept under mosquito nets during the summer, and in the winter tried to stay warm with pot-bellied stoves, which had a tendency to explode after several hours of use, sending the women outside in the snow in their nightclothes. Once, when a typhoon hit, the WACs moved into a cement barracks for safety, and had to cling to ropes to get to the dining hall when the winds were at their peak. The episode became just another experience to write home about.[37]

WACs said there also was much to enjoy about service on Okinawa. They had maid service, including laundry, for five dollars a month. During the evening, many went dancing at the Stateside Club on base. The island was only eight miles wide, and the Army often allowed WACs to take out motor pool vehicles for picnics along the shore.[38]

One Red Cross worker, Shirley Peck (Barnes), called her time on Okinawa in 1953 "my most memorable experience." Secretary to the staff surgeon of the 20th Air Force, she lived in a Quonset at the end of the flight line. "In addition to the inconveniences of a remote island, with typhoons reaching 170 mph [and] uncontrollable mildew," she recalled that "huge rodents and bugs of every species—as well as wild boar and snakes—dominated the terrain." But she also got to be a part of history being made. "Excitement erupted at the presence of the Russian MIG that defected over the 38th parallel of Korea," she said in her registration for the Women In Military Service For America Memorial. And "during the American/Korean prisoner exchange, I was in awe at the sight of the 7th Fleet, alert and anchored off White Beach."[39]

Okinawa was not the only island where military women faced typhoons and strange creatures during the Korean War. Approximately seventy Navy nurses were stationed on Guam, living in Quonset huts and doing frequent battle with the geckoes (chameleon-like lizards) that tried to live with them. One of the nurses there, Lieutenant Commander Joan Heath (Steyn), was a former World War II Cadet Nurse. She had joined the NNC in August 1950, following in the footsteps of a beloved aunt, an Army nurse who had been wounded along with two other nurses during the Normandy invasion. "Aunt Lois" had warned Heath against the military, insisting that a military nurse's life was hard, both physically and emotionally; but the suggestion that she should seek an easier life made Heath even more determined.[40]

Stationed in Guam along with Heath, Iris Stock remembered that the nurses spent their free time exploring. Squadrons of airmen were training on the island, and pilots sometimes would take the nurses flying. A typhoon interrupted that idyll. Stock was on duty when orders came through to evacuate the hospital to the Marine barracks in the Navy supply depot, and was responsible for deciding which supplies and equipment to take. "One of the dependents was having a baby, so we took a delivery table with us," she recalled.[41]

On Midway, the excitement was a tidal wave. The Navy nurses moved out, patients and all, to the top of the highest hill on the island; fortunately, the tidal wave was not so high as had been expected, and the hospital received only minor damage.[42] Midway, which figured in the famous World War II naval battle of the same name, was used during the Korean War as a refueling station for medical evacuation flights and as a haven where aircraft in trouble could land. The small hospital cared for military personnel stationed on the island and their dependents. Midway's nurses also relieved Air Force flight nurses when their medical evacuation flights landed there to refuel, taking over patient care so that the flight nurses could rest. Lieutenant Commander Carolyn Shearer recalls Midway for other reasons as well. In addition to the island's famous black-footed albatross or "gooney bird," there was a ground-nesting bird, nicknamed the "moaning bird," which would "cry at night like a tortured human being. When we first arrived there we had to get used to all the squalling and carrying on each night."[43]

While military women stationed in Japan and the Pacific Islands were somewhat removed from the Korean War Theater, servicewomen serving in the European Theater during those years experienced periods of heightened tension at the beginning of what would be a forty-year Cold War. The communists, the enemy, were right across the border, with troops located in the Soviet sectors of Germany and Berlin, in Czechoslovakia, Hungary, and Yugoslavia. Servicewomen participated in frequent drills to practice emergency procedures, and helped devise evacuation plans in case of attack. They also learned to keep a low profile when not on duty. While serving in England in the early 1950s, Airman Second Class Jacquelyn Tomasik (Anderson) of Holyoke, Massachusetts, remembered being warned not to wear her uniform "when away from base for fear of attracting unwanted attention from Communists. We didn't go anyplace where they could gather a crowd." May Day (May 1 is a major communist holiday) was the worst. "The word would go out. 'Don't go into London on the first.'"[44]

U.S. planners assumed that Europe, with its highly developed resources but postwar political fragility, would be the place where the communists would try to expand, and both politicians and military leaders believed that it was necessary to reinforce troops already there. With the troops went larger numbers of military women as part of the support services: Army and Air Force nurses, WACs, Air Force and Navy women, and a few Women Marines. Staff Sergeant Mary Boyd, one of three Women Marines assigned to NATO's Headquarters Allied Forces Southern Europe, credited the fact that Women Marines were included to Assistant Secretary of Defense Anna Rosenberg. "When she learned of the plan to send 36 women to Naples she insisted that four of the Navy's allotment of eight females be WMs."[45]

Women from various service branches worked closely together at NATO headquarters in Paris. Navy Lieutenant (jg) Helen Weaver (North) was Eisenhower's personal secretary, while WAC Sergeant First Class Arline Davis helped answer his mail. (Weaver also was a member of the Navy and Marine Corps women's pistol team and had won twenty medals in competition, among them the Navy Expert Medal and the National Rifle Association's Sharpshooter Badge.)[46]

In 1950, the Navy assigned another seven Navy women—one lieutenant and six yeomen, all volunteers for overseas duty—to NATO's multiservice staff. They joined the more than one hundred women already working at headquarters, including twenty-two WACs, thirteen Air Force women, nineteen French, and five Dutch servicewomen, all under the command of a WAC captain. Another unit of women assigned to NATO head-quarters was a group of fifty-six Army Signal Corps WACs, who worked at telephone switchboards and at teletype communications message centers. The military women all lived together in three barracks of about forty each, two to a room.[47]

In January 1951, WAC Private First Class Maxine Powell became a clerk in General Dwight Eisenhower's Paris headquarters. By the middle of 1951, nineteen additional WACs from Heidelberg were sent to set up communications facilities at SHAPE HQ. They were an advance team for the 7th Signal Battalion, a WAC detachment that would join with French, Dutch, and British servicewomen at SHAPE.[48]

Throughout Europe, servicewomen worked at military hospitals, managed communications networks, and worked in intelligence, public information, finance, and personnel. Many held positions requiring top-secret clearances. For example, the WACs working at the Army's 7774th Signal Battalion in Heidelberg were involved in a highly specialized communications operation that relayed classified messages between the European Command and Army in Washington, as well as various European commands and American embassies in Europe.[49]

When Captain Jeanne M. Holm arrived in Germany in January 1949 on her first Air Force assignment, her job at Erding Air Base entailed reviewing all the top-secret war plans from Air Force headquarters in Europe and incorporating the instructions into Erding's own planning. It was assumed that if the Soviet Union decided to advance into Europe, that base would be among the first targets. Holm frequently drove the narrow, winding roads of Bavaria, familiarizing herself with potential traffic bottlenecks while reconnoitering the best and fastest route to the Swiss border. (At that time, German drivers still were occasionally hostile toward Allied personnel they encountered on the roads, but Holm said she never felt as though she were in danger. She did, however, carry a loaded pistol in the glove compartment of her car.)[50]

First Lieutenant Mildred Inez Bailey (later Brigadier General Bailey) had received orders to Germany in September 1949 and became the commanding officer of the WAC Detachment at the 98th General Hospital in Munich where she supervised from 130 to 140 enlisted women, most of whom were medical technicians. Bailey also was very much involved in contingency planning should the Korean War expand into Europe. U.S. forces in Europe were on alert for that possibility for the first months of the war, before it became apparent that the war could probably be contained in

Korea. Had the Soviets invaded, however, Bailey and her WAC detachment would have remained in Munich where their services would be needed at the hospital. Dependents, and there were many living in Munich by that time, were to be evacuated as quickly as possible in the event of an attack.[51]

Military women serving in the European Theater during the Korean War years experienced a period of heightened tension. Bailey recalled: "All of a sudden security and plans for evacuation and plans for what would happen if fighting broke out became top priority. We had to do things that no one paid any attention to before, and we had not been required to do before. I was commanding a WAC unit, and I had never participated in field training, because we weren't doing it when I went through Officer's Candidate School. . . . So I had never learned to pitch a tent. . . . My company clerk who knew how to pitch a tent taught me how to pitch one in the back of the building where we had the orderly room, because we suddenly found ourselves being required to take marches, to spend the night out in tents, to bivouac, that sort of thing."[52]

Few of the WACs in Europe had experienced living and working in field conditions, Bailey said, but they all had to learn, whether they worked at military hospitals, or if they managed communications networks, or worked in intelligence with top-secret security clearances. No one was too important to carry a field pack and pitch a tent, whether a veteran of World War II or a relative newcomer to the Army.

"Our first experience was a ten mile hike," she said. "I had never walked 10 miles in my life, and it was the first time I had worn field clothing, boots, helmets, that sort of thing. None of the women in my unit were experienced in bivouacing in the field and marching, and the average age of the women in my unit was 40. But not a single one of my women fell out during that march. . . . their pride would not permit them to do so."[53]

Europe was still rebuilding from the devastation of World War II, and servicewomen's quarters, even in fabled cities replete with fairy tale–like castles, were sometimes uncomfortably cold and bleak. Recreation facilities were not much better. Army Captain Constance Bennett (Van Hook) of Lake Wales, Florida, a physical therapist and avid golfer, remembers "an abandoned tank and shrapnel" on the golf course in Berlin's American sector. "Several . . . holes abutted the Russian territory and if you hit your ball over, you didn't go get (it) because the Russians were supervising the fence."[54]

But despite the Cold War tensions, Europe was a popular duty station, and the service branches were never short of volunteers for European assignments, as the experience of Marine Staff Sergeant Mary Boyd (Lum) attests. Her job as a stenotypist [sic] at NATO's Headquarters Allied Powers Southern Europe included travel to Rome and Paris. "I was able to get to the opera, visited Capri and Mt. Vesuvius, and was billeted in a first class hotel for nine months," she noted. "I was completely spoiled by the time I returned to Quantico."[55]

European postings had a special interest for many servicewomen—shopping. By 1953, WAC Private First Class Cathy Morgan of the 7812th Station Complement at Panzer Kaserne had her choice of coveted Hummel figures in a Kaiserlautern shop.[56] But in immediate postwar Germany, while shopping was not verboten, it was difficult for most American servicewomen. With goods scarce and money nonexistent, bartering became a way of life and cigarettes the most common medium of exchange. "Our quota was a carton and a half a week," recalled Army Major Beatrice Seelav (Stecher) of New York City who was stationed in Frankfurt during the late 1940s. "I smoked [but] I managed to save three packages each week to use for barter." A package of cigarettes was worth ninety to one hundred dollars in American money to the Germans.

WAC Private First Class Cathy Morgan shops for Hummel figurines, Kaiserslautern, Germany, 1953. U.S. Army photo, National Archives (111-SC-424079).

The Army also allowed servicepeople to use cans of coffee, cocoa, and shortening to barter for goods and services in the open market. Seelav and her WAC roommates paid a German one pack of cigarettes to repair a wall in their apartment and "sometimes we gave [the] Germans coffee and cocoa and we would get a pocketbook . . . or a vase."

Although it could mean court-martial, many service personnel also bought things on the black market. Seelav went with friends to a bombed-out building where, after giving a prearranged signal, they were shown into an apartment where "you couldn't see anything on the floors but [sterling silver] platters, coffee sets, tea sets. It looked like all the sterling silver of Hanau [the largest silver-making city in Germany]." The group hid their booty "in the Army car that was driving us so that we could make it through the MP block."

> Seelav had one of the most unusual overseas jobs in the postwar American Army. The former legal secretary supervised two Frankfurt jails for criminal displaced persons. More than thirty different nationalities were represented in the prison population.[57]

Corporal Gladys Hahn (Romanoff) had joined the WAC hoping to be sent overseas, and got her wish when she was sent to Mannheim, Germany, after her first field assignment. As there were no barracks for WACs at Mannheim, she and the other women lived and took their meals at Patton Barracks, a former SS troops facility in Heidelberg, and were bused to and from work twice every day.[58] Another Army Signal Corps teletypist there at that time, Corporal Lucille Marquis (Regan), recalled the 4th Signal Group had three other enlisted and one captain, Elaine Lamm, living with other WAC units at Patton Barracks, "five of us to a room, but the rooms were huge and we had maid service."[59]

In 1951, First Lieutenant Janet Rasmussen had completed a tour of duty in Vienna, Austria, immediately after World War II, and was back in the States as the commander of a detachment of WACs at Fort Hamilton in Brooklyn, New York, when she decided to request another overseas tour. She had hoped to be sent to Japan, but the Army wanted her back in Austria where she took over a Salzburg detachment. After a year, she was reassigned to G-2 at Army headquarters there, where she was responsible for all the files and personnel records seized from the Nazis and used by the U.S. State Department to do background checks on job applicants and displaced persons.

Between her tours in Austria, the comfort level for American forces had improved greatly. The WAC enlisted in Salzburg lived in a guesthouse, with their own kitchen and mess, dayroom, laundry facilities, and executive office. Their officers lived in a nearby hotel in Salzburg, but ate in the WAC mess at a separate table. Rasmussen particularly remembered the officers' waiter, "Pop," who often brought them fresh vegetables from his own garden. "I was more comfortable in Salzburg during the Korean War than I had been earlier in Vienna. By 1950, rationing was over, restaurants were back in business, and Army personnel had a bit more freedom for sightseeing. There [still] was a displaced persons' camp outside of Salzburg, but we felt very comfortable walking by it."[60]

While postwar tensions eased, Cold War tensions continued to grow. In 1948, ANC Captain Dorothy Looby (Manfredi), a World War II veteran of the southwest Pacific, had requested assignment to the European Theater, where the Army Nurse Corps staffed hospitals in the United Kingdom, Germany, France, and Italy. Sent to the 7th Station Hospital in Trieste, Italy, she was constantly aware of being in a hot spot. Trieste was a deep-water port much coveted by Yugoslavia, which had five thousand soldiers poised at the border. Italy, Great Britain, and the United States had significant numbers of troops on alert in Trieste to counter the Yugoslavian threat. Trieste was also the site of many cold war intelligence operations, and Looby recalled that occasionally the hospital was called upon to treat intelligence operatives.

In January 1950, Looby became assistant chief nurse at the 10th Field Hospital in Regensburg, Germany, located about thirty miles from the Soviet-patrolled border. The presence of the Soviets nearby was an accepted fact of life at the 10th Field Hospital. Looby and a group of nurses traveling on their day off once became lost and ran into a patrol of armed Soviet soldiers. Realizing that they had strayed too close to the border, they simply turned around. Another time, Looby was summoned to a ward to care for and try to calm a Russian woman who had defected with her scientist husband.[61] Every summer, the hospital practiced emergency field medicine, living and working in tents, staging convoy hospital moves, and setting up field hospitals under combat conditions. Hospital personnel also drilled on techniques necessary to protect themselves from and treat victims of chemical and biological warfare.[62] First Lieutenant Muriel Raymond (Batcheller), the bride who ended up in Germany sans spouse and helped establish the 120th General Hospital in Landstuhl, recalled frequent middle-of-the-night evacuation drills in case the Soviets attacked.[63]

All newly arrived Army nurses had to take medical field service training to prepare for possible hostilities in Germany, as did those in France, where Army nurses lived and worked under field conditions. (Most Army hospitals outside of Paris were field hospitals.) The fourteen-day course taught the nurses how to pitch tents, read maps and compasses, and treat patients under less than optimal conditions. ANC Captain (later Colonel) Margaret Bailey remembered how wet the ground was during her two weeks of field training. "I assure you," she said, "this was no picnic."[64]

Members of the new Women's Medical Specialty Corps (WMSC) stationed in Europe during the Korean War faced the same Cold War drills. Every month hospital staff were required to participate in field training. At one hospital, during each December's field training, they made a point of setting up near a spruce tree and decorating the tree with the tiny foil wrappings from Hershey's Kisses.[65]

Major Katharine Manchester, dietetic consultant to the European Command during this period, reported that the overriding problem of dietitians was not the Cold War but the black market. Hospital food, far better quality than what was available locally—even at military commissaries—was constantly being pilfered both by Germans employed at the hospitals and by Americans. The Army's Frankfurt hospital was a virtual sieve, with underground tunnels connecting it with the train station and supplies moving mysteriously from hospital storage rooms down the tunnels to the train station and out into the countryside. Coffee, butter, and hamburger were extremely hard to keep in stock.

The pilferage proved almost impossible to stop and put the dietitians, who were responsible for feeding patients and accountable for the food used, in very difficult positions. The problems ranged from double sets of books being kept by higher-ups at one hospital to multiple storage-room keys floating around other hospitals. One night when Manchester and her visiting father were conducting an item-by-item inventory, a door slid open. Manchester grabbed a can and threw it at the offender, who ducked out. The Manchesters sealed the storage-room door with tape so they would be able to tell whether if the thief returned after they left. The next morning, Manchester saw that the door had been opened.[66]

> Pilfering was not a problem in German hospitals because there was little to steal. Army Captain Constance Bennett (Van Hook) of Lake Wales, Florida, described conditions in one local hospital as "shocking." Assigned to teach the staff the latest polio treatment methods during an epidemic, Bennett, a physical therapist, found the hospital lacking even the most basic items. "They were using paper for sheets."[67]

Second Lieutenant Constance Bennett (Van Hook), U.S. Army physical therapist, in a 1944 photograph. Courtesy Constance Bennett Van Hook.

The Air Force was still a fledgling struggling to find its own identity separate from that of the Army during the Korean War. Moreover, as the place and future of women in the new organization was far from clear, assignments for Air Force women commensurate with their rank and training were scarce, especially in Europe. Captain Jeanne M. Holm, a World War II

WAC veteran who rejoined the Army after the 1948 Women's Armed Services Integration Act passed, was one of just five newly minted women Air Force officers at Erding. However, a detachment of enlisted women, assigned throughout the base in supply, medical records, and maintenance, also worked there, as did a handful of WAF assigned to radio maintenance, so the rules against assigning women to isolated situations were observed.[68]

Yet in Nuremberg, Major Corinne Edwards, who served as the information and education officer for the 433rd Troop Carrier Wing, was the only military woman, officer or enlisted, with the unit. A part of her job, in effect, was doing advance public relations for women in the Air Force. At the European Command's School at Dachau, Germany, she was a frequent lecturer—to all-male audiences of up to two hundred—on the need for women in the armed services.[69]

During the Korean War, the vast majority of American servicewomen were assigned to stations on the home front where they replaced men assigned overseas. Whether they served in offices, communications centers, military hospitals, control towers, or laboratories, they felt the impact of the war, and they enabled the U.S. military to field more efficient combat and defensive forces around the world. The Fort Dix, New Jersey, WAC detachment commanded by Captain (later Major) Isabelle Biasini had approximately two hundred women working in thirty-five of the four hundred noncombat positions open to WACs. A sample of their jobs gives a picture of those opportunities. Corporal Bessie Mumford was a machine records specialist; Private First Class Edith Huffstuffer, a photographer; Private Dorlamae Turck, a pediatric assistant; Private First Class Bonnie Adams, an Army orders control clerk; Corporal Elsie Davis, an entertainment specialist; and Corporal Lorraine Basham was an information specialist.[70]

Other WACs proved themselves in situations that were unusual for women during the Korean War era. Sergeant First Class Gladys Nielsen, U.S. Army Reserve, a beautician in civilian life, made news demonstrating her proficiency with the Army carbine when she outshot six hundred soldiers of a transportation unit from Brooklyn Army Base during two weeks of active duty training in August 1950. Nielsen had acquired her skill during weekly unit practices.[71]

Not all WACs worked at Army organizations. Sergeant First Class Elizabeth Darwin, U.S. Army Reserve, was recalled to active duty in September 1950 and assigned to the 373rd Transportation Major Port unit at Hampton

Roads Port of Embarkation, near Norfolk, Virginia. She and other WACs worked with Navy women and were billeted with them at the naval air station.[72]

The outbreak of the war provided some Navy women with unique job opportunities. In 1952, Lieutenant Ruth Carolyn White became the first woman officer on active duty to be designated as an engineer and classified as a Navy engineering duty officer, electronics. White, assigned at the Bureau of Ships in Washington, D.C., was involved in training electronics personnel. She traveled frequently and worked with the men aboard ships and in shipyards to develop training modules.[73] Lieutenant Genevieve Koester, a civil aviation liaison officer with the Joint Staff, Commander in Chief, Pacific Fleet, represented the Navy in the U.S. delegation to the fourth session of the International Civil Aviation Organization's air traffic rules division in Montreal in 1950. A certified commercial pilot, she had been a research associate in guided missiles at the aeronautical engineering department of the University of Michigan.[74] Chief Jean W. Duncan was an instructor in the Navy Department's Link Trainer unit in Washington, D.C., instructing Navy pilots on instrument flight.[75]

While small naval medical facilities, such as the infirmary at Chincoteague, Virginia, and the Marine Air Station at Cherry Point, North Carolina, saw no patients from Korea, larger institutions, such as the Philadelphia Naval Hospital, received several dozen patients at a time, many of them severe frostbite cases, and the hospital in Oakland, California, became the psychiatric center for all patients from Korea and the Pacific.[76] Meanwhile, others such as the Army's Tripler Hospital in Hawaii, where the NNC's Captain Geraldine Houp and Lieutetnant Eveline Kittilson (McClean), were serving, had a continual stream of casualties. "They came in huge plane loads . . . many of them still had the dirt from the battlefield on them. They received hot meals, hot baths, and had their dressings changed," Houp recalled.[77]

Those waves of patients came in on the C-54 Skymasters and the C-97 Globemasters. Outfitted as complete medical stations and staffed by two Air Force flight nurses and two male technicians, they carried some 150 patients a trip. The nonstop 3,921-mile flight from Tokyo to Honolulu was fifteen hours, then it was on to Kelly Field near San Antonio, Texas, the hub for patients destined for hospitals east of the Mississippi. Similar numbers came through Travis Field in California, the switching point for patients destined for the western half of the United States. In the first ten months of the war, from July 1950 through April 1951, the Military Air Transport Service (MATS) flight nurses evacuated 22,300 war casualties and patients from the Pacific to the United States, more than 6,000 in December 1950 alone.[78]

By the time the Korean War broke out in June 1950, flight nurse Janice Feagin (Britton) had already served one tour of duty transporting American military patients from Korea to Japan. She had also taught flight nursing techniques stateside. Given her experience, the Montgomery, Alabama, first lieutenant expected to immediately ship out to the theater of war. Instead, Feagin was sent to Alaska on special maneuvers.

Back in the Orient late in 1950, Feagin found flight nursing in a combat zone demanding—and sometimes dangerous. Although American forces controlled the airspace between Korea and Japan, accidents sometimes happened. Once, Feagin recalls, the plane she was traveling on actually ran out of gas on the runway. "The co-pilot told me afterward he was scared until he saw me in the cabin putting on my lipstick."

Working on the ground could be equally

First Lieutenant Janice Feagin (Britton), an Air Force flight nurse, loads a C-46 with blankets, Thermos bottles of coffee and water, and a tank of oxygen in preparation for an air evacuation flight from Korea, December 1950. U.S. Air Force Photo, Janice Feagin Britton Collection, Women's Memorial Collection.

hazardous. Feagin remembers evacuating a group of Korean orphans ("the babies in dresser drawers") as the enemy hovered nearby. Waiting for patients to arrive from a close-in combat area on another occasion, Feagin and her crewmates heated their C rations on a fire in a burning supply depot while listening to the sound of enemy guns and mortars.

Hardest of all, though were the irregular hours caused by weather and events at the front. At one point Feagin flew twenty-one straight days "from 4 or 5 A.M. 'til as late as 1 A.M." Other times her squadron did "literally nothing." The rigors of the job sometimes dampened the women's morale, but when sixteen flight nurses fresh from the states arrived in 1951, "all of a sudden no one wanted to leave."[79]

Stateside, Lieutenant Patricia Bright (McClain)'s experience was typical of many Air Force nurses. Bright was on duty in the operating room at the 3750th Medical Group at Sheppard AFB, Texas, when six airmen, critically injured in an automobile accident, arrived. She received a letter of commendation for her actions that evening, and another in March 1953 when another accident involving five airmen from Sheppard taxed the resources of the small Bowie, Texas, clinic where they had been taken. Three of the airmen were stable enough to be transported to the base hospital, but two were too critical to be moved and the base sent an emergency medical team to Bowie to help, with Bright as the officer in charge.[80]

WAF were assigned to more than twenty Air Force bases around the country during the Korean War. More than half were engaged in technical work, including maintaining and installing radio and radar equipment, rigging parachutes, and translating coded messages. Others worked in administrative positions supplying, feeding, and transporting troops, and paying the resulting bills. Many worked as medical technicians, as dental assistants, radiologists, and therapists. Women could be assigned to 450 different jobs and to thirty-four of forty-two airman career fields.[81]

Airman Third Class (later Second Class) Elizabeth Alden (Roe) and Airman First Class Frances Hourihan had one of the Air Force's more glamorous jobs: flight attendants with the Military Air Transport Service. Westover AFB, Massachusetts, was the home of the 5th WAF Squadron, which had 265 airmen, most of whom worked in ground-based jobs. Alden acknowledged that while she and Hourihan did get to go shopping and dining in Europe, their job still could be routine, boring, and occasionally even dangerous. Most flights were to Germany with a stop at the Azores, but weather played havoc with the schedules. Other destinations for the giant, double-decker C-97 Stratocruisers, which had a capacity of 130 passengers or twenty tons of cargo, included Tripoli, Iceland, and Labrador. Passengers included enlisted personnel and officers and their families, as well as civilian employees and their families. Occasionally, Air Force women flew aboard medical evacuation flights to attend the crew, while flight nurses and corpsmen took care of patients. Women were not included on flights to Greenland because there were no accommodations for them there.[82]

Other Air Force women earned less traditionally female assignments. Sergeant Viola McLarnin was an engineer in an altitude chamber, where she was responsible for training pilots to withstand unpressurized conditions when flying above ten thousand feet. Part of her preparation for this assignment was completion of a six-month course in medical aviation.[83] Staff

Sergeant Josephine DeAcetis (Schell) was the only woman at the 513th Reserve Wing of the 512th Troop Carrier Wing in Wilmington, Delaware, again breaking the rule that women were not to be assigned to any station alone.[84]

During the Korean War the Air Force also gradually increased the number of women assigned to replace male airmen at USAF Headquarters in the Pentagon. Initially, sixty women were added every two months, then sixty WAF per month, until a total of 475 had been met.[85]

In the same time period, the 1063rd WAF Communications Squadron at Maxwell AFB pioneered a new, nationwide, 128,000-mile, push-button high-speed teletype network that operated twenty-four hours a day. Sixty-five selected women and eleven male airmen were trained by Western Union and Air Force instructors. The switching section was capable of handling 1,200 messages an hour and averaged 3,400 words per minute.[86]

Women assigned to the 1060th Communications Group manned a state-of-the-art communications terminal located deep within the Pentagon, described in one service magazine article as "long aisles filled with tall machines covered with push buttons and colored electric lights, which make a muffled clatter like high speed typing." Machine language "is a maze of holes punched through a paper tape, plus some weird jumbles of printed letters and figures." More than half of the personnel of the 1060th were women (the Air Force was aiming for 70 percent) and they clearly impressed the visiting *Armed Forces Talk* reporter. "With speed and efficiency, they make sense of what could be a chaotic mess in just a few minutes."[87]

The Air Force maintained four other modern communications terminals across the United States, all tied to a worldwide network. The Air Force sent women communications technicians to relay stations, wire and radio rooms, and code and cryptographic centers linked to Army and Navy communications centers as well. One of the teletype relay centers was located at Carswell Air Force Base in Texas. Sergeant Jacquelen McCracken (Henderson) and (no rank available) Medelon Marshall (Hook) were among WAF enlisted assigned there in 1952.[88]

In early 1952, by now Major Jeanne M. Holm, became the first WAF officer to attend the Air Command and Staff College at Maxwell AFB in Alabama. The World War II WAC veteran was fresh from her only Air Force assignment in Germany and fully conscious of her pioneer status. She knew she needed to prove to the Air Force that women were capable of excelling, especially at a school known to be a place where the Air Force prepared leaders. As the lone woman in a class of 499 male officers, Holm buckled down to learn Air Force lingo, command philosophy, how the Air Force believed it should fight wars, how to put a staff together and how to function on a commander's staff. Later that year, she moved into a Pentagon job as staff administration officer of WAF Director Mary Jo Shelly's office.[89]

As the Korean War was nearing its end, it seemed probable that Air Force women's battle to maintain their place in the military had been won, or at least that was the impression left by recruiting material. A 1953 WAF recruiting brochure entitled "Smart Women" claimed that, while the majority of assignments were in administration, medical service and supply, "there are plenty of jobs open to WAF that are directly linked with the flying program such as weather observers and forecasters, control tower operators, flight stewards, parachute riggers, and radio and radar technicians." The brochure profiled women in these jobs, but failed to profile any women assigned to the more traditional clerical jobs to which most Air Force women were assigned. Instead it boasted of air traffic specialists (flight attendants on MATS flights), who attended a Kelly AFB course that familiarized them with the Boeing C-97 Stratocruisers, Douglas C-54 Skymasters, and Douglas C-74 Globemasters on which they would work. It showed Sergeant Ida B. Arenson, a parachute rigger, who received the ultimate praise: "Working alongside 12 male airmen at the parachute repair shop at Westover AFB Mass, she is proving daily that women can handle this exacting responsible work as well as men can." It went on to chronicle her training at Parachute Riggers School at Chanute AFB in Rantoul, Illinois, after basic training. As a senior parachute rigger, she was responsible for inspection, repairs, and modifications on about one hundred parachutes each month. In addition, she inspected and maintained emergency devices such as life rafts and oxygen masks.

The brochure promised swift promotions for women in meteorology and climatology. Would-be weather observers would be sent to Chanute AFB for twelve weeks of training toward the rating. The brochure exclaimed, "Whether it's aiding a fighter, bomber or transport pilot in formulating his flight plan, or transmitting local information quickly around the world, the WAF finds that weather observing grows more interesting every day. Trained Air Force technicians can predict weather up to 48 hours in advance with 85 percent accuracy."[90]

The WAF Band, or 543rd Air Force Band, was another highly touted and highly visible recruiting aid. Former WAC Marybelle J. Nissly, who conducted the first WAC band during World War II, had been invited back into the military in 1951 to start an Air Force women's band. The offer included captain's bars and she didn't resist. The WAF band performed at ceremonies and celebrations across the country.[91] She retired as Major Nissly.

The majority of Air Force women, however, served in assignments of a more traditional nature. For example, the Air Force contracted with Oklahoma A & M University to train 275 stenographers starting in July 1951. Air Force women at Carswell AFB in Texas also served as cheerleaders for the Carswell Air Force Bombers football team.[92]

Nonetheless, by the end of the Korean War, American servicewomen had again established a presence around the globe. They had been integrated into each branch of the service. And once more they taught the military a valuable lesson. To quote again the *New York Times Magazine:* "if the military wants capable, enthusiastic and ambitious young women as well as young men in the service, it must give them opportunities for progress in a particular career field."[93]

The nurses who served during the Korean War era lacked no such opportunities, and it is their story to which we now turn.

CHAPTER 7

The Nurses in Korea—Under Fire and on the Move

It seemed we were never safe, never settled and all the while the casualties
kept coming.
—Captain Phyllis LaConte, chief nurse of the 8055th MASH[1]

Our duty hours are as long as we can keep standing.
—Army nurse Captain Oree Gregory (Michaels), 25 July 1950[2]

Our convoy was attacked, and the nurses spent the remainder of the night
in a ditch lit up by gunfire and burning vehicles. About sun-up we got out
and started treating the wounded, who by this time were coming in pretty
fast. All that day we worked on the roadside: operating, treating for shock.
We lost eight.
—Captain Eunice Coleman, chief nurse of the 1st MASH and one of the
"Lucky Thirteen" who survived a 9 October 1950, attack[3]

I T IS FITTING that the only American military woman on
duty in Korea 25 June 1950, the day the army of Commu-
nist North Korea crossed the 38th Parallel and invaded South Korea, was an
Army nurse, Captain Viola McConnell. The nurses and the few medical
specialists who served in theater during the Korean War would once again
prove how essential military nurses are in war. The example they set of military women performing under fire in time of war cannot be disputed.
There would be a handful of other American military and civilian women
in Korea during the years of the conflict, but it was the nurses whose role in
that war would become the stuff of near legend within the military. For the
general public, however, the image of Korean War–era nurses that too often
comes to mind is a distortion drawn from popular culture. The movie and

later television series *M*A*S*H*, the most prominent example, reflects the relatively static second and third years of the war. During its horrific first months, military women, like men actually fighting the war, were almost constantly under fire and on the move.

The United States had withdrawn its occupation forces from Korea a year before the war started, a quid pro quo to the Soviet Union's withdrawal. Both former allies had left behind military missions to aid North and South Korea in establishing their own "defense forces." McConnell was assigned to the Army dispensary at Camp Sobinggo, near Seoul, part of a group of five hundred or so U.S. military personnel identified as the Korean Military Advisory Assistance Group. Her duties included caring for the families of other U.S. military personnel and acting as a consultant to Korean Army nurses.[4]

The day after the invasion, McConnell escorted 643 American military dependents out of the country on the only vessel available, a Norwegian freighter. Captain McConnell had her hands full during the journey. The evacuees included four pregnant women close to term, an individual with a skull fracture, a baby with pneumonia complicated by chicken pox, another baby with a strangulated hernia, five babies with diarrhea, and two elderly women, one of whom was senile and the other suffering from advanced arthritis. Three of the pregnant women went into labor during the journey, and the fourth began to show signs of miscarrying.[5]

The *Rheinholt,* which usually carried fertilizer, had been built to accommodate a maximum of twelve passengers. Its crew gave their bunks to the sickest passengers. McConnell quartered the women with young children in the kitchen. The women who did not have children and those with older children slept on G.I. blankets in the holds of the ship. "We had 277 children under the age of one aboard," McConnell remembered. "We also had several missionaries aboard [one missionary was a woman doctor] who helped tremendously, and a wonderful United Nations nurse from the Netherlands." After two days, the freighter arrived at Fukuoka, Japan, where the evacuees found shelter at the 118th Station Hospital. (McConnell would receive a Bronze Star, with the Oak Leaf Cluster for extraordinary contributions in evacuating the dependents from the war zone. She would also return to the war zone for another assignment.)[6]

DEPLOYING INTO DANGER: 1 JULY – 15 SEPTEMBER 1950

> As the North Korean Army pushed U.N. forces southward down the peninsula, Mobile Army Surgical Hospital (MASH) units deployed into the theater and set up at the port of Pusan and the towns of Taejon and Taegu to

the north. The 8054th MASH remained in Pusan throughout this period. The 8055th MASH retreated with U.N. forces from Taegu and followed them southwards toward Pusan. Other MASH were also pushed south. U.N. forces established a perimeter around the port of Pusan, which they were ordered to hold at all costs. Casualties were high, and as many as possible were taken to Japan by hospital ship. Army hospitals in Japan expanded rapidly, stretching staff to capacity.

The medical departments of each of the services struggled to get medical units, including nurses, into the Korean Theater as rapidly as possible. They succeeded; the first two MASH units arrived in Pusan on 6 July five days after the arrival of Task Force Smith. The majority of Army nurses assigned to Korea worked in MASH units, with others in field, evacuation, and station hospitals. Nonetheless, nurses were in short supply in the theater in the early days of the war, with only about one hundred on duty two months into fighting.[7]

Living conditions in Korea were miserable for American military personnel. During August, a severe drought and high temperatures caused more Marine casualties than the enemy. Fleas and flies were extremely difficult to deal with and helped to spread the numerous "fevers of undetermined origin" that felled high numbers of soldiers. Malaria cases began appearing before the war was a month old. Water was scarce and had to be imported and rationed. Wounds from the battlefield were often contaminated with dirt, rice, human excrement (used by Korean farmers as fertilizer), maggots, and gangrene. In August, when the war was going badly for U.N. forces, psychiatric admissions skyrocketed.[8]

Originally, MASH units had been intended to be sixty-patient mobile treatment facilities, just one step up from battalion first aid stations manned by male physicians and medics. Their mission was to treat nontransportable patients from the battalion-level aid stations and move them to field, evacuation, or station hospitals as soon as possible. Because of the large numbers of casualties in the early days of the war, however, MASH units rapidly evolved into two hundred–bed ("half-scale") or larger evacuation hospitals.[9]

The first Army nurses to arrive in Korea were those of the 8054th and 8055th MASH, both of which deployed from Yokohama, Japan. Captain Ann Steele, chief nurse of the 8054th MASH, remembered the terse announcement that informed her she was going to Korea. "On the morning of July 2, there was a knock at the door, and a messenger stated, 'Be ready to move in four hours, destination unknown.'" Other members of the unit were similarly startled by their sudden orders.[10]

With twenty-one other Army Nurse Corps (ANC) officers, Steele picked up field equipment and medical supplies and moved out 3 July arriving at Pusan three days later. The hospital set up in Pusan because the port city was accessible by rail and there were abandoned buildings that could be used—a mixed blessing at best. Steele's unit set up the hospital in an abandoned middle school that had no water or electricity. Classrooms became hospital wards, and the school science laboratory was turned into the operating room with the addition of five portable operating tables that had been packed in footlockers.

In a deserted American housing area formerly occupied by American military advisers and their families (who had left on the *Rheinholt*), the nurses found tables, dishes, mops, and brooms. Working around the clock, they scrubbed floors, walls, and windows, tore up sheets for bandages, washed towels in pails, and—one day after they landed—began caring for battle casualties from the 19th Infantry Regiment of the 24th Infantry Division. This was day five of the war. In the following twenty-four hours, 750 casualties (including North Koreans) poured into the hospital, which had barely enough room for four hundred patients.[11] Within weeks, the hospital had grown to twelve hundred beds and had expanded into four different buildings scattered around the city. During the months of August, September, and October the units had five operating tables in use twenty-four hours a day.[12]

The 8055th MASH was activated on 1 July and assembled at the 155th Station Hospital in Yokohama with twelve nurses who had been working at Tokyo General Hospital. They were the chief nurse, Captain (later Major) Phyllis LaConte, plus Captains Margaret Tollefson, Cecilia Kerschling, and Elmira Dalrymple, and Lieutenants Mary Keefe, Margaret Blake, Beulah Annspach, Neta Zinn, Marie McMinn, Eleanor Church, Ethel Cole, and Mary E. Angelich.

The dozen nurses had two days to get ready. They packed bedding rolls, tents, mess gear, gas masks, helmets, field shoes, and fatigues. The one-piece, dark green fatigues for field wear were novelties to the women who were used to wearing neat duty dresses. Novelty aside, the nurses soon discovered that the field clothing did not fit them; everyone ended up with clothing that was either too large or too small. But there was no time for alterations; they just had to make do.

On 3 July with each nurse carrying her own field pack, the unit boarded the train that would take them to their port of embarkation. Forty hours later, at 7:00 A.M. on 5 July, they detrained at the Sasebo railroad yard and were treated to C rations for breakfast. That afternoon, they boarded the USS

Titania. Escorted to Korea by a destroyer, they docked at Pusan early on 7 July, and were trucked to their temporary home, a school building. The group spent the rest of the day uncrating, sorting, and repacking surgical equipment and other medical supplies; the next day, 8 July, they left Pusan aboard a dirty Korean train for Taejon, where they were to support the 24th Infantry Division. They arrived in Taejon around 7:30 in the morning of 9 July and received their first casualties at two that afternoon. As with the 8054th the crush of patients was almost double the unit's capacity. LaConte recalled, "Supplies were scarce. Among the patients were U.S. and U.N. soldiers, and North Korean POWs, some of whom were three-year-old children injured by hand grenades. Seeing these children upset many of the nurses. Some of the prisoners had gaping, festering wounds several weeks old. They had been hiding in the hills, afraid to surrender."[13]

Blake, McMinn, and Church received the patients in the preoperative and shock wards, cutting away clothing to expose wounds, starting blood and administering penicillin. After a physician assessed the patients, corpsmen moved them to the operating room. Tollefson supervised the OR with Dalrymple as her assistant. Keefe was scrub nurse, Kerschling was anesthetic supervisor, and Zinn was anesthetist. The OR could handle up to four patients at once and remained open twenty-four hours a day. The anesthetist simultaneously cared for two surgical patients. Angelich was in charge of post-op, aided by Cole and Annspach. Patients usually remained twenty-four hours before being transferred from the 8055th to another hospital.[14]

During the rest of July and into early August, Taejon fell to the enemy and the 8055th MASH was constantly on the move. The months of July and August and the first half of September were disastrous for U.N. forces, as they retreated south down the Korean peninsula, closer and closer to the port of Pusan. Time and again, the nurses packed and unpacked as they set up the hospital in barns, schoolhouses, rice mills, and churches. They became so proficient at setting up that they were able to break down or rebuild their hospital within two hours.[15]

After five days in Taejon, the unit was ordered south to Yongdong. The four-hour, flea-infested train ride to their new station seemed endless, the nurses recalled. LaConte remembered Kerschling saying, "The train didn't need an engine, the fleas could have pushed it." At Yongdong, the unit occupied what had been a school for agriculture. Housing facilities at both Taejon and Yongdong were crowded and equally bug-infested. All the nurses and their gear were crowded into one room. Water had to be hauled from a nearby well. They bathed using their helmets.[16]

After several days at Yongdong, they were ordered to move south again, this time to Taegu, where the hospital set up in a large, clean building that had formerly been a teachers college. Throughout this entire period, the nurses worked twelve-hour days. The 8055th MASH remained in Taegu only until 18 August, when it moved south back to Pusan.[17]

Working together, the medical services rapidly established an efficient chain of evacuation for U.N. casualties. The wounded were flown by helicopter from the front lines to MASH units and field hospitals, and then placed on hospital trains rather than trucks (the Korean roads were treacherous) to the coast. Throughout the war, usually only one nurse, accompanied by a medical corpsman, was assigned on each eighteen-hour train journey to the coast. Initially, the hospital trains consisted of a few converted boxcars and coaches. The trains were slow and inefficient and the nurse was kept frantically busy. For example, early in July Chief Nurse Steele of the 8054th found herself the lone nurse tending one hundred wounded men on the eighteen-hour trip from Kumchon. The train "crawled

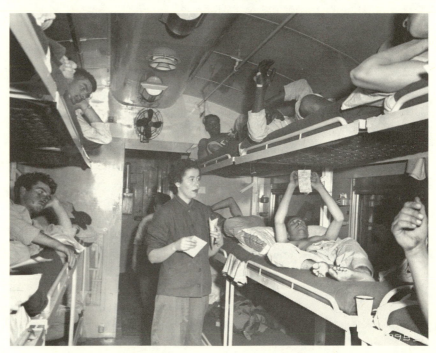

Army nurse First Lieutenant Catherine F. Malvey checks emergency medical tags of wounded patients being evacuated via hospital train from Tai Tong, Korea, 2 December 1950. U.S. Army photo, National Archives (111-SC-353955).

over a 50-mile length of narrow gauge track, sidetracked constantly by military movements. Several times, the track was blocked by Korean refugees, who tried to claw their way aboard. The two MPs assigned to the train were kept busy pushing Korean refugees away from the doors of the train," *Newsweek* reported in March 1951.[18]

First Lieutenant Ida Haegele arrived in Korea in July 1950 and was assigned to duty aboard hospital trains. She described them as "really flea-infested passenger coaches, with litters laid across the backs of the seats, and most of the windows kicked out so that ambulance men could get the patients aboard. Much of my time was taken up by keeping flies and disease-bearing dust from the wounded, and bracing the litter cases against the jolting shocks from the uneven road beds."[19]

Once the trains reached Pusan, the patients were placed aboard a ship and evacuated to Japan. Casualties were taken to Japan solely by ship until mid-September, when U.N. forces consolidated their hold on southern Korea and were able to complete an airstrip capable of handling the heavy aircraft used for medical evacuation. Although the Navy had assigned three of its hospital ships to the Korean Theater at the start of the war, the first to arrive, the *Consolation*, did not reach Pusan until 16 August. Until then, patients were evacuated via an assortment of transport vessels. Army nurses served aboard the USNS *Keathley*, the USNS *Miller*, and the HMHS *Maine*, which plied back and forth from Korea to Japan. Sometimes it was also necessary to press into service old ferries (nicknamed "Red Ball" ships after the Red Ball Express highway of World War II fame). When the *Consolation* finally arrived, she was hailed with joy and relief. On board was Lieutenant Commander Bernice R. Walters, MD USNR, the first woman doctor assigned to a Navy ship, plus 29 male doctors, 30 Navy nurses, and 600 corpsmen and sailors.[20]

The air-conditioned *Consolation* was designed to carry 750 patients. During a push, however, that number could jump to more than one thousand. Each OR could handle two or three patients at a time. During busy periods, patients were lined up in the corridor outside the operating rooms and doctors and nurses worked around the clock. One nurse aboard the *Consolation*, Captain Helen Brooks, remembered that the intensity of the work varied dramatically: heavy loads of wounded in the first two to three days after a military engagement, OR staff nonstop for several days, then a gradual tapering off. Head wounds and orthopedic cases predominated.[21]

The first Army nurses assigned to the Korean Theater had been issued field equipment that they did not need; some things which they *did* need, however, were almost impossible to get, including uniforms that fit properly. Some nurses were issued firearms, although few of them had training in their use and care. Still, they were responsible for the weapons and the other heavy field equipment that they had to pack and carry. The shortage of clean water complicated both personal hygiene and professional tasks. The constant packing, moving, unpacking, repacking, and moving again was frustrating and exhausting. "It seemed as though we were never safe, never settled," said Chief Nurse LaConte. "And all the while the casualties kept coming."[22]

Medical personnel rapidly learned how to adapt to the difficult field environment, including, according to Major Mary Zoschak of the 8063rd MASH, the operating tent's dirt floors and operating tables perched on wooden platforms. "Our instrument and linen packs were sterilized in a steam autoclave outside the OR tent, (the steam) generated by gasoline. We used small individual instrument packs for debridements (the cleaning of large wounds prior to surgery) and minor wounds, and large instrument trays for major cases. We only had two portable lights. The overhead (operating) lights were improvised by using four light bulbs on a cross bar of wood with tin cans put over the bulbs for reflectors."[23]

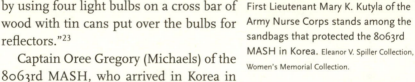

First Lieutenant Mary K. Kutyla of the Army Nurse Corps stands among the sandbags that protected the 8063rd MASH in Korea. Eleanor V. Spiller Collection, Women's Memorial Collection.

Captain Oree Gregory (Michaels) of the 8063rd MASH, who arrived in Korea in mid-July kept a diary of her experiences. Her account shows the constant upheavals medical units faced:

July 15—Due to sail with the 1st Cavalry Division.

Pohang, Korea, July 18—Disembarked . . . An ambulance took us seven miles to our first "home." . . . Slept under mosquito nets for the first time.

July 19—My helmet "bathtub" has been taken over by a friendly little green toad. If I take him out, he just sits there waiting for me to drip water from my washcloth on him. . . .

July 20—Tents torn down early this morning and we boarded our first train in Korea. Dirty, no toilet facilities. All we had to eat was C rations. It took us 12 hours to go a few miles.

July 21—An ambulance met us last night and took us to another tent home through pelting rain. One of the tents blew down, but we were so tired we slept through most of it. Up at seven this morning and ready for travel. Decided we could do with less equipment. Lieutenant Flannagan decided her shawl could go. Lieutenant Carrier had been out and came back bearing the lost article. When I thought I was unobserved, I dropped my gas mask in the tall weeds nearby. As I ducked back toward my tent, a GI called out "Captain, you've lost your gas mask." Finally I discovered he wanted it for himself. He got it. Still pouring when we got into trucks for the next lap. Our new home is an old dirty former school.

July 22—The heat is intense. Dirt and filth and flies as never before. We've been using everything available as mops, brooms, cleaning. We've got to be ready in 24 hours to receive patients.

July 23—I'll never forget these casualties; in all my 17 years of experience I've never seen such patients. Blind, or with legs, arms or buttocks blown off. Many chest and abdomen injuries. Many died despite skilled surgery.

July 25—Our duty hours are as long as we can keep standing. The boys are wonderful. I've never heard so many quiet "Thank you's" for the slightest service. No laundry facilities, we have to do it all by hand. The flies are green, large and heavy. They work in shifts with the mosquitoes. These were thin until the Americans arrived, but now they're so big and strong you think they'll break through the netting.

July 26—Our quarters are next to the mess hall—and no doors. So we bathe and the chow line marches slowly by. The operating room was in front of us and an armed guard walks constantly by the rear window. We've even lost any wish for privacy.

July 28—We are being evacuated. Last night we were told to stay dressed and keep near us anything we ourselves could carry by hand. We were in total blackness. The sky grew brighter and brighter from bursting shells. All packed and ready to leave when I saw Mac—silhouetted against the light from the guns—putting on make up in the dark! We left at 9:30 P.M.

Back to Pusan. But we didn't actually get away until 2 A.M. We waited in the open with our things for four-and-a-half hours. Light rain was falling like a mist and the mosquitoes had a double shift on the job. Finally a boxcar came into sight. . . . Commercial fertilizer mixed with chicken feathers and other trash was about an inch deep on the floor. We turned off flashlights. It's better not to know sometimes.

July 29—Slept well and arrived in Taegu at 7 A.M. We were welcomed at the 8055th hospital with a hot meal and hot water for a helmet bath. Heard that Major Smith died in a C-47 crash on her way to join us. Left at 1 P.M. for Pusan. Reached the 8054th Hospital at 2:30 A.M. on 30th. But an officer met us in front with the news that they had no room for us. We were directed to empty schoolhouse two blocks away.

August 2—This is a nice setup. Cool breeze from the sea of Japan and only four of us to a room. We're leaving for Chongwon on the Masan front. . . .

August 6—Arrived in Chongwon at noon with five new nurses. A school is again our home—but we are 17 to a room. Fleas and rats are added to flies and mosquitoes. Can't open the windows for air, because the rats walk up the sides of the building and get in.

August 8—We have patients everyplace—every type of wound and burn. . . . All the men have bloodstained letters they never had time to read. . . . Sometimes when they heard our voices, the boys would think they were back in the States. One private said: "My God! Not a real American nurse! Remove my bandages so I can see her!" But he was blind.

August 15—Flown to Chinja. The hospital is in buildings, but personnel is [sic] in tents on the ground. No lights and little heat. Our toilets are as usual "open air."

August 17—Our first American prisoners of war. Sad, happy, hungry, wounded, sick, lousy, cold—and very much afraid . . . even of fellow Americans. We did what we could. They're being evacuated by air to Japan as soon as they are able to travel.[24]

In November 1950 in Pusan, the 8054th MASH's generator exploded, destroying half of the unit's supplies. Fires and explosions were a little-acknowledged hazard of service at medical installations in both Korea and Japan during pushes when facilities were strained to the maximum extent.[25]

Particularly during the first year, medical personnel in the combat theater were plagued by staff and supply shortages. Getting supplies to hospitals was made more difficult by the low capacity of the ports and airports, none of which were near major cities. Shortages of critical items grew as supply vessels backed up waiting to enter narrow harbors. Captain Cathy Boles of the 8076th MASH reported that supplies were so difficult to obtain in the first full month of the war, July 1950, that the nurses ripped up sterilized bedsheets to make bandages. Her chief nurse, Captain Elizabeth N. Johnson, washed sheets, pillowcases, and blankets by hand to keep her unit supplied.[26] In a letter to the chief of the Army Nurse Corps, Johnson herself said only that she "pinch hit as general utility gal and laundress." In the battle theater and in Japan, nurses who saw a way to fill a need stepped in and performed, regardless of rank or seniority.[27]

The start of the war had a tremendous impact on the Army's station and general hospitals in Japan, as they had to expand rapidly to accommodate the flood of patients. In many cases, the older buildings in which hospitals were located were not up to the new demands, and the Army was forced to upgrade electrical, water, heat, and ventilation systems. But some hospitals were mushrooming well before these systems could be upgraded, creating more difficult living and sometimes even hazardous working conditions for patients and staff. Early in 1951 a fire in nurses' billets at the 8th Station Hospital injured two nurses, one of whom was returned stateside.[28]

The mission of the Army's 5th Station Hospital also changed dramatically with the start of the war. Charged with the care of personnel at Johnson Air Base and surrounds, including Yokota Air Base and the 43rd Engineer Construction Battalion, its patient census had been dwindling before the start of the war and only eleven Army and Air Force nurses were assigned. Shortly before the war started, the staff received orders to shut down. Instead, as wounded poured in from Korea, the hospital mushroomed and by August 1950, the second month of the war, there simply were not enough nurses, forcing those already on duty to work drastically extended hours. Many patient evacuees had preexisting medical disorders (such as peptic ulcers) exacerbated by combat stress, and a surprising number were evacuated due to severe diarrhea, caused by drinking contaminated rice paddy water. Korea also seemed rife with infectious hepatitis.[29]

When the war began, the 118th Station Hospital on Kyushu, Japan had a five hundred–bed hospital with forty-two ANC and two WMSC assigned. Huge numbers of evacuees poured in, including 643 women and children dependents of military personnel that left Korea on the USS *Rheinholt*. By the end of July, that hospital's nurses were working twelve-hour days and seven-day weeks caring for casualties, even though there was a steady transfer of patients on to Osaka and Tokyo via hospital trains.

In August and September, encephalitis, relatively rare in the U.S., reached epidemic proportions among troops, and the 118th received 280 cases, requiring intensive nursing care and medical attention. From the war's onset through the end of 1950, the typical workweek for nurses was eighty to one hundred hours.[30] First Lieutenant Clarissa Hicks, a physical therapist assigned to the 118th in the midst of the epidemic, had a patient load of forty encephalitis victims who suffered from a lack of coordination, muscular rigidity, and tremors and were at risk for permanent disability due to muscle shortening.[31]

The small number of Army and Air Force medical specialists assigned to Japan were, like Hicks, quickly overwhelmed during the first months of the war. As the patient load in military hospitals soared, physical therapists and dietitians were faced with impossible numbers of patients. Although military hospitals were often able to hire Japanese nurses to supplement Army and Navy nurses, there was no local pool from which to draw dietitians and PTs. Although new hospital units arrived in Japan, each with two dietitians and two PTs, the medical specialists who were in place when the war started had to wait a long time for additional help or rotation out. No occupational therapists would be assigned to Japan until the following year.[32]

Despite the suddenness of the war and the considerable environmental and physical barriers present in Korea, within two and a half months, the medical services had (through considerable cooperative efforts) established a workable evacuation scheme. Army, Navy and Air Force nurses were an integral part of the medical care and evacuation process. The Air Force could not evacuate casualties from the Korean theater as rapidly as needed until engineers built up the existing runways to accommodate heavy aircraft, putting increased pressure on the Navy. The Navy made ready two hospital ships, the USS *Repose* and the USS *Benevolence,* to supplement the beleaguered *Consolation,* but the *Benevolence* never made it to Korea. On the ship's trial run off the coast of California, it was rammed by a freighter and sank within minutes. The *Repose* arrived in Pusan on 20 September 1950, just in time to accept casualties from the Inchon invasion.

The Military Air Transport Service (MATS) was responsible for evacuating sick and injured soldiers and sailors from Japan to the United States. At the war's start, MATS controlled 202 C-54s, but the majority of those were assigned outside the Pacific. The forty-eight C-54s available for use in the

Far East were restricted to carrying ambulatory patients, so the command called on a small fleet of larger C-47s to evacuate litter-bound cases. Twenty-four USAF flight nurses were assigned to the 1453rd Medical Air Evacuation Squadron based both at Hawaii's Hickam Field and in Haneda, Japan. As the war continued, MATS assigned forty more transports to the Pacific, taking them from the European and Continental divisions. The command found it more difficult, however, to find the necessary flight nurses to accompany the additional aircraft.[33]

At the beginning of the Korean War, the AFNC was 1,088 strong, with eighty-three on duty in the Far East where the war was quickly creating a shortage of trained flight nurses. Some flew as many as three evacuation missions a day during emergencies, with some flight nurses averaging more than three hundred flying hours a month. In an attempt to lighten their load, the Air Force eventually assigned general duty nurses to aid evacuation flights. Because many of these nurses had not received flight training, experienced flight nurses had to be assigned to partner them.[34]

Military transports flew from Tokyo or Haneda to Guam, to Kwajalein (an atoll in the Marshall Islands), to Johnston Island, to Hickam Field, Hawaii, and finally to Travis AFB in California. Before the war was a month old, the first load of Korean War casualties were evacuated from Haneda (20 July 1950) and reached Travis after a total flying time of forty-two hours. Cabin noise aboard the C-54s was so loud that the Air Force moved to limit the number of hours personnel were in the air to one hundred per month to prevent hearing loss. This meant that the command needed even more flight nurses. By the end of September, 106 Air Force nurses and 22 Navy nurses were flying Pacific routes. Usually one nurse and two technicians worked aboard C-54s, and two nurses and two technicians were assigned aboard C-47 flights. MATS airlifted a total of 3,650 patients in September 1950, month three of the war.[35]

Captain Catherine Danker (Dombrowski) had been stationed at Vance AFB in Oklahoma when she received a call from her chief nurse telling her to pack her bags for a yet-to-be-determined station in the Pacific. Danker was eager to go; she wanted to become more directly involved in the war. She had applied to flight nurse school, but the call to the Pacific came in first, and she flew air evacuation missions from Tachikawa AFB in Japan to Midway and Wake Islands, all without the benefit of flight nurse training. One flight in particular stood out to Danker: the navigator became disoriented over the ocean and flew off course. The aircraft made it to Wake Island, but with just fifteen minutes of fuel to spare.[36]

VENTURING NORTH OF THE 38TH PARALLEL: 15 SEPTEMBER – 25 NOVEMBER 1950

In mid-September, three months into the war, U.N. forces conducted a surprise invasion of the port of Inchon, easily defeating the North Korean defenders. Relishing victory at last, U.N. forces drove the remnants of the North Korean Army far beyond the 38th Parallel. The 1st MASH, the 8055th MASH, the 64th Field Hospital, and other Army hospitals followed U.N. forces northward. The rail and road chain of evacuation to medical installations and hospital ships in Pusan was stretched both in distance and time. The Air Force alleviated the situation somewhat by establishing medical air evacuation from Korea to Japan. Navy hospital ships continued to evacuate patients. Meanwhile, Army hospitals in Japan continued to expand and grow in number.

Thirteen Army nurses with the 1st Mobile Army Surgical Hospital landed on the beach at Inchon on 15 September in support of X Corps. Their chief nurse, Captain Eunice Coleman, described their frequent moves and the supply problems the unit faced in letters to her family in the States. The unit frequently set up operations in tents, and they quickly ran out of tent-repair kits. They had problems heating the tents, and had to use gasoline because fuel oil was not always available. The two biggest supply problems, Coleman wrote, were blood and blankets. Nurses and others frequently donated their own blood and gave up their blankets for patients.[37]

Because mobile and evacuation hospitals followed the troops and battle lines were extremely fluid in Korea, Army nurses often found themselves closer to the front lines than planners had anticipated, despite the similar experiences of World War I and II nurses. When the nurses of the 1st MASH were en route from Inchon to Pusan during the early morning of 9 October 1950, with the 7th Infantry Division, the convoy was attacked. "The nurses spent

Major Eunice Coleman, chief nurse of the 1st MASH, packs equipment in preparation for another of the unit's rapid moves with the troops, February 1951. National Archives (111-SC-358196).

the remainder of the night in a ditch. . . . The whole sky was lit up by gun-fire and burning vehicles," Coleman wrote her family. "About sun-up we got out and started treating the wounded, who by this time were coming in pretty fast. All that day, until 1500, we worked on the roadside: operating, treating for shock and putting the wounded in the ambulances for care. We lost eight men and quite a number of supplies and vehicles. When all was clear, the convoy started again and arrived at Pusan by midnight."[38] After the ambush, the thirteen nurses in the unit began calling themselves the "Lucky 13."[39]

"Enduring hardships seldom, if ever, equaled by U.S. Army nurses . . . 13 nurses of the 1st Mobile Army Surgical Hospital (MASH) have carried lipstick, cologne, and tender care to the battlefields on both sides of the Korean Peninsula," Pacific *Stars and Stripes'* reporter Tom A. Hamrick told his G.I. readers in a story picked up by many papers in the United States—especially in the nurses' hometowns, which were always mentioned. Pictures of the nurses washing their tin mess gear in steaming garbage cans and "lingerie" (actually G.I.-issue long johns) in their helmets were splashed across more than two pages of the paper.

They were nicknamed the Lucky 13 after surviving some twelve hours trapped in a ditch—while providing care to six critically wounded men—when

First MASH's "Lucky 13" nurses in their tent in Korea, 14 February 1951. National Archives (111-SC-358193).

a battalion of communist forces surprised a thousand-yard-long line of U.S. and U.N. vehicles snaking single file through a mountain pass at 3 A.M. Though several were World War II veterans, "most had never before heard a shot fired in conflict. All through the night they huddled together . . . as tracers penciled lines in the night overhead and ricochets screamed from the hillside rock." The siege lasted twelve hours and then recurred a mile further.

"But even in this there was a touch of humor." Hamrick wrote, "Twice Major [Eunice S.] Coleman (Duke, Oklahoma) whispered out their names—all but one answered. Finally she resorted to crawling down the line of Army Nightingales, touching each one. Then she found First Lieutenant Marie Smarz (Shelton, Connecticut). Why hadn't the lieutenant answered? 'I was afraid the Reds would hear me.'"

The Thirteen, who adopted a pocket-sized Mickey Mouse as their lucky charm, "have asked for no special privileges. . . . Not that the men of the 1st MASH would not have been happy to offer any and everything, but there has been nothing to offer. . . . [Compared to World War II in Europe and the Pacific,] Korea has been colder, with the temperature ranging downward to 20 below zero. Korea has been a seesaw, with the unit continually moving. . . . Korea has been shattered, leaving only Army canvas for a roof."

"On February 8, the MASH nurses observed the 50th anniversary of the Army Nurse Corps, six days late because the unit had been on the road."

Ten of the Lucky 13 posed in the bare-bones tent Hamrick called their "boudoir." They are, left to right, Captain Mary Ward; Captain Eleanor Faust, Kingston, Pennsylvania; Major Coleman; Lieutenant Smarz; Lieutenant Olive Rockabrand, "'Rocky' to everybody back in Oconto, Wisconsin"; Captain Marion Benninger, Shillington, Pennsylvania; Lieutenant Clara Kehoe, Bealton, Virginia; Lieutenant Ann Haddock, Morgantown, West Virginia; Captain Jane Thurness, Columbus, Georgia; and Captain Margaret Zane (Fleming), Utica, New York. Not pictured are other 1st MASH nurses First Lieutenant Faye Sullivan, Seattle, Washington; First Lieutenant Winifred Jensen, Milwaukee, Wisconsin; Second Lieutenant Cornelia Newton, Calistoga, California, and First Lieutenant Margaret Brosner, Columbus, Ohio.[40]

The 121st Evacuation Hospital landed at the port of Inchon on 25 September. The unit was short of anesthetists, so on the voyage from Yokohama, six ward nurses were instructed in the fundamentals. They observed the anesthetist at work for several days after the landing and by the time the unit reached Yongdong were functioning surgical anesthetists. This enabled the 121st to keep eight operating tables going day and night.[41] The 121st was not the only unit to face a shortage of anesthetists. Anesthetists were in such short supply that during the 8076th MASH's first week in country their sole nurse anesthetist, Lieutenant Katherine Wilson, was obliged to hop among as many as six operating tables until she herself was "nearly anesthetized from the fumes."[42]

Then Captain Anna Mae McCabe (Hays), who later was chief of the Army Nurse Corps and the first woman general in the U.S. military, recalled the 4th Field Hospital's landing at Inchon harbor "15 days after Marines. We had to climb down the side of the ship on rope ladders to reach landing crafts that took us to shore. We went into the first building we saw, and someone said 'The nurses can sleep here.' And, it was filled with excreta. I remember taking my shovel, cleaning out this excreta, and putting down my canvas bedding roll."

Several of the male officers scouted the Inchon area looking for a suitable building, McCabe (Hays) said, and located an old two-story school, where her unit moved and set up the hospital. The "mess hall" was a group of picnic tables, where the staff took meals despite very cold weather and, McCabe (Hays) remembered, "a distinct odor of excrement that seemed everywhere in the country." She added, "When I compare Korea with my experiences in World War II, I think of Korea as even worse than the jungle in World War II, because of the lack of supplies and lack of warmth."[43]

After the successful U.N. landing at Inchon, the 8055th MASH received orders to Taegu. U.N. forces were finally advancing again on territory they had earlier been forced to abandon. After just four days in Taegu the 8055th was again ordered forward, this time to Kumchon. The hospital moved slowly in trucks, jeeps, and ambulances over poor, rutted, dusty, narrow, and winding roads. At Kumchon, the hospital and living quarters were in an old school building "recently made air conditioned by the artillery raids," wrote LaConte in her monthly report. The staff ate C rations and warmed themselves at bonfires. Korean civilians, badly burned during bombing raids, were discovered in nearby hills hiding and afraid, and given medical care.[44] The 8055th remained in Kumchon two days before receiving orders to Taejon. Passing Yongdong en route, they discovered that the agricultural school they had recently called home had been destroyed. Later at Taejon, in an accident on duty, Captain Margaret Blake sustained the second-degree burns on her face and hands that got her evacuated to Tokyo Army Hospital, then back home to recruiting duty.[45]

Because of Korea's primitive road, rail, and port facilities, transporting patients by ambulance often meant traversing dirt trails that snaked through mountains and valleys. Some of the worst fighting occurred in these rocky, six thousand–foot mountainous areas of Korea, where ambulances and other motorized vehicles were unable to go; litter bearers often had to carry the wounded for miles on terrible terrain.[46] Although the Army relied on trains during the first months of the war, the Korean rail network was limited. Large areas in the countryside were untouched by rail lines, and the war had damaged many of the existing lines. Even if there had been time and materials to repair bombed-out bridges and railroad tracks, few rail facilities could be counted on during the first year of the war. The fluid front lines only complicated the already hazardous rescue of wounded; because of the condition of the roads and railroads, travel on either was extremely hard on sick or wounded soldiers.[47]

The hospital ship *Repose* had arrived at Pusan five days after the Inchon invasion and served as a station and general hospital until 27 October, when it evacuated 189 casualties back to Japan.[48] Larger than the *Consolation*, eight decks deep and equipped to feed and service fifteen hundred people, its medical personnel included fifteen nurses, thirty doctors, three dentists, and 150 corpsmen. It was a fully functioning hospital with modern X-ray equipment, a laboratory, and physical therapy equipment such as whirlpool baths and infrared lamps. The patients even had bedside lights and multi-station radios near their beds, a stark change for war-weary soldiers evacuated from a rice paddy.[49]

Ensign (later Commander) Lura Jane Emery remembered that the *Repose* arrived in Pusan harbor with only fifteen Navy nurses aboard instead of the normal complement of thirty. The Navy was having problems staffing its ships and hospitals because so many recalled reserve nurses were ineligible for service. Although the shortage allowed each nurse on the *Repose* to enjoy her own stateroom, the fifteen worked exceptionally long hours for the first two weeks in Pusan. "Patients from the Inchon invasion started coming in after noon on the day of our arrival. Trainload after trainload of them. The patients were hoisted up from the dock to the ship. Most of them had just received first aid. They had been lying in buildings and other facilities. The doctor would triage on deck and assign the men to wards. I was the ward nurse in charge of the neurosurgery patients. Those first two weeks, we were lucky if we got two hours' sleep out of every 24 hours. We worked 'round the clock. We air-evacuated patients out to Japan after three days. After the first couple of weeks, things calmed down somewhat and we only had to work from 8 A.M. to 10 P.M. every day. It was months before we got additional nurses."[50]

Working long hours on a hospital ship left little time for recreation but Lieutenant (jg) Lura Jane Emery of Cambridge, Pennsylvania, and her fellow nurses occasionally went to the beach and once toured Pusan with one of the

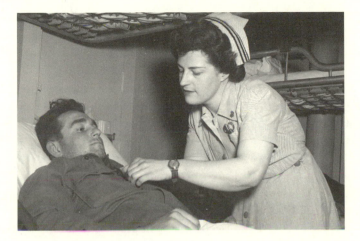

Aboard the USS *Repose*, Navy nurse Lieutenant (jg) Lura Jane Emery listens to Sergeant Paul E. Robinson, U.S. Marine Corps Reserve, C Company, 7th Marines, tell how he stopped a sniper's bullet, Korea, December 1950. U.S. Navy Bureau of Medicine and Surgery Archives.

ship's chaplains. Sometimes the women would be invited to other military units for dinner and dancing. Holidays were always celebrated as well. Emery remembers her first Thanksgiving in Korea, when the cooks on the *Repose* were "roasting turkeys all night for the Marines." At Christmas, the nurses filled empty penicillin bottles with different colored water and hung them on the tree that the ship's supply officer found for them. Mail too was a welcome diversion, although it was often slow in arriving. "When we played bridge," Emery recalls, "we used to bet on the number of bags coming in."[51]

Although milk was difficult to obtain in the Far East, the hospital's menu included most stateside dishes including ice cream, a huge morale booster. The ship made its own for patients, but could not produce enough to send ashore.[52]

By then the war had developed a standard procedure. Army hospitals at the front would administer first aid, after which the wounded would be evacuated to the hospital ships via train, which took twelve to twenty-four hours. According to Ensign Eveline Kittilson (McLean), a nurse on the *Repose*, the train patients usually arrived in Pusan late in the day, but in better shape than those who arrived by helicopter at all hours. The latter were usually in critical condition, needing immediate surgery, and—coming straight from the field—were often dirty and lice-infested as well.[53] Kittilson's colleague Emery remembered, "I caught lice from the patients. Took me two weeks to get rid of them."[54]

The Navy's sea transport service ships (MSTS), which carried troops and supplies to the battle theater, became a way to evacuate the wounded from the battlefield back to Japan. The Navy put eight of these ships into use as hospitals on their return trips, usually with two nurses aboard. Dolores Cornelius (no rank available), who sailed in August 1950 from San Diego to Kobe, Japan, with a unit of Marines, recalled, "the sea was so rough that many of the men took seasick. . . . We had . . . two appendectomies the first night out. I had taken anti–sea sickness pills before I knew about the two operations, and I was worried that I wouldn't be alert enough to work. But I was in such distress that I was fine." During the Inchon landing, Cornelius's MSTS ship was in harbor and took on casualties for transport to the *Repose* when the landing was over.[55]

In late September, air evacuation emerged as the critical element of the evacuation chain as engineers completed reinforcing the runways of certain airports to support large transport aircraft. The Air Force began using C-47 Skytrains and C-54 Skymasters for medical evacuation. Patients whose recovery was expected to take longer than thirty days now could be air-evacuated to Ashiya or Itazuke air bases in Japan, and from there, to the nearby 118th Station Hospital.[56]

As winter moved in on the 8055th during the month of October, the MASH unit moved four times in twenty-two days. LaConte went to the quartermaster of the 24th Division to obtain winter clothing for her nurses, who were suffering, and hit the jackpot. She brought back long johns, undershirts, water-repellent outer pants and wool sweaters. "We are wearing the same winter issue the men do and the smallest shoe they have is a size 8. We wear lots of extra socks with the shoes," she wrote home.[57]

On 16 October, while stationed at Kaesong, the 8055th's nurses traveled to a portable shower unit operated by the 1st Cavalry Division. They were delighted; it was their first opportunity to shower since 27 September, having since that time indulged only in helmet baths. A relaxed atmosphere permeated the American units. For the first time, the war seemed winnable. U.N. forces had crossed the 38th Parallel during the first week of October, and by the nineteenth they captured the North Korean capital of Pyongyang, where a MASH unit set up operations.

When the 8055th moved to Sinmak, north of the 38th Parallel, the nurses made the trip in an ambulance convoy. The hospital was located in tents on the edge of an airstrip, the first time the unit had set up in tents. It was here that the hospital treated North Korean POWs for the first time. The prisoners were on their way to the 4th Field Hospital near Seoul.[58]

The 8063rd and the 8076th MASH units passed the 8055th at Sinmak on their way to the north. Within days, the 8055th followed them and set up at Pyongyang, where nurse Lieutenant Nan L. Porter wrote, "October 29 was a day to remember, as we had our first fresh meat and eggs in several weeks. Everyone raved about the delicious hamburgers. We were even happier over the honest-to-god steaks the following day and the ham that night for supper."[59] The nurses also enjoyed hot showers, courtesy of the 2nd Division's portable shower unit. To the south, other medical units established hospitals at Inchon, Seoul, and again at Taegu, strengthening the chain of evacuation. The Army established a hospital at Kimpo Air Base, and flight nurses of the 801st Squadron set up a hospital tent and provided care to the wounded awaiting air evacuation. Three C-54 flights a day ferried casualties from Kimpo to Itazuke.[60]

By 1 November, U.N. troops had reached as far northward as Wonson and Hamhung. The 24th Infantry Division was north of the Chong Dong River and only eighteen miles from the Yalu River, the border between North Korea and China. Chinese troops briefly harassed units of the 24th Infantry and 1st Cavalry Divisions in late October, only to vanish in early November. The lull was deceptive; the Chinese had not faded back into China as it appeared, but were massing in preparation for another onslaught. The Yalu River froze in mid-November, allowing the Chinese to sneak troops and supplies across into North Korea, where they concealed their presence in the Taebaek Mountains.[61]

On 22 November, twenty-seven U.N. POWs were released by the enemy and treated at the 8055th, still at Pyongyang.[62] In October, a rotation policy was established for nurses who had been in the country for three months. In many units the majority of the nurses applied for rotation. Replacements for nurses who had been in-country ninety days arrived throughout November. Major Luluah Houseknecht Martin became chief nurse Thanksgiving Day, when Captain LaConte rotated out to Japan.[63]

U.S. troops were moving north so rapidly that they began to anticipate a rapid end to the war. Confident, they paused to celebrate a traditional Thanksgiving. The mess sergeants of the 8055th pulled out all the stops and provided the unit with roast turkey with all the trimmings.[64] Sailors aboard the hospital ship *Repose* prepared Thanksgiving dinner for more than seven hundred Army personnel, who were by then far in advance of their own mess facilities. The food arrived on shore ready to eat.[65] To Army troops and medical personnel who had been living on "Class B" food supplies, that Thanksgiving was special indeed. Class B rations are described in one of the

121st Evacuation Hospital's monthly reports as "canned Vienna sausage, luncheon meat, salmon, beef and gravy, pork and gravy, and corned beef, a rotation which rapidly became unpalatable to staff and patients."[66] The respite was short; fighting resumed almost immediately.

26 NOVEMBER 1950 – 15 FEBRUARY 1951

> *A Chinese counterattack drove U.N. forces back down the Korean Peninsula, and Army hospitals moved with the troops. Taken by surprise, some medical units were forced to flee right ahead of the enemy. Casualty numbers spiraled upward, complicating the hospital moves. The Air Force conducted a mass evacuation of patients to Japan and safety, and Navy vessels evacuated exhausted troops from Hungnam Beach. The Navy hospital in Yokosuka was inundated with soldier and Marine casualties. On 23 December, the 8th Army suffered another setback when its commander, General Walton Walker, was killed in a jeep accident. General Matthew Ridgway replaced Walker, and managed to instill confidence into his shaken troops. U.N. forces continued to lose ground throughout the first weeks of 1951, however, and by February both Inchon and Seoul had fallen to the enemy.*

In late November, General Walton Walker's 8th Army retreated rapidly from the Chongchon River to Pyongyang, pressed hard by overwhelming numbers of Chinese communist troops. The hospital ship *Repose* was ordered to proceed upriver to Chinnampo, which required the ship to creep through thirty miles of dangerously shallow water. "The most perilous part of the assignment was the task of steering the ship along the narrow, winding channel without running aground," said the ship's captain, C. H. Perdue. "We couldn't use the main channel because it was heavily mined. The channel we used was only 26 feet deep in places and the *Repose* draws 25 feet 6 inches. We didn't have much water under our keel."[67] Ensign Lura Jane Emery recalled, "We had two mine sweepers go up the channel, one on either side, looking for the mines that were supposed to be there. They didn't find any."[68]

At Chinnampo, the ship took on casualties around the clock for two and a half days, evacuating 750 wounded U.N. troops before they could be trapped by the Chinese. "We didn't pull out until our wards were full to the brim," Perdue said.[69] Emery added, "We put all the weapons and ammunition the patients had on them into the hold of the ship. That added to the weight of the ship . . . [and we] had to wait for a very high tide."[70]

ANC Lieutenant Genevieve Connors (McLean) had been working as an OR nurse in Japan when the war broke out, and volunteered for duty in the combat theater. She joined the 8055th MASH at Pyongyang on Thanksgiving eve, just in time for the disastrous Chinese invasion. Connors remembered the evacuation helicopters and their loads of wounded soldiers arriving at the hospital from the front lines. "The choppers, with a patient locked on an outdoor stretcher-holder on each side of the aircraft, touched down on a road of mud six inches deep outside the door of a schoolhouse that had been converted into a hospital," she said. "Medics carried the wounded into the receiving room of the hospital where portable X-ray equipment was used to diagnose the damage and view chunks of metal still inside bodies [before] the soldier was then quickly carried into the operating room."[71]

At the time of the Chinese attack, the 64th Field Hospital also was at Pyongyang and was quickly inundated with casualties from the north. According to the unit report for November, "On the evening of November 29th, a communist light plane added to the excitement by dropping some nuisance bombs on the outskirts of the airport adjacent to the hospital." The 64th was bombed the next night as well. The word "excitement" was an understatement; during this period, all forward clearing stations were evacuating their patients to the presumed safer 64th. The 64th's personnel worked around the clock until the unit was ordered south. Because the enemy was so close, the nurses were flown out of Pyongyang to Ascom City.[72]

Pyongyang fell to enemy forces on 5 December, but the 8055th did not leave the city until 4 December. The unsigned monthly report said, "December 3 will be remembered by all for a long time. . . . [H]our after hour past our hospital was the sight of retreating troops in trucks, trailers and tanks. Everyone was wondering what would be in store for us. . . . Before the night was over and without warning the sky lighted up not very far from us followed by terrific explosions and severe blasts. . . . No one wasted any time dressing. . . . [T]he remainder of the night . . . what sleep could be had . . . was with our combat boots on." The 8055th moved south the next morning, with the nurses flying to Kimpo.

Before the month was over, the 8th Army had fallen back nearly three hundred miles and air-evacuated all its forward hospitals. Medical units withdrawing with the 8th Army had to care for massive casualties. The 8055th MASH moved six times during the six months Connors was with

them. "We went where the action was," she said, "either forward or backward, depending on the front line's location." Some dozen trucks hauled
the staff and equipment. Medical personnel often had to chip ice out of the
wash basin in order to scrub and their hands were constantly raw and red.

"We all worked round the clock when the patient load was heavy," Connors recalled. "Our steel helmets served as washbasins for our faces and
clothes. At night, sleeping was difficult because we were all squeezed into
one room on cots only 16 inches apart. The potbellied stoves had to be shut
off at night to conserve oil. This forced us to bed down in long johns, topped
off by pajamas and sweaters. Once at about midnight, enemy fire struck the
ammo dump near us, and it exploded like an earthquake. The glass wall of
our bedroom burst inward onto our cots. We all jumped up in the darkness
and hopped in our sleeping bags—like kangaroos—to the safety of the op-
posite wall."[73]

The 8055th's chief nurse, Major Houseknecht, remembered that first
winter in Korea very well. "The troops were moving so fast and we were
right behind them all the time. If we weren't busy taking care of the patients, we were packing up and moving on. Sometimes the hospital packed
up after staying only one night."[74] Among the casualties the MASH nurses
treated were soldiers of the 8th Army's 2nd and 7th Infantry Divisions,
which had been at the Yalu River on Thanksgiving and narrowly managed to escape being completely enveloped by the enemy. The 2nd Division
was ambushed at Kunu-ri, losing three thousand of its seven thousand
soldiers.[75]

The 8th Army's retreat exposed the 1st Marine Division, which had been
on the Army's west flank and did not receive orders to retreat until it was almost too late. The enemy circled and trapped the Marines in the high
mountain passes along the northeast coast of the peninsula. The Marines
fought their way out of the Chosin Reservoir along narrow, ice-slick trails,
with Chinese forces holding the high ground above them, constantly lacing
the roadway with mortar and machine-gun fire. The temperature plummeted to 24 degrees below zero. "The men were ragged, their faces swollen
and bleeding from the icy wind. A few were without hats, their ears blue
from the cold. Others were barefoot, because they couldn't get their frost-
bitten feet into their shoepacs," wrote war correspondent Marguerite Higgins.[76] Casualties were enormous, but the Marines stayed together in a col-
umn and struggled with their equipment, their wounded and their dead, all
of whom were carried out. Their ammunition dwindling, they forged on-
ward despite mounting casualties. Finally, they made it to the ports of Hung-

nam and Hamhung, where Navy vessels awaited them. The 1st Division's casualties were taken to the naval hospital at Yokosuka.[77]

At Hungnam Beach, the 1st MASH took care of a great many "worn, weary and frozen Marines,"[78] one of whom recalled, "The medics brought me out of the hills, put me in a pre-op room. And then this girl—this nurse—took over. Bathed me. Got the anesthetic ready. She looked deader than I did. On her feet for two days, two nights. I was gonna tell her she should have been on the stretcher instead of me. But I conked out."[79]

The by now famous "Lucky 13," the nurses of the 1st MASH, remained with the troops on Hungnam Beach until 13 December, days before the beach fell to the North Koreans. As the nurses climbed aboard the landing craft that was to take them to the waiting Navy vessel, the remaining soldiers watched grimly. "Everything seemed all right as long as you nurses were here," one young man said sadly.[80]

Between 13 December and Christmas, "We were on ship and close enough to shore to see the activities of the enemy," Captain Eunice Coleman, chief nurse of the 1st, recalled. "The enemy air force was active at night, so it was necessary to black out the ship then. On Christmas Eve, the ship sailed out with all the other Allied vessels. We arrived in Pusan Harbor on December 25 and transferred the patients onto the hospital ship *Consolation*. The nurses of our unit debarked on December 27, and were conveyed by vehicles to another school house." (Captain Coleman received the Bronze Star with the V Device for valor for her service in Korea.)[81]

At Yokosuka, some two hundred Navy nurses worked around the clock treating frostbite and wounds. During the months of December and January, the hospital received some five thousand Marine casualties, and the nurses worked three to four days straight without respite. Loaded hospital trains arrived every three to four hours. Soon, the wounded were stacked in bunks in every ward; when room ran out there the wounded were placed on litters that lined the hallways. The living quarters of nurses, corpsmen, and doctors were pressed into service as wards, and personnel doubled up, then tripled up in the remaining quarters.[82] "We were getting patients in so fast," remembered Navy nurse Florence Alwyn (Twyman), "that when we left our quarters in the morning we wouldn't know whether or not we would have a bed to sleep in that night, because they kept moving us around to take patients. We had patients in triple decks."[83]

A line of litters that seemed never-ending caused gridlock in the hallway outside the three-table OR. Many of the most serious injuries caused by frostbite and land mines resulted in amputations. Lieutenant Commander

Helen Fable, who supervised the nurses and corpsmen in the OR, said, "The operating room was called the 'Dirty Room,' because that's where all the worst cases were sent. The staff performed triage in the hallway, deciding which patients should be operated on first."[84] After a hellish several weeks, things calmed down again and the patient census dropped somewhat. Some patients were sent back into the theater, while others moved on to specialized treatment centers. Those who would never fight again went home. By springtime, the staff at Yokosuka was working regular shifts.

With the Chinese communist attack, air evacuation became more important. The staff at Army hospitals throughout Korea worked in cooperation with Air Force medical personnel to empty Army hospitals by airevacuating as many patients as possible to Japan. The 801st flight nurses staffed aircraft that lifted Marine patients from Yonpo Airfield to Itami Air Base and Army patients from Yonpo to Itazuke. On 5 December, when the 8th Army decided to evacuate Pyongyang and all forward hospitals, cargo command lifted 3,925 patients, the Korean War's largest single-day medical airlift.[85]

Major Marguerite H. Liebold, of the 801st Medical Air Evacuation Squadron (MAES), a particular flight during which the crew was told that if they

Army nurse Lieutenant Nancy Cahill (Newton) with children of the Taejon, Korea, orphanage, 1952. The children's clothing was donated by Sears, Roebuck and Co. The 171st Evacuation Hospital staff provided medical care, medicine, food, and construction crews for the orphanage. Nancy Cahill Newton Collection, Women's Memorial Collection.

saw a white sheet on the field they could land; otherwise, the enemy had taken the field and they should get away as quickly as possible. They landed and got their patients out minutes before the field fell. Liebold received the Air Medal for her actions.[86]

Not all the evacuees were American military personnel. AFNC Lieutenant Grace Chicken of the 301st MAES, who served in Korea from September 1950 until January 1952, vividly recalled the air evacuation of a thousand Korean War orphans, in fourteen aircraft, from Kimpo to the United States via Japan. It was December 1950, just after the Chinese attack; the children were undernourished and many had no winter clothing. Chicken was responsible for eighty-six children, including twelve infants; the oldest was eight. The children "kept staring at me with big eyes and strained little faces the entire trip. I couldn't do anything for them.

Navy nurse Lieutenant (jg) Rose Ellen McCluskey (McCullough) gives a small Korean girl a treat at a Mother's Day orphan's party aboard the hospital ship USS *Haven*, Pusan, Korea, 13 May 1951.
Rose Ellen McCluskey McCullough Collection, Gift of William I. McCullough, Women's Memorial Collection.

I'd have given half a month's salary for some candy or crackers." The planes landed in Japan, where the children spent the night, then left for the United States the next day. After landing in Japan with the orphans, Chicken was getting ready for bed when she was asked to fly back to Korea to pick up two critical patients. She quickly ate a bowl of soup and returned to duty. By the time she returned to her quarters from that second trip, she had been on duty twenty-four hours. She slept the next day through.[87]

At the air base in Tachikawa, personnel of the 13th Medical Group, which included fourteen Army and Air Force nurses, worked in a cantonment hospital (one composed of temporary structures). The hospital was far from comfortable. In one ward the maximum temperature "on a good day" might be between thirty-four and forty-eight degrees, and as the patient census grew, so did the rat problem. The two hundred–bed capacity hospital had expanded to three hundred beds in November, but even this 50 percent increase was no match for the increase in patient load—364 percent. During the expansion the hospital also lost three nurses to reassignment. Begin-

ning then and each month thereafter, the hospital received nearly two hundred additional ambulatory patients evacuated from Korea. To make room,
all enlisted men moved out of their barracks and into tents. Corridors and
hallways became wards. Nurses worked twelve-hour days. All leaves and
passes were canceled. In addition to regular duty, nurses spent long hours
training corpsmen how to handle shock, administer plasma, and operate
oxygen equipment.

The incoming wounded were in terrible shape. Many suffered from frostbite and trench foot. The average combat soldier had lost from twenty to
thirty pounds; although food had been available, many were unable to eat
because of nerves.[88] In December 1950, the first brutal winter of the war in
Korea, the Army established a special cold injury center affiliated with
Osaka Army Hospital in Japan. More than four thousand soldiers were
treated there the first winter, and the program was resumed the following
winter. Second Lieutenant Catherine Owen (Horne) was assigned to frostbite cases, and treated U.N. troops from a wide variety of nations. She remembered that she and her boss, Chief Physical Therapist Inez Moffet,
treated as many as 225 patients a day, with the help of three enlisted technicians. The work was demanding and tiring. Before patients could go into
surgery, they often had to be bathed in whirlpool baths to remove debris
from the field that could cause postoperative infections.[89]

AFNC Captain Barbara Northrup (Thomas), remembered that the first
thing frostbite patients were required to do was quit smoking, because nico-
tine could shut down small capillaries and impede blood flow to damaged
skin and extremities, compounding the risk of amputation. Patients also
were required to exercise ten minutes out of every waking hour to restore
and maintain a maximum range of motion. Consequently, the cold injury
center constantly needed physical therapists.[90]

Army nurses in Korea knew that despite the unflattering bulk of their
clothes (mostly men's winter issue that they wore to combat the cold), their
presence invariably cheered the exhausted, demoralized soldiers. Nurses
realized that the patients enjoyed being cared for and even just talking to
women from home. MASH First Lieutenant Margaret Zane (Fleming) told
a reporter that she made a point of wearing bright red lipstick every day. She
also confided that although she did not have much room for clothing in her
pack, she made sure to bring a pair of filmy red pajamas because simply
having them with her made her feel more feminine.[91] "Patients complain
when we don't have our lipstick on," Second Lieutenant Margaret Feil (Reese)
of the 4th Field Hospital told the *New York Times*, adding, "I don't feel like I

am making a big sacrifice here. If they offered to let me go [home], I wouldn't. I want to finish this."[92]

When General Matthew Ridgway, the well-known World War II airborne commander, replaced 8th Army Commander General Walton Walker after Walker's accidental death two days before Christmas, he found American troop morale exceptionally low. Reeling from the unexpected entry of the Chinese communists into the war, humiliated to be once again in retreat, and bitterly disappointed that they were not "home for Christmas" as MacArthur had promised, the troops' misery was exacerbated by one of the worst winters in Korean history.

Ridgway knew soldier morale had to be restored if U.N. forces were to accomplish anything in Korea. A dynamic, positive-thinking individual— his troops affectionately called him "Old Iron Tits" because of the two grenades he wore on his chest—he had a reputation for being always on the go, always willing to listen to complaints and do something about them. Ridgway had no patience for negative thinking: he was not interested in subordinates' defensive plans; he wanted to know how they were planning to attack. But the U.N. troops were not yet ready to go on the offensive.

In early January 1951, U.N. forces were forced to evacuate Inchon and Seoul, which the Chinese had invaded in December. The 4th Field Hospital hurriedly evacuated to Taegu. ANC Captain Anna Mae McCabe (Hays) remembered "traveling south from Inchon to Taegu by train in the middle of the night—not knowing when a railroad trestle over which we traveled would be blown up." Once set up at Taegu, she recalled that in one night alone, seven hundred patients came in to the four hundred–bed hospital. A Quonset hut OR had eight operating tables going at once, each separated by sheets draped on wires and held in place with shower clips. McCabe (Hays) recalled that the unit had to request more neurosurgeons.

The OR functioned twenty-four hours a day. Surgeons and nurses had hardly any time to sleep, and dentists were pressed in to assist. "We wore woolen underwear, fatigues, and a pile-lined jacket under a white scrub dress. It wasn't a dress. It was a patient's gown. We always kept our hats on our heads and the hat was covered with a white gauze covering. And we always wore men's woolen socks and boots. But we were still cold,"[93] McCabe (Hays) said.

Three months before women won the right to vote in 1920, United States Army nurses won relative rank—officer titles but not full officer status. Both achievements acknowledged the World War I contributions of thousands of nurses and other American women volunteers. Although the 1920 Army Reorganization Act did not guarantee nurses full equality with male officers, it was an important first step. Another Army nurse born that year trailblazed through many of the next steps and went on to become the first woman general in the history of the U.S. military.[94]

Army nurse Captain Anna Mae McCabe (Hays), 4th Field Hospital, Korea, in 1950 or 1951.
Courtesy Anna Mae McCabe Hays.

The child of Salvation Army officers of Irish and Welsh descent, Anna Mae McCabe (Hays) grew up in an atmosphere of profound religiosity, patriotism, self-sacrifice, and very little material wealth. "What probably made me want to become a nurse was the fact that my father was always talking about my being a (nurse) missionary," said the Buffalo, New York, native.[95]

Within months of Pearl Harbor, McCabe (Hays) joined the University of Pennsylvania's 20th General Hospital. She served in the China-Burma-India Theater in Assam, India, "one of the worst malarial districts in the whole world . . . (and) very busy with combat casualties from Burma (and) the famous Merrill's Marauders."[96]

In 1947, McCabe (Hays) returned stateside to Fort Dix, New Jersey, and two significant promotions; she made captain, and she applied for integration into the Regular Army when the Army-Navy Nurse Act of 1947 (Public Law 36-80) granted permanent equal pay and commissions for nurses. "Selected officers were given the opportunity to apply. . . . I didn't even think twice about it."[97]

McCabe (Hays) was head nurse of the Fort Myer, Virginia, outpatient clinic when the Korean War began in June 1950. By August, she had deployed with the Army's 4th Field Hospital. "The Marines entered Inchon. We landed about 15 days later."[98] In the next fourteen months, she and thirty-one other nurses treated more than 25,000 patients.

During two unforgettable weeks that first September, U.N. forces tried to recapture Seoul. With nearly a quarter-million soldiers engaged in intense fighting as the Navy's 7th Fleet shelled Korea's eastern coast, somewhere in the middle the 4th Field Hospital coped. "A little scary. . . . The USS *Missouri* was firing over us. . . . And we were close to Kimpo Air Base when it was bombed," she recalled.[99]

"The operating room was open 24 hours. . . . Most nights we had only three or four hours of sleep." On her thirty-first birthday, 16 February 1951, wounded were lined up "on litters covering the entire . . . floor, with hardly an inch of pathway. . . . (The) cold . . . probably affected us more than anything. When an abdomen was opened, steam rose from the body. . . . Water was scarce and (when) we had to scrub our hands for surgery, the water would drip one drop at a time, from a handmade tank. We had deep cuts in our fingers. . . . We would carefully boil the instruments and then, at the end of the day, we would carry the remaining water back to our quarters . . . to wash our clothes."[100] McCabe (Hays) soon earned the necessary twenty-eight points in a forward area to rotate out to Japan. "After working in Korea . . . I thought that Tokyo would be just a lark. But we were working 12 hours or more each day."[101]

In early 1952, McCabe (Hays) returned home, reassigned to the Army hospital at Indiantown Gap, Pennsylvania. "I always went to school wherever I was. I always wanted to improve myself." She remembers she wasn't in uniform but wearing "a pretty green and white Irish skirt . . . looking at the bulletin board to see what courses they were giving and this gentleman came up behind me and he said, 'Can I help you?'" She and William Hays, dean of students at Lebanon Valley College, married in 1956.[102]

Following other prestigious tours of duty (including Walter Reed Army Institute of Research and a stint as one of three Army nurses assigned to President Eisenhower), she returned to a changed Korea in October 1960 as chief nurse of the 11th Evacuation Hospital in Pusan. "It was peaceful and absolutely delightful."[103]

On 8 November 1967 President Lyndon B. Johnson signed Public Law 90-130 removing the rank ceiling on military women and Hays made full colonel. "I was extremely proud . . . there had been only five colonels in the Army Nurse Corps as late as 1966."[104] Two months later, she became the thirteenth chief of the Army Nurse Corps during the most ferocious fighting of the Vietnam War. Four years later on 11 June 1970, Army Chief of Staff General William C. Westmoreland pinned a brigadier general's single star on her shoulder, then one star on the shoulder of WAC Director Colonel Elizabeth P. Hoisington, and planted kisses on two new general officers, saying "I hereby establish a new protocol for congratulating lady generals!"[105]

General Hays retired in 1971 with the Distinguished Service Medal and the Legion of Merit with an Oak Leaf Cluster. After nearly thirty years military service and three major wars, she noted that the "forgotten war," Korea, remains the most difficult for her to forget.

"Would I do it again? Absolutely!" she said. "I wish I could go right now."[106]

On 9 January, the 121st Evacuation Hospital was ordered east of Taegu and forced to locate in the midst of rice paddies because personnel could find no other level terrain. The hospital set up in tents, and the resulting cold, dampness, and drainage problems made for an extremely uncomfortable month and a half, until the unit again received orders to relocate.[107]

In mid-January, U.N. forces once again established a defensive line at the 38th Parallel and halted the Chinese-led offensive. In February, the 8055th MASH was ordered to Chonan. Nurses picked up, packed up, and traveled by ambulance to Chochiwon, where they boarded a hospital train for the rest of the journey. A lone male medical officer acted as the nurses' escort. On 7 February, the 8055th moved again, this time to Suwon by ambulance bus, where general duty nurses went on twelve-hour shifts to accommodate the wounded.[108]

Several Navy nurses remembered air raid drills at Yokosuka during this time. Each time, the staff was instructed to collect all the ambulatory patients, as well as those who could be safely moved on litters, and take them into a series of tunnels or caves that had been constructed by the Japanese during World War II. There, patients' litters were mounted on rails affixed to the walls. Patients in traction could not be moved from the wards, so some nurses and corpsmen were assigned to remain with them. The nurses remembered only one actual air raid that was real and not a drill.[109]

Like other hospitals in the evacuation chain, the Army's 8th Station Hospital in Kobe, Japan, a five-story brick building, had tripled its capacity from one hundred to three hundred beds in the second month of the war. By September it had 560 beds, and by December, eight hundred. The number of nurses, eleven plus one WMSC, remained the same. When the Chinese attacked in November, the hospital began getting the first frostbite cases. Now, in February, the eighth month of the war, an explosive outbreak of atypical pneumonia, which the staff labeled "K fever" after the Kobe hospital, felled forty-five persons, including eight of the eleven nurses.[110]

ANC Lieutenant J. E. "Jake" Jacoby, assigned to the Far East Theater the previous November, traveled to Japan on a troop ship with eight thousand soldiers and just twelve new nurses—"fillers" assigned to hospitals that had lost nurses due to rotation into Korea. At the orthopedic ward of the 382nd Station Hospital, set up in an old factory building some fifteen to twenty miles outside Osaka, "The first thing they told me to do was to go to my ward and set up ninety beds," she recalled. "I was amazed. I said, 'In one ward?' 'Yup!'" Within a week, a ship loaded with casualties arrived from Korea. "The first thing we did was get them into beds. The nurses would start undoing bandages, because some of them had been in transit for some time, cutting off casts, and looking at the wounds. Basically, these guys had been debrided at least once in Korea, put in casts, and thrown on the ship. When we started taking off casts, we saw maggots."[III]

Another concern was amputees who might become suicidal. Jacoby recalled she was always warning other nurses, "If they go to the latrine then you tell your personnel, 'If they are not out of that latrine in two to five minutes, you get in there! And don't care what they say.' One of the young nurses found one in the bathtub with his head tied under the water. She pulled him out, and she later thanked me, saying 'I really didn't believe you, Jake.'"[112]

THE UNCERTAIN SPRING: 15 FEBRUARY – 23 JUNE 1951

> *That spring, U.N. forces halted the Chinese offensive and slowly began to push the Chinese north beyond the Han River, recapturing Seoul. In early April, the president recalled MacArthur, and replaced him with Ridgway, who had been commanding the 8th Army. Increasingly dissatisfied with MacArthur's tendency to ignore orders, Truman wanted a man he could trust in the top job. On April 22, the Chinese communists launched another offensive north of Seoul. Although the communists were contained north of the Han River, U.N. casualties were extremely high. During May, the Chinese continued to push hard against U.N. forces north of Seoul. In June, the U.N. forces attacked the Chinese and drove them back. Casualties were high, and medical evacuations continued apace.*

In late February 1951, the 1st MASH moved forward from Suwon to Chechon, where except for the surgery, which had the luxury of being housed in a wrecked bank, the hospital was in tents. Communist forces advanced to within a few miles, gunfire punctuated conversations and headquarters left it to the commanding officer's discretion whether to pull back. Because of the condition of the roads and the large number of wounded at the hospital, he had little choice but to remain.[113]

By March, the 8055th was at Suwon, occupying a school. On 9 March, a helicopter crashed on takeoff in the hospital's "backyard" after dropping its load of patients; another went down that same day while rescuing G.I.s off a ridge at the front. Fighting was still fierce, but U.N. troops recaptured Seoul on 14 March. By 20 March, the 8055th was newly ensconced in Yongdong, in what one recalled as "the best building we ever had." The nurses were allotted three different rooms for quarters, as well as a "day room" with gauze curtains that looked "almost stateside." In less than a month, it was on the move again, and again in tents in Uijonbu on 11 April.[114]

"Jake" Jacoby rotated into the 8055th MASH that April and was immediately assigned twelve-hour night duty in the surgical tent, which left her with a lifelong hatred of tents. "At the time a lot bothers you because you're cold, you're hungry, and you are on duty. I won't even go to a circus if it is in a tent any more. A year in a tent—and in the cold and hot weather of Korea—is enough."[115]

Chinese communist forces launched a spring offensive on 22 April, pitting 250,000 men against U.N. forces along the now forty-mile front line north of Seoul. They broke through near the Imjin River and, on 23 April, U.N. wounded came pouring into the hospital by helicopter, ambulance, and rail. That evening, even the hospital itself was on the run, the nurses scrambling by ambulance for Seoul and temporarily separated from the unit. The next days were pure chaos.

Two days later the nurses rejoined the 8055th at Yongdong, where the hospital staff gratefully set up inside a building, but barely in time for the more than seven hundred wounded who came in 25 April. This time patients came in so fast that the wards could not fit them in. Even the corridors couldn't hold them. Some ended up in stairwells.

By 26 April the nurses were back at Suwon and back under tents, but for less than a day. Abruptly, the unit was ordered to repack and return to Yongdong, where they reestablished the hospital. Rumor had the enemy five miles from Seoul. Artillery fire sounded throughout the night. The rumbles shook the nurses' quarters, but, the author of the monthly report boasted, no one let it bother her.[116]

For many of the moves of the 8055th, its nurses rode in Army buses converted into ambulances. The only problem with this deluxe mode of travel, or so they told a newspaper reporter, was a dearth of places at which to relieve themselves in private.[117] The nurses of the 1st MASH confirmed this, laughing to a newspaper reporter about "holding up blankets to form improvised latrine walls during rest stops." They also told the reporter that they had used vivid red "Fatal Apple" nail polish to paint a "Nurses' Latrine" sign they put up wherever they happened to be camping.[118]

Air Force First Lieutenant Louise Ann Jenkins of Lansing, Michigan, was one of the relatively few African American nurses who served in the battle theater. A flight nurse with the 801st Medical Air Evacuation Squadron of the 315th Air Division (Combat Cargo), she provided care for wounded being evacuated from

Korea to Japan on huge Globe-masters.[119]

So uncommon were black nurses that when the U.S. Transport *Aultman* arrived in Yokohama in early 1951 carrying the first eight Army nurses assigned to Far East Command—all first lieutenants—it made news back home in the African American press.[120] Eight months later in September 1951, when one of those nurses, now Captain Eleanor E. Yorke, of Orange, New Jersey, rotated out of a MASH unit in Korea, she told the *Baltimore Afro-American,* "It was a terrible eight months, but I was too busy to be scared. We received the wounded 20 to 45 minutes after they were hit. . . . The helicopters flew continuously from dawn to dusk and the ambulances rolled on constantly. It got pretty rough at times, working under artillery bombardment . . . many times I was rocked to sleep in my Army cot from the reverberations."[121]

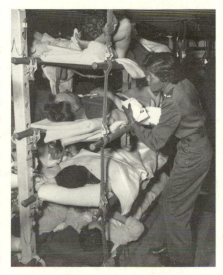

Air Force flight nurse First Lieutenant Louise A. Jenkins checks her patients on a C-124 Globemaster before an air evacuation flight from Korea to Japan, January 1953. U.S. Air Force Photo, Lillian Kinkela Kell Collection, Women's Memorial Collection.

When the 1st MASH moved forward again in mid-April, this time to Chunchon, they were too far forward when the Chinese Army closed in and had to be uprooted once more, returning to Wonju.[122] Nurses of the Army's 11th Evacuation Hospital arrived in early May. When hemorrhagic fever struck U.N. forces in 1951, the 11th Evac pioneered the use of the new Kolff artificial kidney on patients who went into kidney failure. The forerunner of modern-day renal dialysis machines, there were just thirty Kolff units in the United States.[123]

Soon after the war started, the Navy had ordered the USS *Benevolence* to Korea along with the *Consolation* and the *Repose.* When it was rammed and sunk during a test run, the Navy ordered the *Haven* into service as a replacement. Far from ready to deploy, the *Haven* did not reach Korea until early 1951. Medical personnel aboard numbered thirty nurses, twenty-five doctors, one pharmacist, 194 hospital corpsmen, three dental officers, and six dental corpsmen. The *Haven* was able to accommodate 797 patients in double-decker bunks in its eighteen wards, which varied in size from twenty-six to fifty-eight patients.[124] Once in theater, the *Haven* supported the 1st Marine Division. Although the ship did not have a helicopter platform, the crew rigged up a way for helicopters to land on pontoon barges and evacuate seriously wounded Marines to the ship in under twenty minutes. Whenever the 1st Marines saw action, the *Haven* was deluged with casualties. During the Chinese communist offensive of late April 1951, the *Haven*'s three large ORs went nonstop for seventy-two hours straight.[125] (In late 1951, the *Consolation* was ordered to California, where a helicopter pad was installed. By December, helicopters could ferry patients directly to that ship as well.)[126]

PEACE TALKS BEGIN: 23 JUNE – 22 AUGUST 1951

> *In June, a Soviet U.N. delegate indicated that the Chinese communists and their North Korean allies might finally agree to starting peace talks. During initial talks at Kaesong fighting was sporadic, as both sides held back and watched the peace table for signs of progress. Unfortunately, the respite would be short.*

When it became clear that the communists were interested in starting peace talks, President Truman told Far East Theater Commander Ridgway to inflict as much loss as possible on the enemy without inciting the North Koreans or Chinese into anything major. Ridgway ordered field commanders to submit for approval any proposed action involving more than a battalion, effectively limiting U.N. offensives.[127]

The peace talks began oddly. "At the first meeting of the delegates, I seated myself at the conference table and almost sank out of sight," recalled Vice Admiral Turner Joy, head of the U.N. delegation. The head of the communist delegation, North Korean General Nam Il, had purposely provided Joy with an unusually low chair, presumably so that Nam would appear tall and Joy would have to look up to him across the table. Joy switched chairs. It took the two groups ten days just to decide what they would discuss.

The discussions that followed were even more difficult, with the communists intent on portraying themselves as victors. Within weeks, outside events began having a negative impact on the talks. On 5 August U.N. negotiators suspended the talks after communist soldiers intruded into previously agreed-on neutral ground nearby. Five days later, talks resumed, but on 22 August the communists suspended them when U.N. aircraft violated the neutral area.[128]

The peace talks did seem to stem the tide of patients at military hospitals in Korea and Japan after July 1951, and supply shortages began to ease. Medical personnel at mobile, field, and evacuation hospitals all noticed significant improvements in their food. Staff at the 121st Evacuation Hospital actually got fresh meat and vegetables for the first time since they had been in-country. These Class A rations were a big morale booster to both patients and staff heartily tired of Vienna sausage.[129]

Despite recruiting problems at home, the handful of Army station hospitals in Korea were assigned at least one dietitian and physical therapist. The experiences of these professionals were as exemplary and varied (and under the same very difficult circumstances) as those of their nurse colleagues; at least one hospital commander complained, however, that they were women and not men. "It is the considered opinion of the undersigned [John G. Baxter, Colonel, Medical Corps, Commanding] that insofar as this theater is concerned a male officer should head the mess department and not a member of the WMSC, and it is doubtful as to whether the mess department of any numbered unit should be headed by a woman. The hours are long and strenuous requiring travel to ration dumps in cold and inclement weather. Strict disciplinary control over 40 enlisted men is another requirement more suited to a male officer."

Another of Baxter's complaints in the report, however, makes it clear he objected to women officers in any field situation. "This hospital has functioned near the combat zone all year, and we could have used more surgeons and male medical officers rather than the dietitians and physical therapists that have been assigned."[130] Baxter's report contained no specific complaints about less than adequate performance on the part of his women officers.

That WMSCs were more than capable of performing their duties under less than optimum field conditions is clear from the example of Major Ethel M. Theilmann, who received the Legion of Merit for her work in Korea as a physical therapy consultant to Army hospitals there. On assignment in Japan in 1950–51, Theilmann was asked to set up a rehabilitation program for several thousand civilian Korean amputees in three hospitals in Pusan. The Army had agreed to supply prostheses and trained technicians; it was left to Theilmann to organize this tremendous effort. Although she had difficulty obtaining translators, she was able to teach local doctors and nurses how to train technicians to carry out the program throughout Korea.[131]

Army PTs stationed at hospitals in Japan were very busy. "Never have I been in a situation where there was so much to do to help others and such an opportunity to do so much about it," one wrote a former schoolmate. "We get the patients soon after injury, so we can clean up the open wounds in whirlpool, and what is so important, keep the joints mobile before adhesions and contractures set in. The more serious cases are sent on to the States, but we are able to teach them how to exercise en route and thereby shorten their hospitalization." [132]

Another Army physical therapist wrote from Yokohama emphasizing the variety of nationalities of the patients she worked with. "We are currently treating Greeks, Netherlanders, Turks, Thailanders, Belgians, French and Ethiopians, none of whom speak or understand English, but learn fast and never cease chattering," she said, confessing she sometimes felt frustrated because she couldn't explain to them, "I know it hurts, but I can't always stop this treatment because of pain." Identified only as "Leith" in the professional journal that printed her letter, she added, "We need more people like you, Ruth, with training and experience, to pitch in and help us. . . . Knowing how you feel about citizenship and its responsibilities, I expect the return address on your next letter to read Lieutenant Ruth Jones, U.S. Army."[133]

PEACE TALKS COLLAPSE AND FIGHTING RESUMES: 22 AUGUST – 25 OCTOBER 1951

> With the collapse of the peace talks in August, both sides returned to the fight with increased determination, attempting to gain as much ground as possible. The 1st Marine Division seized Bloody Ridge at the cost of 2,700 casualties; the 2nd Infantry Division took Heartbreak Ridge with 3,700 casualties. Five I Corps divisions then advanced to what became the Jamestown Line in the Old Baldy area at the cost of four thousand more U.N. casualties. Medical units were exceptionally busy. At the same time, they had to deal with increasing numbers of POWs. With U.N. troops slowly seizing more ground, the communists begin to reconsider peace talks.

A major sticking point in the original peace negotiations had been the fate of the 132,000 North Korean and Chinese soldiers held prisoners of war by U.N. forces. Although the United States had originally agreed to repatriate all POWs, half of the communist POWs reportedly did not want to go home and the United States was reluctant to repatriate them forcibly. Communist negotiators, however, were insistent.[134]

Army nurses, responsible for nursing Korean civilians, Korean and Chinese soldier POWs, and U.N. forces, soon learned that Asians had very different ideas of hospital life than their American caretakers. They objected strongly to being bathed, and many Koreans wanted their relatives to be allowed into the hospital to cook for them. Hungry patients frequently attempted to steal food from weaker patients. Nurses found themselves acting as referees and police officers. The language barrier added to the frustrations.[135]

By the time Army Captain (later Lieutenant Colonel) Barbara Cullom of Mount Olive, Illinois, volunteered to go to Korea in 1950, she had been an Army nurse for nearly ten years including service in World War II Europe. That foreign experience stood her in good stead when she served as chief nurse in the 8029th MASH located south of Heartbreak Ridge in 1951–1952. In its neurological unit she cared for head wound patients from many different countries who fought under the auspices of the United Nations. "I took care of soldiers from Colombia and Ethiopia. Others were French or British. We also had patients from New Zealand and Australia as well as from Turkey. At one time I was able to name thirteen representative countries."

Chief Nurse Captain Barbara Cullom, Army Nurse Corps, and Commanding Officer Lieutenant Colonel Donald Reiner, Medical Corps, 8209th MASH, somewhere north of the 38th Parallel, eastern zone, Korea. Courtesy Barbara Cullom.

To get around the language barrier, Cullom and her colleagues devised an international language. "Everyone knew what 'okay' meant," she said. "Japanese words were used for 'large' and 'small.' Courtesies were expressed in French and sign language was also [used]. It was a collection. We worked at it until there was understanding."

Improvisation included "a special flag that went up when we had an influx of patients . . . called our 'blivet flag.' I don't know exactly what blivet meant. [It] was made of a few strips that had been sewn together. We hoisted it when we needed additional help or to let others know that we were busy."

Among Cullom's memorable patients: "a massively built Ethiopian soldier with a bullet right between his eyes" that the doctors thought it best not to extract. "He spoke fine Italian, learned from Italian troops who had occupied Ethiopia before and during World War II."[136]

All of the patients at the 171st Evacuation Hospital in Taegu were North Korean POWs, who were often hysterical, defiant, or rigid with fear because of propaganda that portrayed Americans as cruel and sadistic. The nurses placed postoperative patients in with the newly admitted, so new patients could see that North Koreans were very well cared for. U.N. authorities attempted to separate the North Korean and Chinese POWs from North Koreans who claimed to be anticommunist in order to avoid fights between POWs with opposing political views. Counterinsurgency was a problem when, due to large influxes of prisoners and general confusion, opposing groups inadvertently were mixed and one group attacked and harmed patients of other groups.[137]

The 3rd and 4th Field Hospitals were combined to house POWs who claimed to be in the North Korean Army against their will, while the 64th Field Hospital was assigned to the U.N. POW Camp 1 on the island of Koje-do, which held Chinese communist POWs. At its largest, Koje-do held 183,000 military and civilian internees. The hospital had five thousand beds but could expand to six thousand beds in an emergency. The majority of patients, thousands of cases, were hospitalized for tuberculosis and dysentery. The hospital also experienced a severe epidemic of conjunctivitis and encountered lung fluke, a parasitic respiratory disease difficult to distinguish from TB, among the POWs.[138]

POW hospitals had other unique problems. Prisoners often destroyed cots, blankets, and towels, damaged latrines, and passed hospital supplies over the wall to civilians in exchange for local goods, including alcohol. Chinese patients "would rather die in their tents than submit to western medical care," reported the monthly unit report of the 64th.[139]

Ralph Matthews, war correspondent for the *Baltimore Afro-American*, visited the prisoner-of-war camp on the island of Koje-do near Pusan. Hospital commander, Lieutenant Colonel Cary Tucker, described overcrowded hospital conditions. "We take care of 10,000 patients with a staff hardly large enough to take care of one-third that many," he told Matthews,

Newspaper photo of Army nurse Juanita Long taking a break from conducting classes for Korean nurses near the Pusan prisoner of war camp, September 1951. *Afro-American* Newspapers Archives and Research Center.

then dispatched a courier so the reporter could meet Lieutenant Juanita Long, one of the few African American nurses serving in country.

"I expected the courier to return with a strapping military figure, but instead he was accompanied by a wisp of an olive brown girl who hardly reached his elbow and, except for her dungarees, was as dainty and unruffled as a vacationer at Highland Beach," Matthews wrote.

Long, daughter of a Boston minister and wife of an Army captain stationed in nearby Pusan, had graduated from Boston University and interned at Boston City Hospital before joining the Army Nurse Corps. In Koje-do, she was in charge of training 135 Chinese and Korean women POWs to help take care of other prisoners.

"We found that among the hundreds of women captured, very few of those listed as nurses had any real knowledge of our methods of patient care," Tucker explained. "They were in uniform, but . . . they were little more than camp followers and some of them were confessed prostitutes. But they will be nurses before they leave here if Lieutenant Long keeps up her good work." According to Tucker, Long could "train auxiliary help like they turn out cars on an assembly line."[140]

There were several riots at the POW camps during which prisoners were shot or otherwise injured. During the worst, POWs in Compound 76 at the 64th captured the commander, Brigadier General Francis T. Dodd. Compound 76 was located directly in front of the hospital, and only one narrow road led from the hospital to the headquarters area and the outside gate. Tension was high. The entire hospital was placed on alert; nurses were evacuated. The rebellion lasted for several days. After Dodd's release, the new camp commander, Brigadier General Haydon L. Boatner, ordered the nurses confined to compound headquarters during the night and escorted to and from the hospital by a heavily armed guard as security measures.[141] Working with POWs, reported the combined 3rd and 14th Field Hospitals' monthly report, "seriously tested this hospital's ability to function and provide treatment."[142] POWs were frustrating duty for the nurses. Prisoner patients did not show the appreciation American soldiers did, and there were obvious additional dangers and strains.

In October 1951, MATS tested giant C-124 Globemasters for evacuation flights. Three flight nurses and technicians accompanied 103 litter and 62 ambulatory patients on the first two-hour flight from Pusan to Itami airfield. The huge plane could carry 127 litter or 200 ambulatory patients and be loaded and unloaded faster than the several planes required for

The 801st Medical Air Evacuation Squadron personnel prepare for an air evacuation flight out of Korea. U.S. Air Force photo, Gift of Peter A. Foley, Women's Memorial Collection.

equivalent patient loads. Although it was an efficient use of staff and pa-tients liked the big plane, nurses and medics worried that they would be un-able to save all their charges if a C-124 had to ditch at sea. C-124s could fly out of Seoul and Taegu, but they were too heavy for the airfields at Pusan, where the majority of air-evacuation patients were sent. The C-124s instead became the plane of choice for the long, trans-Pacific flight from Japan to the United States.[143]

PEACE TALKS RESTART AND TRENCH WARFARE BEGINS: 25 OCTOBER 1951–APRIL 1952

In October 1951 the peace talks started again, this time at Panmunjom. By November, the front had stabilized. From this point on, trench warfare reminiscent of World War I characterized the battlefield. Casualties still kept coming, but at a slower pace.

By the time First Lieutenant Mary Pritchard rotated into Korea and the 343rd General Hospital in 1952, the war had settled into a stalemate around the 38th Parallel. Even then, though, duty in Korea was still very difficult, as Pritchard would soon discover. She and several others were issued new gear before leaving Japan. "That was the first time we ever had fatigues and boots on. The fatigues were made for men. They made us wear neckties and we didn't know how to tie a necktie, but the G.I.s helped us get ready. We were also issued the winter uniform, trousers and wool shirts and fur-lined vests. We took them to the Korean tailors and had the fly taken out of the front and a zipper put in the side," she said. "It was difficult getting shoes to fit if you had a narrow foot because we all wore men's boots. Often the nurses leaving Korea left their boots behind to help out incoming women with small feet. Small boots were almost impossible to get."

Pritchard was alone on the last leg of her train journey from Taegu to the 21st Evacuation Hospital in Pusan, where she got an unpleasant welcome. While she waited at the station for transport, a Korean man spat on her feet. "I was surprised because I had assumed that U.N. forces were helping the South Koreans and that they should be grateful," she said. Pritchard was also surprised at how restricted she and her fellow nurses were. "We were not allowed to go outside the compound unless we had a driver and someone to ride shotgun. Women were not allowed to drive themselves. Nurses with escorts and drivers could go to the main PX downtown and a couple of restaurants. Or they could visit other compounds, such as the British hospital or the 22nd Evacuation Hospital, which took care of POWs."

The conditions at Pusan—especially the prevailing cold and additional precautions—took some getting used to. The wooden building that housed the hospital was so poorly insulated that it was possible to see daylight through the walls, she recounted. "It was very, very cold. Gasoline heaters were used in the wards; they were very noisy and not particularly effective."

The nurses monitored all medications with extra vigilance. "All antibiotics had to be signed for every time they were dispensed, to keep a strict accounting because of the black market. All medicine vials had to be broken after use to prevent them from being taken and refilled with something made to look like medicine and then sold on the black market. Medications such as penicillin and streptomycin were in great demand. Our VD rate was very high. We used a lot of Demerol, a lot of morphine, and a lot of sulfa. We had a great many smallpox cases among GIs, who had lied about having received the vaccine for it."

"We were at the end of the [line for the] hospital train, so we had to take [all remaining] patients no matter how many were on the train. When a train came in and you weren't on duty, you had to go to the emergency room and help admit them. . . . The hospital train came all the way from the north, dropping off patients and picking them up at various points along the line. We were the last stop in Pusan."

In addition to the workload and privations, the food was awful, Pritchard recalled. "Everything was canned, including the butter that we had. We had a lot of Spam, a lot of string beans, a lot of turkey. We had powdered eggs and sometimes the eggs were so bad they were green [and] we didn't serve them to the patients. We had reconstituted milk or canned milk."[144]

The hospital ship *Repose*, which had arrived in-theater in September 1950, was not sent home until January 1952. Nurse Lura Jane Emery, who had been promoted to lieutenant (jg) in late 1951, remembered the crew of the *Repose* was tired, but proud of the fact they'd had only seven deaths during their cruise, with two of those from smallpox. The soldiers who came to the ship suffering napalm burns were "unforgettable," as were those who "had done so well that they were afraid they would be sent back to the field. So they tried to hide their charts from the staff."[145]

THE JAMESTOWN LINE: APRIL 1952 – OCTOBER 1952

In April, the 1st Marine Division was ordered to the Jamestown Line, forty miles northwest of Seoul and four miles southeast of Panmunjon, where the peace talks continued. This time strategists had decided to keep the pressure on the communists by aggressively fighting as negotiations dragged on. The division's mission was to repel Chinese thrusts in the direction of Seoul. The Chinese probed and shelled the line, causing numerous casualties. In May, Lieutenant General Mark Clark replaced Ridgway as head of Far East Command and as commander in chief of United Nations Command. The communists accused the United Nations of germ warfare, which the U.N. denied. Throughout the summer and into the fall of 1952, fighting remained vicious and bitter, and soldiers fought to take and retain individual hills they named "Pork Chop," "Jane Russell," and "Bunker." Finally, on 8 October, the U.N. Command adjourned the armistice talks indefinitely.

Even this late into the war—two years—Army hospitals were still experiencing shortages, but reports from the field indicate that the shortages had become more annoying than critical. At the 121st, for example, typewriters were scarce, increasing the administrative burden on staff. Linens and blankets were constantly being pilfered and were in short supply. There were other irritants: outdoor latrines and showers, air raid alerts and blackouts.[146]

ANC First Lieutenant Joyce Gillespie, assigned to the 171st Evacuation Hospital at Taejon, arrived in Korea in April 1952. On her twelve-hour train trip from Taegu, Gillespie saw a great deal of desolation and destruction: roads filled with debris, knocked-out tanks covered with graffiti, rubble everywhere, and Koreans living in shacks they had thrown up in place of bombed-out buildings.

Gillespie's patients included local civilian men called KSCs (for Korean Service Corps), men who were either too young or too old for the Korean Army (ROK). The KSC supported the American Army and others. "Because roads were so poor, transportation was impossible," Gillespie said. "Jeeps and other Army vehicles did not work. There was no way to get supplies to men on the front lines in the mountains. KSCs carried the supplies on A-frames, wooden logs latched together and tied to their backs. The men were capable of carrying 450 to 500 pounds on these wooden platforms. They walked up the mountains and made their deliveries, and sometimes the North Koreans shot them on their way back down." Army hospitals and American nurses provided medical care.

There was a steady stream of incoming wounded, "a total of 250 casualties a day," Gillespie recalled. As the patient load grew, the number of wards for which each nurse had charge grew accordingly, and supplies often could not be stretched far enough. "Twice we ran out of dressings. . . . We ran out of food one time. Twice we ran out of eggs. During one period, we ate hamburger three times a day. Of the sixteen months I lived in Korea, we had raw vegetables one time—tomatoes and cucumbers. We were not allowed to eat any [fresh vegetables] grown in Korea. . . . Because Koreans had parasites, the food they grew was also infested with them."

Shower time for nurses of the 171st was once a day at 4 P.M., and Gillespie often missed out because she had trouble getting off her shift in time. As the nurses complained of "Peeping Toms," however, she said she sometimes was just as glad. The nurses lived in Quonset huts, seven to a hut, with a stove at either end. In the tight quarters, Gillespie's roommates discovered that she ground her teeth at night, something she realized was an indication of stress.[147]

ANC Lieutenant Carmela Filosa (Hix) arrived at the 8063rd MASH early in 1952, and was assigned to the operating tent. A seasoned twenty-nine-year-old, Filosa still remembers the first surgery she attended there, "a young man about eighteen. They were trying to stem the bleeding from a carotid artery. They failed and the boy died. I watched him die. I can still see his face." The OR at the 8063rd had only two tables, but during a push it was not unusual to work twenty-four hours straight. "Everything was improvised," she said. "The sink was a big water heater tank cut in half. During that first winter, I was so cold I wore flannel pajamas under my scrubs. We didn't have any winter coats, and I caught pneumonia."[148]

A surgical nurse in a MASH unit, Lieutenant Carmela Filosa (Hix) of Brooklyn, New York, saw all kinds of battlefield wounds and injuries. Some were obvious such as the intestinal traumas where the surgeons had to cut out the wounded area and join the healthy parts together. Others, like napalm burns, were subtler. To find them, the medical staff put soldiers in a tub of magnesium. "The spots where the skin sizzled were the spots where the napalm had hit." Most insidious of all was hemorrhagic fever, a highly contagious summertime threat spread by mites. "The patients would be in shock when they arrived," Filosa recalls. "Often, they were unconscious or comatose and their bodies would be covered with small red dots. Some men pulled out of it and some [didn't]." The medical staff's only protection against infection was wearing elastic bands around their sleeves and pant legs. However primitive, the bands kept the mites at bay. None of the medical staff of the 8063rd MASH caught the disease.[149]

First Lieutenant Carmela Filosa (Hix), U.S. Army Nurse Corps. Women's Memorial Register.

Although the front had stabilized, the opponents probed and tested each other's defensive lines, and the Navy and Air Force continued to evacuate patients. In one twenty-four-hour period in September 1952, some sixty-two helicopters packed with wounded landed on the small flight deck located on the *Consolation*'s fantail. Total time shore to ship was five minutes. Before the war ended, *Consolation* would evacuate about twelve thousand casualties to Japan and treat seventeen thousand more.[150] AFNC First Lieutenant Agnes Zuverink (Norman) remembered flying on C-124s, C-54s, and C-48s. Many of the planes lacked heat and weren't pressurized. On one flight, while trying to give a patient a shot, she noticed that her fingertips were blue and that her hands were shaking from lack of oxygen. Another time, the landing gear of the plane broke on a seawall in Japan. The pilot had to keep flying the aircraft to get rid of the fuel, while Zuverink and the rest of the staff prepared the patients for a crash landing that fortunately was avoided.[151]

When her rotation to the 8055th MASH in theater was over in May 1952, ANC Lieutenant "Jake" Jacoby returned to Japan and the Sapporo Army hospital, a six-story former factory in "a little country town clear out in the woods with a river." No longer was there the sound of gunfire nearby, but death still plagued the soldiers in her care. Jacoby said that during a three-month hepatitis epidemic, "I was so mad one night. There was a patient that wouldn't eat (the only available treatment was diet and bed rest), wouldn't cooperate, and he would pull his IVs out. It should have gone okay, but this guy was not normal. I raised havoc, and when he died on me it made me even madder. I made every patient in the other two wards come in and look at that guy. Darn, we tried to save him and do what we could, but we had to have a little cooperation. I don't know if it was a good or bad thing to do, but they went back to their beds and kind of hung their heads a little bit. I know I threw them all into a depression, but we had better co-operation."[152]

Nurses were not the only military women in Japan caring for soldiers from the Korean front. At Tokyo Army Hospital, large numbers of WACs who had been trained as medical technicians worked under nurses. One of these, Muriel Scharrer (Wimmer), was assigned to the colostomy ward; she and her colleagues worked twelve-hour days, six days a week, changing dressings, giving shots, and doing whatever else was necessary for the multinational patients. "One of my favorite patients was an Ethiopian soldier. He was very badly shot up, but he was unfailingly patient and good-humored," she recalled. "We also had Turkish, Colombian, and Greek patients on the ward. Two of the Colombian soldiers were so young, no more than fourteen or fifteen; that shocked me." [153]

POLITICS ENTER THE PICTURE: OCTOBER 1952 – MARCH 1953

In the presidential elections of 1952, Republican candidate and World War II hero Dwight D. Eisenhower promised to end the war in Korea if he were elected. After his election in November, he toured the Korean front, lifting morale in-theater and at home, and reinforcing the will of the United Na-

tions to end the war. By late 1952, political considerations weighed heavily in the minds of U.N. commanders. Although the armistice talks had been recessed, negotiators did not want to discourage the communists from returning to the peace table. Commanders were expected to maintain equilibrium along the 140-mile front while at the same time keeping casualties to a minimum. All proposed forays against the Chinese had to be cleared with the military hierarchy. The Chinese, meanwhile, suffered no such restraints and launched attacks against Old Baldy and Pork Chop Hill. In March, the world was shocked by the sudden death of Soviet Premier Joseph Stalin. With the communist leader gone, it was unclear whether China and North Korea could count on political and military support from the Soviet Union. In late March, the communists indicated that they were willing to again begin negotiations.

For the nurses and other servicewomen in Korea and Japan, very little changed when negotiations stalled. There were still patients to care for, shortages to finesse, and occasional moments of heightened awareness that the war was still alive. By January 1953, there were seventeen Army WMSC PTs in Japan and one on Okinawa. Medical personnel had discovered that hydrotherapy and therapeutic exercises were especially good for patients who suffered from large open lesions and burned areas.[154]

NNC Lieutenant Nancy Crosby noticed that security around the *Haven* increased dramatically after the ship had been in port for several months. As Crosby noted in her diary, "Communist action along the rear area is increasing, and gas masks have been issued to all patients and personnel aboard the ship. Male officers have been issued side-arms to wear whenever they left the ship, but we nurses have not been issued guns." The tensions lasted about two weeks before they simmered down.

Crosby served two tours on the *Haven* during 1952 and 1953. During her first tour, when she was a novice at shipboard life, her diary reveals that she worried constantly about keeping supplies on shelves when the ship dipped and rocked. While dining, "one's chair moved about so much that one often found oneself sitting in front of someone else's plate." She shared a tiny room with another nurse, and commented, "If one of us exhales while the other is inhaling and vice versa, it just might work." When the ship arrived in Pusan, a group of the new-to-theater doctors and nurses went ashore to explore. Crosby was shocked by the "poverty, filth, desolation and frightened animals that were once people [who] made up the population. Didn't see any article of food in their stores that we would even feed the pigs. Saw no vegetables, only dead and dried fish and octopus. The odor turned my stomach."[155]

CEASE-FIRE: APRIL–JULY 1953

> *In early April, U.N. and communist negotiators arranged to exchange sick and wounded POWs. Operation Little Switch began on 20 April. The communists released 684 disabled U.N. POWs, while the U.N. command released 6,670 communist POWs. Throughout June and July, the communists made several last-ditch efforts to gain territory. These skirmishes, mainly against ROK divisions, inflicted heavy casualties on both sides and gained the communists only a few thousand yards. Finally convinced that there could be no substantial ground gained without tremendous casualties, the communists accepted the cease-fire line at the 38th Parallel. The treaty formally ending the conflict was signed 27 July 1953. Only then was Operation Big Switch, the exchange of the rest of the POWs, begun. Big Switch lasted one month, with the last prisoner exchange held on 5 September.*

The U.N. prisoners returned by the communists during Operation Little Switch were weak with illness, injuries, and malnutrition. They were taken to Army hospitals in Japan for a week, while two Army dietitians worked to build up the POWs' strength for the trip home. The signing of the armistice itself was very low-key. The two principal signers, Lieutenant General William K. Harrison, senior U.N. delegate, and North Korea's chief negotiator, Nam Il, sat at separate tables and did not even look at each other. After signing, each rose and left the room. The terms of the armistice imposed a cease-fire, the withdrawal of all troops from a two-and-a-half-mile neutral zone along what had been the front line, the exchange of all prisoners, and a political conference to be held ninety days after the signing.[156]

The U.N. POWs returned during Big Switch appeared to be in much better shape than those returned in the previous exchange, and consumed "huge" quantities of ice cream and cookies. Red Cross personnel heard many tales of privation and torture. The former POWs claimed that the communists had been hardest on American officers. After three years in captivity, the highest-ranking POW, Major General William Dean, said, "It is a wonderful thing, like a dream. You look much better to me than I am sure I look to you."[157]

All told, the communists returned 12,757 prisoners: 7,848 South Koreans, 3,597 Americans, and 1,312 from other nations within the U.N. Command. The United Nations turned over 75,823 prisoners to the communists, about 70,000 of them North Koreans and the rest Chinese. More than 22,000 POWs refused to be repatriated.

According to the terms of the cease-fire, each North Korean and Chinese POW who refused to be repatriated was marched into a tent and subjected to a communist harangue, in an attempt to get him to change his mind. Only a handful altered their decisions.[158]

The Korean War was responsible for the death of fifty-four thousand American soldiers. Although no servicewomen died in Korea, thirteen nurses died en route to assignments in the battle theater and three Air Force flight nurses died on medical evacuation flights into or out of the theater.[159]

In mid-September 1950, the Navy Nurse Corps lost eleven nurses en route to the Yokosuka naval hospital when their plane crashed on takeoff after refueling on Kwajelein Island. One, Ensign Marie Margaret Boatman, age twenty-five, of San Antonio, Texas, had been in the Navy less than three years. Another, Lieutenant (jg) Margaret Grace Kennedy, a World War II veteran from Webster, Massachusetts, had joined the Navy Reserve and volunteered for Korea.[160]

Another fifteen nurses were aboard the USS *Benevolence* on the dark, foggy night of 5 August 1950, when the freighter *Mary Luckenbach* rammed and sunk it off San Francisco. The nurses ended up tied together, hanging onto wooden rafters to keep afloat in the rough cold seas until an Army tug picked them up.[161] One of the fifteen, Ensign Wilma Ledbetter of Chillicothe, Texas, who carried dried bluebonnets in her Bible and was known to friends as "Leddy," later died from shock and exposure. Seventeen sailors also lost their lives when the *Benevolence* sank.[162]

The sole Army nurse casualty, Major Genevieve Smith, died in early July 1950 when the C-47 transporting her from Yokohama to her new assignment as chief of Army nurses in Korea crashed into the sea.[163] The Air Force nurses died in two separate incidents. Before dawn on 26 September 1950, a C-54 carrying military personnel, including two flight nurses, crashed in the Sea of Japan, drowning many passengers, including Captain Vera Brown. Lieutenant (later Captain) Jonita Bonham (Bovee) although injured, assisted others and was subsequently awarded the Distinguished Flying Cross. The last Korean War servicewomen to die, two flight nurses of the

801st MAES, Lieutenant Margaret Perry and Lieutenant Virginia McClure, were killed while on a December 1952 evacuation flight in southern Korea.[164]

The point is not that so few American military women died in the Korean War—only thirteen nurses compared to fifty-four thousand soldiers, sailors, and Marines—it is that once again as they have since the American Revolution and before, women citizens risked their lives for their country. Too often, the debate about women and war is colored by lurid Hollywood images of women blazing away in ground combat or hand-to-hand fighting. The reality is that by simply being there and doing whatever jobs they are assigned, women, too, lose their lives.

CHAPTER 8

Recurring Issues Relating to Military Women

She is an efficient type woman and for a woman does an exceptional job.
—Efficiency report given then Captain and later Brigadier General
   Mildred Inez Bailey[1]

I was still in my full uniform, hadn't gained any weight and they were short
of help. . . . I was five-and-a-half months pregnant.
—First Lieutenant Muriel Raymond (Batcheller)[2]

On every roster, every order, those four girls always had an asterisk after
their names with the footnote: "negroid." I thought it was grossly unfair.
—Airman Second Class Joyce Blackstock (Lester), a white WAF from
   Dacula, Georgia[3]

DURING THE KOREAN WAR ERA, both the military
and American society struggled with issues related to
women's military service that were in many ways ghosts of the past. Some
had already been dealt with during World War II. Others were at least anticipated if not resolved in the postwar debates surrounding the 1948
Women's Armed Services Integration Act and the acceptance of women in
the peacetime military. Still others were new twists on age-old notions
about how society saw itself and the half of its population who were women,
among them whether women had any place in a war zone, and whether
men had any place in previously all-female health professions.

The most surprising of these issues, of course, was the attempt to remove military nurses from the battle theater. Some Army commanders and
their own chief nurses questioned whether, as women, nurses might become

"a distinct liability to themselves and the troops."[4] It is a given that the military's policies on women in dangerous or isolated assignments reflected 1950s' attitudes, as did military policies about servicewomen wives and mothers. Equally a reflection of those attitudes was the military's institutional willingness but frequent individual balking at the full integration of minority women. Some of these remain contentious even today. That persons of color are now accepted at the highest levels of the military and society is encouraging; that the women in combat issue, however, has yet to be resolved indicates how complex and unresolved women's full participation in society still is. The reality remains, however, whether or not the military was completely comfortable with them there, during the Korean War, with very few exceptions, only nurses served in the combat theater.

The calm efficiency with which Army, Navy, and Air Force nurses performed their duties in difficult and dangerous situations argued that other military women could be as capable in the combat theater. Nonetheless, military leaders refused to permit more than a handful of WACs and no WAF to serve in Korea during the war. This decision held even after General James A. Van Fleet, commander of the 8th U.S. Army in Korea, requested that a unit of six hundred WACs be sent to work at the U.N. headquarters in November 1951.[5]

At the time, Assistant Secretary of Defense Anna Rosenberg had just returned from visiting troops near the front lines during a two-week European trip in September 1951 and another fifteen-day trip to the Far East in October—attired in "a WAC uniform, paratroop boots and an alligator handbag," a Pennsylvania newspaper noted.[6] One of the purposes of her trip was to talk in person with the troops about their individual concerns and morale. As she expected, soldiers wanted to know when they could go home. Rosenberg knew that if WACs and WAF could be assigned to the Korean Theater, it would be much easier for DOD to rotate soldiers out; when she returned from Korea, she announced DOD approval for sending six hundred WACs to Van Fleet's 8th Army headquarters. Rosenberg elaborated that Army leaders anticipated using WAC clerk typists, photo interpreters, and laboratory technicians as far forward as Seoul.[7] Shortly afterwards, DOD announced that because of WAC recruitment failure, the deployment would not happen.[8]

In 1952, Army and Air Force commanders in Korea both signed a memo to DOD requesting units of servicewomen. DOD seriously considered the second request because they believed the front line had finally stabilized. Once again, however, they decided not to send servicewomen into Korea, again blaming poor recruitment and the fact that neither the WAC or the WAF had enough women to send units to Korea without taking them from critical jobs in the United States.[9]

The Army finally allowed three WACs into Korea. In December WAC Master Sergeant Carolyn James and two WAC Corporals Louise Farrell and Christine Chrones were sent to 8th Army Headquarters in Seoul.[10] Later in 1953, General Richard Whitcomb, the commander of ports, specifically requested Captain Martha Voyles, who had worked for him in the States before his assignment to Korea. According to Voyles, "WAC leadership was willing to assign me to Korea, but they believed that I should be ac-companied by at least two other women, so that I wouldn't feel completely isolated. So two WAC sergeants were found to go with me."

Once the orders had been approved, Voyles and the two enlisted women flew by military transport to Korea. "When the plane arrived in Pusan, everyone was allowed to get off except the three of us. We were held on board and not allowed to disembark for several hours. It was extremely hot aboard the plane, and we were wearing our winter uniforms. Finally, they told us what the problem was. It was the United Nations Command. Everyone who came into Korea had to be replacing another individual, and as there were no WACs in [Pusan], so we could not be replacing existing individuals. Finally, General Whitcomb arrived and managed to convince the U.N. Command that he had authorization to allow us into the country."[11]

Master Sergeant Carolyn H. James, left, and Corporal Louise M. Farrell, the first two WACs and the first two non-medical military women to be assigned to the Eighth Army, arrive in Korea, 18 December 1952. National Archives (111-SC-414255).

What is particularly inexplicable about the American military's hesitation to send servicewomen other than nurses into the combat theater is that civilian women, including those working alongside the military for organizations such as the American Red Cross, the USO, and DOD's education service, were in and out of Korea throughout the war. These women, like their nurse colleagues, endured with little complaint the air raid drills and subzero nights in tents. The experiences of journalist Marguerite Higgins,

The American Red Cross's Jane Seaver Kirk hands out doughnuts to 2nd Infantry Division soldiers guarding 180,000 prisoners of war, Koje-do Island, Korea, 22 April 1952. Jane Seaver Kirk Collection, Women's Memorial Collection.

a correspondent for the *New York Herald Tribune* during the opening days of the war, should have demonstrated once and for all that women were tough enough to take what the combat theater had to offer. Under fire in the air and on the ground, Higgins ignored both the danger and her gender and simply concentrated on getting the story and making sure it got out. Few military leaders were inclined to learn much from Higgins's exploits, however. Most only wanted to make certain that she did not get killed, wounded, or captured while she was in their area of responsibility. For this reason, the more cautious among them ordered her out of the theater or attempted to place limits on where she could go.[12]

Higgins, for her part, insisted that she did not want her newspaper to be scooped simply because its correspondent was a woman. In her famous account of the early days of the war, *War in Korea,* Higgins said the most trouble came from "officials who had never themselves been on the firing lines."[13] When Lieutenant General Walton Walker, 8th Army commander, ordered her out of the theater because "there are no facilities for ladies on the front,"[14] Higgins appealed his order all the way up to General MacArthur. She argued that General William Dean, 24th Infantry Division commander, said she proved "the lack of facilities was immaterial."[15] "Lack of facilities" is, in itself, a recurring issue for military women and one that usually proves to be a red herring. When the need for trained personnel is great enough, "suitable" facilities can generally be found in order for service-*women* to fill the *man*power need. When MacArthur rescinded Walker's ex-pulsion order, Walker ordered Higgins into his office and told her, "Just be careful and don't get yourself killed or captured."[16]

Higgins remembered only one time in Korea when she felt less than ad-equate because of her gender. She and three male correspondents were traveling through Korea one night by jeep when the driver put the vehicle into a ditch. "I didn't have the strength to help pull it out, so I walked to a nearby farmhouse and rousted out a farmer and his son to help us," man-aging to contribute to the success of the group.[17] And there was at least one time she herself was seriously inconvenienced because of her gender, but only because of military intransigence. During the invasion of Inchon, the Navy decided that Higgins could not remain overnight on an assault trans-port because she was an unescorted female. For the next several nights she, still an unescorted female, was forced to sleep rolled up in a ground cloth with the troops in the field while her male press corps colleagues took nightly hot showers and slept in real beds on the transport.[18]

Like Higgins, women who performed with the USO in Korea during the war also found themselves roughing it in difficult and dangerous situa-tions. After World War II, the USO had closed operations areas around the world and was caught with its doors shut in June 1950. Though it made hur-ried contact with DOD to provide much needed social and recreational sup-port for troops, the fluid and inconclusive character of the first six months of the war meant camp shows were slow to arrive in Korea. Eventually, 126 USO units put on 5,400 shows for military personnel in Korea. During 1952, there was a USO show in Korea every day. By the end of the war, there were 113,394 USO volunteers in the United States and nearly three hundred USO centers overseas.[19]

Carole Blakeman (Russell), who performed under the shortened last name Blake, was eighteen years old and living with her Air Force pilot brother when she decided to volunteer with the USO, hoping the experi-ence would launch her singing career. Blake was billed as a "velvet-voiced vocalist" in the five-woman, five-man troupe. The other women were re-ferred to as "an outstanding young dancing artiste," a "lovely soprano," "the pet majorette of the Los Angeles Rams," and one-half of a "husband and wife music and comedy act." The men included a country-and-western singer, a "master of mirth," a trombonist, and an accordion player. Troupe

Carole Blake (Russell), center, and her USO troupe mates under the 40th Infantry Division sign announcing their "Hollywood Showcase" performance, Korea, January 1953. Carole Blake Russell Collection, Women's Memorial Collection.

members were required to get twenty inoculations, and "my arm swelled to double its normal size," Blake recalled. In February 1953, the group made the thirty-six-hour trip to the Far East Theater on a MATS propeller-powered aircraft. "Korea was freezing cold and the troupe was billeted in tents with potbellied stoves, and no water or bathrooms. Our first day, an Army sergeant showed us to our tent. A little disconcerted, I asked him 'Where's the shower?' He looked at me funny, picked up a bucket, and said, 'Here's the shower, lady.' I'll never forget it.

"We performed at least once a day and usually twice a day. We traveled across the country in jeeps and helicopters, sometimes in blackout conditions. We played at Seoul, Inchon, Taegu, Wonson—anywhere the troops were. We were always billeted in tents. One night, we had an air raid. When we grabbed our coats and ran to our assigned foxholes, I picked up a lipstick and put in my pocket. Then, once I was in the foxhole, I proceeded to remove the curlers from my hair. My troupe mates asked me what I was doing, and I said 'If I am going to die, I want to look attractive while I'm at it!' They thought that I was crazy," Blake recalled.

"I always wore a strapless evening gown for my performance, no matter how cold it was outside—we usually performed outside. My mother sent me a pair of red long johns, which I wore under the gown. One night, a gust of wind blew my dress up and the GI's got a good look at my long red underwear. They loved it!"[20]

Dancer Lorraine Gist, a member of a USO production sponsored by the American Broadcasting Corporation, spent several months traveling around Korea doing "a continual series of performances on makeshift outdoor field stages, theaters, and hospitals, and [using] dressing rooms [that] varied from administration areas, to tents to dispensaries."

The troupe was usually billeted over night in tents, and the women were required to have an MP escort to the bathroom. Troupe members ate at the officers' mess, wore Army uniforms whenever they were not performing, and had to be "ready for anything. . . . [Once] there was a fire in one of the tents and a soldier was rushed into our dressing room, which happened to be the dispensary. The medic, working quickly to clean the [wounded soldier's] burned area, requested my help. . . . The twenty-year-old was in great pain, and asked me for a cigarette. I lit a cigarette and gave it to him. In one breath, he inhaled the entire thing down to the filter, and I removed it from his mouth. The medic got him stabilized and the show went on as always."

One night, as the troupe traveled from one engagement to another in Chonson in a convoy of jeeps, ambulances, and trucks during a blinding rainstorm, "I looked out the back window and I saw the saturated road just crumble away behind the last few vehicles in the convoy. Fortunately those vehicles were carrying equipment, not people, because they ended up in the river. We lost the two drivers." Gist herself was injured while on tour and evacuated to Tokyo.[21]

Ann Zoss (Roberts), a DOD civilian teacher, ran the Air Force education center at Air Base K-13 (51st Fighter Interceptor Wing) outside of Suwon, sixty miles south of Seoul. "I thought that I had rocks in my head, because I had given up my job [as director of the Army education center] in Tokyo for the most desolate place I had ever seen. There were no trees and no grass, just squatty little buildings. The wind blew all the time. I was billeted all by myself in a little wood-framed building with a guard, because I was the only woman on base with five thousand airmen." Zoss was less concerned about safety or being isolated than she was with the condition of her quarters: "the dirtiest room I ever saw . . . furnished with little more than a chair and a bed. The Korean maid and I cleaned and cleaned, and finally made it livable."

Zoss immediately got to work to set up the nonexistent education center. "I asked for an office," she said, "and the command politely gave me a chair.

Then I asked for paper and pencils and started the program by writing 'advertisements' which I posted to catch the interest of fellows seeking high school [equivalency] diplomas. The response was terrific, because we were all confined to the base, even on off-duty hours." She ate in the officers' mess, and "worked from eight in the morning until ten at night because there really wasn't anything else to do." Given those conditions, the education center became very popular with the troops. She recruited college graduate officers to teach science and civics. "The only problem came when my instructors were sent on flying missions. I was left with as many as seventeen classes to teach myself," she said.

Department of Defense teacher Ann Zoss (Roberts), one of many civilian women who worked within the war zone in Korea, rings the bell to start the first day of classes for 51st Fighter Interceptor Wing airmen at her new school at Air Base K-13, near Suwon, Korea. Courtesy Ann Zoss Roberts.

"The program grew so big, and was so well accepted that the command ran out of office space for classrooms. So the base built me a wood-frame, two-room schoolhouse, complete with a school bell. We called the school Suwon U." Eventually, the command garnered a librarian for the education center, and "After the first librarian left, the command got another, because they didn't want me to be all alone on base."

Zoss wore khaki slacks and shirts comparable to uniforms worn by the airmen on base. Most of the men did not wear their rank on their uniform in case the base was overrun and they were captured. All personnel were required to carry gas masks with them at all times; when the air raid alarm sounded (as it frequently did in the evenings) all were required to go to the revetments (waist-high lines of sandbags) for protection.[22]

At the same time, of course, military bases in Europe were constantly on the alert, and some male military members wondered whether servicewomen there should just be sent home in the event of an attack. The director of the WAF, Colonel Geraldine May, encountered some of this thinking when she visited WAF units in Europe in early 1950, as she reported.

I have just returned from a trip to England and Germany. I was over there at a time when it might have been possible to have a small incident disrupt the world. I visited a few bases in Germany, and the first thing that came from the officers, male, was "Now when we put all the dependents on the airplanes, we will put the WAF on too, won't we?" I was horrified by that suggestion. These are women who are regular members of the Air Force over there in what might be a danger zone at any time. I said, "Of course not. They are members of the Air Force and will stay at their duty post." Well, it turned out that the easiest way to have the dependents cared for on the return trip was to send the WAF home with them.[23]

The assignment of servicewomen to geographically isolated bases anywhere, not just overseas, or to bases where there were few other women was a recurring issue during the Korean War era. The armed forces, at the urging of the women's service directors, were reluctant to assign servicewomen singly or in small groups out of concern for their personal safety and morale, although at times this concern seemed out of step with local perception. Staff Sergeant Josephine DeAcetis (Schell) was the only WAF at the 513th Reserve Wing of the 512th Troop Carrier Wing in Wilmington, Delaware. To a newspaper reporter who did a story on the unit, neither DeAcetis nor her male colleagues appeared to think that there was anything particularly unique about her assignment.[24] And, as we have seen, civilian agencies seemed to have had fewer qualms about assigning lone women to remote areas; Evelyn "Hopsie" Higgins was the only female at the tiny, isolated Misawa Air Force Base in northern Honshu, home to an Air Force bomber wing, when the Korean War broke out (the Red Cross veteran was on her third tour of duty there).[25]

It also appears that the military could overlook concerns about isolated women or geographically isolated areas when it was difficult to hire civilian women in an area. In 1953, Major Jeanne M. Holm of the WAF director's office made an inspection trip to just such an isolated WAF squadron at Great Falls, Montana. The Air Force had a difficult time in the remote, rural area finding enough qualified civilians to fill the many administrative jobs on base. What Holm took note of and her conclusions are interesting: Five WAF officers and ninety-one WAF airmen were assigned to twelve different units and attached to a WAF squadron, a situation that conformed to Air Force policy. At that time the Air Force was attempting to phase out smaller WAF squadrons in the interest of efficiency. The women officers' quarters were dingy and unattractive, but they did not complain because the men officers' quarters were worse. Further, the base commander was aware of the situation, but had only recently received money for renovations; new construction was not yet budgeted. The women at Great Falls ate at the same mess as the men and reported that the food was excellent. Moreover, both the base commander and the WAF squadron commander took issue with a recent WAF attitude survey (April–May 1951), claiming that Great Falls WAF were dissatisfied with their jobs. To the contrary, they felt needed and accepted by the men with whom they worked. The sole negative feedback Holm got came from the weather squadron commander, who had difficulties with WAF assigned to him and believed that women were "not suited" to weather work.

Everything Holm saw led her to agree that morale among the WAF on-post was high. Local civilians, however, were not fond of military people and expressly disapproved of women in uniform. This meant that WAF were not often inclined to go to town; as a result, Holm did express concern that Great Falls was probably not the best posting.

Her report also alerted the WAF director of one additional potential problem at Great Falls: eighteen of the ninety-some WAF there were married and lived off base. Although these women planned to remain in the Air Force, they had the same caveat: they would stay with the Air Force as long as they were assigned alongside their husbands and did not get pregnant.[26] Marriage was not the problem, per se. Allowing women to abrogate their service contracts solely on the basis of marriage was creating unacceptable turnover.

There in a nutshell was the challenge for the military with respect to women. As long as society expected women to marry and follow their spouses, all the policies and promises the military dreamed up to recruit and retain women had to be filtered through that expectation. As long as nature took its course—this was a decade or more before the birth control pill was readily available—women got pregnant, and the military by necessity had to deal with the issue of maternity. Regarding the former issue, marriage, the military went back and forth throughout the Korean War, as we have seen. The latter problem, motherhood, would not be acted upon until servicewomen mothers began taking their automatic discharges to court and—in the 1970s—began winning reinstatement and back pay.

Without exception, the women's service organizations interpreted pregnancy discharges as reflecting badly on the organizations. And, because the greatest problem was among enlisted women, who of course had less career potential to entice them not to get married and pregnant, the military

The WAC Drill Team of Fort Lee, Virginia, marches into the world premiere of the movie *Never Wave at a WAC* at RKO Keith's Theater, Washington, D.C., 28 January 1953. National Archives (111-SC-414142).

went round in circles on the policy that allowed an enlisted woman the option of leaving the service once she married. Discharge on marriage was not reinstated for women officers until after the war in September 1953.[27] Yet even here the military appears to have waffled. In 1951, when one highly visible WAC officer was able to leave the service to get married, she made headlines.

Lieutenant Colonel Ruby E. Herman, director of the WAC Training Center at Fort Lee, Virginia, wed the director of *Never Wave at a WAC*, starring Rosalind Russell and Paul Douglas, which filmed at Fort Lee. The movie was Hollywood's humorous look at a wealthy woman's sojourn as an enlisted woman. The Army hoped the movie publicity would help with WAC recruiting, and eventually awarded Rosalind Russell a medal for her aid to recruitment—but an unanticipated publicity result of the filming was Herman's romance and resignation.[28]

It's clear that the services did try to accommodate marriages between service members, both officer and enlisted couples, by assigning married couples to the same general locales, if not always the same installations. This was often a case of the good deed that never goes unpunished. Accommodating one military spouse sometimes led to jealousy on the part of another service member who believed that he or she was better qualified for the job, then saw it go to another in the name of keeping spouses together.

WAC Major (later Lieutenant Colonel) Irene Van Houten Munster, the World War II veteran who delayed wedding bells when the Korean War broke out, went to the top in her request to stay with her new husband after the Army sent him to Germany in 1951. She wrote to Ike himself. "We were newlyweds and really wanted to be together. The general remembered me [from her service as a top-secret document control officer at his head-quarters in France and later in Occupied Germany, 1945 through 1947] and sent a letter to WAC Headquarters requesting me personally. I became the assistant supply officer at SHAPE."[29]

Similarly, WAC Sergeant Patricia Grant (Overacker) was assigned to G-1 at the Counter Intelligence Center at Fort Holabird, Maryland, in 1951, where she met and married. When her husband was assigned to the 430th CIC Detachment in Salzburg, Austria, the Overackers requested that the WAC find a position in Salzburg for her. She was assigned to the 430th as a cryptographer, but had to learn cryptography on the job.[30] WAC Private First Class Muriel Scharrer (Wimmer) was working as a medical technician at Tokyo Army Hospital when she met her future husband. She had been overseas one year and two months and had been in a new assignment for only a short time when she asked for a discharge to marry and return home with her future husband, who was being reassigned. The WAC granted her discharge even though she had not fulfilled her original three-year enlist-ment agreement.[31]

Captain Rebecca Williams Burr, a married Army dietitian, requested an assignment to Germany in 1950 because her husband, an Army MP, was stationed in Bremerhaven. She was assigned to the 97th General Hospital in Frankfurt. She remembered that she sailed to Europe on a troop ship as the only military woman aboard, and was assigned a cabin with three mili-tary wives going to Germany to join their husbands.[32]

It may seem peculiar today in an era in which most families have two wage earners, but the problem of how to treat the spouses of servicewomen presented a real issue for the military. Wives were dependents. But hus-bands? In the 1950s, that idea was almost anti-American. When First Lieu-tenant Mildred Inez Bailey received orders to Stuttgart in September 1949 she had only two options: the future brigadier general could either go to Germany without her World War II veteran husband (now a civilian) or re-sign from the WAC. The Baileys decided that she should accept the assign-ment and that he would join her in Germany as soon as possible. An accountant, he quickly found a U.S. Civil Service job in Stuttgart. But after just three months in Stuttgart as the assistant S-2 (intelligence) officer of the 7824th Service Command, Bailey became commanding officer of the WAC detachment at the 98th General Hospital in Munich. She moved to Munich and commuted to be with her husband in Stuttgart on weekends. The fact that they were a commuting couple, long before that sort of marriage was, if not common, at least not unusual among two spouses with careers, caused an additional problem. As a civil servant, her husband was entitled to a billeted apartment, but only if his wife resided with him. He finally persuaded authorities to give him what had been "the janitor's quarters in the basement of an apartment building," she recalled.

Retired Brigadier General Mildred Inez Bailey's distinguished Army career began as an officer in the Women's Army Auxiliary Corps (WAAC) in 1942.
Courtesy Mildred Inez Bailey.

"He was not entitled to any furnishings, because you could only draw furniture for a family billet, and you weren't entitled to a stove or refrigerator. . . . It was in pretty sad shape, with dirty, ugly old linoleum on the floor, bare light bulbs hanging from the ceiling, walls that had pipes running around them." The Baileys worked hard to fix up the apartment, ordering fabric from Sears, Roebuck to hang on the walls to hide the pipes and repairing "furniture so broken down that no one else wanted it"—only to have the military "try to take it away from us and assign it to a family. My husband went to the commanding general and told him what we had done and he refused to let them take it."

After two years, Bailey finally was assigned to an intelligence position in Stuttgart, enabling her to rejoin her husband. He now was entitled to family quarters as a civil servant with a resident wife; she, however, was not entitled to such housing. Though a rapidly rising Army officer, she was a woman, and women by the definition of the 1950s were the dependents.[33]

ANC Lieutenant Muriel Raymond Batcheller, the bride who returned from her honeymoon to find orders for Japan, was not so lucky. She managed a short reprieve and an assignment stateside, but then was ordered to Germany and not allowed to take her husband with her, although male officers were able to bring along family. It turned out she had brought family with her, too: she did not pass the required pregnancy test once she arrived in Germany. With nurses in such demand, however, she was unable simply to resign her commission as policy required. "I was still in my full uniform, hadn't gained any weight and they were short of help. . . . I was five-and-a-half months pregnant when they finally decided I could go." There were two other women in her condition, but "the captain . . . decided we didn't need to go yet."[34]

"Unusual" was the word Airman Second Class Jacquelyn Tomasik (Anderson), used to describe her status as a married WAF in the 1950s. "Making a career and getting married were novelties" then, and military procedures didn't make dual careers any easier.

She and her husband had a hard time coordinating their leaves just to get married. Almost immediately after the wedding, he was reassigned to England, where there were no billets for WAF. By the time she had submitted her third request for a compassionate transfer, a contingent of WACs from Germany had been assigned to a station in England and her transfer then was approved. There was also an issue of maiden versus married names. When Tomasik first applied for a compassionate transfer, she was told she had to change her name to his "because [of] regulations."

Airman Second Class Jacquelyn Tomasik (Anderson), U.S. Air Force, and her husband on their wedding day. Women's Memorial Register.

Regulations also required that military women could not travel in groups smaller than fifty. In Tomasik's case, that meant she had to wait a week at Camp Kilmer, New Jersey, for enough women to arrive to make up a "shipment." Once in England, regulations specified that females had to be housed within twenty-five miles of assignment. "That way, if something went wrong in the marriage, you just 'went home to mother,'" Tomasik said.

As the only enlisted female WAF on the South Ruslip base, she was the object of some curiosity when she, unlike the other wives, went off to work each morning. "The English had a hard time realizing that I was in the Women's Air Force." On one trip to London with her husband, a hotel desk clerk demanded to see her identification to prove that she was American and not English. "The desk clerk got upset with my husband because he thought he was bringing an [English] lady of the night into the hotel," Tomasik said. "When he found out I was American, he was fine. He didn't care what American military did with each other as long as it didn't involve English girls."

She had hoped to make the Air Force a career, but when she became pregnant, an honorable discharge was her "only option." "At that time no allowance was made for pregnant members of the service. . . . You had to get out, supposedly for the baby's health. At that time I didn't think anything of it, because it was the only thing I could do." Even more discouraging was the attitude of the military doctors and nurses to her pregnancy, she said. "They thought enlisted women were either lesbian or loose, so they looked down their noses at me until I flashed my wedding rings."

She remained in England as her husband's dependent.[35]

As the services learned during the Korean War, in a way perhaps they did not have to during World War II, there is some truth in the old adage that "biology is destiny." There was really nothing the military could do (or, it must be added, anything it would want to do) about young women's propensity to get married and become pregnant except perhaps hope those women would finish their military commitment first. The flip-flops on discharging married women and the hand-wringing about motherhood causing retention problems could be viewed as just another step along a long learning curve regarding utilization of servicewomen.

There were other issues that would prove to be stumbling blocks in the military's treatment of women, of course. Sexual discrimination and sexual harassment on the job would be the most glaring examples, but the language describing these had not yet been coined during the Korean War era. For example, many former servicewomen resented seeing promotions they thought they were due going to a man. "Years later I found out why I wasn't promoted to master sergeant," WAF Technical Sergeant Mary Russ (Veres) said. "The colonel said, 'give it to this guy because he's married' . . . [but] I was supporting my mother and sister."[36]

Behavior that would not be tolerated today appears in the most everyday recollections among the oral histories for this book, although official records of complaints about what is now called a "sexually hostile environment" have not been found. One example, former Marine Sergeant Anna Yachwan, matter-of-factly told of a supervisor who regularly called all his personnel bastards, until she snipped, "I know who my parents are and I can verify the information with a phone call. Can you, sir?" She said he did not respond. She also recalled numerous off-color jokes. If she laughed, he would demand, "Are you a lady, Corporal?" If she didn't laugh, he would mockingly ask her in front of the men, "Didn't you understand?" Like many other servicewomen, Yachwan complained her boss worked her longer hours than the men in the unit "and gave me the worst jobs." Yet when Yachwan contacted the woman supervisor in charge of enlisted Women Marines in a successful attempt to be transferred, she discovered her boss had boasted of all the work he'd gotten out of her.[37]

To date, nothing like the Navy's infamous "Tailhook" incident in 1991 has been found in archival records or come up in military women's oral histories despite repeated attempts to find such material; nor have any statistics or official reports dealing with the incidence of violence against or rape of military women been located. To put this in context, the 1950s was an era when rape was being reported in civilian newspapers as "criminal assault"—if it was reported at all. Some servicewomen were raped, some were murdered, and there are newspaper clippings regarding these incidents in the Women's Memorial files; whatever official records exist, however, seem to be scattered inside "incident reports" filed under the perpetrators' names rather than by the nature of the crimes.

Clearly, the overwhelming concern that each of the women's service components had for the propriety of their women was a defensive reaction to their being viewed either as what we now call sex objects or, worse (what was called "deviant" or "mannish" then) homosexual. Just as clearly, male military leaders were uneasy about servicewomen for the same still unnamed reasons. Why else the preoccupation with glamorous secretarial pools and "proper employment for sisters and girlfriends?" Why else post guards for whole platoons of Women Marines in barracks where they had been housed—sans guards—during World War II?

As for job discrimination, it would be another dozen-plus years before it would become illegal for newspaper Help Wanted ads to list jobs by gender. The military can hardly be faulted for declaring what it considered men's work to be men's work and telling servicewomen to be "more feminine and stick to secretarial work instead of trying to be mechanics, truck drivers and grease monkeys."[38] Can it merely be coincidence, however, that early in her military career the first woman two-star, Air Force Major General Jeanne M. Holm, had been an enlisted WAC truck driver? Or that the Air Force, the service that first tried to integrate women fully was the first branch to award a woman a second star? Discrimination against women simply because they were women was, in the 1950s, as widely accepted in the military as it was then in society, even though women were beginning to recognize it for what it was.

When (by then) Captain Mildred Inez Bailey returned from Europe in 1953 to an intelligence assignment as a records control officer with a counter-intelligence unit in Washington, D.C., she recalls she "encountered a very open and overt act of discrimination because I was a woman." Her immediate supervisor, a major "could not stand the idea of a woman officer, especially a woman officer assigned to him. . . . I discovered that I had no work to do. I would go to the office in the morning and my basket was empty. I was just sitting there. . . . I went to him and said 'Major, I don't know why you aren't giving me any work to do. . . . Is there something wrong with my work? Am I not doing it to your satisfaction?' I could not get a satisfactory answer out of him. . . . With an ugly tone of voice and a disgusted attitude, he would take a stack of folders that contained the work we were supposed to be doing and throw it on my desk. So I would do what had to be done and put them back on his desk. I wouldn't get any more work until I went back and asked for it. . . . I put up with this for about a month . . . walking around all day with a lump in my throat . . . and I decided I wasn't going to live like that. I would leave the Army before I would live like that."

Bailey went to the officer assignment branch of the WAC director's office and demanded they either reassign her or give her resignation papers. They reassigned her to another job in intelligence in Washington. When Bailey later saw the efficiency rating the major had given her, she noticed one particular sentence, "She is an efficient type woman and for a woman does an exceptional job."[39]

Discrimination against African American servicewomen was another area in which military practices and societal attitudes were still in flux. The armed services were required by presidential mandate to racially integrate their forces wherever they were located around the world. Units fighting in Korea were being integrated for the first time, as were those at home and in Europe, but not all Americans were happy about it.

Even as policymakers hammered out a post–World War II role for women in the U.S. Armed Forces in 1948, the decades-old battle over military racial desegregation was a subtext to the debate. The inequities of the "separate but equal" doctrine of the 1896 *Plessy v. Ferguson* Supreme Court decision still shaped public policy and white attitudes, even though positive (if limited) experiences with desegregation during World War II and increased civil rights activism gave weight to arguments for racially unifying the downsized military. Still, many high-ranking military officers and legislators openly opposed desegregation. Even some civil rights supporters feared forcing the armed forces into a position that went against mainstream American thinking.

President Harry S. Truman's Executive Order 9981, mandated "equality of treatment and opportunity for all persons in the armed services without regard to race, color, religion, or national origin." But note the absence of the word "sex," despite the fact the women's integration was happening almost simultaneously. Note also that Truman, hoping to unify a Democratic party sharply divided on racial policy in a critical election year, carefully omitted the term "desegregation" (anathema to conservative Southerners) from his order and purposely left the timing and method of achieving racial equality up to each service. Yet the order addressed the essence of African American and liberal demands and the president's intent was clear. Asked by a reporter whether he actually intended to end racial segregation in the armed forces, Truman responded with a single, emphatic yes, and ordered the policy implemented "as rapidly as possible . . . without impairing efficiency or morale."[40]

The *Chicago Defender* hailed Truman's "dramatic and historic move, unprecedented since the time of Lincoln" with the front-page banner headline "President Truman Wipes Out Jim Crow Segregation in the Armed Forces." The *Defender* ordered readers to "SAVE This PAPER It Marks HISTORY" [*sic*].[41]

Three African American Army nurses broke the color barrier when they were assigned to Frankfurt's 97th Army Hospital in 1951. When three more African American nurses broke the color line—and were the only African American female officers—at the 98th General Hospital in Munich, it seemed that three was some sort of a magic number for desegregation in Army Nurse Corps' facilities. (Black nurses had served with the Army since the Spanish-American War and had been on active duty with the ANC during World War I, though in reserve capacity and—always—segregated situations. In 1941, the ANC began commissioning African American nurses in preparation for World War II.)

> Captain Margaret Bailey, one of the first black Army nurses at the 98th, recalled she and her two colleagues were surprised and dismayed to discover that they had been assigned separate living quarters across the street from the hospital. They had expected to be placed with the other nurses. The three of them always attracted a great deal of attention from German civilians on the street and in the shops, but, Bailey said, "The staff became accustomed to having black nurses around."

There was one incident, however, that reduced her to tears. "Upon completion of rounds, the group usually gathered to discuss the treatment of the patients. . . . The nurse was always part of that group, so I remained with them. On that occasion, one of the doctors said to me 'What are you waiting for?' I was shocked and withdrew to another area of the room to cry. It was the only thing I knew to do at the time. In a moment I felt a hand on my shoulder. One of the doctors came over to me and said, 'Captain Bailey, dismiss his behavior. He is no gentleman.' Following this incident, I had to make a mental adjustment in order to be effective in my work, for I would be seeing this person daily. Strangely enough, he was very kind to me thereafter, which I took as an apology for his behavior. From that time things went well."[42]

First Lieutenant Margaret E. Bailey, U.S. Army Nurse Corps, 1946. Army Nurse Corps Collection, Office of Medical History, Office of the Army Surgeon General.

The slow pace of desegregation was frustrating to black Americans; African American leaders said, it revealed the hypocrisy in America's vaunted freedoms. "The Germans say rather bluntly that the occupation by the U.S. Army [has] anything but a salutary effect on their belief in [d]emocracy, for the hierarchy of the [A]rmy, both in its military sphere and in its social sphere, is highly undemocratic." So reported the president of the National Council of Negro Women, Dr. Dorothy Ferebee, who in 1951 visited Germany on a fact-finding mission as part of an eleven-member panel representing America's largest women's organizations. The successor to Mary McLeod Bethune, who had been much involved in bringing black women into the WACs in World War II, Ferebee and group were expected to "interpret the role of women's organizations in a democratic society and to help the German people to fuller understanding of life in a democracy." Formed at the invitation of Germany, the panel was sponsored by the U.S. Department of State and the International Division of the Women's Bureau of the U.S. Labor Department.

Ferebee complained that segregated units in the Occupation forces were "something the German mind could not comprehend. If, they reasoned, democracy means respect for individual worth, freedom and equality, why were Negroes brought as separate units to a country where a new democracy was striving to be born? . . . It gave the average German the feeling that this pattern was no different from the racism they had been taught."

After the mission, Ferebee wrote to President Truman requesting a meeting to discuss her conversations with "Negro units" at several installations. "I need not tell you that the presence of the segregated military units . . . wreaks damage. . . . Although I attempted to interpret the difference between the Nazi brand of racism and that which despoils our own nation, I was aware of the fact that the pattern of our own American military units made bitter mockery of my words."[43]

She especially recalled trying to encourage "new Negro WACs" stationed near Munich to be "the best possible exponents of American ideals of justice and of democratic living [but] I knew from the faces of those girls that they shared with me the leaden burden of the American dilemma."[44]

Then First Lieutenant Mildred Inez Bailey, herself a white southerner, was one of the officers charged with making integration work as commander of a WAC unit at the 98th General Hospital in Germany. "We received information that we were going to get black women in the company. . . . Someone said, 'Well, we'll just put four of the women together in one room and two in another.' I said, 'No, they have got to be absorbed into the company where people get to know one another as individuals. . . . If you give the black women a chance to keep to themselves and the whites a chance to ignore them, it will create problems.

"Only one woman complained to me about sleeping in the same barracks room with a black woman. I told her that the black WACs would be placed into the rooms with empty beds, and if the woman's room had an empty bed in it, she would have to get used to the idea of having a black roommate." Bailey said she later heard that the woman had taken her complaint higher through the chain of command. "They all supported me because how could they do otherwise?"[45]

The pace of American military desegregation in Germany continued to move slowly. As late as 1 March 1952, a headline in the *Baltimore Afro-American* declared, "Pentagon Brass Decrees Certain Number of All-Colored Units," adding, "Segregation . . . is Army Policy." A letter to the paper from General Thomas Handy, commander in chief of American troops on the Continent, written in response to a reporter's inquiries, explained that orders to maintain all-colored male troops emanated from the Pentagon— but, the general boasted, "All WACs are integrated. . . . All colored women, enlisted and officers, are assigned to units not designated as colored."[46]

In Germany, however, "not designated as colored" scarcely meant equality. African American WACs complained of unfair treatment, menial assignments, segregated living quarters, and failure to receive promotions for which they qualified. When seven African American WACs at Signal Battalion Headquarters of the European Command questioned why they had not advanced in rank, their white duty sergeant reportedly was blunt. "It is a shame, but you girls have to be twice as intelligent as whites before you can be promoted."[47]

The Army lagged behind the other services and took almost two years even to develop its desegregation plan. In 1948, four African American officers and 121 enlisted women had been on active duty; until 1950, however, all black women volunteers received automatic assignment to the segregated Company B, 1st Battalion, at the WAC Training Center in Fort Lee, Virginia. It was staffed entirely by African American officers and noncommissioned officers. Although Officer Candidate School (OCS) and specialist training already were integrated, after their training most African Americans still faced careers in segregated work assignments, housing, eating arrangements, and social gatherings. In 1950, when the Army officially desegregated, the WAC Training Center reported, "We noted the change in the Army's system of segregation as we welcomed the last Company B into 405 School [WAC clerical training]."[48]

Throughout the armed forces, black servicewomen tested the new policies. Navy servicewomen had already served in desegregated assignments, but their numbers were few. In early 1948, the Navy claimed only one African American woman officer and six African American enlisted women among an enlisted force of seventeen hundred. By 1950, the service included two African American nurses and twenty-five enlisted WAVES, but no non-nurse officers. Under the headline "Navy Welcomes Women," the *Chicago Defender* reported in 1950, "In the relatively short span of eight years, the Navy has moved from a policy of complete exclusion of Negroes from general service and officer ranks to . . . a policy of complete integration. Undoubtedly public opinion has been a factor . . . but chiefly the Navy had been influenced by considerations of military efficiency and the need to economize human resources."[49]

The first two African American women joined the Marine Corps in the summer of 1949 and a third volunteered early in 1950. In 1949, the Air Force officially disbanded Jim Crow units and desegregation appeared successful. In 1950, an African American WAF sergeant talked about job assignments and living conditions in the Air Force with the regional secretary of the National Association for the Advancement of Colored People (NAACP), during the latter's surprise visit to Randolph Air Force Base, Texas. "Essentially, we had integration in the WAFs even before the order. There were few of us Negro girls, and I suppose it would have been practically impossible to make a distinction."[50]

In 1951, the year when the Air Force commissioned its first three black officers—Edwina Martin of Danville, Virginia; Jane Cotton of Jackson, Michigan; and Evelyn Brown of Shreveport, Louisiana—officials credited the success of desegregation at Lackland to the commitment of commanding officers.[51] An African American WAF noted, however, that when the Human Resources School administered psychological tests, the testing cards of African American women were each marked with a red X. She wondered why.[52] One white WAF who joined the Air Force in 1952 remembered that the four black women in her training flight were always kept together and that their race was always noted. "On every roster, every order, those four girls always had an asterisk after their names with the footnote: 'negroid.' I thought it was grossly unfair."[53]

It is intriguing to note here what may or may not have been coincidence. A phrase that has haunted the full inclusion of servicewomen was used (perhaps even coined) in a complaint about Assistant Secretary of Defense Anna Rosenberg and racial integration. In March 1952, when the House of Representatives voted down Universal Military Training (UMT), forty Southern Democrats—usually among the first to vote pro-military—stunned observers by joining isolationist Republicans against the bill. UMT had once again raised the issue of a female draft, but the resistance to it was clearly about race. Representative John Williams of Mississippi had written Rosenberg requesting her assurance that segregation would be maintained. According to the *New Republic,* when her answer came back "a blunt 'No,'" one congressman said, "this measure is . . . an Anna Rosenberg *social integration* scheme."[54]

Institutional and official histories rarely reflect the personal slights and problems encountered by their minority members; the leaders set the story line based on their own perceptions. The women who headed the women's components of the various military branches in their early days, from World War II through the passing of the 1948 Women's Armed Services Integration Act and the Korean War, were no different. They recorded how they anticipated problems related to integration, took steps to eliminate prospective problems before they began, then breathed a sigh of relief when problems did not materialize or were not reported to them. Looking back on that time in 1980, Marine Colonel Helen A. Wilson wrote:

> I can recall that at MCAS, Cherry Point, I was very much concerned about the acceptance and treatment of my Negro enlisted women, who arrived in 1950. . . . I consulted my trustee, Sergeant Major Alice J. Connolly, and together we decided . . . they would be billeted in an area with . . . a devout Christian woman, and if there were any problems, they would be referred to the commanding officer. How antiquated this decision now seems to be. But in retrospect, it was important that we placed the two Negro women in areas where there would be minimal or no rejection—and of course it worked.[55]

The perspectives of the African American women being integrated into the predominantly white force were frequently different, but less frequently collected in official records. Chief Warrant Officer Second Class Annie Laurie Grimes, the third of the women who had helped integrate the Women Marines, said of her twenty years in the Marine Corps, "Looking back, I thor-

Private Annie L. Grimes, the third African American woman to join the Marine Corps and later the Marines' first black woman officer, with her recruit platoon during boot camp, Parris Island, South Carolina, 1950.
U.S. Marine Corps photo.

oughly enjoyed my career. . . . I made many lifelong friends. The positive experiences completely overshadowed the negative ones." When specifically asked by a Marine Corps historian what the negative experiences were, Grimes replied, "Oh, nothing really terrible. Just little things, like happen in regular life to black people every day."[56]

In researching this book on the servicewomen who served their country during the Korean War and early Cold War period, similar attitudes become apparent. None regretted her service, though some had specific complaints that have lingered through the years regarding differences in treatment or in dependents' benefits. All were proud of their contributions to the war effort. Almost all voiced the wish that they had been permitted to do more.

"The Old Dividing Line"

The old dividing line between "a man's job" and "a woman's job" is fast
disappearing. Short of combat, we think women can do virtually any job in
the armed forces. However . . . this far, women have not pulled their share
of the load.
—General George C. Marshall, *Poughkeepsie New Yorker*, 14 January 1952[1]

In every time of crisis women have served our country in difficult and
hazardous ways. . . . Women should not be considered to be a marginal
group to be employed periodically only to be denied opportunity to satisfy
their needs and aspirations when unemployment rises or a war ends.
—Former World War II Navy Officer John Fitzgerald Kennedy, upon
    establishing his President's Commission on the Status of Women,
    14 December 1961[2]

W HEN THE KOREAN WAR officially ended 27 July 1953,
the armistice agreement established a border four
thousand meters wide and 151 miles long across Korea, down the middle of
which ran a demarcation where the fighting stopped. Known as the Demilitarized Zone (DMZ), it exists to this day, one of the last remnants of the
hostilities in Korea and one of the last landmarks of the Cold War.[3]

Although the United States continued to face Cold War responsibilities
around the world, its armed forces underwent significant demobilization
after the Korean War ended. The number of Americans in uniform fell
from 3.7 million to under three million, still the highest peacetime levels in
history.[4] That count would rise and fall with each new Cold War crisis—
ranging between 2.5 and 2.8 million—until the crisis in Southeast Asia

escalated into another "limited" war. The military's women's components quickly reverted to their tiny prewar sizes, and remained significantly under-strength throughout the remainder of the 1950s.[5]

An opinion survey among 4,420 women of all services in the spring of 1953 demonstrated that recruiting and retaining servicewomen would continue to be a problem. Only 27 percent of the servicewomen taking the survey indicated that they planned to reenlist when their tour was up; of those who had other plans, half indicated marriage was their plan. Older women in their thirties and forties and those with longer service records were more likely to reenlist. More worrisome, less than 25 percent of active duty women said that they would "definitely and without reservations" advise a friend to join and just a scant 18 percent more—less than half—"probably" would advise a friend to join, but "with reservations." Tellingly, the longer a woman had been in service, the less likely she was to recommend it. Lack of job satisfaction appeared to be the major contributing factor in the disillusionment uniformed women had about military service.[6]

None of this was news, and perhaps servicemen were equally as negative about reenlisting or recommending that a friend join up, especially those who had been drafted or who had joined to avoid the draft. But, again and again, each survey the services designed and administered during the Korean War indicated that servicewomen felt they were not really needed or appreciated, and that those who felt stuck in dead-end jobs planned to be the first out the door. During World War II, servicewomen had been willing to put up with dead-end jobs, fight pernicious gossip by setting a fine example, and make do with less than optimal living conditions because they believed that they were needed and were contributing to a higher cause. The American public didn't perceive the Korean War as a true national emergency, nor did servicewomen. "Except for nurses, servicewomen were too few, and their assigned work too readily done by others [soldiers or civilians], to become a vital part of the military establishment. As long as the draft could produce the varying quantity of raw manpower needed, service women seemed little more than a dispensable vestige [of World War II]. The Korean War did nothing to change that."[7] Given the conditions, if the military wanted servicewomen, it had to reaffirm that need in its treatment of them or it had to draft them, which it could not do. And, with the booming postwar economy, it had to compete for them with civilian employers.

For Navy women, the post–Korean War period was particularly bleak. Promotions were slow and opportunities to enter technical fields were far fewer than in World War II.[8] The ratings open to enlisted Navy women declined throughout the 1950s as the Navy steered more and more women into clerical and administrative fields. In 1952, some thirty-six Navy ratings were open to women; by 1956, only twenty-five were open. Only twenty-one remained open in 1962. Moreover, women did not actually have opportunities in all the ratings open to them. Ninety percent of the enlisted women were relegated to just two occupational groups, administrative/clerical and medical/dental. The draft and the threat of it (volunteers could choose their service, draftees could not) provided enough young men to fill most of the technical billets that led to lucrative civilian jobs, shutting young women out of the kind of training for which they'd joined.

During this time the Navy Women's Reserve saw a rise in disciplinary problems because of the youth of recruits, the shortage of female petty officers, and male petty officers who complained they couldn't figure out how to "handle" women. The latter situation, it almost goes without saying, was blamed exclusively on the women.[9] Recruiting and retaining high-caliber women was also difficult, as reflected in the fact that the number of women enrolled in officer training declined. In 1952 and 1953, there were seventy or more women in each class at the Navy's Newport school. That number dropped to ten in 1956.[10]

Other Navy women felt threatened—or cheated—by their treatment. In 1953 reservist Kathleen Amick, a World War II veteran and aviation electrician's mate, received a low grade on her quarterly evaluation. She investigated and found out a suspicious number of seasoned women mechanics also had received inexplicably low marks. "It was as if someone wanted us to look bad. I think some people thought it wasn't appropriate for women to be in the mechanic's ratings," said Amick. She insisted that her grade be changed to reflect her performance more accurately. When she later discovered that the correction had not been recorded, "I made them change it right then and there."[11]

Reenlistment and retention problems plagued the entire armed forces, not just the women's components throughout the Korean War. Before its start, the reenlistment rate for all services, including men and women, was 59.3 percent. By the end of the war it had fallen to 23.7 percent. Extremely concerned, Secretary of Defense Charles Wilson appointed a committee that concluded that military pay had not kept pace with the cost of living in the postwar boom. Another significant factor in losing G.I.s: a decline in public respect for military service, low morale, and an increase in disciplinary problems. The committee recommended increasing reenlistment incentives, retirement programs, and military pay.[12]

When WAF Director Mary Jo Shelly resigned in January 1954, her outgoing report concluded that the WAF would have to remain small and exclusive. The Air Force did not have a choice in the matter, Shelly maintained. Women in the U.S. Armed Forces were volunteers in the full sense; unlike men, women were under no obligation to serve. It was this freedom from obligation that determined, beyond any service branch's control, not only how many women would heed the call to service, but who they were, what they wanted, and what they would and would not do for the privilege of wearing Uncle Sam's uniforms. This overriding reality, not any decision of the Air Force, would shape the WAF program. If the Air Force or any other branch wanted women of a certain caliber, it might get a small number of such women. If it insisted on a larger force, the quality of women would decline.[13]

Shelly offered one insight that put much of this in context. Despite American women's impressive World War II record, military service was the newest, least accepted, and most misunderstood profession for them. With the exceptions of the half-century-old Army and Navy Nurse Corps and the brief, temporary service of Yeomen (F) and Women Marines during World War I, women had been a part of the military just since 1942, barely a dozen years. The first generation of regulars was still on active duty. In this light, Shelly said, it should be no surprise that few women seriously contemplated military service in peacetime, and that for the most part only very young and unskilled women had opted to serve during the Korean War, a period boasting the highest-ever civilian employment level in American history.[14]

"Why didn't [the Korean War] inspire women to join the services?" Shelly asked rhetorically. (Her question was equally applicable to both sexes. Korea hardly inspired men to join, but uninspired men could be drafted.) Shelly said two things allowed Americans to ignore the Cold War threat to democracy: the nation's small military commitment relative to its World War II effort, and the fact that the economy was no longer so intertwined with the war effort as it had been a decade earlier.[15]

In 1953, WAF Second Lieutenant Betty Miller (White) of Palmyra, Pennsylvania, was planning her wedding to a fellow Air Force officer when she was asked to take a WAF recruiting course. She said "No, thank you," but the Air Force prevailed and Miller postponed her wedding. After completing the ninety-hour course she married and was sent to New Jersey to recruit women in New England and the Mid-Atlantic. Her job was daunting. At first, because the Army

At the end of the Korea War, Ruth Cheney Streeter, the former director of the World War II Marine Corps Women's Reserve told a Princeton, New Jersey, civic group that qualified women still were needed in all the service branches and then introduced a fashion show of current duty and dress uniforms, 21 October 1953. Models left to right: Navy Reserve Lieutenant M.E. Mitchell, Air Force Lieutenant Betty L. Miller White, Marine Corps Reserve Lieutenant Hazel D. Gausch, Women's Army Corps Lieutenant Julia McNeely, Navy Yeoman First Class Betty B. Burke, Marine Corps Sergeant Marie A. Pandolfi, Women's Army Corps Sergeant First Class Betty Blackburn, and Air Force Staff Sergeant Jean Northam. U.S. Army photo.

and Air Force were doing joint recruiting, she had two bosses: an Army lieutenant colonel and a WAF officer. "If a woman walked in [to the recruiting office] and knew she was interested in the Air Force, I dealt with her. If she didn't know which service she was interested in, I had to present both."

Outside the office, Miller found it "difficult to recruit women and difficult to combat the sexual innuendo that surrounded the topic." In speeches before community groups she tried to counter the traditional arguments against women in the service by stressing the sense of self gained from being in the service and the high moral character of female enlistees. "Response was generally positive," she said, adding, "If the men did not agree with me they did not confront me. They would say something to the person sitting next to them." Young people could be openly derisive. During a local high school career day, "some snickered. I was a novelty. They had never seen a woman in uniform." However, the fact that she had gone to college in the area proved to be a plus because "the school's reputation reflected well on me and on the Air Force."

> Women audiences were generally more open. Miller recalls a fashion show in Princeton, New Jersey, that featured Ruth Cheney Streeter, the first director of the Women Marine Reserves, and military women modeling the uniforms of their various services. "Response [was] very positive."
>
> Throughout her fifteen months as a recruiter Miller never had a quota to fill. "I was recruiting at a time when quality was more important than quantity."[16]

In the aftermath of the Korean War, the military itself was still not clear about its need for women or their place in the defense of the nation. Reflective of this attitude was a 1954 thesis entitled "Why WAF?" submitted to the Air War College Air University by Colonel James R. Bearly. He declared the WAF program a failure because it was too small to be a credible mobilization base—a valid criticism and one that women's directors had recognized almost from the start. Bearly further criticized the WAF recruiting effort during the Korean War, claiming rightly that the promised "Career Choice, Travel, and Training Opportunities" set up expectations in recruits that the Air Force could not match. Only 10 percent of the WAF were assigned overseas during the war, said Bearly, and most women did not even have a choice about their training and assignments. Their resulting negativity and low morale (for which the women of the WAF were hardly to blame) were extremely difficult to combat.[17]

The truly disturbing thing about Bearly's report is its bias against women; he was, after all, an Air Force colonel who had commanded WAF in the field. He not only blamed the women for every problem associated with them, he recirculated many of the slanderous World War II rumors about their morals and sexuality. Notably, he neglected to discuss WAF job performance and abilities, or make a comparison with male recruits of the same age. In this Air Force colonel's opinion, the WAF should be discontinued.

It would not be surprising if Bearly's attitude had been reflected in many male officers under him, as well as the airmen under them. How many male officers simply had a knee-jerk reaction that the military was no place for women and that the women's components should be disbanded? And was this problem unique to the Air Force, or were male leaders and soldiers in the other services just as negative about women in the military? One shudders for the morale of the servicewomen who worked under this and similar-thinking commanders.

When women gained permanent status in the military in 1948, the attitude that they were interlopers on an all-male preserve did not change. As permanent members of the service, women potentially now competed with men for assignments, ratings, and promotions; as Army historian Colonel Bettie Morden noted, however, only a limited number of "imperturbable, confident, and good-humored" women were successful in climbing the supervisory ladder.[18]

The military is a reflection of the society it serves, and American society had changed very little between 1948 and 1953. Newspapers and magazines constantly reassured the public that the new "businesswomen" filling outer offices were not trying to compete with men, but only wanted to be an effective part of the team. It was a message that women military leaders adapted as their own, stressing that servicewomen weren't viewed as "replacing" men but "complementing" them. One reporter wrote after a visit to Lackland Air Force Base, "The mass of military men cling strongly to the idea that if women won't stay in the kitchen, they should surely go no further than the typewriter or the filing cabinet."[19] At the same time, housewives were lavishly praised by social commentators. Their jobs were now "more complex . . . they were expected to be domestic scientists, a category that encompassed child psychologist, economist, nutritionist, chemist, physicist, biologist and of course . . . a good cook."[20] Anyone could read between the lines: woman's place was in the home.

Given the societal values of the 1950s, the limitations placed on women's options outside the home, and the disapproval from many Americans—not just military men—of the presence of women in the ranks, it is not surprising that servicewomen's job options were extremely limited throughout the Korean War and its aftermath. It was a no-win situation, and yet the women's programs, just by surviving that time period, *did* win. Nonetheless, until society changed its attitudes about women in the military, the servicewomen's programs would remain small, limited organizations that would be severely challenged in times of emergencies.

Coincident with Shelly's final report some six months after the war ended, Secretary of State John Foster Dulles announced the "New Look" defense strategy, a doctrine of a massive and instant nuclear retaliation. In effect, the bomb made the idea of a massive, protracted mobilization of manpower obsolete. If manpower (massive reliance on combat soldiers) was becoming obsolete, could the need for womanpower (support personnel who freed men to fight) also become obsolete? That had been the raison d'être for the women's line components as defined in the 1948 Women's Armed Services Integration Act.[21] What no one stopped to consider at the time, what perhaps could not even be conceived of in the 1950s, was that

New Look's reliance on technology rather than combat suggested that the military technologist's gender might be irrelevant. "Short of combat, we think women can do virtually any job in the armed forces," General Marshall had said. New Look may have been the first indication that "the old dividing line between 'a man's job' and 'a woman's job'" might someday disappear.

After peaking at 48,700 women in October 1952, the number of women in the military dropped off to slightly more than 35,000, or less than 1 percent of the total military force in June 1955. For the postwar women's services (other than the always necessary nurse corps and medical specialists), the next ten to twelve years would become a period of survival in an inhospitable environment.[22] The military continued to employ women primarily in the jobs that "women did better than men," repetitive tasks such as typing, filing, and switchboard work. Generals and admirals competed for attractive young female junior officers for administrative assistants and protocol officers as office decoration.[23] And the women's directors believed that if they rocked the boat by making too many demands, the military might move to abolish the women's programs altogether.[24]

Jerry Robb joined the Marine Corps right out of high school at the end of the Korean War and for no other reason than that a friend had done so. Underage at eighteen, her mother had to sign a permission form. She freely admitted that she hated the discipline, the regimentation, the climate at Parris Island, and particularly loathed the amount of time she spent ironing her uniform. But she also remembered her personal pride in being a Marine—and that the Corps instilled in her a belief that she could accomplish anything she wanted to. "I came out of boot camp thinking I was absolutely, really something." And, she added, "that is not such a bad thing to teach young women."

"Look at all the wrinkles! They really look nice in the morning, but by the end of the day they look like they've been slept in," wrote Private First Class Jerry Robb about her Marine Corps utility uniform during boot camp, Parris Island, South Carolina, 1953. Courtesy Jerry Robb.

> When the Corps discovered that Robb was a high-speed typist and could take high-speed dictation, she was sent directly from boot camp to Marine Corps Headquarters in Washington where she worked for visiting VIPs. But despite her pride and her high-profile job, Jerry Robb left the Marine Corps at the end of her first enlistment. She said she never even considered reenlisting.[25]

The high attrition rate of first-term enlisted women that had plagued the services during the Korean War continued unabated throughout the 1950s. Into the early 1960s, 70 to 80 percent of enlisted women left the service before or when their first terms were up, raising serious questions about the cost-effectiveness of the women's programs. Those concerns were not without irony. During the same time period, male draftees had a higher attrition rate. Yes, analysts did question the cost of training women only to have them leave before they completed the jobs they had contracted to do, but the services continued to allow women to leave upon marriage, believing it would be bad public relations not to. Yes, women did get married and pregnant and leave the service, but men had families the services had to support. Most military men simply did not want to acknowledge the high cost of dependents to the military. Writing about this era in her landmark *Women in the Military: An Unfinished Revolution,* Major General Jeanne M. Holm pointed out the "basic hypocrisy in the service's hand wringing over female attrition. . . . [T]hose who viewed the losses with the most alarm often were those most reluctant to change the policies that generated the losses, by, for example, requiring married women to fulfill their contracts. . . . No matter that men actually cost more in the long term."[26]

During the same period, there were some solid steps toward equality. Because of the dire scarcity of women military nurses and women medical specialists during the Korean War, a few male physical therapists were commissioned in the Air Force, and a series of bills to gender-integrate the nurse corps and medical specialist corps were introduced into Congress during and after the war. Ohio Representative Frances Payne Bolton sponsored five of these legislative efforts before she succeeded in getting one passed.[27] Finally, in 1955, male nurses were allowed into the Reserves of the Army, Navy, and Air Force nurse and medical specialist corps.[28]

The Defense Advisory Committee on Women in the Services (DACOWITS), created early in the Korean War (1951), was one of the lasting legacies of that era. Initially given three objectives—inform the public of the need for servicewomen, persuade parents that the service was a good place for their daughters, and boost the recruitment of sufficient top-quality women—DACOWITS proved a worthy champion.[29] From its earliest years, members of the committee made personal field trips, observed servicewomen on the job, inspected their living quarters and talked to them about their experiences, problems, and aspirations. Again and again DACOWITS's members reported back that servicewomen simply wanted the opportunity to do their best work and receive fair compensation.[30] DACOWITS made appropriate recommendations to the DOD; if the DOD did not act upon the recommendations quickly, DACOWITS made the same recommendation the following year, in some cases for as long as twenty years before the DOD adopted a proposal.[31]

Many of the committee's most critical and controversial recommendations took years to come to fruition. For example, in 1956 DACOWITS recommended that married military women be permitted to live off-post and collect an allowance for quarters, just as married servicemen did. They proposed it a third time in 1959, then every year throughout the 1960s until the inequity was righted in early 1971.[32] Brigadier General Mildred Inez Bailey, U.S. Army (Ret.), praised DACOWITS for its "almost bulldog tenacity. . . . When they identified the really important issues they hung in there until [they were] . . . finally resolved."[33]

DACOWITS's tenacity has earned it enemies as well as friends. In recent years, as sizable numbers of women have taken part in combat support in the Balkans, Afghanistan, and the Middle East, DACOWITS has pushed for ever broader roles—and its enemies have become more vocal regarding where "the old dividing line between a 'man's job' and a 'woman's job'" should be drawn.

Even as the post–Korean War military faced challenges complicated by the nation's New Look defense philosophy, the United States was in the process of becoming embroiled in its next limited war: Vietnam. That war would eventually challenge the services' ability to recruit or even to draft young men. Navy nurse Marie Eberhardt (no rank available) was stationed at the U.S. Naval Hospital in Yokosuka, Japan, in 1954 when the French military was forced out of Vietnam.[34] The Navy sent vessels from Yokosuka to aid in the evacuation. With Navy nurses and a woman pharmacist, Commander Kay Keating, aboard, the hospital ship *Haven* sailed up the Saigon River in September 1954 to evacuate some 721 French army, navy, and Foreign Legion casualties.[35]

That every U.S. military branch had servicewomen ready to deploy in that emergency and those that have followed meant servicewomen had proved themselves to be, as Captain Joy Bright Hancock had argued in 1948 they were, "a national defense weapon known to be of value." Their organizations had been kept in "working order and not allowed to rust or to be abolished." Each new generation of servicewomen might have to prove themselves and face new equality battles, but the military would never again have "to start from scratch . . . duplicate effort . . . make the same mistakes," as WAC Director Colonel Mary Hallaren had warned would occur were the nation to forget women's contributions—until it needed them again to help wage another war.

NOTES

INTRODUCTION (PP. 1–12)

1. Joy Bright Hancock, Captain, U.S. Navy (Ret.), *Lady in the Navy: A Personal Reminiscence* (Annapolis, Md.: Naval Institute Press, 1972), 228.

2. Mildred McAfee Horton, Lieutenant Commander and former director of the WAVES, U.S. Navy, "Why Not Draft Women?" excerpt from February 1951 *Ladies Home Journal*, reprinted in the *AWS* (All Women's Services) *Journal* (February 1951), 2, Grace L. Mueller Collection, Women's Memorial Collection.

3. Though historians may debate which of several events marked the first battle of the Cold War, Winston Churchill coined the phrase in a 5 March 1946, speech at Westminster College in Fulton, Missouri, as quoted by David McCullough, *Truman* (New York: Simon and Schuster, 1992), 489: "From Stettin in the Baltic to Trieste in the Adriatic an iron curtain has descended. . . . Behind that line lie all the capitals of the ancient states of Central and Eastern Europe. Warsaw, Berlin, Prague, Vienna, Budapest, Belgrade, Bucharest and Sofia, all these famous cities and the populations around them lie in what I must call the Soviet sphere."

4. Emma Jane Riley, Colonel, U.S. Air Force (Ret.), report, Papers of Jeanne M. Holm, Major General, U.S. Air Force (Ret.), U.S. Air Force Academy Archives.

5. Jeanne M. Holm, Major General, U.S. Air Force (Ret.), *Women in the Military: An Unfinished Revolution*, rev. ed. (Novato, Calif.: Presidio, 1992), 162.

6. Lorry M. Fenner, Colonel, U.S. Air Force, "Ideology and Amnesia: The Public Debate on Women in the American Military 1940–1973" (Ph.D. diss., University of Michigan, 1995), 324.

7. Joseph Goulden, *The Best Years: 1945–1950* (New York: Atheneum, 1976), 93–95, 107.

8. McCullough, *Truman*, 467.

9. Ibid., 486–490.

10. Sherie Mershon and Steven Schlossman, *Foxholes & Color Lines: Desegregating the US Armed Forces* (Baltimore, Md.: Johns Hopkins University Press, 1998), 168–169.

11. John Egerton, *Speak Now Against the Day* (Chapel Hill: University of North Carolina Press, 1994), 360–366; Thomas Sugrue, *The Origins of the Urban Crisis: Race and Inequality in Postwar Detroit* (Princeton, N.J.: Princeton University Press, 1996), 7–8.

12. Eleanor Roosevelt, letter submitted with remarks by Rep. Helen Gahagan Douglas, 20 February 1947, to the *Appendix to the Congressional Record,* in regard to the pending legislation, "Elimination of Unfair Discrimination Based on Sex," 635.

13. Fenner, "Ideology and Amnesia," 312.

14. The full names of the World War II women's components were the Women's Army Auxiliary Corps (WAAC), which became the Women's Army Corps (WAC); the Navy Women's Reserve (WAVES); the Marine Corps Women's Reserve; and the Coast Guard Women's Reserves (SPARs). Because the Coast Guard is not part of the military during peacetime, the Coast Guard was not initially included in these efforts to gender-integrate the armed forces.

15. Women's Armed Services Integration Act of 1948, Eightieth Congress, Second Session, 12 June 1948.

16. The Army Nurse Corps ordered "reserve" nurses to duty as early as 1911 when several skirmishes broke out along the U.S.-Mexican border. At that time, however, the Army Nurse and Navy Nurse Corps reserves consisted of nurses who had enrolled in the American Red Cross and had agreed to be subject to a call-up. During World War I more than ten thousand Red Cross reserve nurses served on active duty in the Army and eleven hundred in the Navy. Throughout the 1930s, the Army began acquiring reserve nurses directly from nursing schools rather than the Red Cross. The Navy, on the other hand, quietly terminated all its reserve nurses, and only established a small reserve list in 1940 as war began to appear imminent. The massive mobilization effort required for World War II forced both services to take even more control over their reserve nurses. In 1944 Public Law 350 granted Army and Navy nurses temporary commissions equal to those of male officers and assigned the responsibility for procuring reserve nurses to the armed services rather than the Red Cross. The 1947 Army-Navy Nurse Act, which provided military nurses with permanent commissions equal to those of male officers, also established the first actual Army and Navy Nurse Officers' Reserve Corps.

17. Mary T. Sarnecky, Colonel, U.S. Army Nurse Corps (Ret.), *A History of the Army Nurse Corps,* (Philadelphia: University of Pennsylvania Press, 1999), 271.

18. Army Memorandum, 10 March 1958, miscellaneous folder, Korean War, Historian's Files, Women In Military Service For America Memorial Foundation, Inc. (hereafter Women's Memorial).

19. Esther Strong, Ph.D., Representative of Women's Interests, Personnel Policy Board Staff to WAC Lt. Colonel Geneva McQuatters, DACOWITS Executive Secretary, 25 February 1952, Folder 1, Staff Signature File, Record Group 330, Office of the Assistant Secretary of Defense for Manpower, Personnel and Reserves, Anna Rosenberg, National Archives, College Park, Maryland.

20. Transcript, Conference of Civilian Women Leaders, 21–22 June 1950, sponsored by the Personnel Policy Board of the Pentagon, Historian's Files, Women's Memorial.

21. Recommendations of the Defense Advisory Committee on Women in the Services Meeting, 17–18 March 1952, Staff Signature File, Record Group 330, Office of the Assistant Secretary of Defense for Manpower and Personnel, Anna Rosenberg, National Archives, College Park, Maryland.

22. Hazel Baird Macquin, dean, College of Nursing, University of Utah, to the Honorable Daniel A. Kimball, Secretary of the Navy, 30 December 1952, Administration Division General Correspondence 1952–1971, File A4–1/AH12 [USS HAVEN] Record Group 52, BUMED, National Archives, College Park, Maryland.

23. Dorothy G. Horwitz, ed., *We Will Not Be Strangers: Korean War Letters Between a MASH Surgeon and His Wife,* foreword by James I. Matray (Urbana: University of Illinois Press, 1997), 94, 99, 104, 131, 229; Annual Reports, 8225th MASH, 1952–1953, (AMEDD) Records 1947–1961, File HD 319.1, Record Group 112, Office of the Surgeon General, Army, U.S. Medical Department, National Archives, College Park, Maryland.

24. Dorothy Brandon, "Men to Replace Nurses Up Front Urged by Korea Nurses' Leader," *New York Herald Tribune,* 5 May 1952, n.p.; Dorothy Brandon, "Calls Army Nurses 'Hazard to Troops,'" *Washington Post,* 1 June 1952, 17, Gift of Bert Hartry, Women's Memorial Collection.

25. Fenner, "Ideology and Amnesia," 326.

26. Letter of Appreciation, Commanding Officer 98th Bombardment Wing to Commanding Officer 8043 Signal Service, re: Sergeant Alice R. O'Connor, Alice R. O'Connor Collection, gift of Margaret J. Wieschhaus, Women's Memorial Collection.

27. Unit reports from Army hospitals in Korea indicate the 3rd Station Hospital had one dietitian as of December 1950 and the 10th Station Hospital had one dietitian and one physical therapist by the end of the war. Two dietitians were sent to Korea at the end of the war to assist in Operation Little Switch, a prisoner of war exchange. Annual Reports of Medical Units in the Far East Theater, 1950–1953, RG 112, OSG U.S. Medical Dept. (AMEDD) Records 1947–61 File HD19.1, National Archives, College Park, Maryland.

28. Carl Mydens, "Girl War Correspondent," *Life Magazine,* (1 December 1952), 51–60.

29. Fenner, "Ideology and Amnesia," 344.

30. Brett Harvey, *The Fifties: A Woman's Oral History* (New York: HarperCollins, 1993), 69.

CHAPTER 1. WOMEN'S PLACE—AND THE SERVICEWOMAN'S PLACE— IN POST–WORLD WAR II AMERICA (PP. 13–30)

1. Jeanne M. Holm, Major General, U.S. Air Force (Ret.), *Women in the Military: An Unfinished Revolution,* rev. ed. (Novato, Calif.: Presidio, 1992), 113.

2. Mattie Treadwell, Lieutenant Colonel, Women's Army Corps, *The Women's Army Corps* (Washington, D.C.: Office of the Chief of Military History, 1954), 748.

3. Holm, *Women in the Military,* 105.

4. Doris Weatherford, *American Women and World War II* (New York: Facts on File, 1990), 307; Susan Hartman, *The Homefront and Beyond: American Women in the 1940s* (Boston: Twayne, 1982), 209–217; William Chafe, *The American Woman: Her Changing Social, Economic and Political Role, 1920–1970* (New York: Oxford University Press, 1972), 199–225.

5. Penny Coleman, *Rosie the Riveter: Women Working on the Home Front in World War II* (New York: Crown, 1995), 97.

6. Stephanie Coontz, *The Way We Never Were: American Families and the Nostalgia Trap* (New York: Basic Books, 1992), 23–41; Betty Friedan, *The Feminine Mystique,* rev. ed. (New York: Dell Publishing, 1984), 15–32.

7. Caroline Bird, *Born Female: The High Cost of Keeping Women Down* (New York: David McKay, 1968), 43–44.

8. *Historical Statistics of the United States: Colonial Times to 1970,* Part 1, Bureau of U.S. Census, 1975, 19.

9. Bird, *Born Female,* 43–75; Chafe, *American Woman,* 181–182; *Statistical Abstracts of the United States,* 81st ed. (Washington, D.C.: GPO, 1960), 81.

10. Coontz, *The Way We Never Were,* 27, 32–33; Friedan, *Feminine Mystique,* 16, 204.

11. William Chafe, *The Unfinished Journey: America Since World War II* (New York: Oxford University Press, 1991), 85.

12. *Statistical Abstracts of the United States,* 86th ed. (Washington, D.C.: GPO, 1965), 228; Bird, *Born Female,* 43–75; *Statistical Abstracts of the United States,* 81st ed. (Washington, D.C.: GPO, 1960), 81.

13. Bird, *Born Female,* 47; Chafe, *American Woman,* 181–182; Chafe, *Unfinished Journey,* 84.

14. Chafe, *Unfinished Journey,* 79.

15. Coleman, *Rosie the Riveter,* 99.

16. Chafe, *Unfinished Journey,* 84.

17. Stephen Galpin, "Women: They're Grabbing Off A Greater Share of Jobs in Office and Factory," *Wall Street Journal,* 24 May 1950, 1.

18. Ibid.

19. Bird, *Born Female,* 43–75.

20. Weatherford, *American Women,* 307.

21. Florence Kitchelt, "Letters to the Editor," *Wall Street Journal,* 5 June 1950, n.p.

22. Holm, *Women in the Military,* 105.

23. Jean Ebbert, Lieutenant (jg), U.S. Navy, and Marie Beth Hall, *Crossed Currents: Navy Women in a Century of Change,* rev. ed. (Washington, D.C.: Brassey's, 1999), 113.

24. Joy Bright Hancock, Captain, U.S. Navy (Ret.), *Lady in the Navy: A Personal Reminiscence* (Annapolis, Md.: Naval Institute Press, 1972), 222.

25. Ebbert and Hall, *Crossed Currents,* 114.

26. Treadwell, *Women's Army Corps,* 748.
27. Ebbert and Hall, *Crossed Currents,* 113; Holm, *Women in the Military,* 104.
28. U.S. House of Representatives, 79th Congress, 2nd Session, Naval Affairs Committee Hearings on H.R. 5915, 9 May 1946, 3322.
29. Janann Sherman, *No Place for a Woman: A Life of Margaret Chase Smith,* (New Brunswick, N.J.: Rutgers University Press, 2000), 69.
30. Hearings on H.R. 5915.
31. Janann Sherman, "'They either need these women or they do not': Margaret Chase Smith and the Fight for Regular Status for Women in the Military," *Journal of Military History* (January 1990), 65.
32. Bettie J. Morden, Colonel, U.S. Army (Ret.), *The Women's Army Corps, 1945–1978* (Washington, D.C.: U.S. Army Center of Military History, 1992), 43.
33. Morden, *Women's Army Corps,* 35–36; Ebbert and Hall, *Crossed Currents,* 110–112.
34. Edith Sullivan, Captain, Women's Army Corps, letters of 24 August 1946; 6 October 1946; and 26 August 1947 to her parents, Mr. and Mrs. Benjamin Franklin Sullivan of Chazy, New York, Edith Sullivan Moss Collection, Gift of Marcia J. Moss, Women's Memorial Collection.
35. David McCullough, *Truman* (New York: Simon and Schuster, 1992), 521–523, 642–652; David Halberstam, *The Fifties* (New York: Villard Books, 1993), 9–10.
36. Doris M. Sterner, Captain, U.S. Navy Nurse Corps (Ret.), *In and Out of Harm's Way: A History of the Navy Nurse Corps* (Seattle, Wash.: Peanut Butter Publishing, 1997), 63, 123–124, and 160.
37. U.S. Senate, Subcommittee of the Committee on Armed Services, Testimony 2 July 1947, on the Women's Armed Services Integration Act.
38. Hancock, *Lady in the Navy,* 228.
39. U.S. Senate, Subcommittee of the Committee on Armed Services, Testimony 2 July 1947, on the Women's Armed Services Integration Act.
40. Mary Agnes Hallaren, Colonel, U.S. Army (Ret.), oral history conducted by Donald R. Hargrove, Colonel, U.S. Army and Milton L. Little, Lt. Colonel, U.S. Army, 7 March 1977, Historian's Files, Women's Memorial.
41. Hallaren, oral history.
42. Morden, *Women's Army Corps,* 40–44.
43. Ibid; Mary A. Hallaren, Colonel, U.S. Army (Ret.), biography, www.wic.org/bio/mhallare.htm (accessed 10 January 2005).
44. Morden, *Women's Army Corps,* 109.
45. Ibid., 45–46.
46. Sherman, *No Place,* 70.
47. James Schnable, *The Joint Chiefs of Staff and National Policy, 1945–1947* (Washington, D.C.: Office of the Chairman of the Joint Chiefs of Staff, 1996), 109–113.
48. McCullough, *Truman,* 726–741.
49. Ebbert and Hall, *Crossed Currents,* 120–121.
50. Holm, *Women in the Military,* 103–119; Morden, *Women's Army Corps,* 48–49.

51. U.S. House of Representatives, Armed Services Committee, Testimony on S. 1641, 18 February 1948.

52. Hancock, *Lady in the Navy*, 231.

53. Holm, *Women in the Military*, 50–54.

54. Hancock, *Lady in the Navy*, 230.

55. "Who Was Joy Bright Hancock?" www.usna.edu/JBHO/jbh_biography.htm (accessed 10 January 2005).

56. Ibid.

57. Hancock, *Lady in the Navy*, 220–232.

58. Lorry M. Fenner, Colonel, U.S. Air Force, "Ideology and Amnesia: The Public Debate on Women in the American Military 1940–1973" (Ph.D. diss., University of Michigan, 1995), 259.

59. Morden, *Women's Army Corps*, 53.

60. Ibid., 52.

61. Ibid., 54; Kenneth W. Condit, *The Joint Chiefs of Staff and National Policy, 1947–1949*, History of the Joint Chiefs of Staff, vol. 2 (Washington, D.C.: Office of Joint History, Office of the Chairman of the Joint Chiefs of Staff, 1996), 61–85, 100–101.

62. Holm, *Women in the Military*, 118.

63. Ibid.

64. Ibid., 122.

65. Ibid.

CHAPTER 2. SERVICEWOMEN'S INTEGRATION: "PRAYERFUL ASSUMPTION" VERSUS "PREVAILING AMBIVALENCE" (PP. 31–64)

1. Frances P. Bolton, "Women Should Be Drafted," *American Magazine*, (June 1949), 47.

2. Emma Jane Riley, Colonel, U.S. Air Force (Ret.), report, Papers of Jeanne M. Holm, Major General, U.S. Air Force (Ret.), U.S. Air Force Academy Archives, Colorado Springs, Colorado (hereafter Holm Papers).

3. Anne Peregrim, Master Sergeant, U.S. Marine Corps (Ret.), 9 October 2000 interview, Historian's Files, Women's Memorial.

4. Bettie J. Morden, Colonel, U.S. Army (Ret.), *The Women's Army Corps: 1945–1978*, (Washington, D.C.: U.S. Army Center of Military History, 1992), 56–58.

5. Mary Stremlow, Colonel, U.S. Marine Corps Reserve (Ret.), *A History of the Women Marines, 1946–1977*, (Washington, D.C.: Headquarters, U.S. Marine Corps, 1986), 40–43.

6. Jeanne M. Holm, Major General, U.S. Air Force (Ret.), *Women in the Military: An Unfinished Revolution*, 2nd ed. (Novato, Calif.: Presidio, 1991), 133.

7. Ibid., 149.

8. Pearl Faurie, Master Chief Yeoman (Ret.), U.S. Coast Guard, 18 August 1999, oral history, Historian's Files, Women's Memorial.

9. Betty Splaine, Chief Warrant Officer 4 (Ret.), U.S. Coast Guard, 23 August 1999, oral history, Historian's Files, Women's Memorial.

10. Holm, *Women in the Military*, 131.

11. Ibid., 137.

12. Ibid.

13. Ibid., 134.

14. *New York Times*, 25 January 1950, 29 and 4 April 1950, 27.

15. Stremlow, *History of the Women Marines*, 18.

16. Although the Army's authorized strength was 837,000, it maintained ten divisions with difficulty and its actual strength as of 30 June 1950, was just 593,167. The Navy and Marine Corps combined were authorized 666,882 men, but had only 456,908 as of the end of June. The Air Force was authorized 502,000 and had 411,277.

17. James F. Schnable and Robert J. Watson, *The Joint Chiefs of Staff and National Policy, 1950–1951: The Korean War, Part One*, History of the Joint Chiefs of Staff, vol. 3 (Washington, D.C.: Office of the Chairman of the Joint Chiefs of Staff, 1988), 21.

18. Morris MacGregor, *Integration of the Armed Forces 1940–1964* (Washington, D.C.: U.S. Army Center of Military History, 1981), 614–619; *Who's Who in America*, 40th ed. (Chicago: Marquis, 1979).

19. Schnable and Watson, *Joint Chiefs of Staff*, 28.

20. Joan DeAngelo Fogelstrom, Airman Second Class, U.S. Air Force, 21 January 2001, oral history, Historian's Files, Women's Memorial.

21. Dorothy Looby Manfredi, Captain, U.S. Army Nurse Corps, 21 September 1999, interview, Historian's Files, Women's Memorial.

22. Irene Michels Sorrough, Major, U.S. Army, 28 July 1999, interview, Historian's Files, Women's Memorial.

23. Irene Van Houten Munster, Lieutenant Colonel, U.S. Army (Ret.), 24 March 1999, oral history, Historian's Files, Women's Memorial.

24. Morden, *Women's Army Corps*, 56–61.

25. Ibid., 3; Karen Salisbury, "The WAC," *Newsweek* (21 May 1951), 28–30.

26. "A Career as a WAC," 2, Sally Laven Wicht Collection, Women's Memorial Collection.

27. Mildred K. Lehman and Milton Lehman, "The Lady Privates of Company D," *Cosmopolitan* (October 1951), 68.

28. Ibid.

29. Salisbury, "The WAC," 28–30.

30. Morden, *Women's Army Corps*, 83.

31. Ibid., 84.

32. Jean Ebbert, Lieutenant (jg), U.S. Navy, and Marie Beth Hall, *Crossed Currents:*

Navy Women in a Century of Change, rev. ed. (Washington, D.C.: Brassey's, 1999), 131–134.

33. Ibid., 134.
34. Gloria Minich Finucane, Personnelman Third Class, U.S. Navy, 1 May 1991, oral history, Colonial Dames Collection, Women's Memorial Collection.
35. Joy Bright Hancock, Captain, U.S. Navy (Ret.), *Lady in the Navy: A Personal Reminiscence,* (Annapolis, Md.: Naval Institute Press, 1972), 236–238.
36. "Navy Means Blisters to 19 Girls," *New York Times,* 20 June 1950, 29.
37. Ibid.
38. Donna Fournier, Lieutenant Commander, U.S. Navy Reserve, *The Few, The Proud: A History of Women Marines* (Quantico, Va.: Women Marines Association), Esther D. Waclawski Collection, Women's Memorial Collection.
39. Mary Stremlow, Colonel, U.S. Marine Corps Reserve, draft, "A History of the Women Marines, 1946–1977," Historian's Files, Women's Memorial, 23–59.
40. Peter Soderbergh, *Women Marines in the Korean War Era* (Westport, Conn.: Greenwood, 1994), 50.
41. Holm, *Women in the Military,* 136.
42. Gertrude Samuels, "'It's Hup, 2, 3, 4' and 'Yes, Ma'am,'" *New York Times Magazine* (3 September 1950), 88.
43. Holm, *Women in the Military,* 134–136.
44. Mattie Treadwell, Lieutenant Colonel, Women's Army Corps, *The Women's Army Corps* (Washington, D.C.: Office of the Chief of Military History, 1954), 559; Morden, *Women's Army Corps,* 24.
45. Salisbury, "The WAC," 28–30.
46. Irene Van Houten Munster, oral history.
47. Esther Pulis Corcoran, Lieutenant Colonel, U.S. Army, 4 December 2001, oral history, Historian's Files, Women's Memorial.
48. Ebbert and Hall, *Crossed Currents,* 133.
49. Joy Bright Hancock, Captain, U.S. Navy (Ret.), presentation, Conference of the Chief of the Army Nurse Corps with Civilian Consultants and Army Chief Nurses (hereafter Nurse Corps Conference), 15–17 February 1950, Washington, D.C., printed by the Department of the Army, Surgeon General, 1950, Virginia Dailey Collection, Gift of Mary Golden, Women's Memorial Collection; Hancock, *Lady in the Navy,* 236.
50. *New York Times,* 18 January 1950, 33.
51. Holm, *Women in the Military,* 138.
52. Dorothy Crawford Ulrey, Airman Second Class, U.S. Air Force, 18 April 2001, oral history, Historian's Files, Women's Memorial.
53. Joan Eastwood Neuswanger, Staff Sergeant, U.S. Air Force, 26 April 2001, oral history, Historian's Files, Women's Memorial.
54. Corinne Gogue Cook, Corporal, U.S. Air Force, 27 March 2001, oral history, Historian's Files, Women's Memorial.

55. Geraldine Pratt May, U.S. Air Force, WAF Director, Report to the Chief of Staff of the Air Force, 11 June 1951, Subject: WAF Program 1948–June 1951 (hereafter, May Report) Appendix D-6, Historian's Files, Women's Memorial.

56. "Percentage Distribution of WAFs in Career Fields," Ad Hoc Committee Report of WAF Program, 15 January 1951, Jackie Cochran file, Historian's files, Women's Memorial.

57. Memorandum to Geraldine Pratt May, Colonel, U.S. Air Force, and director, Women's Air Force (WAF), from Susan Barlow, Lieutenant Colonel, U.S. Air Force Reserve, 28 June 1950, Holm Papers, U.S. Air Force Academy Archives, Colorado Springs, Colorado.

58. Morden, *Women's Army Corps,* 86.

59. Mary Teague Smith, First Lieutenant, U.S. Army, 26 August 1999, interview, Historian's Files, Women's Memorial.

60. Ernestine Johnson Thomas, Staff Sergeant, U.S. Air Force, 15 March 2001, oral history, Historian's Files, Women's Memorial.

61. Lucy Bond, Lieutenant Colonel, U.S. Army (Ret.), 5 December 2001, oral history, Historian's Files, Women's Memorial.

62. Morden, *Women's Army Corps,* 86.

63. Teague Smith interview.

64. Soderbergh, *Women Marines,* 23.

65. Ibid.

66. Gogue Cook, oral history.

67. Ibid.

68. Ernestine Johnson Thomas, Staff Sergeant, U.S. Air Force, 14 October 1998, interview, Historian's Files, Women's Memorial.

69. Authors' conversation with Major General Jeanne M. Holm, U.S. Air Force (Ret.), 7 March 2003, Women's Memorial offices.

70. *New York Times,* 10 February 1950, 20.

71. Mildred Inez Bailey, Brigadier General, U.S. Army (Ret.), interview, 23 September 1999, Historian's Files, Women's Memorial.

72. "WAF Colonel Wins a Wolf Whistle; Blushing, She Credits New Uniform," *World Telegram and Sun,* 19 January 1951, 3, Geraldine Pratt May folder, Historian's Files, Women's Memorial.

73. Joan DeAngelo Fogelstrom, Airman Second Class, U.S. Air Force, 24 January 2001, oral history, Historian's Files, Women's Memorial.

74. Crawford Ulrey, oral history.

75. Mary Russ Veres, oral history, Historian's Files, Women's Memorial.

76. Ebbert and Hall, *Crossed Currents,* 131.

77. Stremlow, "History of the Women Marines," 162–164.

78. Enlistment Survey, Marlene Denbrock Knopp Collection, Women's Memorial Collection.

79. *New York Times,* 18 February 1950, 10.

80. Ibid.

81. Ibid.

82. Report, "The Attitudes of Enlisted Women to Reenlistment," Files 250–291.3, 1952, Mail and Records Section Decimal File, Record Group 330, Assistant Secretary of Defense, Manpower and Personnel, Anna Rosenberg, National Archives, College Park, Maryland.

83. Stremlow, "History of the Women Marines," 42.

84. Peter Soderbergh, *Women Marines in World War II Era* (Westport, Conn.: Praeger, 1992), 20.

85. John D. Rice, Chief, Personnel Planning and Analysis Branch, Resources Analysis Division, U.S. Army, presentation, Nurse Corps Conference.

86. Between 1921 and the passage of the Army-Navy Nurse Act in 1947, Army nurses were granted a second-class type of rank called Relative Rank, which did not carry the command authority or benefits of Regular Rank. A nurse captain, for example, received less pay than a male captain in the Army and was ranked below him. Army nurses temporarily were accorded Regular Rank during World War II.

87. Carolyn Feller, Lieutenant Colonel, U.S. Army Nurse Corps Reserve, and Constance Moore, Major, U.S. Army Nurse Corps, *Highlights of the Army Nurse Corps* (Washington, D.C.: U.S. Army Center of Military History, 1995); Mary T. Sarnecky, Colonel, U.S. Army Nurse Corps (Ret.), *A History of the Army Nurse Corps* (Philadelphia: University of Pennsylvania Press, 1999), 291–293.

88. Sarnecky, *History of the Army Nurse Corps,* 291–293.

89. Mary G. Phillips, Colonel, Chief, Army Nurse Corps, presentation, Nurse Corps Conference.

90. U.S. Air Force Medical Services Digest, vol. 5, no. 9, September 1954, Dorothy J. Christison Collection, Gift of Mr. and Mrs. Robert B. Christison, Women's Memorial Collection.

91. Verena Zeller (Pettoruto Seberg), Captain and Acting Chief, Air Force Nurse Corps, presentation, Nurse Corps Conference.

92. Nellie DeWitt, Captain, and Chief, U.S. Navy Nurse Corps, presentation, Nurse Corps Conference; Doris M. Sterner, Captain, Nurse Corps, U.S. Navy Reserve, *In and Out of Harm's Way: A History of the Navy Nurse Corps* (Seattle, Wash.: Peanut Butter Publishing Company, 1997), 230.

93. Robert L. Black, Colonel, Army Medical Service Corps, presentation, Nurse Corps Conference.

94. Mary G. Phillips, Colonel and Chief, U.S. Army Nurse Corps, presentation, Nurse Corps Conference.

95. Looby Manfredi, interview.

96. As the Korean War began, the Army WMSC had 149 regular officers, including 64 dietitians, 59 physical therapists, and 26 occupational therapists, supplemented by 191 reserve officers, including, 77 dietitians, 76 physical therapists, and 38 occupational therapists.

97. Emma Vogel, Colonel and Chief, U.S. Army Women's Medical Specialist Corps, presentation, Nurse Corps Conference.
98. Eleanor Mitchell, Lieutenant Colonel, U.S. Army Women's Medical Specialist Corps, Nurse Corps Conference.
99. Ibid.
100. Record Group U.S. Government, Department of Defense, Box 22, Army, Folder 2, American Physical Therapy Association, Alexandria, Virginia.
101. Ibid.
102. Record Group U.S. Government, Department of Defense, Box 21, Navy, Folder 1, American Physical Therapy Association, Alexandria, Virginia.
103. Robert L. Clark, director of the National Security Resources Board Manpower Office, Nurse Corps Conference.
104. Bolton, "Women Should Be Drafted," 47.
105. Report of Emma J. Riley, Colonel and WAF Director, U.S. Air Force, Papers of Jeanne M. Holm, Major General, U.S. Air Force (Ret.), U.S. Air Force Academy Archives, Colorado Springs, Colorado.
106. Transcript, Conference of Civilian Women Leaders, 21–22 June 1950, Personnel Policy Board, the Pentagon, Historian's Files, Women's Memorial.
107. Ibid.
108. Ibid.
109. Ibid.

CHAPTER 3. RECRUITING AND RETAINING "AMERICA'S FINEST WOMEN" (PP. 65–87)

1. "First WACs Slated for Duty in Korea," *New York Times*, 6 November 1951, 36.
2. Michael Clarke, " The Girls Get Ready to Serve," *Collier's Magazine*, (3 March 1951), 16, Gift of Frank Bisogno, Women's Memorial Collection.
3. Gertrude Samuels, "The WACs (Age 10) Take the Salute," *New York Times*, (11 May 1952), 18.
4. James F. Schnable and Robert J. Watson, *The Joint Chiefs of Staff and National Policy, 1950–1951; The Korean War, Part One,* History of the Joint Chiefs of Staff, vol. 3 (Washington, D.C.: Office of Joint History, Office of the Chairman of the Joint Chiefs of Staff, 1988), 25–50.
5. Ibid., 20.
6. Edwin Overholt, Colonel, MD, U.S. Army (Ret.), Conference of Army Historians, 5 June 2000, Arlington, Virginia, Historian's Files, Women's Memorial.
7. Donald M. Goldstein and Harry J. Maihafer, *The Korean War* (Washington, D.C.: Brassey's, 2000), 33.
8. Ibid., 53, 76.

9. Marguerite Higgins, *War In Korea* (New York: Lion Books, 1952), 32–33, Eleanor V. Spiller Collection, Women's Memorial Collection.

10. Schnable and Watson, *Joint Chiefs of Staff*, 53–57.

11. Ibid., 78.

12. Bettie J. Morden, Colonel, U.S. Army (Ret.), *The Women's Army Corps, 1945–1978* (Washington, D.C.: U.S. Army Center of Military History, 1992), 94.

13. Alba Martinelli Thompson, Major, Women's Army Corps, 8 August 2001, interview, Historian's Files, Women's Memorial.

14. Doris M. Sterner, Captain, Nurse Corps, U.S. Navy (Ret.), *In and Out of Harm's Way: A History of the Navy Nurse Corps* (Seattle, Wash.: Peanut Butter Publishing, 1997), 242.

15. Records of the U.S. Government, Department of Defense, Army Folder 2, Box 22, American Physical Therapy Association, Alexandria, Virginia.

16. Morden, *Women's Army Corps*, 97.

17. Lisle A. Rose, *The Cold War Comes to Main Street: America in 1950* (Lawrence: University Press of Kansas, 1999), 187–192.

18. Authors' conversation with Major General Jeanne M. Holm, U.S. Air Force (Ret.), 7 March 2003, Women's Memorial offices.

19. Schnable and Watson, *Joint Chiefs of Staff*, 84–93.

20. Rose, *Cold War Comes to Main Street*, 227–228.

21. Mildred McAfee Horton, Lieutenant Commander and former director of the WAVES, U.S. Navy, "Why Not Draft Women?" excerpt from February 1951 *Ladies Home Journal* reprinted in the *All Women's Services Journal* (February 1951), 2, Grace L. Mueller Collection, Women's Memorial Collection.

22. Morden, *Women's Army Corps*, 92.

23. Ibid., 100.

24. *New York Times*, 19 November 1951, sec. 4, 13.

25. *Milwaukee* [Wisconsin] *Sentinel*, 13 November 1950, gift of Bert Hartry, Women's Memorial Collection.

26. *New York Times*, 10 November 1950, 1.

27. Anna M. Rosenberg, guest columnist, "A Women's New York," *Poughkeepsie New Yorker*, 14 January 1951, news clipping, Helen Mannion Doyle Collection, Women's Memorial Collection; Eric Pace, "Anna Rosenberg Hoffman Dead; Consultant and 1950's Defense Aid," *New York Times*, 10 May 1983, D 25; Frances Levison, "'Aunt Anna' Captures the Pentagon," *New York Times Sunday Magazine* (18 March 1951), 8.

28. Jeanne M. Holm, Major General, U.S. Air Force (Ret.), *Women in the Military: An Unfinished Revolution*, rev. ed. (Novato, Calif.: Presidio, 1992), 150–152. Morden, *Women's Army Corps*, 100.

29. Clarke, "The Girls Get Ready to Serve," 16.

30. Morden, *Women's Army Corps*, 98.

31. Clarke, "The Girls Get Ready to Serve," 16.

32. *New York Times*, 10 March 1951, 15.
33. Richard Thruelsen, "Women at Work: Flying WAF," *Saturday Evening Post* (25 April 1953), 28, 29, 136, 137, 138, 140, 142, Elizabeth Alden Roe Collection, Women's Memorial Collection.
34. Newsletter, 382nd Hospital, Kyoto, Japan, 27 April 1951, Catherine Owen Horne Collection, Women's Memorial Collection.
35. Goldstein and Maihafer, *Korean War*, 87–90, 99, 102–103.
36. Army Memorandum, 10 March 1958, Miscellaneous Folder, Korean War, Historian's Files, Women's Memorial.
37. Handwritten journal, Nancy J. Crosby, Lieutenant, Nurse Corps, U.S. Navy, 2 January 1952–September 1953, USS *Haven*, Nancy J. Crosby Collection, Women's Memorial Collection.
38. *Fresno* [California] *Bee*, 5 July 1951, Jacquelen McCracken Henderson Collection, Women's Memorial Collection.
39. Series of memoranda between E. C. Lynch, Major General, U.S. Air Force, and Anna Rosenberg, August 1951–January 1952, File 291.3, Mail and Records Section Decimal Files 248.4–293.6, Record Group 330, Office of the Secretary of Defense, Anna Rosenberg, Assistant Secretary of Defense for Manpower and Personnel, National Archives, College Park, Maryland.
40. Sarah Cook, Lieutenant (jg), U.S. Navy Nurse Corps, telephone interviews, 26 August 1999 and 9 September 2004, Historian's Files, Women's Memorial.
41. Joan Eastwood Neuswanger, Staff Sergeant, U.S. Air Force, 26 April 2001, oral history, Historian's Files, Women's Memorial.
42. Ernestine Johnson Thomas, Staff Sergeant, U.S. Air Force, 15 March 2001, oral history, Historian's Files, Women's Memorial.
43. DeAngelo Fogelstrom, oral history.
44. Mildred Stumpe Kennedy, Sergeant, U.S. Marine Corps, 26 June 2001, oral history, Historian's Files, Women's Memorial.
45. Mary Russ Veres, Command Master Sergeant, U.S. Air Force Reserve (Ret.), 25 April 2001, oral history, Historian's Files, Women's Memorial.
46. Jacquelyn Tomasik Anderson, Airman Second Class, U.S. Air Force, 23 January 2001, oral history, Historian's Files, Women's Memorial.
47. Jacqueline Gates Reichert, Staff Sergeant, U.S. Marines Corps, 26 June 2001, oral history, Historian's Files, Women's Memorial.
48. Anna Yachwan, Staff Sergeant, U.S. Marine Corps, 5 June 2001, oral history, Historian's Files, Women's Memorial.
49. Jerry Robb, Private First Class, U.S. Marine Corps, 2 December 1999, oral history, Historian's Files, Women's Memorial.
50. Jean Ertwine Disterdick, Captain, U.S. Air Force Medical Specialist Corps, 27 March 2001, oral history, Historian's Files, Women's Memorial.
51. Janice Feagin Britton, U.S. Air Force Nurse Corps, 9 May 2001, oral history, Historian's Files, Women's Memorial.

52. Dorothy Russian Horne, First Lieutenant, U.S. Air Force Nurse Corps, 28 September 1998, oral history, Historian's Files, Women's Memorial.

53. Muriel Raymond Batcheller, First Lieutenant, Army Nurse Corps, 7 May 2001, oral history, Historian's Files, Women's Memorial.

54. Russ Veres, oral history.

55. Holm, *Women in the Military*, 151.

56. Defense Advisory Committee on Women in the Services 45th Anniversary Book (Washington, D.C.: DACOWITS, 1996), 23–38.

57. Mary Hallaren, Colonel, U.S. Army, and director of Women's Army Corps, text of speech given to the first DACOWITS, 18 September 1951, Hallaren File, Historian's Office, Women's Memorial.

58. Ibid.

59. E. C. Lynch, Major General, U.S. Air Force, note to Anna Rosenberg, 25 September 1951, File 291.3, Mail and Records Section Decimal Files 248.4–293.6, Record Group 330, Office of the Secretary of Defense, Anna Rosenberg, Assistant Secretary of Defense for Manpower and Personnel, National Archives, College Park, Maryland.

60. "Development of the Uniform for Women in the Air Force," Tab G, Report, Office of Geraldine Pratt May, Colonel, U.S. Air Force, Director, WAF, June 1948–June 1951, Historian's Files, Women's Memorial.

61. Bess Furman, "Services to Open Drive for Women," *New York Times*, 27 September 1951, 21.

62. Mark L. Gnerro, "Woman's Place At Home or In Uniform," *Washington* [D.C.] *Star*, 29 September 1951, Helen Mannion Doyle Collection, Women's Memorial Collection.

63. Ibid.

64. Anna Rosenberg, letter to Senator Hubert Humphrey, 6 November 1951, File 291.3, Mail and Records Section Decimal Files 248.4–293.6, Record Group 330, Office of the Secretary of Defense, Anna Rosenberg, Assistant Secretary of Defense for Manpower and Personnel, National Archives, College Park, Maryland.

65. Helen Mannion Doyle, First Lieutenant, Nurse Corps, U.S. Air Force, explanatory statement accompanying assorted newspaper clippings in her collection, Women's Memorial Collection.

66. Anna Rosenberg, memorandum to the Secretary of the Air Force, 22 October 1951, File 291.3, Mail and Records Section Decimal Files 248.4–293.6, Record Group 330, Office of the Secretary of Defense, Anna Rosenberg, Assistant Secretary of Defense for Manpower and Personnel, National Archives, College Park, Maryland.

67. "Korean Casualties Flown by Trained Nurses," undated Corpus Christi, Texas, newspaper clipping, Helen Mannion Doyle Collection, Women's Memorial Collection.

68. "Hospital Planes Drone in Daily at Kelly Field," *New York Herald Tribune*, 9 November 1951, Helen Mannion Doyle Collection, Women's Memorial Collection.

69. Dorothy Russian Horne, First Lieutenant, Air Force Nurse Corps, 28 September 1998, oral history, Historian's Files, Women's Memorial.

70. "PBW to Sponsor Visit of Nurses," undated *Ponca City* [Oklahoma] *News*, Helen Mannion Doyle Collection, Women's Memorial Collection.

71. "Servicewomen Paid Honors at Football Game," undated Austin, Texas, newspaper clipping, Helen Mannion Doyle Collection, Women's Memorial Collection.

72. "Servicewomen's Week Scheduled November 11–18," *Binghamton* [New York] *Sun*, 6 November 1951, Rosenberg File, Historian's Files, Gift of Bert Hartry, Women's Memorial Collection.

73. John A. Giles, "Marines Top Recruiting Costs with $120-Per-Man Expenses," *Washington* [D.C.] *Star*, 8 November 1951, Rosenberg File, Historian's Files, Gift of Bert Hartry, Women's Memorial Collection.

74. Constituent letter to Senator Margaret Chase Smith forwarded by her to Women's Army Corps director's office through Rosenberg's office, File 291.3, Mail and Records Section Decimal Files 248.4–293.6, Record Group 330, Office of the Secretary of Defense, Anna Rosenberg, Assistant Secretary of Defense for Manpower and Personnel, National Archives, College Park, Maryland.

75. Women Marines Association, *Women Marines Association Pictorial Review* (Paducah, Ky.: Turner Publishing, 1992), 30–31.

76. Holm, *Women in the Military*, 155–156; Morden, *Women's Army Corps*, 98–104; "Women Ignore Call to Colors," *Washington Post*, 19 March 1952, Helen Mannion Doyle Collection, Women's Memorial Collection.

77. Dorothy Crawford Ulrey, Airman Second Class, U.S. Air Force, 18 April 2001, oral history, Historian's Files, Women's Memorial.

78. "Women Ignore Call to Colors," *Washington Post*, 19 March 1952, Helen Mannion Doyle Collection, Women's Memorial Collection.

79. Memorandum to Anna Rosenberg, Subject: DACOWITS Meeting, 17–18 March 1952, File 291.3, Mail and Records Section Decimal Files 248.4–293.6, Record Group 330, Office of the Secretary of Defense, Anna Rosenberg, Assistant Secretary of Defense for Manpower and Personnel, National Archives, College Park, Maryland.

80. "The Servicewoman as a Public Relations Agent for Her Service," Attitude Research Branch, Office of Armed Services Information and Training, File 291.3, Mail and Records Section Decimal Files 248.4–293.6, Record Group 330, Office of the Secretary of Defense, Anna Rosenberg, Assistant Secretary of Defense for Manpower and Personnel, National Archives, College Park, Maryland.

81. Ibid.

82. "Attitudes of Enlisted Women in the Regular Service to Re-Enlistment," Attitude Research Branch, Office of Armed Services Information and Training, File

291.3, Mail and Records Section Decimal Files 248.4–293.6, Record Group 330, Office of the Secretary of Defense, Anna Rosenberg, Assistant Secretary of Defense for Manpower and Personnel, National Archives, College Park, Maryland.

83. Holm, *Women in the Military,* 153–154.
84. 1948 Postage Stamp File, Historian's Files, Women's Memorial.
85. Ibid.
86. David McCullough, *Truman* (New York: Simon and Schuster, 1992), 912–913.
87. Holm, *Women in the Military,* 153–159.
88. Ibid., 157.

CHAPTER 4. FITTING SERVICEWOMEN IN: FINDING "PROPER EMPLOYMENT FOR SISTERS AND GIRLFRIENDS" (PP. 88–116)

1. Geraldine May, Colonel, U.S. Air Force (Ret.), and Emma Jane Riley, Colonel, U.S. Air Force (Ret.), oral history conducted by Lorry Fenner, Captain, U.S. Air Force, 1990, U.S. Air Force Academy, Historian's Files, Women's Memorial.
2. Department of the Army Pamphlet 20–138, "Leave It To The WAC," 14 September 1951, Edith Sullivan Moss Collection, Gift of Marcia J. Moss, Women's Memorial Collection.
3. Florence Scholljegerdes, Commander, U.S. Navy Nurse Corps, 5 December 2002, oral history, Historian's Files, Women's Memorial.
4. Bettie J. Morden, Colonel, U.S. Army (Ret.), *The Women's Army Corps: 1945–1978* (Washington, D.C.: U.S. Army Center of Military History, 1992), 102.
5. Ibid., 91.
6. Newspaper clippings (n.p.): "Woman Major Fights WAC Rule on Mothers," *New York Times,* 9 January 1952; "Ex-Wac, Fired as Mom, Tells U.S. Facts of Life," *Brooklyn New York Eagle,* 14 January 1952; "Mom Fights Her Army Discharge," *New York World Telegram,* 14 January 1952; "Army 'Shortsighted': WAC Reservist Blasts 'Motherhood' Discharge," *Long Island City* [New York] *Star Journal,* 14 January 1952; "Mother Loses Her Plea To Remain Army Major," *New York Times,* 25 January 1952; "Army Firm in Dismissal Of Major Who Is Mother," *New York Herald Tribune,* 25 January 1952; "Army Knows Best, Mother Gives Up Rank," *New York Daily News,* 25 January 1952, Gift of Bert Hartry, Women's Memorial Collection.
7. "Fighting N.J. Woman Hails Reserve Action: Officer-Mothers Can Keep Status" *New York World Telegram and Sun,* 28 June 1952, n.p., Gift of Bert Hartry, Women's Memorial Collection.
8. The 1948 Women's Armed Services Integration Act, Historian's Files, Women's Memorial.

9. Executive Order 10240, issued 27 April 1951, Historian's Files, Women's Memorial.

10. Morden, *Women's Army Corps,* 94–98.

11. *New York Times,* 29 May 1951, 33.

12. Morden, *Women's Army Corps,* 94–104.

13. Newspaper clipping, "They're in the Army Now," *Evening Star,* 5 December 1951, Dorothy V. Elliott Collection, gift of Wanda Krenz Drose, Women's Memorial Collection; Mary T. Sarnecky, Colonel, U.S. Army Nurse Corps (Ret.), *A History of the Army Nurse Corps* (Philadelphia: University of Pennsylvania Press, 1999), 294.

14. Assorted newspaper clippings, n.d., Dorothy Vanden Oever Barron Collection, Women's Memorial Collection.

15. *AWS* [All Women's Services] *Journal,* September 1950, 5, Grace L. Mueller Collection, Women's Memorial Collection.

16. *AWS* [All Women's Services] *Journal,* March 1952, 8, Grace L. Mueller Collection, Women's Memorial Collection.

17. Betty S. Regan, Corporal, U.S. Army, "She Seeks 30,000 Women to Replace Men for Combat Duty," newspaper clipping, Dorothy Vanden Oever Barron Collection, Women's Memorial Collection.

18. Department of the Army Pamphlet 20–138, "Leave It To The WAC."

19. Yearbook, WAC Detachment, Third Armored Division, Fort Knox, Kentucky, 1952, Doris Kuchlis Maty Collection, Gift of Pauline M. Abraham, Women's Memorial Collection.

20. Morden, *Women's Army Corps,* 108; Executive Office Subject File, Far East 1952, Folder 4, Record Group 330, Assistant Secretary of Defense for Manpower and Personnel, Anna Rosenberg, National Archives, College Park, Maryland.

21. Dorothy Vanden Oever Barron, Women's Memorial Register.

22. Jean Ebbert and Marie Beth Hall, *Crossed Currents: Navy Women in a Century of Change* (Washington, D.C.: Brassey's, 1999), 125, 140–141, 184.

23. Ibid., 150 and 184.

24. Ibid., 150–151.

25. Ibid., 142.

26. Ibid., 145.

27. Jeanne M. Holm, Major General, U.S. Air Force (Ret.), *Women in the Military: An Unfinished Revolution,* rev. ed. (Novato, Calif.: Presidio, 1992), 163.

28. Ebbert and Hall, *Crossed Currents,* 143–144.

29. Joy Bright Hancock, Captain, U.S. Navy (Ret.), *Lady in the Navy* (Annapolis, Md.: Naval Institute Press, 1972), 258–259.

30. *AWS* [All Women's Services] *Journal,* November 1950, 16; February 1951, 11, Grace L. Mueller Collection, Women's Memorial Collection.

31. "Four WAVES Make Sea Debut in Style," *New York Times,* 3 September 1953.

32. *New York Times,* 5 August 1951, 45.

33. Ibid., 136–139, 145; "Women in the Navy Jills of All Trades," *All Hands*, July 1952, 20, Historian's Files, Women's Memorial.
34. *New York Times*, 24 November 1950, 39.
35. D'Anne Aultman Evans, Lieutenant (jg), U.S. Navy, 2 May 2000, oral history, Historian's Files, Women's Memorial.
36. Mary V. Stremlow, Colonel, U.S. Marine Corps Reserve, working draft of "A History of Women Marines 1946–1977," 48, Esther D. Waclawski Collection, Women's Memorial Collection.
37. Ibid.; LaVergne R. Novack Collection, Women's Memorial Collection.
38. *New York Times*, 24 July 1950, 6.
39. Mary V. Stremlow, Colonel, U.S. Marine Corps Reserve, *A History of Women Marines, 1946–1977* (Washington, D.C.: Headquarters, U.S. Marine Corps), 56.
40. Peter Soderbergh, *Women Marines in the Korean War Era* (Westport, Conn.: Greenwood, 1994), 30.
41. Stremlow, *History of Women Marines*, 58.
42. *New York Times*, 22 February 1951, 27.
43. Stremlow, *History of Women Marines*, 52.
44. Ibid., 48.
45. Ibid., 49.
46. Ibid., 52.
47. Ibid., 48.
48. Ibid., 51–57.
49. Ibid., 65–67.
50. Ibid., 60.
51. Ibid., 57.
52. Ibid., 57–59.
53. Ibid., 59.
54. Ibid.
55. Ibid., 62.
56. Ibid., 145.
57. Holm, *Women in the Military*, 139.
58. Ibid., 138.
59. Geraldine May, Colonel, U.S. Air Force, Report to Air Force Chief of Staff, 11 June 1951, WAF Program June 1948–June 1951 (hereafter referred to as May Report), appendix C-3 Historian's Files, Women's Memorial.
60. May Report, appendix C-2.
61. Ibid., appendix C-4.
62. Ibid., appendix D-3.
63. Memorandum for the Acting Deputy Chief of Staff, Personnel, Department of the Air Force, 25 October 1950, Cochran File, Historian's Files, Women's Memorial.
64. May and Riley, oral history (see note 1, this chapter); Lorry M. Fenner, Colonel,

U.S. Air Force, "Ideology and Amnesia: The Public Debate on Women in the American Military, 1940–1973" (Ph.D. diss., University of Michigan, 1995), 355.

65. Holm, *Women in the Military,* 142.
66. Jackie Cochran and Maryann Bucknum Brinley, *Jackie Cochran: The Autobiography of the Greatest Woman Pilot in Aviation History* (New York: Bantam Books, 1987), 244–269.
67. Jacqueline Cochran, *The Stars at Noon* (Boston: Little, Brown, 1954), 130.
68. Memorandum to the Chief of Staff of the Air Force, 6 December 1950, from Jacqueline Cochran, Special Consultant to the Chief of Staff (hereafter referred to as the Cochran Report) 7–8, Historian's Files, Women's Memorial.
69. Cochran Report, 5.
70. Cochran, *The Stars at Noon,* 130.
71. Air Force Committee Response to Cochran Report, Historian's Files, Women's Memorial.
72. Cochran and Brinley, *Jackie Cochran,* 269; Thomas Parrish, *Berlin in the Balance: 1945–1949* (Reading, Mass.: Perseua Books, 1998), 217.
73. Outgoing Clear Message, Department of the Air Force Staff Message Division, 20 December 1950, Historian's Files, Women's Memorial.
74. Fenner, "Ideology and Amnesia," 323; Drew Pearson, "Gen. Vandenberg Wants More Glamorous Women in U.S. Air Force," newspaper clipping, Historian's Files, Women's Memorial.
75. Cochran, *The Stars at Noon,* 132.
76. Ibid., 134.
77. Memorandum to Anna Rosenberg, Assistant Secretary of Defense for Manpower and Personnel, from Major General R. E. Nugent, 12 February 1951, Historian's Files, Women's Memorial.
78. *New York Times,* 12 June 1951, 2; *New York Times,* 17 June 1951, 3.
79. May and Riley, oral history, (see note 1, this chapter).
80. Ibid.
81. Eulogy for Colonel Geraldine Pratt May by Jeanne M. Holm, Major General, U.S. Air Force (Ret.), 10 December 1997, Historian's Files, Women's Memorial.
82. Cochran, *The Stars at Noon,* 134.
83. May Report, Historian's Files, Women's Memorial.
84. *New York Times,* June 1951, 18.
85. Memorandum to Mary Jo Shelly, Colonel, U.S. Air Force, Director, WAF, from Jeanne M. Holm, Captain, U.S. Air Force, Staff Visit to Lackland Air Force Base, 9–15 November 1953, papers of Jeanne M. Holm, Major General, U.S. Air Force (Ret.), Air Force Academy Archives, Colorado Springs, Colorado.
86. Mary Jo Shelly, Colonel, U.S. Air Force, WAF Director, 23 April 1952, Report, 1, Historian's Files, Women's Memorial.
87. Shelly, 15 May 1952, Report, 4, Historian's Files, Women's Memorial.

88. Shelly, 23 April 1952, Report, 3, Historian's Files, Women's Memorial.

89. Shelly, Final Report, 19 January 1954, 6, Historian's Files, Women's Memorial.

90. Shelly, 15 May 1952, Report, 4; Shelly, Final Report, 7.

91. Shelly, 23 April 1952, Report, 8.

92. "Fly Girl Boss Likes Walking But She'll Take to Air When It's Necessary," *Spokesman Review,* 10 June 1951, Historian's Files, Women's Memorial.

93. Holm, *Women in the Military,* 167–172.

94. Ibid.

95. Shelly, 23 April 1952, Report, 5.

96. Ibid., Report, 9–10.

97. Chart, "Educational Level of No Prior Service WAF Enlistees, December 1–31, 1952," Holm Papers, U.S. Air Force Academy Archives, Colorado Springs, Colorado.

98. Jeanne M. Holm, Major General, U.S. Air Force (Ret.), 30 September 1999 interview, Historian's Files, Women's Memorial.

99. Holm, *Women in the Military,* 170; Memorandum for Major General Lloyd P. Hopwood, U.S. Air Force, 1 December 1952, from Colonel J. T. Winstead Jr., U.S. Air Force, Chief, Plans and Programs, Holm Papers, U.S. Air Force Academy Archives, Colorado Springs, Colorado.

100. Holm, *Women in the Military,* 152–153; Memorandum for General Norris B. Harbold, 13 February 1953, from Colonel B. W. Armstrong, Chief, Personnel Procurement Division, subject: WAF Procurement, Historian's Files, Women's Memorial.

101. Mary Jo Shelly, Colonel, U.S. Air Force, Director, WAF, 31 March 1953, Memorandum to the Director, Personnel Policy Division, Assistant Secretary of Defense, Historian's Files, Women's Memorial.

102. Memorandum on WAF Procurement, 3 July 1953, Directorate of Personnel Planning to the Directorate of Training, Holm Papers, U.S. Air Force Academy Archives, Colorado Springs, Colorado.

103. Joan DeAngelo Fogelstrom, Airman Second Class, U.S. Air Force, 14 January 2001 interview, Historian's Files, Women's Memorial.

104. Marjory V. Foster Munn, Captain, U.S. Air Force (Ret.), Women's Memorial Register.

105. Conference Minutes, 8 December 1951, Headquarters, 4th Air Force, Hamilton Air Force Base, California, Holm Papers, U.S. Air Force Academy Archives, Colorado Springs, Colorado.

106. Mary Jo Shelly, Colonel, U.S. Air Force, Director, WAF, 23 April 1952, Report, 6, Historian's Files, Women's Memorial.

107. Mary Jo Shelly, Colonel, U.S. Air Force, Director, WAF, "Status of the WAF Program," 5 March 1953, 2, Historian's Files, Women's Memorial.

108. Jeanne M. Holm, Captain, U.S. Air Force, "Assumptions: Report on WAF Acquisitions and Losses," July 1953, Holm Papers, U.S. Air Force Academy Archives, Colorado Springs, Colorado.

109. Mary Jo Shelly, Colonel, U.S. Air Force, Director, WAF, "Basic Authorization for an Interim WAF Program," Memorandum for the Director of Personnel Planning, 10 December 1953, Historian's Files, Women's Memorial; Shelly, "Final Report of the Director, WAF," 19 January 1954, 12, Historian's Files, Women's Memorial.

110. Jeanne M. Holm, Major General, U.S. Air Force (Ret.), 29 November 2001, interview, Historian's Files, Women's Memorial.

111. Betty Splaine, Chief Warrant Officer 4, U.S. Coast Guard (Ret.), 23 August 1999 interview, Historian's Files, Women's Memorial.

112. Pearl Faurie, Master Chief Yeoman, U.S. Coast Guard (Ret.), 18 August 1999, interview, Historian's Files, Women's Memorial.

CHAPTER 5. A "WOMAN IMPERATIVE"? — MILITARY NECESSITY ERODES OLD BARRIERS (PP. 117–140)

1. *New York Times*, "A Program for Nurses" (editorial), 27 January 1951, 12.

2. Morris A. Wolf, R.N., "Men Nurses in the Services" (letter), *New York Times*, 5 May 1952, 22.

3. Dorothy Armstrong Elias, M.D., Captain, U.S. Air Force Medical Corps Reserve, files, undated newspaper clipping (n.p.), Women's Memorial Register.

4. Record Group U.S. Government, Department of Defense, Army Folder 2, American Physical Therapy Association Archives, Alexandria, Virginia.

5. Ibid.

6. Jeanne Ertwine Disterdick, Captain, U.S. Air Force Medical Specialist Corps, 27 March 2001, oral history, Historian's Files, Women's Memorial.

7. Lorry M. Fenner, Colonel, U.S. Air Force, "Ideology and Amnesia: The Public Debate on Women in the American Military, 1940–1973" (Ph.D. diss., University of Michigan, 1995), 300.

8. According to Luther Christman, Ph.D., R.N., men made up only 3 percent of nurses in the 1950s. www.medzilla.com/press62502.html (accessed 6 January 2005).

9. *New York Times*, "A Program for Nurses."

10. Wolf, "Men Nurses."

11. Mary T. Sarnecky, Colonel, U.S. Army Nurse Corps (Ret.), *A History of the U.S. Army Nurse Corps* (Philadelphia: University of Pennsylvania Press, 1999), 294.

12. Ibid.

13. Susan H. Godson, *Serving Proudly: A History of Women in the U.S. Navy* (Annapolis, Md.: Naval Institute Press, 2000), 143.

14. Public Law 408, 24 June 1952.

15. Sarnecky, *A History of the U.S. Army Nurse Corps*, 295.

16. "Army Medical Service Steps Up Drive As Armed Forces Seek 72,000 More

Women," 1 November 1951, Office of the Surgeon General, Technical Information Office, Historian's Files, Women's Memorial.

17. Sarnecky, *History of the U.S. Army Nurse Corps,* 295–298; Betty Walker, "She Heads Angels in Khaki," *Chicago Sun-Times,* 28 April 1954, 35; Ann Cotrell Free, "Army Nurse Corps Chiefs Are Two Virginia Women," *Richmond* [Virginia] *Times Dispatch,* 14 October 1951, A-3; Mary Sarnecky, "In Memorium: Ruby Fichlin Bryant, Colonel, ANC, 24 April 1906–22 January 2002," *The Connection,* 27, no. 1 (March 2002), 2.

18. *New York Times,* 19 January 1951, 6.

19. *New York Times,* 25 January 1951, 8; 28 January 1951, 7.

20. Carmela Filosa Hix, Captain, U.S. Army Nurse Corps, oral history, 6 July 2000, Historian's Files, Women's Memorial.

21. Doris M. Sterner, Captain, U.S. Navy Nurse Corps (Ret.), *In and Out of Harm's Way: A History of the Navy Nurse Corps* (Seattle, Wash.: Peanut Butter Publishing, 1997), 229.

22. Ibid., 231.

23. Ibid., 231–234.

24. Ibid., 234–235.

25. Ibid., 231.

26. Ibid.

27. Ibid., 249–250.

28. Verena Zeller Pettoruto Seberg, Colonel, U.S. Air Force Nurse Corps (Ret.), interview, 27 August 1999, Historian's Files, Women's Memorial; "The Impact of Korean Hostilities on Aeromedical Evacuation 1950–1953," n.d., Papers of Ethel Kovach Scott, Colonel, U.S. Air Force Nurse Corps (Ret.), Historian's Files, Women's Memorial.

29. Zeller Pettoruto Seberg, oral history.

30. *AWS* [All Women's Services] *Journal* (July 1950), 2, Grace L. Mueller Collection, Women's Memorial Collection.

31. Scott papers (see note 28, this chapter).

32. Zeller Pettoruto Seberg, oral history.

33. *AWS* [All Women's Services] *Journal* (August 1951), 12, Grace L. Mueller Collection, Women's Memorial Collection.

34. Record Group U.S. Government, Department of Defense, Army Folder 2, American Physical Therapy Association Archives, Alexandria, Virginia.

35. Margaret Hartwig Pithkethly, First Lieutenant, U.S. Army Nurse Corps, 26 August 1999, interview, Historian's Files, Women's Memorial.

36. Nell Wickliffe Merrill, Colonel, U.S. Army (Ret.) and Harriet S. Lee, Colonel, U.S. Army (Ret.), "The Korean War, June 1950 to July 1953," in *Army Medical Specialist Corps,* ed. Robert Anderson, Colonel, Medical Corps, U.S. Army (Washington, D.C.: Office of the Surgeon General, Department of the Army, 1986), 377–378, 384.

37. Ibid., 372–374.

38. Ibid., 370.

39. Jessie Fant Evans, "Maj. Vogel Is First Woman To Head Important Army Unit," newspaper clipping, no city, no date. Emma E. Vogel File, Blue Earth County Historical Society, Mankato, Minnesota, Historian's Files, Women's Memorial.

40. Eulogy, Emma E. Vogel, Colonel, U.S. Army (Ret.), presented by Colonel Elizabeth L. Lambertson, U.S. Army (Ret.) at Arlington National Cemetery, 3 September 1981.

41. Record Group U.S. Government, Department of Defense, Navy Folder 1, American Physical Therapy Association Archives, Alexandria, Virginia.

42. Pauline DesRochers Fauser, Ensign, U.S. Navy Medical Corps, letter, 24 August 1999, Historian's Files, Women's Memorial.

43. Record Group U.S. Government, Department of Defense, Air Force Folders 1–4, American Physical Therapy Association Archives, Alexandria, Virginia.

44. Jean Ertwine Disterdick, Captain, U.S. Air Force Women's Medical Specialist Corps, 1 September 1999 interview, Historian's Files, Women's Memorial.

45. Mildred Elson, executive director, American Physical Therapy Association, notes from 23 July 1951, meeting with Colonel Miriam Perry, Chief, Air Force Women's Medical Specialist Corps, American Physical Therapy Association Archives, Alexandria, Virginia.

46. Miriam Perry, Colonel, U.S. Air Force, Chief, Women's Medical Specialist Corps, 11 December 1951, Letter to Margaret Moore, American Physical Therapy Association education consultant, American Physical Therapy Association Archives, Alexandria, Virginia.

47. Mildred Elson, executive director, American Physical Therapy Association, letter to Donald Covalt, M.D., Institute of Rehabilitation and Physical Medicine, 9 January 1953, American Physical Therapy Association Archives, Alexandria, Virginia.

48. Record Group U.S. Government, Department of Defense, Air Force Folders 1–4 American Physical Therapy Association Archives, Alexandria, Virginia.

49. Miriam E. Perry, Lieutenant, U.S. Army, "Three and a Half Years in the Caribbean," *Simmons Review* (August 1944), Simmons College Archives, Boston, Massachusetts.

50. *AWS* [All Women's Services] *Journal* (July 1950), 15, Grace L. Mueller Collection, Women's Memorial Collection.

51. "Miriam Perry Goll," *Simmons Review* (Spring 1981), Simmons College Archives, Boston, Massachusetts.

52. Fenner, "Ideology and Amnesia," 299.

53. *New York Times*, 23 March 1950, 14.

54. *AWS* [All Women's Services] *Journal* (November 1950), 16, Grace L. Mueller Collection, Women's Memorial Collection.

55. Fenner, "Ideology and Amnesia," 299.

56. *AWS* [All Women's Services] *Journal* (February 1951), 9, Grace L. Mueller Collection, Women's Memorial Collection.
57. Fenner "Ideology and Amnesia," 299.
58. Ibid.
59. Fae M. Adams, M.D., Colonel, U.S. Army Medical Corps (Ret.), Women's Memorial Register.
60. Fae Adams, M.D. Colonel, U.S. Army Medical Corps (Ret.), 12 November 2003, oral history, Historian's Files, Women's Memorial.
61. *AWS* [All Women's Services] *Journal* (January 1952), 10; *AWS* [All Women's Services] *Journal* (June 1951), 6, Grace L. Mueller Collection, Women's Memorial Collection.
62. *AWS* [All Women's Services] *Journal* (June 1951), 13–14, Grace L. Mueller Collection, Women's Memorial Collection.
63. Elias files (see note 3, this chapter).
64. Fenner, "Ideology and Amnesia," 333.
65. Jean Ebbert and Marie Beth Hall, *Crossed Currents: Navy Women in a Century of Change* (Washington, D.C.: Brassey's, 1999), 145–146; Katherine Keating, Captain, U.S. Navy Medical Services (Ret.), Women's Memorial Register.
66. Faye Abdellah, Rear Admiral, U.S. Public Health Service (Ret.), 10 September 1998, interview, Historian's Files, Women's Memorial.
67. Margaret DeLawter, Captain, U.S. Public Health Service (Ret.), 8 August 2000, interview, Historian's Files, Women's Memorial.
68. Monthly Unit Report, 8063rd MASH, November 1950, RG 112, OSG, U.S. Medical Dept (AMEDD) Records 1947–1961, File HD 319.1, National Archives, College Park, Maryland.
69. Annual Report, 8055th MASH, 1 January 1951, RG 112, OSG, U.S. Medical Dept (AMEDD) Records 1947–1961, File HD 319.1, National Archives, College Park, Maryland.
70. Annual Report, 64th Field Hospital 1950, RG 112, OSG, U.S. Medical Dept (AMEDD) Records 1947–1961, File HD 319.1, National Archives, College Park, Maryland.
71. Dorothy Brandon, "Men to Replace Nurses Up Front Urged by Korea Nurses' Leader," *New York Herald Tribune*, 5 May 1952, n.p.; Brandon, "Calls Army Nurses 'Hazard to Troops'" *Washington Post*, 1 June 1952, n.p.; Brandon, "Nurses Prove They Can Take Korea in Stride," *New York Herald Tribune*, 29 June 1952, n.p., Army Nurse Corps Historian's Files, Office of Medical History, Office of the Army Surgeon General, Falls Church, Virginia.
72. Elizabeth M. Norman, *We Band of Angels: The Untold Story of American Nurses Trapped on Bataan by the Japanese* (New York: Random House, 1999), 133–138, 225–227.
73. Brandon, "Men to Replace Nurses Up Front Urged by Korea Nurses' Leader."

74. Ibid.
75. Dorothy G. Horwitz, ed., *We Will Not Be Strangers: Korean War Letters Between a MASH Surgeon and His Wife,* foreword by James I. Matray (Urbana: University of Illinois Press, 1997), 94–104, 131, 153, 196, 212, 216, 229; Annual Report, 8225th MASH, 31 December 1952, RG 112, OSG, U.S. Medical Dept (AMEDD) Records 1947–1961, File HD 319.1, National Archives, College Park, Maryland.
76. Horwitz, *We Will Not Be Strangers,* 97 and 131.
77. Ibid., 152–153.
78. Ibid., 196.
79. Ibid., 212 and 216.
80. Annual Report, 8225th MASH, 31 December 1952, RG 112, OSG, U.S. Medical Dept (AMEDD) Records 1947–1961, File HD 319.1, National Archives, College Park, Maryland.
81. Report for the Period January 1–February 1, 1953, 8225th MASH, RG 112, OSG, U.S. Medical Dept (AMEDD) Records 1947–1961, File HD 319.1, National Archives, College Park, Maryland.
82. Horwitz, *We Will Not Be Strangers,* 229.
83. Fenner, "Ideology and Amnesia," 297.
84. Brandon, "Nurses Prove They Can Take Korea in Stride."

CHAPTER 6. "NEEDED IN CADRE" — PROVIDING SUPPORT AROUND THE WORLD (PP. 141–168)

1. Juanita Mooney, Sergeant First Class, Women's Army Corps, letter, 13 July 1950, Germany, Juanita I. Mooney Collection, Women's Memorial Collection.
2. Doris M. Sterner, Captain, U.S. Navy Nurse Corps (Ret.), *In and Out of Harm's Way: A History of the Navy Nurse Corps* (Seattle, Wash.: Peanut Butter Publishing, 1997), 239.
3. Shirley Peck Barnes, U.S. Air Force civilian employee, Women's Memorial Register.
4. Janet Gingrich Preston, First Lieutenant, U.S. Army, 19 August 1999, interview, Historian's Files, Women's Memorial.
5. Dawn Yetman Croshaw, Sergeant, U.S. Army, Women's Memorial Register.
6. Louise Gorski Richardson, Petty Officer Third Class, U.S. Navy, Women's Memorial Register.
7. Mooney, letter, 13 July 1950.
8. Walter Poole, *The Joint Chiefs of Staff and National Policy, 1950–1952,* History of the Joint Chiefs of Staff, vol. 4 (Washington, D.C.: Office of the Chairman of the Joint Chiefs of Staff, 1998), 93.

9. Jacquelynn Janikowski Meakin, Corporal, U.S. Army, Women's Memorial Register.

10. Irene Michels Sorrough, Lieutenant Colonel, U. S. Army (Ret.), 28 July 1999, interview, Historian's Files, Women's Memorial.

11. Sterner, *In and Out of Harm's Way,* 216.

12. Poole, *Joint Chiefs of Staff,* 113–117.

13. Gertrude Samuels, "The WACs (Age 10) Take the Salute," *New York Times Sunday Magazine* (11 May 1952), 18.

14. Irene Van Houten Munster, Lieutenant Colonel, U.S. Army (Ret.), 24 March 1999, interview, Historian's Files, Women's Memorial.

15. Muriel Raymond Batcheller, First Lieutenant, U.S. Army Nurse Corps, 22 April 1999 and 7 May 2001, interviews, Historian's Files, Women's Memorial.

16. Jeanne Hamby Gang Collection, Women's Memorial Collection.

17. Bettie J. Morden, Colonel, U.S. Army (Ret.), *The Women's Army Corps, 1945– 1978* (Washington, D.C.: U.S. Army Center of Military History, 1992), 107; Yearbook, "Quonset, WAC Battalion, 8064th Army Unit, Yokohama Japan, 1951," Jean M. Colby Collection, Women's Memorial Collection.

18. Muriel Scharrer Wimmer, Private First Class, U.S. Army, 21 September 1998, interview, Historian's Files, Women's Memorial.

19. Evelyn Higgins, American Red Cross, excerpts from a letter to her parents, 9 July 1950, Historian's Files, Women's Memorial.

20. Gingrich Preston, interview.

21. Scharrer Wimmer, interview.

22. Yearbook, "Quonset, WAC Battalion, 8064th Army Unit."

23. Scharrer Wimmer, interview.

24. *AWS* [All Women's Services] *Journal* (April 1951), 8–9, Grace L. Mueller Collection, Women's Memorial Collection.

25. Yearbook, "Far East Review, 1946–1952," Florence M. Del Rosso Collection, Women's Memorial Collection.

26. Ibid.

27. Ernestine Johnson Thomas, Staff Sergeant, U.S. Air Force, 14 October 1998, and 15 March 2001, interviews, Historian's Files, Women's Memorial.

28. Johnson Thomas, 15 March 2001 interview.

29. "30 WAF's Arrive: WAF Provisional Squadron # 2 Fills Wing JADF Vacancies," Historian's Files, Women's Memorial.

30. Press Releases, Headquarters, Far East Air Forces, 15 February 1952 and 22 April 1952, found with photographs in RG 342-J-68-B, Still Picture Branch, National Archives, College Park, Maryland.

31. American Red Cross Annual Report for Year Ending June 30, 1951, American Red Cross Archives, Falls Church, Virginia.

32. Sylvia J. Rock, "Japan Intrigued Jersey Girl: Ex-Red Cross Worker Says Yokohama is Like Harlem," *Baltimore Afro-American,* 13 October 1951, magazine section, 7.

33. Annual Report for 1952, 121st Evacuation Hospital, 6 May 1953, RG 112, Office of the Surgeon General, U.S. Medical Department AMEDD Records 1947–1961 HD 319.1, National Archives, College Park, Maryland.

34. Report of Medical Service Activities, 172d Station Hospital, 5 November 1951, and Report of Medical Service Activities 8164th Army Hospital, 1951, RG 112, Office of the Surgeon General, U.S. Medical Department AMEDD Records 1947–1961 HD 319.1, National Archives, College Park, Maryland.

35. Annual Report for 1951, 382nd General Hospital, RG 112, Office of the Surgeon General, U.S. Medical Department AMEDD Records 1947–1961, HD 319.1, National Archives, College Park, Maryland.

36. Dorothy Brandon, "Okinawa 'Not Bad' to 250 Busy WACs," *Washington Post*, 11 June 1952, Margaret R. Gorning Collection, Women's Memorial Collection.

37. Martha Halyak Fogle, Sergeant, U.S. Army, 16 March 1999 interview, Historian's Files, Women's Memorial.

38. Ibid.

39. Shirley Peck Barnes, U.S. Air Force civilian employee, Women's Memorial Register.

40. Joan Heath Steyn, Lieutenant Commander (Ret.), U.S. Navy Nurse Corps, 7 October 1998, interview, Historian's Files, Women's Memorial.

41. Sterner, *In and Out of Harm's Way*, 246.

42. Ibid., 247.

43. Ibid.

44. Jacquelyn Tomasik Anderson, Airman Second Class, U.S. Air Force, 23 January 2001, interview, Historian's Files, Women's Memorial.

45. Peter A. Soderbergh, *Women Marines in the Korean War Era* (Westport, Conn.: Greenwood, 1994), 89.

46. Newspaper clippings, Dorothy L. Matz Collection, Women's Memorial Collection.

47. Ibid.

48. Department of the Army Pamphlet No 20–138, "Leave It To The WAC," 14 September 1951, 3, Elizabeth Cook Jones Collection, Women's Memorial Collection; *New York Times*, 13 January 1951.

49. Ibid.

50. Jeanne M. Holm, Major General, U.S. Air Force, (Ret.), 30 September 1999, interview, Historian's Files, Women's Memorial.

51. Mildred Inez Bailey, Brigadier General, U.S. Army (Ret.), 4 October 1999, interview, Historian's Files, Women's Memorial.

52. Mildred Inez Bailey, Brigadier General, U.S. Army (Ret.), oral history, conducted by Rhoda Messer, Lieutenant Colonel, U.S. Army, U.S. Army War College, U.S. Army Military History Institute Senior Debriefing Program, 1978, 18–20, Historian's Files, Women's Memorial.

53. Ibid.

54. Constance Bennett Van Hook, oral history interview conducted by Connie Slewitzke, Brigadier General, U.S. Army Nurse Corps (Ret.), 26 September 2002,
Historian's Files, Women's Memorial, 7.

55. Soderbergh, *Women Marines in the Korean War Era*, 89.

56. U.S. Army Photo caption, National Archives (111-SC-424079).

57. Beatrice Seelav Stecher, Major, U.S. Air Force, 3 October 2000, interview, Historian's Files, Women's Memorial.

58. Gladys Hahn Romanoff, Corporal, U.S. Army, 7 April 1999, interview, Historian's Files, Women's Memorial.

59. Lucille Marquis Regan, Corporal, U.S. Army, 10 January 2001, telephone interview, Historian's Files, Women's Memorial.

60. Janet Rasmussen, Captain, U.S. Army (Ret.), 16 August 1999, interview, Historian's Files, Women's Memorial.

61. Dorothy Looby Manfredi, Captain, U.S. Army Nurse Corps, 21 September
1999, interview, Historian's Files, Women's Memorial.

62. Ibid.

63. Muriel Raymond Batcheller, First Lieutenant, U.S. Army Nurse Corps, 22 April
1999, interview, Historian's Files, Women's Memorial.

64. Margaret E. Bailey, Colonel, U.S. Army Nurse Corps (Ret.), *The Challenge: Autobiography of Colonel Margaret E. Bailey* (Lisle, Ill.: Tucker Publications, 1999),
52–56.

65. Katharine Manchester, Colonel, U.S. Army Medical Specialist Corps (Ret.), 29
September 1999, interview, Historian's Files, Women's Memorial.

66. Ibid.

67. Bennett Van Hook, oral history.

68. Holm, interview.

69. *AWS* [All Women's Services] *Journal* (July 1952), 8, Grace L. Mueller Collection,
Women's Memorial Collection.

70. "One In A Million: A WAC At Ft. Dix," *AWS* [All Women's Services] *Journal*
(September 1951), 6–7, Grace L. Mueller Collection, Women's Memorial
Collection.

71. *AWS* [All Women's Services] *Journal* (September 1950), 2, Grace L. Mueller
Collection, Women's Memorial Collection.

72. *AWS* [All Women's Services] *Journal* (October 1951), 11, Grace L. Mueller
Collection, Women's Memorial Collection.

73. *All Hands* (July 1952), 20–22, Historian's Files, Women's Memorial; *AWS* [All
Women's Services] *Journal* (May 1952), 3, Grace L. Mueller Collection, Women's
Memorial Collection.

74. *All Hands* (July 1952).

75. Ibid.

76. Sterner, *In and Out of Harm's Way*, 241–242.

77. Ibid., 239.

78. *New York Herald Tribune,* 9 November 1951, Helen Mannion Doyle Collection, Women's Memorial Collection.

79. Janice Feagin Britton, Captain, U.S. Air Force Nurse Corps, 9 May 2002, oral history, Historian's Files, Women's Memorial.

80. Elwanda Patricia Bright McClain Collection, Women's Memorial Collection.

81. Mary Jo Shelly, Colonel, U.S. Air Force, Director WAF, Memorandum for the Chief of Staff, 11 June 1951, Historian's Files, Women's Memorial; Shelly Memorandum for Lieutenant General Laurence S. Kuter, 15 May 1952, Historian's Files, Women's Memorial.

82. Elizabeth Alden Roe Collection, Women's Memorial Collection.

83. *AWS* [All Women's Services] *Journal* (March 1952), 7, Grace L. Mueller Collection, Women's Memorial Collection.

84. *Delaware Magazine, Wilmington Sunday Star,* 16 August 1953, Josephine DeAcetis Schell Collection, Women's Memorial Collection.

85. *AWS* [All Women's Services] *Journal* (June 1951), 6, Grace L. Mueller Collection, Women's Memorial Collection.

86. Ibid., 8–9.

87. "Women in the Armed Forces," *Armed Forces Talk* (November 1952), Elizabeth M. Jones Collection, Women's Memorial Collection.

88. Jacquelen McCracken Henderson Collection, Women's Memorial Collection.

89. Holm interview.

90. "Smart Women," U.S. Air Force Recruiting Brochure, Women's Memorial Collection.

91. "The WAF Band Salutes Marybelle J. Nissly," 1999 Women's Air Force Band Reunion Program Book, (U.S. WAF Band, Springfield, Virginia, 1999).

92. "A&M Turning Out 25 WAFs Every Week," undated newspaper clipping, n.p. Jane Spide Conard Collection, Women's Memorial Collection; Jacquelen McCracken Henderson Collection, Women's Memorial Collection.

93. Gertrude Samuels, "The WACs (Age 10) Take the Salute."

CHAPTER 7. THE NURSES IN KOREA — UNDER FIRE AND ON THE MOVE (PP. 169–219)

1. "Background Information: Captain Phyllis LaConte, Army Nurse Corps," 30 October 1950, RG 112, Office of the Surgeon General (OSG), U.S. Medical Dept. (AMEDD) Records 1947–1961, File HD 211 (Nurses) Korea, National Archives, College Park, Maryland.

2. "Tokyo to Pusan: An Army Nurse's Diary From the Battlefield," Department of the Army Office of the Surgeon General, Technical Information Office, 13 March 1951, RG 112, OSG, U.S. Medical Dept. (AMEDD) Records 1947–1961 File HD 211 (Nurses) Korea, National Archives, College Park, Maryland.

3. "Background Information: Army Nurses in Korea," Department of the Army Office of the Surgeon General Technical Information Office, 2 May 1951, RG 112, OSG, U.S. Medical Dept. (AMEDD) Records 1947–1961 File HD 211 (Nurses) Korea, National Archives, College Park, Maryland.

4. Mary T. Sarnecky, Colonel, U.S. Army Nurse Corps (Ret.), *A History of the Army Nurse Corps* (Philadelphia: University of Pennsylvania Press, 1999), 287, 301–302; "Stand By For Korea," 25–26, Army Nurse Corps Historian's Files, 314.7 History Korea, U.S. Army Center of Military History.

5. Sarnecky, "Stand By For Korea"; Presentation of Colonel Edwin Overholt, U.S. Army Medical Corps (Ret.) at the Conference of Army Historians, June 2000, Arlington, Virginia.

6. Doug DuBois, "Angels of Mercy," *Stars and Stripes,* 14 October 1950, RG 112, OSG, U.S. Medical Dept. (AMEDD) Records 1947–1961 File HD 211 (Nurses) Korea, National Archives, College Park, Maryland.

7. Sarnecky, *History of the Army Nurse Corps,* 303–306; "Stand By For Korea," 39.

8. Richard K. Kolb, "War in the 'Land That God Forgot': Korea, 1950–1953," *VFW Magazine,* December 1991, 28–34; Albert E. Cowdrey, *The Medics' War* (Washington, D.C.: U.S. Army Center of Military History, 1990), 271.

9. Sarnecky, *History of the Army Nurse Corps,* 303–304.

10. Sarnecky, "Stand By For Korea," 33–34.

11. Sarnecky, *History of the Army Nurse Corps,* 306.

12. "Annual Report of Medical Activities 8054th Evacuation Hospital July–December 1950," RG 112, OSG, U.S. Medical Dept. (AMEDD) Records 1947–1961 File HD 319.1, National Archives, College Park, Maryland.

13. "Background Information: Captain Phyllis LaConte; 8055th MASH Monthly Report July 1950," RG 112, OSG (Army) Historical Unit Medical Detachments (HUMEDS) File Essential Medical Data 1950–1951, National Archives, College Park, Maryland.

14. Sarnecky, *History of the Army Nurse Corps,* 305.

15. "8055 MASH Monthly Reports, July 1950 and August 1950," RG 112, OSG (Army) Historical Unit Medical Detachments (HUMEDS) File Essential Medical Data 1950–1951, National Archives, College Park, Maryland.

16. Ibid.

17. Ibid.

18. "Blond Curls and Stern Tasks: Story of an Army Nurse," *Newsweek* (12 March 1951), 28–30, Historian's Files, Women's Memorial.

19. John P. Wooden, "Background On Army Nurses In Korea," Department of the Army, Office of the Surgeon General, Technical Information Office, 12 February 1951, RG 112, OSG, U.S. Medical Dept. (AMEDD) Records 1947–1961, HD 211 (Nurses) Korea, National Archives, College Park, Maryland.

20. "Highlights of Naval Medical History in the Korean Campaign, 1 August 1951," Historian's Files, Women's Memorial; "Annual Report of Medical Activities,

8054th Evacuation Hospital, July–December 1950," RG 112, OSG, U.S. Medical Dept. (AMEDD) Records 1947–1961, File HD 319.1, National Archives, College Park, Maryland.

21. Doris M. Sterner, Captain, U.S. Navy Nurse Corps (Ret.), *In and Out of Harm's Way: A History of the Navy Nurse Corps* (Seattle, Wash.: Peanut Butter Publishing, 1997), 236.

22. "Background Information: Captain Phyllis LaConte, Army Nurse Corps, 30 October 1950," RG 112, OSG, U.S. Medical Dept. (AMEDD) Records 1947–1961, File HD 211 (Nurses) Korea, National Archives, College Park, Maryland.

23. Mary Zoschak, "My Days in a MASH Unit," Mary Zoschak Collection, Women's Memorial Collection.

24. "Tokyo to Pusan: An Army Nurse's Diary From the Battlefield," Department of the Army Office of the Surgeon General, Technical Information Office, 13 March 1951, RG 112, OSG, U.S. Medical Dept. (AMEDD) Records 1947–1961, File HD 211 (Nurses) Korea, National Archives, College Park, Maryland. Note: the entry on 29 July refers to the death of Major Genevieve Smith, who died in early July 1950 when the aircraft taking her to Korea exploded in midair.

25. "Annual Report of Medical Activities 8054th Evacuation Hospital July–December 1950," RG 112, OSG, U.S. Medical Dept (AMEDD) Records 1947–1961, File HD 319.1, National Archives, College Park, Maryland.

26. Doug DuBois, "Angels of Mercy," *Stars and Stripes,* 14 October 1950, quoted in "Background Information: Army Nurses in Korea," RG 112, OSG, U.S. Medical Dept. (AMEDD) Records 1947–1961, HD 211 (Nurses) Korea, National Archives, College Park, Maryland.

27. "Background Information: Army Nurses In Korea," 24 August 1950, Department of the Army Office of the Surgeon General, Technical Information Office, RG 112, OSG, (Army) U.S. Medical Dept. (AMEDD) Records, 1947–1961, HD 211 (Nurses) Korea, National Archives, College Park, Maryland.

28. "Annual Report, Eighth Station Hospital, 1951, 16 January 1952," RG 112, OSG, U.S. Medical Dept. (AMEDD) Records 1947–1961, File HD 319.1, National Archives, College Park, Maryland.

29. "Annual Report, Army Medical Service Activities for Calendar Year 1950, 5th Station Hospital, 1 January 1951," RG 112, OSG, U.S. Medical Dept. (AMEDD) Records 1947–1961, File HD 319.1, National Archives, College Park, Maryland.

30. "Annual Report, 118th Station Hospital, Medical Service Activities, 1950," RG 112, OSG, U.S. Medical Dept. (AMEDD) Records 1947–1961, File HD 319.1, National Archives, College Park, Maryland.

31. Robert S. Anderson, Colonel, U.S. Army Medical Corps, editor in chief, *Army Medical Specialist Corps* (Washington, D.C.: Office of the Surgeon General, 1986), 562.

32. Ibid., 373.

33. "The Impact of Korean Hostilities on Aeromedical Evacuation, 1950–1953," Papers of Ethel Kovach Scott, Historian's Files, Women's Memorial.

34. Ibid.

35. Ibid.

36. Catherine Danker Dombrowski, Captain, U.S. Air Force Nurse Corps, 26 August 1999, interview, Historian's Files, Women's Memorial.

37. "Annual Report, 1st Mobile Army Surgical Hospital, 8 October 1951," RG 112, OSG, U.S. Medical Dept. (AMEDD) Records 1947–1961, File HD 319.1, National Archives, College Park, Maryland.

38. "Background Information: Army Nurses in Korea," Department of the Army, Office of the Surgeon General, Technical Information Office, 2 May 1951, Abstracted from the personal letters of Major Eunice Coleman, Chief Nurse, 1st Mobile Army Surgical Hospital, RG 112, OSG, U.S. Medical Dept. (AMEDD) Records 1947–1961, File HD 211, National Archives, College Park, Maryland.

39. Scrapbook, Margaret Zane Fleming Collection, Gift of Frances Zane, Women's Memorial Collection.

40. Tom A. Hamrick, "The Lucky 13: Army Nurses in Korea Bring Medical Aid and Morale to Frontlines," *Pacific Stars and Stripes*, n.d., 8–9, 14, Margaret Zane Fleming Collection, Gift of Frances Zane, Women's Memorial Collection.

41. "Annual Report of Medical Service Activities, 121st Evacuation Hospital, 18 January 1951," RG 112, OSG, U.S. Medical Dept. (AMEDD) Records 1947–1961, File HD 319.1, National Archives, College Park, Maryland.

42. Doug DuBois, "Angels of Mercy," *Stars and Stripes* 14 October 1950; quoted in "Background Information: Army Nurses in Korea," RG 112, OSG, U.S. Medical Dept. (AMEDD) Records 1947–1961, File HD 211 (Nurses) Korea, National Archives, College Park, Maryland.

43. Anna Mae McCabe Hays, Brigadier General, U.S. Army Nurse Corps (Ret.), oral history conducted by Amelia Carson, Colonel, Army Nurse Corps, U.S. Army War College/U.S. Army Military History Institute Senior Officer, Oral History Program, 1982.

44. Ibid.

45. "8055th Monthly Report, October 1950," RG 112, OSG, U.S. Medical Dept. (AMEDD) Records 1947–1961, File HD 319.1, National Archives, College Park, Maryland.

46. Albert E. Cowdrey, *The Medics' War* (Washington, D.C.: U.S. Army Center of Military History, 1990), 95.

47. Ibid.

48. "History of the U.S.S. *Repose* (AH-16)," U.S. Navy Bureau of Medicine and Surgery Archives.

49. "The Ship With a Heart," *Life and Health* (July 1952), RG 52, BUMED, Administrative Division, General Correspondence 1952–1971, File A4-1/AH, Feb.–Dec. 1952, AH 16 U.S.S. *Repose*, National Archives, College Park, Maryland.

50. Lura Jane Emery, Commander, U.S. Navy Nurse Corps (Ret.), 20 July 2000, interview, Historian's Files, Women's Memorial.
51. Ibid.
52. "The Ship With a Heart."
53. Sterner, *In and Out of Harm's Way*, 237–238.
54. Emery, interview.
55. Sterner, *In and Out of Harm's Way*, 238.
56. "The Impact of Korean Hostilities on Aeromedical Evacuation, 1950–1953," papers of Ethel Kovach Scott, Colonel, U.S. Air Force Nurse Corps (Ret.), Historian's Files, Women's Memorial.
57. "8055th MASH, Monthly Report, October 1950," RG 112, OSG, (Army) Historical Unit Medical Detachments (HUMEDS) File Essential Medical Data 1950–1951, National Archives, College Park, Maryland.
58. Ibid.
59. Ibid.
60. "The Impact of Korean Hostilities on Aeromedical Evacuation, 1950–1953," papers of Ethel Kovach Scott, Historian's Files, Women's Memorial.
61. Donald M. Goldstein and Harry J. Maihafer, *The Korean War* (Washington, D.C.: Brassey's, 2000), 87–88.
62. "8055th MASH, Monthly Report, November 1950," RG 112, OSG, (Army) Historical Unit Medical Detachments (HUMEDS) File Essential Medical Data 1950–1951, National Archives, College Park, Maryland.
63. Ibid.; Sarnecky, *History of the Army Nurse Corps*, 307.
64. "8055th MASH, Monthly Report, November 1950," RG 112, OSG, (Army) Historical Unit Medical Detachments (HUMEDS) File Essential Medical Data 1950–1951, National Archives, College Park, Maryland.
65. "A Review of 2 Years of Operations of the U.S.S. *Repose* in the Korean Theater of Operations September 20, 1950–September 20, 1952," RG 52, BUMED Administration Division, General Correspondence 1952–1971, File A4–1/AH Feb.–Dec. 1952 U.S.S. *Repose*, National Archives, College Park, Maryland.
66. "Annual Report, 121st Evacuation Hospital 1950–1951, 18 January 1951," RG 112, OSG, U.S. Medical Dept. (AMEDD) Records 1947–1961, File HD 319.1, National Archives, College Park, Maryland.
67. Frances Omori, Commander, U.S. Navy, *Quiet Heroes: Navy Nurses of the Korean War, 1950–1953, Far East Command* (Saint Paul, Minn.: Smith House Press, 2000), 111–112.
68. Emery, interview.
69. Omori, *Quiet Heroes*, 112.
70. Emery, interview.
71. "Genevieve McLean Remembers Medicine in the Real Korean War," *Kennebec Observer*, 14 September 1988, Genevieve Connors McLean Collection, Women's Memorial Collection.

72. Annual Report, Medical Service Activities, 64th Field Hospital, 1950, RG 112, OSG, U.S. Medical Dept. (AMEDD) Records 1947–1961, File HD 319.1, National Archives, College Park, Maryland.

73. "Genevieve McLean Remembers"; "8055th MASH Monthly Report, December 1950."

74. *Detroit* [Michigan] *Free Press*, photo caption, no headline or page number, 28 October 1950; Jeff Olesen, "Martin Recalls Duties as Nurse During War," "Meet Your Neighbor" section, *Hillsdale* [Michigan] *Daily News*, date unclear (possibly 25 June 1988), Luluah Houseknecht Martin Collection, Women's Memorial Collection.

75. Goldstein and Maihafer, *Korean War*, 89–90.

76. Marguerite Higgins, *War in Korea* (New York: Lion Books, 1952), 107, Eleanor V. Spiller Collection, Women's Memorial Collection.

77. Omori, *Quiet Heroes*, 19, 33–42.

78. "Background Information: Army Nurses in Korea, 2 May 1951," Department of the Army, Office of the Surgeon General, Technical Information Office, RG 112, OSG, U.S. Medical Dept. (AMEDD) Records 1947–1961 File HD 211, National Archives, College Park, Maryland; *AWS* [All Women's Services] *Journal* (February 1952), 2, Grace L. Mueller Collection, Women's Memorial Collection.

79. Scrapbook, Margaret Zane Fleming Collection, gift of Frances Zane, Women's Memorial Collection.

80. Ibid.

81. "Background Information: Army Nurses in Korea, 2 May 1951," Department of the Army, Office of the Surgeon General, Technical Information Office, Washington, D.C., RG 112, OSG, U.S. Medical Dept. (AMEDD) Records 1947–1961 File HD 211, National Archives, College Park, Maryland.

82. Omori, *Quiet Heroes*, 19, 33–42.

83. Sterner, *In and Out of Harm's Way*, 239.

84. Helen Fable, Lieutenant Commander, U.S. Navy Nurse Corps (Ret.), oral history conducted by Frances Omori, Commander, U.S. Navy, 13 July 1999, Historian's Files, Women's Memorial.

85. "The Impact of Korean Hostilities on Aeromedical Evacuation, 1950–1953," papers of Ethel Kovach Scott, Colonel, U.S. Air Force Nurse Corps (Ret.), Historian's Files, Women's Memorial.

86. Marguerite Liebold, Major, U.S. Air Force Nurse Corps (Ret.), Women's Memorial Register.

87. Grace Chicken Collection, Women's Memorial Collection.

88. "Annual Report, 376th Station Hospital, 9 January 1951," RG 112, OSG, U.S. Medical Dept. (AMEDD) Records 1947–1961, File HD 319.1, National Archives, College Park, Maryland.

89. Catherine Owen Horne, Major, U.S. Army Women's Medical Specialist Corps, telephone interview, 22 June 1999; Historian's Files, Women's Memorial.

90. Barbara Northrup Thomas, Captain, U.S. Air Force Women's Medical Specialist Corps, telephone interview, 2 September 1999, Historian's Files, Women's Memorial.

91. Scrapbook, Collection of Margaret Zane Fleming, gift of Frances Zane, Women's Memorial Collection.

92. Gertrude Samuels, "With Army Nurses Somewhere in Korea," *New York Times*, 15 April 1951.

93. Anna Mae McCabe Hays, Brigadier General, U.S. Army Nurse Corps (Ret.), 23 April 1999, interview, Historian's Files, Women's Memorial; Anna Mae McCabe Hays, Brigadier General, U.S. Army Nurse Corps (Ret.), oral history conducted by Amelia Carson, Colonel, Army Nurse Corps, U.S. Army War College/U.S. Army Military History Institute Senior Officer, Oral History Program, 1982.

94. Carolyn M. Feller and Constance J. Moore, *Highlights in the History of the Army Nurse Corps*, U.S. Army Center of Military History, Washington, D.C., 1995, 11.

95. Anna Mae McCabe Hays, Brigadier General, U.S. Army Nurse Corps (Ret.), oral history conducted by Amelia Carson, Colonel, Army Nurse Corps Senior Army Officers Oral History Program, U.S. Army Military History Institute (AMHI) Project 83–10, 28 October 1983, 5.

96. McCabe Hays, oral history, AMHI, 23.

97. McCabe Hays, oral history, AMHI, 46.

98. McCabe Hays, oral history, AMHI, 57–58.

99. McCabe Hays, oral history, AMHI, 68.

100. McCabe Hays, oral history, AMHI, 60–62.

101. McCabe Hays, oral history, AMHI, 69.

102. Anna Mae McCabe Hays, Brigadier General, U.S. Army Nurse Corps (Ret.), 17 March 2000, interview conducted by Kathleen M. Scott, Historian's Files, Women's Memorial.

103. McCabe Hays, oral history, AMHI, 97.

104. McCabe Hays, oral history, AMHI, 120.

105. Kathleen M. Scott, "An Officer and a Lady: Status and Gender in the U.S. Army Nurse Corps, 1942–1971," Williamsburg, Va.: College of William and Mary, unpublished thesis, 2001, 59.

106. Scott, "An Officer and a Lady," 63.

107. "Annual Report 1951, 121st Evacuation Hospital, 10 January 1952," RG 112, OSG, U.S. Medical Dept. (AMEDD) Records 1947–1961, File HD 319.1, National Archives, College Park, Maryland.

108. "8055th MASH, Monthly Reports, January and February 1951," RG 112, OSG, Army Historical Unit Medical Detachments (HUMEDS) File Essential Medical Data 1950–1951, National Archives, College Park, Maryland.

109. Oral history interviews conducted by Frances Omori, Commander, U.S. Navy; Marilyn Ewing Affleck, Lieutenant, U.S. Navy Nurse Corps, 22 May 1999; Betty Jo Alexander, Ensign, U.S. Navy Nurse Corps, 24 June 1999; Jean Eliza-

beth Ellis Young, Lieutenant Commander, U.S. Navy Nurse Corps (Ret.), 27 June 1999; Lois Colgate Merritt, Commander, U.S. Navy Nurse Corps (Ret.), 15 July 1999; Helen Fable, Lieutenant Commander, U.S. Navy Nurse Corps, (Ret.), 13 July 1999; and Virginia Miriam Jennings Watson, Lieutenant (jg) U.S. Navy Nurse Corps, 15 September 1999, Oral History Collection, Women's Memorial.

110. "Unit Historical Report for 1950, Hq 8th Station Hospital, 8 January 1951," RG 112, OSG, U.S. Medical Dept. (AMEDD) Records 1947–1961, File HD 319.1, National Archives, College Park, Maryland; "Annual Report 1951, 8th Station Hospital, 16 January 1952," RG 112, OSG, U.S. Medical Dept. (AMEDD) Records 1947–1961, File HD 319.1, National Archives, College Park, Maryland.

111. J. E. Jacoby, Lieutenant Colonel, U.S. Army Nurse Corps (Ret.), oral history conducted by Wynona Bice-Stephens, Major, U.S. Army Nurse Corps, and Susan Steinfield, Major, U.S. Army Nurse Corps, at the 1988 convention of the Retired Army Nurse Corps Association, Seattle, Washington.

112. Ibid.

113. "Annual Report, 1st Mobile Army Surgical Hospital, 8 October 1951," RG 112, OSG, U.S. Medical Dept. (AMEDD) Records 1947–1961, File HD 319.1, National Archives, College Park, Maryland.

114. "8055th MASH, Monthly Report, March 1951," RG 112, OSG, Army Historical Unit Medical Detachments (HUMEDS) File Essential Medical Data 1950–1951, National Archives, College Park, Maryland.

115. Jacoby, oral history.

116. "8055th MASH, Monthly Report, April 1951," RG 112, OSG, Army Historical Unit Medical Detachments (HUMEDS) File Essential Medical Data 1950–1951, National Archives, College Park, Maryland.

117. "8055th MASH, Monthly Reports, July 1950–April 1951," RG 112, OSG, Army Historical Unit Medical Detachments (HUMEDS) File Essential Medical Data 1950–1951, National Archives, College Park, Maryland.

118. Scrapbook, Margaret Zane Fleming Collection, Gift of Frances Zane, Women's Memorial Collection.

119. U.S. Air Force photo, "Flight Nurse Checks Her Patients," 14 January 1953, Lillian Kinkela Keil Collection, Women's Memorial Collection.

120. Newspaper photo, *Chicago Defender*, 29 January 1949, 9.

121. "Army Nurse Home After Eight Months in Korea," *Baltimore Afro-American*, 23 October 1951, 4.

122. "Annual Report, 1st Mobile Army Surgical Hospital, 8 October 1951," RG 112, OSG, U.S. Medical Dept. (AMEDD) Records 1947–1961, File HD 319.1, National Archives, College Park, Maryland.

123. Sarnecky, *History of the Army Nurse Corps*, 311–312.

124. Sterner, *In and Out of Harm's Way*, 248.

125. Ibid.

126. Omori, *Quiet Heroes*, 93–95.

127. James F. Schnable, *The Joint Chiefs of Staff and National Policy, 1950–1951; The Korean War, Part One,* History of the Joint Chiefs of Staff, vol. 3 (Washington, D.C.: Office of the Chairman of the Joint Chiefs of Staff, 1998), 216.

128. Kathiann Kowalski, "Two Years of Talking," in *The Korean War, 1950–1953* (Peterborough, N.H.: Cobblestone, 1999), 20.

129. "Annual Report, 121st Evacuation Hospital, 1951, 10 January 1952," RG 112, OSG, U.S. Medical Dept. (AMEDD) Records 1947–1961, File HD 319.1, National Archives, College Park, Maryland.

130. "Annual Report of Army Medical Service Activities, 10th Station Hospital, 1950," 8 January 1951, RG 112, OSG, U.S. Medical Dept. (AMEDD) Records 1947–1961, File HD 319.1, National Archives, College Park, Maryland.

131. *Physical Therapy Review*, 33, no. 5, (May 1953), 259; *Physical Therapy Review* 33, no. 6 (June 1953), 306, American Physical Therapy Association Archives, Alexandria, Virginia.

132. *Physical Therapy Review*, 31, no. 9, 401, American Physical Therapy Association Archives, Alexandria, Virginia.

133. Ibid.

134. Kowalski, "Two Years of Talking," 21.

135. Sarnecky, *History of the Army Nurse Corps*, 313–314.

136. Barbara Cullom, Lieutenant Colonel, U.S. Army Nurse Corps (Ret.), oral history conducted by Major Carol Reineck, 12–13 April 1986, 5, 7, 12, 14–15, 24, U.S. Army Center of Military History, Army Nurse Corps Oral History Transcripts, Korean War, vol. 1.

137. Ibid.

138. "Annual Medical Report, 4th Field Hospital, 1950, 15 January 1951," RG 112, OSG, U.S. Medical Dept. (AMEDD) Records 1947–1961, File HD 319.1, National Archives, College Park, Maryland; "Annual Report, 3rd Field Hospital, 1950, 13 January 1951," RG 112, OSG, U.S. Medical Dept. (AMEDD) Records 1947–1961, File HD 319.1, National Archives, College Park, Maryland.

139. "Annual Report, Medical Service Activities, 64th Field Hospital, 1952," RG 112, OSG, U.S. Medical Dept. (AMEDD) Records 1947–1961, File HD 319.1, National Archives, College Park, Maryland.

140. Ralph Matthews, "Camp in Korea Men's Hopes Tied to Cease-fire Parleys," *Baltimore Afro-American,* 4 September 1951, 14.

141. "64th Field Hospital Secret Security Information, 1952," RG 112, OSG, U.S. Medical Dept. (AMEDD) Records 1947–1961, File HD 319.1, National Archives, College Park, Maryland.

142. "Annual Report, 3rd and 14th Field Hospitals, 1950," n.d. and "Annual Report, 3rd and 14th Field Hospitals, 1952, 14 April 1953," RG 112, OSG, U.S. Medical

Dept. (AMEDD) Records 1947–1961, File HD 319.1, National Archives, College Park, Maryland.

143. Ethel Kovach Scott Papers, Historian's Files, Women's Memorial.

144. Mary Pritchard, Lieutenant Colonel, U.S. Army Nurse Corps (Ret.), oral history conducted by Jude Larkin, Lieutenant Colonel, U.S. Army Nurse Corps, at the 1988 Retired Army Nurse Corps Association Convention (RANCA) in Seattle, Washington, Historian's Files, Women's Memorial.

145. Emery, interview.

146. "Reports of the 121st Evacuation Hospital, 1950, 1951, and 1952," RG 112, OSG, U.S. Medical Dept. (AMEDD) Records 1947–1961, File HD 319.1, National Archives, College Park, Maryland.

147. Joyce Gillespie, Colonel, U.S. Army Nurse Corps (Ret.) oral history conducted by Constance J. Moore, First Lieutenant, U.S. Army Nurse Corps, RANCA convention, Washington, D.C., 1986.

148. Carmela Filosa Hix, Captain, U.S. Army Nurse Corps, 5 July 2000, oral history, Historian's Files, Women's Memorial.

149. Ibid.

150. Sterner, *In and Out of Harm's Way*, 247.

151. Agnes Zuverink Norman, Major, Air Force Nurse Corps, (Ret.), Women's Memorial Register.

152. Jacoby, interview.

153. Muriel Scharrer Wimmer, Private First Class, Women's Army Corps, 21 September 1998, oral history, Historian's Files, Women's Memorial.

154. "Annual Report 1953 HQ U.S. Army Forces Far East, 4 October 1953," RG 112, OSG, U.S. Medical Dept. (AMEDD) Records 1947–1961, File HD 319.1, National Archives, College Park, Maryland.

155. Handwritten journal, Nancy J. Crosby, Lieutenant, U.S. Navy Nurse Corps, 2 January 1952–September 1953, USS *Haven*, Nancy J. Crosby Collection, Women's Memorial Collection.

156. *The Unicorn Book of 1953 Outstanding Events of the Year* (New York: Unicorn Books, 1954), 244.

157. Ibid., 248.

158. Goldstein and Maihafer, *Korean War*, 125.

159. Casualty File, Historian's Office, Women's Memorial.

160. Ibid.

161. Sterner, *In and Out of Harm's Way*, 233.

162. Ibid.; Casualty File, Historian's Office, Women's Memorial.

163. Sarnecky, *History of the Army Nurse Corps*, 303.

164. 801st MAES Yearbook, Carolyn Allen Johnson Collection, Women's Memorial Collection; *History of Air Evacuation*, Sarah P. Wells Collection, Women's Memorial Collection.

**CHAPTER 8. RECURRING ISSUES RELATING TO MILITARY WOMEN
(PP. 220–243)**

1. Mildred Inez Bailey, Brigadier General, U.S. Army (Ret.), oral history conducted by Rhoda Messer, Lieutenant Colonel, U.S. Army War College/U.S. Army Military History Institute Senior Officer Debriefing Program, 1978, 39–40.
2. Muriel Raymond Batcheller, First Lieutenant, U.S. Army Nurse Corps, 7 May 2001, telephone interview, Historian's Files, Women's Memorial.
3. Joyce Blackstock Lester, Airman Second Class, U.S. Air Force, 18 September 2001, oral history, Historian's Files, Women's Memorial.
4. Dorothy Brandon, "Men to Replace Nurses Up Front Urged by Korea Nurses' Leader," *New York Herald Tribune,* 5 May 1952, n.p.; Brandon, "Calls Army Nurses 'Hazard to Troops,'" *Washington Post,* 1 June 1952, 17; Brandon, "Nurses Prove They Can Take Korea in Stride," *New York Herald Tribune,* 29 June 1952.
5. Dorothy Brandon, "First WAC Unit Going to Korea for Van Fleet," *New York Herald Tribune,* 6 November 1951, 1.
6. "A Feminine Report on a Tough War," *Pathfinder,* Philadelphia, Pennsylvania, 14 November 1951, gift of Bert Hartry, Women's Memorial Collection.
7. "First WACs Slated for Duty in Korea," *New York Times* 6 November 1951, 36.
8. Bettie J. Morden, Colonel, U.S. Army (Ret.), *The Women's Army Corps, 1945–1978* (Washington, D.C.: U.S. Army Center of Military History, 1992), 108.
9. Memorandum from the Assistant Secretary of Defense for Manpower and Personnel to the Secretary of Defense, 8 December 1952, Folder 4, Executive Office Subject File, RG 330, Office of the Assistant Secretary of Defense for Manpower and Personnel, Anna Rosenberg, National Archives, College Park, Maryland.
10. Morden, *Women's Army Corps,* 108.
11. Martha Voyles, Lieutenant Colonel, U.S. Army (Ret.), 23 February and 1 March 2000, telephone interviews, Historian's Files, Women's Memorial.
12. Marguerite Higgins, *War in Korea* (New York: Lion Books, 1952), Eleanor V. Spiller Collection, Women's Memorial Collection.
13. Ibid., 55.
14. Ibid., 52.
15. Ibid., 55.
16. Ibid., 60–62.
17. Ibid., 23.
18. Ibid., 85.
19. Peter Soderbergh, *Women Marines in the Korean War Era* (Westport, Conn: Greenwood, 1994), 86; *USO: A Tribute to 45 Years of Dedicated Service* (Washington, D.C.: USO World Headquarters, 1987), 48–49.

20. Carole Blakeman ("Blake") Russell, USO performer, telephone interview, 14 March 2000, Historian's Files, Women's Memorial.

21. Lorraine Gist Miller, USO performer, telephone interview, 21 March 2000, Historian's Files, Women's Memorial.

22. Ann Zoss Roberts, DOD teacher, telephone interview, 17 March 2000, Historian's Files, Women's Memorial.

23. Minutes of the Conference of Civilian Women Leaders, Personnel Policy Board, Pentagon, 21–22 June 1950, 155, Historian's Files, Women's Memorial.

24. *Delaware Magazine, Wilmington Sunday Star,* 16 August 1953, Josephine De-Acetis Schell Collection, Women's Memorial Collection.

25. Evelyn Higgins, American Red Cross, interview, 21 July 1999, Historian's Files, Women's Memorial.

26. Jeanne M. Holm, Major, U.S. Air Force, Report on inspection of the Great Falls, Montana, Air Force Base, 13 July 1953, Holm Papers, U.S. Air Force Academy Archives, Colorado Springs, Colorado.

27. Memorandum for Deputy Assistant Secretary of Defense Military Manpower and Personnel Policy, 22 July 1992, subject: Presidential Commission on the Assignment of Women in the Armed Forces, 3.

28. Morden, *Women's Army Corps,* 110.

29. Irene Van Houten Munster, Lieutenant Colonel, U.S. Army (Ret.), interview, 24 March 1999, Historian's Files, Women's Memorial.

30. Patricia Grant Overacker, Sergeant, U.S. Army, interview, 16 July 1999, Historian's Files, Women's Memorial.

31. Muriel Scharrer Wimmer, Private First Class, Women's Army Corps, interview 21 September 1998, Historian's Files, Women's Memorial.

32. Rebecca Williams Burr, Captain, U.S. Army Medical Specialist Corps, interview, 4 April 2001, Historian's Files, Women's Memorial.

33. Bailey, 1978 MHI oral history transcript, (see note 1, this chapter), tape 3, side 1, 15.

34. Muriel Raymond Batcheller, First Lieutenant, U.S. Army Nurse Corps, telephone interview, 7 May 2001, Historian's Files, Women's Memorial.

35. Jacquelyn Tomasik Anderson, Airman Second Class, U.S. Air Force, oral history, 23 January 2001, Historian's Files, Women's Memorial.

36. Mary Russ Veres, Command Master Sergeant, U.S. Air Force Reserve (Ret.), oral history, 25 April 2001, 27, Historian's Files, Women's Memorial.

37. Anna Yachwan, Staff Sergeant, U.S. Marine Corps, oral history, 5 June 2001, Historian's Files, Women's Memorial.

38. Lorry M. Fenner, Colonel, U.S. Air Force, "Ideology and Amnesia: The Public Debate on Women in the American Military, 1940–1973" (Ph.D. Diss., University of Michigan, 1995), 323.

39. Bailey, 1978 MHI oral history transcript, tape 3, side 2, 37–41.

40. Sherie Mershon and Steven Schlossman, *Foxholes & Color Lines: Desegregating*

the *U.S. Armed Forces* (Baltimore, Md.: Johns Hopkins University Press, 1998), 184–185.

41. *Chicago Defender,* 31 July 1948, 1.
42. Margaret E. Bailey, Colonel, Army Nurse Corps (Ret.), *The Challenge: Autobiography of Colonel Margaret E. Bailey* (Lisle, Ill.: Tucker Publications, 1999), 52–56.
43. Dorothy Ferebee, President, National Council of Negro Women, Inc., letter to President Harry S. Truman, 19 July 1951. Digitized Collections: Desegregation of the Armed Forces, Truman Presidential Museum and Library. http://www.trumanlibrary.org
44. Draft Report to the National Council of Negro Women, Inc., Papers of Dorothy Boulding Ferebee, 1919–1980. Manuscript Division, Moorland-Spingarn Research Center, Howard University, Washington, D.C.
45. Bailey, 1978 MHI oral history transcript, tape 3, side 2, 23–27.
46. Claude A. Barnett, "Commander Admits Army in Europe is Segregated," *Baltimore Afro-American,* 1 March 1952, 5.
47. "WACS in Germany Find Discrimination Disgusting," *Baltimore Afro-American,* 13 October 1951, 14.
48. Final Report, WAC Training Center, June 1950, Archives, General Files, U.S. Army Women's Museum, Fort Lee, Virginia.
49. "Navy Welcomes Women," *Chicago Defender,* 26 August 1950, 6.
50. Donald Jones, "No Jim Crow at Randolph," *Crisis,* November 1950, 617.
51. James Hicks, "30,000 Train in Harmony in Texas," *Baltimore Afro-American,* 13 June 1951, 13.
52. Ibid.
53. Lester, oral history.
54. "UMT—Not Now," *New Republic* (17 March 1952), gift of Bert Hartry, Women's Memorial Collection.
55. Mary Stremlow, Colonel, U.S. Marine Corps Reserve (Ret.), *A History of the Women Marines, 1946–1977* (Washington, D.C.: Headquarters, U.S. Marine Corps), 33.
56. Soderbergh, *Women Marines in the Korean War Era,* 23.

CONCLUSION: "THE OLD DIVIDING LINE" (PP. 244–254)

1. Anna M. Rosenberg, "A Woman's New York," *Poughkeepsie New Yorker,* 14 January 1952.
2. President John Fitzgerald Kennedy's announcement of the establishment of the President's Commission on the Status of Women, Executive Order 10980, 14 December 1961, Records of the President's Commission of the Status of

Women, December 1961–October 1963, Federal Records Collection, John F. Kennedy Library, Boston, Massachusetts.

3. "General Information on U.S. Army Hospitals in Korea," Elizabeth A. Twining Collection, Women's Memorial Collection.

4. Jeanne M. Holm, Major General, U.S. Air Force (Ret.), *Women in the Military: An Unfinished Revolution*, rev. ed. (Novato, Calif. Presidio, 1992), 157.

5. Ibid.

6. Jeanne M. Holm, Major, U.S. Air Force, Office of the WAF Director, "Historical Summary, 1 July 1952–30 December 1952," Holm Papers, U.S. Air Force Academy Archives, Colorado Springs, Colorado.

7. John Shy, Ph.D., University of Michigan, memo, 3 December 2003, Historian's Files, Women's Memorial.

8. Jean Ebbert and Marie Beth Hall, *Crossed Currents: Navy Women in a Century of Change* (Washington, D.C.: Brassey's, 1999), 150.

9. Ibid., 151.

10. Ibid., 161.

11. Ibid., 157–158.

12. Bettie J. Morden, Colonel, U.S. Army (Ret.), *The Women's Army Corps, 1945–1978* (Washington, D.C.: U.S. Army Center of Military History, 1992), 142.

13. Mary Jo Shelly, Colonel, U.S. Air Force, WAF Director, Final Report, 15 January 1954, Historian's Files, Women's Memorial.

14. Ibid.

15. Ibid.

16. Betty Miller White, Second Lieutenant, United States Air Force, 24 July 2001, interview, Historian's Files, Women's Memorial.

17. James R. Bearly, Colonel, U.S. Air Force, "Why WAF?" (master's thesis, Air War College Air University, 1954), Holm Papers, U.S. Air Force Academy Archives, Colorado Springs, Colorado.

18. Morden, *Women's Army Corps*, 171.

19. Lorry M. Fenner, "Ideology and Amnesia: The Public Debate on Women in the American Military, 1940–1973" (Ph.D. diss., University of Michigan, 1995), 271.

20. Ibid., 347.

21. Holm, *Women in the Military*, 161.

22. Ibid., 157.

23. Ibid., 160.

24. Ibid., 158.

25. Jerry Robb, Private First Class, U.S. Marine Corps, 2 December 1999, interview, Historian's Files, Women's Memorial.

26. Holm, *Women in the Military*, 162–164.

27. Record Group U.S. Government, Department of Defense, Army Folder 2, American Physical Therapy Association Archives, Alexandria, Virginia.

28. Mary T. Sarnecky, Colonel, U.S. Army Nurse Corps (Ret.), *A History of the Army Nurse Corps* (Philadelphia: University of Pennsylvania Press, 2000), 297; Fenner, "Ideology and Amnesia," 340–342.

29. Thirty-Fifth Anniversary: Highlights of the Defense Advisory Committee on Women in the Services (DACOWITS Office, The Pentagon), 2.

30. Record Group 330, Records of the Assistant Secretary of Defense for Manpower and Personnel, 190/26/35, boxes 265 and 266, National Archives, College Park, Maryland.

31. Jeanne M. Holm, Major General, U.S. Air Force (Ret.) and Mildred Inez Bailey, Brigadier General, U.S. Army (Ret.), "Report on DACOWITS 1951–1971," 4–5, DACOWITS file, Historian's Office, Women's Memorial.

32. Ibid.

33. Ibid., 16.

34. Doris M. Sterner, Captain, U.S. Navy Nurse Corps (Ret.), *In and Out of Harm's Way: A History of the Navy Nurse Corps* (Seattle, Wash.: Peanut Butter Publishing, 1997), 258.

35. Ibid., 258–259; Katherine Keating, Captain, U.S. Navy Medical Services (Ret.), 1 October 1999, interview, Historian's Files, Women's Memorial.

Page numbers in **bold** indicate photographs. Entries that begin with numbers are alphabetized as though spelled out, e.g., "1063rd" is alphabetized as "ten sixty-third."

Abdellah, PHS Rear Admiral Faye G., **135**, 135–136

Adams, USA Private First Class Bonnie, 162

Adams, USA First Lieutenant Fae M. (M.D.), 133–134

African American servicewomen, 2, 36–37, 49–52, 149–151; discrimination against, 236–241; in Europe, 237–240; in Japan, 150; in Korea, 202–203, 208–209; integration of, 49–52, 240–241

Air Force Nurse Corps (AFNC), 2, 119; casualties, 218–219; establishment of, 57; number of, 58, 71, 124–125, 181; nurses in Japan, 151, 180–181; nurses in Korea, 164, 180, 194–196, 214–215; nurses in United States, 82, 165; recruiting, 81–82, 124–126; responsibilities, 120; shortage, 181; training, 125; transfer from ANC, 57, 59; uniforms, 53

Air Force Women's Medical Specialist Corps (AFWMSC): assignments, 129; established, 59; in Europe, 129; in Japan, 129, 180; male physical therapists, 130–131, 252; number of, 59–60, 129; recruiting, 60, 129–130; shortage of, 60, 119, 130; transfer from Army, 59–60; uniforms, 53

Alaska: Cold War tension and drills, 38, 164; Medical specialists assigned to, 61; Navy nurses assigned to, 58; Navy women assigned to, 96

Alden, USAF Airman Third Class Elizabeth (Roe), 74, **74**, 165

Alwyn, USNNC Florence (Twyman), 193

American Red Cross (ARC), 11, 147, 151; African American women serving in, 151–152; in Japan, 147–148, 151–153, 228; in Korea, 223; in Okinawa, 153

Amick, USN Master Chief Petty Officer Kathleen, 246

Anderson, Jacquelyn Tomasik. *See* Tomasik, USAF Airman Second Class Jacquelyn (Anderson)

Andrews, Walter G. (congressman, New York), 24, 28

Angelich, USANC Lieutenant Mary E., 172

Annspach, USANC Lieutenant Beulah, 172–173

Arenson, USAF Sergeant Ida B., 167

Armstrong, USA Major General George E. (Army Surgeon General), 138

Army–Air Force Female Physicians Bill of 1950, 132–133

Army Divisions: 1st Cavalry, 66, 188, 189; 2nd Infantry, 206; 7th Infantry, 66, 182; 24th Infantry, 66, 172, 189; 25th Infantry, 66

Army Medical Reserve Corps, 133

Army-Navy Nurse Act of 1947: applying for Regular status under, 57, 198; and the establishment of the Army Women's Medical Specialist Corps, 118, 120; limitations on age, grade, and retirement, 118; limitations on command authority, 120–121; passage of, 22, 31; stipulations of the dependents of Navy nurses, 121, 133

Army Nurse Corps (ANC), 2; anesthetists, 58–59, 184–185; casualties,
218; dependents, 121; establishment,
120; in Europe, 38, 59, 145; in Japan,
151, 179–180, 200–20; in Korea, 122–
123, 169–219; number of, 57, 71, 118,
121; qualifications for, 57; recall of,
120; recruiting, 69, 122–123; Regular
status, 57; Reserve, 57; responsibilities, 120; transfer to AFNC, 57, 59;
uniforms, 52
Army of Occupation: in Austria, 14, 67; in
Germany, 14, 37, 67, 142–143,
155–162; in Japan, 14, 67, 146–153
Army Special Services, 55, 145–146
Army Women's Medical Specialist Corps
(AMSC): call ups, 68, 126; dependents,
121; established, 59, 118, 120, 128; in
Europe, 127, 157, 160–161; in Japan,
127, 179–180, 196, 205–206, 216; in
Korea, 127, 205; number of, 59–60,
126; recall of, 126; recruiting, 60, 127;
shortage of, 60, 119; transfer to Air
Force, 59; uniforms, 52
Ascom City (Korea), 191
Atom bomb, Soviet detonation of, 37, 143
Attrition: problems pertaining to, 8,
10–11, 111–114, 252; rates of, 11, 64,
111–114, 252
Aultman, USNR Lieutenant (jg) D'Anne
(Evans), 97
Austin, Myrtle (DACOWITS), **79**
Austria, 14, 23, 67, 159

Bailey, USA Brigadier General Inez
Mildred: on assignment to Germany
accompanied by husband, 231–232,
232; as captain on uniform design, 52;
on DACOWITS, 253; as lieutenant on
contingency planning in Germany,
156–157; on racial integration, 239; on
sexual harassment 220, 236
Bailey, USANC Colonel Margaret: as
captain on field training in Germany
160; on integrating the 98th General
Hospital, 237–238, **238**
Bainbridge (Maryland), 95
Baker, Kay (shipyard worker), 17

Ball, USCG Lieutenant Commander
Beatrice V., **110**
Ballentine, USAF Colonel Frances, chief
of Air Force Medical Specialist Corps:
at signing of Public Law 90–130 open-
ing promotions for women to general
and flag ranks (8 November 1967), **x**
Baltimore Afro-American: Army nurse
Eleanor Yorke on duty in Korea, 203;
on ARC in Japan, 151–152; on deseg-
regation in the armed forces, 239;
on POW camp on Koje-do Island and
Army nurse Juanita Long, **208**,
208–209
Bankowski, USA Private First Class
Marie, 55
Barnes, Shirley Peck. *See* Peck, Shirley
(Barnes)
Barneycastle, USAFNC Captain Made-
line, 82
Barron, Dorothy J. Vanden Oever. *See*
Vanden Oever, USA Sergeant Dorothy
J. (Barron)
Bartering, 158
Basham, USA Corporal Lorraine, 162
Basic training: cut by Army, 92; for
Marine Corps women, 42, 98; for
Navy women, 95; for WACs, 40, 92;
for WAF, 43, 103, 108
Batcheller, Muriel Raymond. *See* Ray-
mond, USA Lieutenant Muriel
(Batcheller)
Baxter, USA Colonel John G.: questioning
assignment of Army Women Medical
Specialists to combat theater, 205
Bearly, USAF Colonel James: on "Why
WAF?" 249
Belgium, 23, 67
Belka, USN Ensign Debbie, 97
Benevolence, USS (Navy hospital ship):
Navy nurse casualty on, 218; sinking
of, 123, 180, 203, 218
Bennett, USA Captain Constance (Van
Hook), 157, 161, **161**
Benninger, USANC Captain Marion, **183**,
184
Berlin: Airlift, 28–29, 37, 142; city of, 37,
143, 157; travel by train to, 39, 143

Bethune, Mary McLeod (president, National Council of Negro Women), 238

Biasini, USA Major Isabelle, 162

Bigelow, USMC Corporal Regina, 77

Bisard, USA Sergeant Olive, 153

Bishop, USMC Colonel Barbara J., director of Women Marines: at signing of Public Law 90–130 opening promotions for women to general and flag ranks (8 November 1967), **x**

Blackburn, USA Sergeant First Class Betty, **248**

Black market, 158, 161

Black servicewomen. *See* African American servicewomen

Blackstock, USAF Airman Second Class Joyce (Lester), 220

Blake, USANC Captain Margaret: as a captain injured while with 8055th MASH and evacuated to United States and recruiting duty, 185; on the first MASH into Korea, 123; as lieutenant with the 8055th MASH, 172–173

Blakeman, Carole (Russell) (USO), 224, **225**, 226

Blanding, Sarah Gibson (DACOWITS), **79**

Bloody Ridge (Korea), 206

Boatman, USNNC Ensign Marie Margaret, 218

Boatner, USA Brigadier General Haydon L., 209

Boles, USANC Captain Cathy, 179

Bolling Air Force Base (Washington, D.C.), 79

Bolton, Frances P. (representative, Ohio): and attempts to gender-integrate the military nurse and medical specialist corps, 252; on drafting women, 62, 81; on enough women volunteering to serve, 31; introducing a bill to eliminate the word "women" from the Army Women's Medical Specialist Corps, 118, 131

Bond, USA Lieutenant Colonel Lucy, 50

Bonham, USAFNC Captain Jonita (Bovee), 218

Bovee, Jonita Bonham. *See* Bonham, USANFC Captain Jonita (Bovee)

Boyd, USMC Staff Sergeant Mary (Lum), 155, 157

Bradley, USA General Omar N. (Army chief of staff), 26

Brandon, Dorothy (journalist) 140

Bremerhaven (Germany), 141

Bright, USAFNC Lieutenant Elwanda Patricia, 165

Britton, Janice Feagin. *See* Feagin, USAFNC Captain Janice (Britton)

Brooke Army Hospital (San Antonio, Texas), 119, 129, 131

Brooks, USNNC Captain Helen, 175

Brooks, Marietta Moody (DACOWITS), **79**, 83

Brosner, USANC Lieutenant Margaret, 184

Brown, USAF Airman First Class Doris, 151

Brown, USAF Lieutenant Evelyn, 241

Brown, USANC Captain Mary E., **151**

Brown, USAFNC Captain Vera, 218

Bryant, USANC Colonel Ruby F. (chief of Army Nurse Corps): career of, 121–122, **122**; and gender-integrating the ANC, 137–138; and the planning of the nurse-less MASH, 137–138

Bulshefski, USNNC Captain Veronica, chief of the Navy Nurse Corps: at signing of Public Law 90–130 opening promotions for women to general and flag ranks (8 November 1967), **x**

Bunker Hill (Korea), 212

Burke, USN Yeoman First Class Betty B., **248**

Burr, Rebecca Williams. *See* Williams, USA Captain Rebecca (Burr)

C-46 aircraft, 164

C-47 Skytrain, 76, 103, 181, 188, 218

C-48 Skytrooper, 214

C-54 Skymasters, 163, 180–181, 188–189, 214, 218

C-74 Globemasters (later C-124), 82, 163, 167, 203, 209–210, 214

C-97 Stratocruisers, 82, 165

Cahill, USANC Lieutenant Nancy (Newton), **194**

Carnegie, Hattie (fashion designer), 52

Carswell Air Force Base (Texas), 166, 168

Carter, USMC Sergeant Ila (Holzbauer), 83–84

Casualties, servicewomen, 218–219

Cate, USANC Captain Elizabeth M., 140

Cavalry Division, 1st: casualties of, 75; and the 8055th MASH, 188–189; part of the Eighth Army in Japan at the start of the war, 66

Cease-fire, 217

Chanute Air Force Base (Illinois), 43, 51, 167

Chase, Edna Woolman (editor-in-chief, *Vogue*), 52

Chechon (Korea), 201

Chiang Kai-Shek, 15

Chicago Defender: on inclusion of African American women in the Navy, 240; on President Harry S. Truman and desegregation of the armed forces, 237

Chicken, USAFNC Lieutenant Grace, 195

China, 15, 37, 69, 143–144

Chinja (Korea), 178

Chinnampo (Korea), 190

Chochiwon (Korea), 200

Chonan (Korea), 200

Chongwon (Korea), 178

Chosin Reservoir (Korea), 75, 192

Chrones, USA Corporal Christine, 222

Chunchon (Korea), 203

Church, USANC Lieutenant Eleanor, 172–173

Church, USA Major Ruth E. (physician), 133

Churchill, Winston (Iron Curtain speech), 4, 142

Civil Rights Movement, 4; civil rights activism and supporters, 236

Clark, USA Lieutenant General Mark (commander in chief, U.N. Command), 135, 212

Coast Guard Headquarters (Washington, D.C.), 33, 115

Coast Guard women, returning to duty during the war, 33–35, 115

Cochran, Jacqueline (consultant to Air Force chief of staff), 103–108

Cold War, 5; in Asia, 37, 143–144; in Europe, 37–39, 142–144, 156–157, 159–160

Cole, USANC Lieutenant Ethel, 172–173

Coleman, USANC Captain Eunice S., 169, **182, 183**, 183–184, 193

Collins, USA Corporal Harold, **69**

Communism, 37, 143–144, 155

Congressional debate: on the Army-Navy Nurse Act of 1947, 22, 31; on legislation proposed by Congresswoman Frances P. Bolton on gender-integrating the nurse and medical specialist corps, 118, 131, 252; on Universal Military Training, 29, 72, 241; on the 1948 Women's Armed Services Integration Act, 20–29

Connolly, USMC Sergeant Major Alice, 242

Connors, USANC Lieutenant Genevieve (McLean), 191–192

Consolation, USS (Navy hospital ship): and Lieutenant Commander Bernice Walters, 132; arriving off coast of Korea, 175; compared to the *Repose*, 186; receiving casualties via helicopter, 214; receiving helicopter pad, 203–204; receiving Marines from the Chosin Reservoir, 193; sole hospital ship in Korea, 180

Cook, Corinne Gogue. *See* Gogue, USAF Corporal Corinne (Cook)

Cook, USNNC Ensign Sarah Jim, **76**

Corcoran, Esther Pulis. *See* Pulis, USA Lieutenant Colonel Esther (Corcoran)

Cornelius, USNNC Dolores, 188

Cotton, USAF Lieutenant Jane, 241

Couch, USANC First Lieutenant Mary I., **69**

Cowles, Fleur, 106

Coyne, USN Lieutenant Florence, 96

Craighill, Margaret (M.D.), 64

Crawford, USAF Corporal Dorothy (Ulrey), 46–47, **47**, 54, **54**, 84, **84**
Crews, USN Lieutenant Anita, 96
Crosby, USNNC Lieutenant Nancy: on hospital ship life, 216–217; on wearing uniform off-duty, 75
Croshaw, Dawn E. Yetman Youells. *See* USA Sergeant Yetman, Dawn E. (Youells Croshaw)
Crowder, Camp (Missouri), 134
Cullom, USANC Captain Barbara, 207, **207**
Czechoslovakia, 15, 28, 145–146

DACOWITS. *See* Defense Advisory Committee on Women in the Services (DACOWITS)
Dalrymple, USANC Captain Elmira, 172
Danker, USAFNC Captain Catherine (Dombrowski), 181
Darwin, USAR Sergeant First Class Elizabeth, 162
Davis, USA Sergeant First Class Arline, 155
Davis, USA Corporal Elsie, 162
DeAcetis, USAF Staff Sergeant Josephine (Schell), 228
Dean, USA Major General William: as highest ranking POW, 217–218; on allowing Marguerite Higgins in the battle theater, 222
DeAngelo, USAF Airman First Class Joan (Fogelstrom): as aircraft control and warning specialist, 38, **38**; on malassignment, 112–113; reasons for joining up, 76; on uniforms, 54
Defense Advisory Committee on Women in the Services (DACOWITS): establishment of, 3, 72, 79; legacy of, 252–253; recommendations of, 8, 85; and recruiting, 79–81, 83, 84; and Anna Rosenberg, 72
DeLawter, Margaret (PHS nurse), 136
Demilitarized Zone (DMZ), 244
Demobilization, of armed services after World War II, 13–14
Denfeld, USN Vice Admiral Louis E. (chief of naval personnel), 15, 26

Dentist, first Army woman, 134
Department of Defense (DOD): and assignment of women to Korea, 221–222; and buildup of military personnel 6; and civilian women assigned to Korea, 11; and clarifying the responsibilities of military nurses, 120; and DACOWITS, 8, 253; and discharge on marriage policy, 3, 84, 90, 95, 229–230; and enlisted medical women, 76; and lowered enlistment standards for women, 98; and manpower studies, 62–63, 76; and nationwide recruitment campaign, 69–70, 79–81, 84–87; and the Reserve, 74–75; and servicewomen with children, 90–91
Dependents, policies on servicewomen's, 36, 90–91, 121
Desegregation. *See* Integration, racial
Dietitians: Air Force, 129; Army, 161; in Europe, 161; in Japan, 129, 180; in Korea, 205
Discharge: on marriage, 3, 84, 90, 95, 229–230, 231, 252; for pregnancy, 3, 229–230, 234; as a result of acquiring underage dependents, 36, 90–91, 121
Discrimination: gender, 4, 234–236; racial, 4, 36–37, 236–241
Diseases in Korea: encephalitis, 127, 180; hemorrhagic fever, 203, 214; infectious hepatitis, 127, 179; lung fluke, 208; smallpox, 211–212; tuberculosis, 208
Disterdick, Jean Ertwine. *See* Ertwine, USA Lieutenant Jean (Disterdick)
Doctors, women. *See* Physicians, women
Dodd, USA Brigadier General Francis T., 209
Dombrowski, Catherine Danker. *See* Danker, USAFNC Captain Catherine (Dombrowski)
Dougherty, Ann (Army Special Services), **146**
Douglas, Helen Gahagan (congresswoman, California), 5
Doyle, Helen Mannion. *See* Mannion, USAFNC Lieutenant Helen (Doyle)

Draft: and fathers, 3; of nurses, 6; public support for, 68; restoration of the all-male draft, 31, 44, 92; and start of the Korean War, 65; and using women to avoid a draft, 15; and using women to minimize the extent of, 29; of women, 62, 70; and women and the ERA, 5

Duke, USMC Corporal Sara, 77

Dulles, John Foster (secretary of state), 250

Duncan, USN Chief Jean W., 163

Dunlap, USANC Captain Lillian (later brigadier general and chief of Army Nurse Corps), 82

Eastern Europe, 14, 28

East Germany, 15

Eastwood, USAF Staff Sergeant Joan (Neuswanger), 47, **47**, 76

Ebeling, Lena (DACOWITS), **79**

Eberhardt, USNNC Marie, 253

Edwards, USAF Major Corinne, 162

Edwards, India (DACOWITS), **79**

Eighth Army, 66; assignment of WACs to, 221–222; casualties, 192; forward hospitals evacuated to, 194; retreat of, 191, 194; Ridgway replaces MacArthur, 201; Ridgway replaces Walker as commander of, 197; Walton Walker, as commander of, 190, 197

8164th Army Hospital (Kyoto, Japan): ARC activities for patients at, 152

Eisenhower, USA General Dwight D.: and presidential election of 1952, 73, 86–87, 215; as supporter of women in the U.S. Armed Forces, 2, 13, 15, 19, 22, 25; as Supreme Allied Commander of NATO, 44, 144, 155–156

Elias, USAF Captain Dorothy (M.D.), 117, 134

Elson, Mildred (director, American Physical Therapists Association), 126, 130

Ellington, USA Private First Class Nettie, 55

Emery, USNNC Lieutenant (jg) Lura Jane, 186–187, **187**, 190, 212

Employment of servicewomen: malassignment of, 112–113; Marine women, 97, 100–101; Navy Women, 45–46, 96–97, 163, 246; WACs, 93–94; WAF, 46, 48, 73–74, 102, 112–113, 165–168. *See also* Military Occupational Specialty (MOS)

England: Air Force Medical Specialists assigned to, 129; Cold War tensions, 155; no billets for WAF in, 233–234; safe place for servicewomen, 228

Enlistment, reasons for, 76–78

Equal Rights Amendment (ERA), 5

Erding Air Force Base (Germany), 109, 156, 162

Ertwine, USA Lieutenant Jean (Disterdick), 78, **118**, 118–119; transferred to Air Force 129–130

Evacuation, air, 188–190, 194, 203, 209–210; chain of, 174–175, 180–182; and flight nurse casualties on evacuation flights, 218–219; helicopters used in, 191, 204; of Korean War orphans, 195

Evacuation hospitals: 11th, 199, 203; 21st, 211; 22nd, 211; 121st, 152, 184, 190, 199, 205, 212; 171st, 208, 213

Evans, D'Anne Aultman. *See* Aultman, USNR Lieutenant (jg) D'Anne (Evans)

Executive Order No. 9981 (ending segregation and racial discrimination in the military), 36–37, 51, 237

Executive Order No. 10240 (discharge of servicewomen who became mothers), 91

Fable, USNNC Lieutenant Commander Helen, 193–194

Far East Command, Japan, 146

Farrell, USA Corporal Louise M., **222**

Faurie, USCGR Chief Yeoman Pearl: on returning to duty during the Korean War 33–35, **34**, 115

Faust, USANC Captain Eleanor, **183**, 184

Fahy, Charles O.: and the Fahy Report, 50; and racial integration of the armed services, 37, 50

Fauser, USN Ensign Pauline, 129

Feagin, USAFNC Captain Janice (Britton), 78, 164, **164**
Federal budget cuts, impact on women's components, 36, 57
Feil, USANC Lieutenant Margaret (Reese), 196–197
"Female ghettoes," 44
Ferebee, Dorothy (president, National Council of Negro Women), 238–239
Field hospitals: 3rd, 208–209; 4th, 185, 188, 196–197, 208; 10th, 160; 14th, 209; 64th, 137, 182, 191, 208–209
Films: *Flight Nurse*, 126; *M*A*S*H*, 10, 169–170; *Never Wave at a WAC*, 230
Filosa, USANC Lieutenant Carmela (Hix), 123, 213–214, **214**
Finletter, Thomas (secretary of the Air Force), 110
Finucane, Gloria Minich. *See* Minich, USN Personnelman Third Class Gloria (Finucane)
First Marine Hospital (Tientsin, China): Navy nurses stationed to, 144
Fitzsimons General Hospital (Denver, Colorado), 123
543rd WAF Band (Lackland Air Force Base, Texas), 83, 167
513th Reserve Wing, 512th Troop Carrier Wing (Wilmington, Delaware): Sergeant Josephine DeAcetis (Schell) sole WAF assigned to, 166, 228
Fleming, Margaret Zane. *See* Zane, USANC Captain Margaret (Fleming)
Flight Nurse, 126
Flight training, 125
Floyd Bennett Air Station (Brooklyn, New York), 42
Fogelstrom, Joan DeAngelo. *See* De Angelo, USAF Airman First Class Joan (Fogelstrom)
Fogle, Martha Halyak. *See* Halyak, USA Sergeant Margaret (Fogle)
Forrestal, James V. (secretary of the Navy), 25, 26
Fort Dix (New Jersey), 55, 162
Fort Holabird (Maryland), 100
Fort Jackson (South Carolina), 142

Fort Jay (New York), 52, 55
Fort Knox (Kentucky), 94
Fort Lee (Virginia), 39, 50, 230, 240
Fort Lewis (Washington), 21, 50
Fort Monmouth (New Jersey), 55
Fort Sam Houston (Texas), 124, 131
Fort Slocum (Georgia), 100
Foster, USAF Lieutenant Marjory V., 113
433rd Troop Carrier Wing (Nuremberg, Germany): WAF Major Corinne Edwards, as sole military woman assigned to, 162
France, 23, 67
Frances E. Warren Air Force Base (Wyoming), 47
Frankfurt (Germany), 158, 161
Frostbite, 127, 163; and Chosin casualties, 193–194; cold injury center in Japan and, 196; and increasing numbers of cases after Chinese attack in November 1950, 200; and tobacco, 196; and treatment by physical therapists, 196
Fullam, USCG Irene, **34**

Galpin, Stephen (writer, *Wall Street Journal*), 17–19
Gang, Jeanne Hamby. *See* Hamby, Jeanne (Gang)
Gates, USMC Staff Sergeant Jacqueline (Reichert), 77, 78
Gausch, USMCR Lieutenant Hazel D., **248**
Gender: discrimination, 4, 234–236; job-based within the medical profession, 119, 130–131; rank limitations imposed by the Women's Armed Services Integration Act of 1948, 29; rank limitations removed, 199
General hospitals: 97th, 231, 237; 98th, 156, 232, 237–239; 120th, 160; 343rd, 210
Germany: assignment of women to, 228; bartering, 158; Black market, 158, 161; Berlin, 143, 39, 157; Berlin Airlift, 37; Bremerhaven, 141–142, 231; Cold War tensions, 39, 155 –157, 160; Erding Air Force Base, 156, 162; Four

Germany *(continued)*
    Powers, 37, 143; Frankfurt, 159, 161,
    231, 237; Hanau, 158; Heidelberg,
    39, 47, 156, 159; integration of quar-
    ters, 237–240; Kaiserslautern, 158;
    Landstuhl, 160; malassignment of
    WAF in, 112–113; Mannheim, 159;
    medical specialists assigned to, 61;
    Military Air Transport flights to, 165;
    Munich, 156–157, 232; no place for
    servicewomen's dependents, 145;
    Nuremberg, 162; Regensberg, 39,
    160; servicewomen not entitled to
    housing for spouses in 232; SHAPE
    Headquarters, 44–45; Stuttgart, 231;
    WAF assigned to, 109
G.I. Bill, 68, 72, 133, 136
Gibson, USNNC Captain Winnie (chief
    of the Navy Nurse Corps), **123**, 123–
    124
Gilbreth, Lillian Moller (DACOWITS),
    79
Gillespie, USANC Lieutenant Joyce, 213
Gingrich, USA Lieutenant Janet (Preston),
    141, 148
Gist, Lorraine (USO), 226
Gogue, USAF Corporal Corinne (Cook),
    47, **48**, 51
Goll, Miriam Perry. *See* Perry, USAF
    Colonel Miriam E. (Goll)
Gordon, Camp (Georgia), 93
Gorski, USN Petty Officer Third Class
    Louise (Richardson), 142
Graham, USMC Private First Class Annie
    E., 51, **51**
Grant, USA Sergeant Patricia (Overacker),
    231
Great Falls (Montana), 38, 228–229
Great Lakes Naval Training Center (Illi-
    nois), 41–42, 95, 100
Gregory, USANC Captain Oree
    (Michaels), 169, 176–178
Grimes, USMC Chief Warrant Officer
    Second Class Annie L., 51, **242**,
    242–243
Gritsavage, USANC Lieutenant Colonel
    Alice M., 137

Guam, 58, 181; Navy nurses stationed in,
    154
Gunter Air Force Base (Alabama), 125

Haddock, USANC Lieutenant Ann, **183**,
    184
Haegele, USANC Lieutenant Ida, 175
Hahn, USA Corporal Gladys (Romanoff),
    159
Hall, USA Sergeant Jerrie, 153
Hallaren, USA Colonel Mary: career of
    23, 23–24; Congressional testimony
    on behalf of Women's Armed Services
    Integration Act, 13, 22, 30; with
    DACOWITS, **72**; DACOWITS and
    recruiting women, 79–80; on draft-
    ing women 70; on higher ranks for
    servicewomen 64; and Geraldine
    May, 107; and the recruitment cam-
    paign, 92–93; responding to negative
    attitudes about servicewomen 83; as
    supporter of servicewomen, 254;
    as WAC Director 40; with women
    service directors, **110**
Halouska, USA Sergeant Veva R., 55
Halyak, USA Sergeant Margaret (Fogle),
    153
Hamby, Jeanne (Gang) (Army Special
    Services), 145, **146**
Hamhung (Korea), 189, 192–193
Hamrick, USA Colonel Mary L., chief
    Army Medical Specialist Corps: at
    signing of Public Law 90–130 opening
    promotions for women to general and
    flag ranks (8 November 1967), x
Hancock, USN Captain Joy Bright: career
    of, 26–27, **27**; Congressional testi-
    mony on behalf of the 1948 Women's
    Armed Services Integration Act, 1, 22,
    26, 253; with DACOWITS, **72**; draft-
    ing legislation to provide women with
    a permanent place in the Navy, 19; on
    the use of the acronym WAVES, 94;
    with women service directors, **110**
Haneda Air Base (Japan), 149, 151, 181
Han River (Korea), 201
Harrison, USA Lieutenant General

William T.: signs armistice ending Korean War, 217

Hartley, USMC Warrant Officer Lillian, 101–102

Hartwig, USA Lieutenant Margaret (Pithkethly), 126–127

Haven, USS (Navy hospital ship), 9, 75, 135, 203–204, 216, 253

Hawaii: Hickam Air Force Base, 109, 181; Honolulu, 163; Kanehoe Bay, 100; Pearl Harbor, 99, 123; Tripler Army Hospital, 141, 163; Women Marines assigned to, 99

Hayes, Helen (DACOWITS), 79

Hays, USANC Brigadier General Anna Mae McCabe: as captain with the 4th Field Hospital, 185, 197; as colonel and chief of the Army Nurse Corps at signing of Public Law 90–130 in November 1967, **x**; career of, 197, **198**, 198–199

Heartbreak Ridge (Korea), 206, 207

Heath, USNNC Lieutenant Commander Joan (Steyn), 154

Heidelberg (Germany), 39, 156, 159

Henderson, Jacquelen McCracken. *See* McCracken, USAF Sergeant Jacquelen (Henderson)

Herman, USA Lieutenant Colonel Ruby E., 230

Hickam Air Force Base (Hawaii), 109, 181

Hicks, USA Lieutenant Clarissa, 180

Higgins, Evelyn "Hopsie" (ARC), 147, **147**, 228

Higgins, Marguerite (war correspondent), 11; fighting to remain in battle theater regardless of gender, 222–224; on Marines at Chosin Reservoir, 192; performing job near front lines, 66–67

Hill, USMC Captain Elsie E., 43

Hix, Carmela Filosa. *See* Filosa, USANC Lieutenant Carmela (Hix)

Hoisington, USA Colonel Elizabeth P., director Women's Army Corps: at signing of Public Law 90–130 opening promotions for women to general and flag ranks (8 November 1967), **x**

Holm, USAF Major General Jeanne M.: on the Air Force's "obsession" with comparing WAFs to WAVES, 36; on attrition, 252; as a captain at Erding Air Base (Germany), 156, 161; as a captain in the WAF Director's office, 112; as director of Women in the Air Force at the signing of Public Law 90–130 in November 1967, **x**; as first two-star woman in U.S. military, ix; inspection trip to WAF squadron (Great Falls, Montana), 228–229; as a major at the Air Command and Staff College 166; on relationship between military uniforms and morale, 52; as WWII WAAC, **ix**; as WWII WAC truck driver, ix, 235; on women volunteers, 87

Holzbauer, Ila Carter. *See* Carter, USMC Sergeant Ila (Holzbauer)

Honolulu (Hawaii), 163

Hook, Medelon Marshall. *See* Marshall, USAF Medelon (Hook)

Horne, Catherine Owen. *See* Owen, USA Lieutenant Catherine (Horne)

Horne, Dorothy Russian. *See* Russian, USAFNC Lieutenant Dorothy (Horne)

Horton, Mildred McAfee. *See* McAfee, USN Captain Mildred (Horton)

Horwitz, USA Lieutenant Melvin: on the "nurse-less MASH," 138–140

Hospital trains, 174–175, 186, 211

Houp, USNNC Captain Geraldine, 141, 163

Hourihan, USAF Airman First Class Frances, 165

Houseknecht, USANC Major Lululah (Martin), 189, 192

Housing: Air Force civilian in Korea, 226; Air Force problems with, 111; ANC quarters in Korea, 201–202, 213; ARC in Yokohama, 152; integration of servicewomen's quarters in Germany, 237–240; lack of billets for WAF in England, 233; Navy women's overseas assignments limited due to, 96; new housing for WAF women, 114; NNC

Housing *(continued)*
quarters on USS *Haven*, 216; quarters
for servicewomen's dependents overseas not authorized, 231–232; racial
integration of WAC billets, 50; WAC
barracks during basic training, 40;
WAC quarters in Europe, 159; WAC
quarters in Japan, 148; WAC quarters
on Okinawa, 153; WAF quarters in
Great Falls Montana, 228; for Women
Marines at Camp Pendelton (California), 99;
Huffstuffer, USA Private First Class
Edith, 162
Humphrey, Hubert H. (senator, Minnesota), 81; as vice president at signing of Public Law 90–130 opening
promotions for women to general and
flag ranks (8 November 1967), x
Hungnam Beach (Korea), 190, 192–193
Hylton, USAF Private First Class
Dorothy, 73

Imjin River (Korea), 202
Inchon (Korea), 69, 182, 185, 188, 198,
225
Infantile paralysis, 117–118, 161
Infantry Division: 2nd, 192, 206; 7th, 66,
182, 192; 23rd, 75; 24th, 66, 172,
188–189; 25th, 66
Infantry Regiment: 19th, 172; 21st, 66;
34th, 66
Integration: gender, 35, 49; racial, 36–37,
49–52
Involuntary recall, 67–68
Iron Curtain, 4, 142
Itami Air Base (Japan), 194, 209
Itazuke Air Force Base (Japan), 147–148,
189, 194

Jackson, USAF Private Eleanor, 48
Jacoby, USANC J. E. "Jake," 200, 215
James, USA Master Sergeant Carolyn H.,
222
Jamestown Line (Korea), 206
Jane Russell Hill (Korea), 212
Janikowski, USA Corporal Jacqueline
(Meakin), 143

Japan, 10, 14, 65, 67, 146; Air Force
Medical Specialists assigned to, 129,
180; Air Force nurses assigned to, 151,
180–181; ARC workers assigned to,
147–148, 151–153, 228; Army Medical
Specialists assigned to, 127, 179–180,
196, 205–206, 216; Army nurses
assigned to, 151, 179–180, 200–220;
end of occupation, 147; Navy nurses
assigned to, 123–124, 193–194, 200;
WAC assigned to, 10, 141, 146–148,
151; WAF assigned to 109, 148–151
Japan Air Defense Force (Nagoya): WAF
assigned to, 150
Japan Logistical Command, 146
Jenkins, USAFNC Lieutenant Louise
Ann, 202–203
Jensen, USANC Lieutenant Winifred, 184
Joint Chiefs of Staff (JCS), 2; concerns
about Europe during the Korean
War, 144; formalized as an entity, 24;
and the greater utilization of women,
31, 44; obtained increase in Army's
authorized strength, 67; policy state-
ment on the utilization of military
women, 63
Johnson Air Base (Japan), 179
Johnson, USANC Captain Elizabeth N.,
179
Johnson, USAF Staff Sergeant Ernestine
(Thomas): overseas duty in Japan,
149–150; on racial segregation in
Japan, 49, 50, 51–52; reasons for
enlisting, 76
Johnson, Le Roy (representative, California), 28
Johnson, Louis (secretary of defense), 63
Johnson, Lyndon Baines (senator, Texas),
81; and Jacqueline Cochran 103; and
Public Law 90–130, x, 199
Joy, USN Vice Admiral Turner: and peace
talks, 204
Juhre, USMC Ellen, 98

Kaesong (Korea), 188, 204
Kaiserslautern (Germany), 158
Keathley, USNS, 175
Keating, USN Captain Katherine, 135, 253

Keefe, Mary, 172–173
Keesler Air Force Base (Mississippi), 43
Kefauver, Estes (senator, Tennessee), 5
Kehoe, USANC Lieutenant Clara, **183**, 184
Kelly Air Force Base (San Antonio, Texas), 82, 163, 167
Kennedy, USNNC Lieutenant (jg) Margaret Grace, 218
Kennedy, Mildred Stumpe. *See* Stumpe, USMC Sergeant Mildred (Kennedy)
Kerschling, USANC Captain Cecilia, 172–173
Kilmer, Camp (New Jersey), 233
Kimpo Air Base (Korea), 189, 191, 195, 198
Kinnibreu, USAF Private Bettyjean, **48**
Kirk, Jane Seaver. *See* Seaver, Jane (Kirk)
Kitchelt, Florence, L.C. (chairman, Connecticut Committee for the ERA), 19
Kittilson, USNNC Lieutenant Eveline (McClean), 163; as ensign on USS *Repose*, 187
Kobe (Japan), 188, 200
Koester, USN Lieutenant Genevieve, 163
Koje-do Island (Korea): location of prisoner-of-war camp, 208–209, **223**
Korean Service Corps (KSC), 213
Korean War: popular support for, 68–70, 75, 86–87, 215–216; start of, 65, 169
Kovach, USAFNC Colonel Ethel R., chief of Air Force Nurse Corps: at signing of Public Law 90–130 opening promotions for women to general and flag ranks (8 November 1967), x
Kumchon (Korea), 174, 185
Kumchow (Korea), 123
Kunu-ri (Korea), 192
Kutyla, USANC Lieutenant Mary K., **176**
Kwajalein Island, 123–124, 181, 218
Kyoto (Japan): 8164th Army Hospital, 152
Kyushu (Japan), 179

Lackland Air Force Base (Texas): basic training at, 43; Cochran's visit to, 104; difficulties outfitting and housing recruits at, 80; 543rd WAF Band, 83, 167; hospital at, 82; integrated basic training begins at, 52; newspaper coverage of, 250; Operation Independence recruits arrive at, 76; quality of recruits at, 111; 3743rd (Colored) WAF Training Squadron, 51; uniforms issued at, 54; WAF Director's Office inspection trip to, 108
LaConte, USANC Major Phyllis: quoted, 69; rotated out of Korea, 89; with the 8055th MASH, 172–173, 185, 188
Lamb, USMC Private First Class Ann Estelle, **51**
Lamm, USA Captain Elaine, 159
Landstuhl (Germany), 160
Langley Air Force Base (Virginia), 79
Larson, USNNC Margaret, 68
Lauer, USN recruit Alice, 42
Ledbetter, USNNC Ensign Wilma, 218
Legislation: Army-Air Force Female Physicians Bill of 1950, 132–133; Army-Navy Nurse Act, 22, 31, 57, 118, 120–121, 133; Executive Order No. 9981 (ending segregation and racial discrimination in the military), 36–37, 51, 237; Executive Order No. 10240 (discharge of servicewomen who became mothers), 91; 1948 Women's Armed Services Integration Act, 2, 5–6, 22–31, 48, 91, 97, 99–100, 121, 220, 241, 250; Public Law 90–130 (removing rank ceilings on military women), 199
Lejeune, Camp (North Carolina), 100
Lenihan, USN Captain Rita, assistant to the chief of naval personnel (women): at signing of Public Law 90–130 opening promotions for women to general and flag ranks (8 November 1967), x
Leone, Lucille Petry (PHS Chief Nurse), 135
Leslie, Joan (actress, *Flight Nurse*), 126
Lester, Joyce Blackstock. *See* Blackstock, USAF Airman Second Class Joyce (Lester)
Letterman Army Hospital (San Francisco, California), 94
Lewis, Ruth Rohan. *See* Rohan, USCG Ruth (Lewis)

Liebold, USAFNC Major Marguerite H., 194

Lindbergh, Charles, resemblance to Air Force Chief of Staff Hoyt Vandenberg, 105

Long, Juanita, USANC Lieutenant, **208**, 208–209

Looby, USANC Captain Dorothy (Manfredi): on assignment as a nurse anesthetist, 59, **59**; on Communist threat in Europe, **38**, 38–39, 59–160;

Lord, Mary Pillsbury (DACOWITS), 64, 79

Lowe, USA Private First Class Vivian, **151**

Lowry Air Force Base (Colorado), 43

"Lucky 13" (nickname of Army nurses of the First MASH), **183**, 183–184, 193

Lum, Mary Boyd. *See* Boyd, USMC Staff Sergeant Mary (Lum)

Lura, USA Lieutenant Colonel Edna, 68

MacArthur, USA General Douglas: and African American WAFs, 50; designated Commander in Chief of U.N. Forces in Korea 67; Headquarters in Tokyo, 148; and Marguerite Higgins's battle to remain in Korea, 223–224; and the Inchon invasion, 69, 124; relieved by President Truman, 75, 150, 201; speaks of bringing U.S. soldiers home "in time for Christmas," 70;

MacDonald, USA Captain Mary G., 93

Macquin, Hazel Baird (dean, University of Utah College of Nursing): comments on slow career progression of Navy nurses, 9, 10

Mainbocher, designs uniform of Women Marines, 54

Maine, HMHS, 175

Malvey, USANC Lieutenant Catherine, **174**

Manchester, USA Major Katherine, 161

Manfredi, Dorothy Looby. *See* Looby, USANC Captain Dorothy (Manfredi)

Mannheim (Germany), 159

Mannion, USAFNC Lieutenant Helen (Doyle), 81–82

Mao Tse-Tung, 15, 37

Marine Corps, women: enlisted women's training, 42, 98; in Europe, 155; in Hawaii, 99–100; jobs, 97, 100–101; number of, 32, 71, 80, 97, 101; officer training, 43, 98; quarters for, 99; racial integration of, 240–243; recruiting, 83–84, 98; Reserve platoons, 43, 97–98; stateside, 99–100; specialty schools, 100; uniforms, 8, 54–55; of World War I, 247; of World War II, 14

Marine Corps Air Station: Cherry Point (North Carolina), 99; El Toro (California), 99; Kanehoe Bay (Hawaii), 100

Marine Corps Reserve Depot (San Diego, California), 99

Marine Division, 1st, 192–193, 204, 206

Markel, Hazel (DACOWITS), 79

Marquis, USA Corporal Lucille (Regan), 159

Marriage, policies pertaining to, 2–3, 84, 90, 231, 229–234

Marshall, George C. (secretary of defense): and appointment of Anna Rosenberg as assistant secretary of defense, 71; and creation of DACOWITS, 79; as supporter of women in the armed forces, 251

Marshall, USAF Medelon (Hook), 166

Martin, USAF Lieutenant Edwina, 241

Martin, Lululah Houseknecht. *See* Houseknecht, USANC Major Lululah (Martin)

Martinelli, USA Major Alba (Thompson): recalled to active duty 67–68; discharged due to pregnancy, **90**, 90–91

Mary Luckenbach (freighter), 218

MASH. *See* Mobile Army Surgical Hospital

*M*A*S*H* (television series and movie), 10, 170

Matta, USMC Maria, 98

Maxwell Air Force Base (Texas), 166

May, USAF Colonel Geraldine Pratt: on assignment of WAF to greater numbers of Air Force jobs, 46, 48, 73; and the Cochran episode, 103, 106–107,

107, 108; on integrating WAF into the Air Force, 88, 102; as a lieutenant colonel in the WAC, 21; replaced as WAF director, 36, 106–108; on selection of WAF uniform, 53; on sending overseas servicewomen home in event of an attack, 227–228; and Mary Jo Shelly, 110–111

Mayes, Rose (Mrs. Gilford) (DACOWITS), **79**

McAfee, USN Captain Mildred (Horton): as director of WWII WAVES, 27; on drafting women, 70, 81; on the male impulse to protect servicewomen, 1

McClean, Eveline Kittilson. See Kittilson, USNNC Lieutenant Eveline (McClean)

McClure, USAF Lieutenant Colonel Kathleen, 104

McClure, USAFNC Lieutenant Virginia, 219

McCluskey, USNNC Lieutenant (jg) Rose Ellen (McCullough), **195**

McConnell, USANC Captain Viola, 169

McCracken, USAF Sergeant Jacquelen (Henderson), 166

McCulloch, USA Private Audrey, 55

McCullough, Rose Ellen McCluskey. See McCluskey, USNNC Lieutenant (jg) Rose Ellen (McCullough)

McLarnin, USAF Sergeant Viola, 165

McLean, Genevieve Connors. See Connors, USANC Lieutenant Genevieve (McLean)

McMinn, USANC Lieutenant Marie, 172–173

McNeely, USA Lieutenant Julia, **248**

Meakin, Jacqueline Janikowski. See Janikowski, USA Corporal Jacqueline (Meakin)

Media. See Publicity and press coverage

Medical Air Evacuation Squadron (MAES): 801st, 189, 194, 202, 210, 219; 301st, 195; 1453rd, 181

Medical Group, 13th, 195

Menninger Clinic, 68

Meyers, USA Lieutenant Helen E. (DDS), 134

Michels, USA Major Irene (Sorrough), 39, **39**, 143

Midway Island, 58, 153, 181; Navy nurses stationed on, 154

Military Air Transport Service (MATS): assigning more transports to the Pacific Theater, 180–181; flight attendants with, 165, 167; number of evacuations, 164; and a shortage of flight nurses, 124; testing C–124 Globemasters, 209; transporting USO members to Korea, 225

Military Occupational Specialty (MOS), 2, 11, 44

Military Sea Transport Service (MSTS): enlisted women aboard ships, 134; evacuating wounded from Korea to Japan, 188; Mid-Pacific Honolulu, 96; Navy nurses aboard, 58, 89

Military women: attrition of, 8, 10–11, 64, 85–86, 112, 245–246, 252; cap on number of, 30, 32; career possibilities for, 29; dependents of, 36; draft of, 70; gossip about, 83; numbers of, 71, 73; retention of, 8, 10–11, 85–86, 112, 245–246; reputation of, 64, 75, 83; shortages of, 71; surveys of, 85–86, 245–246; testing of, 102. See also individual women's services

Millar, Nancy (Army Special Services), **146**

Miller, USAF Lieutenant Betty (White), 247, **248**, 249

Miller, USNS, 175

Minich, USN Personnelman Third Class Gloria (Finucane), 42

Misawa Air Force Base (Japan), 228

Mitchell, USNR Lieutenant M. E., **248**

Mitsubishi Building, Tokyo (Japan), **41**, 141, 148, 150,

Mobile Army Surgical Hospital (MASH), 9, 136, 170; 1st, 123, 182, 193, 201–203; 8029th, 207; 8054th, 171, 174, 178; 8055th, 136, 171–174, 182, 185, 188–189, 191, 200, 202, 215; 8063rd, 136, 176–178, 213–214; 8076th, 179, 185, 189; 8225th (experimental MASH), 9, 138–140

Moeller, USN Captain Ruth, chief of Navy Medical Specialist Corps: at signing of Public Law 90–130 opening promotions for women to general and flag ranks (8 November 1967), **x**

Moffet, USA Chief Physical Therapist Inez, 196

Mooney, USA Sergeant First Class Juanita I., 141–142,

Moore, USAF Private Geraldean, **48**

Morden, USA Colonel Bettie, 250

Morgan, USA Private First Class Cathy, 158, **158**

MOS. *See* Military Occupational Specialty

Moseley, USNNC Lieutenant Eugenia, 82

Moss, USA Captain Edith (Sullivan), 21, **21**

Motherhood, policies on, 8, 90–91, 229–234

Movies. *See* Films

Mumford, USA Corporal Bessie, 162

Munich (Germany), 156–157, 232, 237–239

Munster, Irene Van Houten. *See* Van Houten, USA Lieutenant Colonel Irene (Munster)

Murphy General Hospital (Waltham, Massachusetts), 55

Musemeci, USMC enlistee Connie, 98

Nagoya Air Force Base (Japan), 109; Japan Air Defense Force, WAF assigned to, 150; 6101st Air Base Wing and Headquarters, WAF assigned to, 150

Nam Il, 204, 217

National Foundation for Infantile Paralysis, 118

National Security Act, 24

Naval Air Station (Lakehurst, New Jersey), 97

Naval Air Technical Training Center (Memphis, Tennessee), 97

Naval Supply Center (Oakland, California), 97

Navy, women: at sea, 134; attrition, 95; basic training, 95; enlisted women's training, 41–42, 95; in Europe, 155;

jobs, 45–46, 96–97, 163, 246; number of, 32, 70, 80, 95, 246; officer training, 41–42, 95, 246; overseas assignments, 96; petty officer shortage, 95; post–Korean War, 245–246; racial integration, 240; Reservists, 95; stateside, 142, 163; uniforms, 8, 54; use of WAVES acronym, 94–95

Navy Bureau of Aeronautics (Washington, D.C.), 26–27

Navy Bureau of Ships (Washington, D.C.), 163

Navy Nurse Corps (NNC), 9, 119; aboard hospital ships, 123, 175, 186–187, 190–191, 204, 212, 214, 216; aboard MSTS ships, 58, 188; assignments, 58, 163; casualties, 123, 218; dependents, 121; establishment, 120; on Guam, 154; in Japan, 123–124; on Midway Island, 154; number of, 58, 124; pay for, 120; quarters, 124; recall, 123; Reserve, 120, 123–124; responsibilities, 120; training, 124; at Yokosuka (Japan), 193–194, 200

Navy Women Medical Specialists, 61, 129

Nenni, USA Sergeant Concetta, 55

Nesom, USA Private First Class Jimmie, **45**

Netherlands, 67

Neuman, Charlcia, 15

Neuswanger, Joan Eastwood. *See* Eastwood, USAF Staff Sergeant Joan (Neuswanger)

Never Wave at a WAC, 230

Newport (Rhode Island), 41, 95, 100, 129

Newspaper coverage. *See* Publicity and press coverage

Newton, USANC Lieutenant Cornelia, 184

Newton, Nancy Cahill. *See* Cahill, USANC Lieutenant Nancy (Newton)

Nielsen, USA Sergeant First Class Gladys, 162

Nimitz, USN Fleet Admiral Chester W.: testifying on behalf of the 1948 Women's Armed Services Integration Act, 22, 26

19th and 307th Bomb Wings (Okinawa):

WAF and former WWII WASP Lieutenant Marjory V. Foster grounded due to gender, 113

Nissly, USAF Major Marybelle J., 167

Noncommissioned officer (NCOs), 6

Norman, Agnes Zuverink. *See* Zuverink, USAFNC Lieutenant Agnes (Norman)

North, Helen Weaver. *See* Weaver, USN Lieutenant (jg) Helen (North)

Northam, USAF Staff Sergeant Jean, **248**

North Atlantic Treaty Organization (NATO), 37, 142–144; Headquarters, northern Europe, 155–156; Headquarters, southern Europe, 155, 158

North Korea, 65, 144; troops in, 69

Northrup, USAFNC Captain Barbara (Thomas), 196

Nugent, USAF Major General R. E., 106

Nuremberg (Germany), 162

Nurse anesthetists, 58–59, 184–185

Nurses, male, 9, 137

Oak Knoll Naval Hospital (Oakland, California), 68

O'Connor, USAF Sergeant Alice, 10, 12

Odlum, Floyd, 103

Okinawa, 113, 141, 153–154

Olathe (Kansas), 100

Old Baldy, area in Korea, 206

O'Neil, USAF Staff Sergeant Margaret, 151

Operation Big Switch (POW Exchange), 217–218

"Operation Independence" (recruiting drive), 75

Operation Little Switch (POW Exchange), 217–218

Ordstrom, USA Captain Mercedes M., 93

Organized Reserve Corps (United States Army Reserve): WACs in, 91–92

Orphans, Korean War: assisted by 171st Evacuation Hospital, **194**; evacuation of, 164, 195; Mother's Day orphan's party on USS *Haven* in May 1951, **195**

Osaka (Japan), 180, 200; Osaka Army Hospital, 196

Overacker, Patricia Grant. *See* Grant, USA Sergeant Patricia (Overacker)

Overholt, USA Colonel Edwin, 66

Overseas assignments: Air Force Nurse Corps, 151, 164, 180–181, 194–196, 214–215; Air Force Women's Medical Specialist Corps, 129, 180; Army Nurse Corps, 38, 59, 122–123, 145, 151, 169–219; Army Women's Medical Specialist Corps, 127, 157, 160–161, 179–180, 196, 205–206, 216; Marine Corps, 155; Navy Nurse Corps, 58, 123–124, 154, 175, 186–188, 190–191, 193–194, 200, 204, 212, 214, 216; Navy, 96, 155; WAC, 10, 141–143, 146–148, 153, 155–159, 221–222; WAF, 47, 84, 109, 113, 148–151, 155, 221–222, 228

Owen, USA Lieutenant Catherine (Horne), 196

Palmer, USN Captain Jean, 20

Pandolfi, USMC Sergeant Marie, **248**

Panmunjom (Korea), 210

Parris Island (South Carolina), 42, 97, 100, 251

Patton, USA General George C., 71

Peace talks, 204–206, 212, 217

Pearl Harbor (Hawaii): Naval Hospital at, 123; Women Marines arrive, 99

Pearson, Drew (columnist), 105

Peck, Shirley (Barnes) (ARC), 141, 153–154

Pendleton, Camp (California), 99

Pentagon: communications center, 47; WAF assigned to, 166

Percy Jones Army Hospital (Battle Creek, Michigan), 127

Peregrim, USMC Master Sergeant Anne, 32

Permanent status. *See* Women's Armed Services Integration Act (1948)

Perry, USAFNC Lieutenant Margaret, 219

Perry, USAF Colonel Miriam E. (Goll) (director of Air Force Women's Medical Specialist Corps), 59–60; 129–131, **131**

Perry, USCG Ruth V., **34**

Pharmacists, Navy woman, 135

Philadelphia Naval Hospital (Pennsylvania), 129, 163

Phillips, USANC Colonel Mary G. (chief of the Army Nurse Corps), 58, **72**, 121

Physicians, women: Air Force Medical Corps, 132–134; Army Medical Corps, 132–134; Navy Medical Corps, 132

Pithkethly, Margaret Hartwig. *See* Hartwig, USA Lieutenant Margaret (Pithkethly)

Platoon 7, first racially integrated unit in Marine Corps, 51

Polio. *See* Infantile paralysis

Porkchop Hill (Korea), 212

Porter, USAFNC Lieutenant Nan, 189

Powell, USA Private First Class Maxine, 156

Powers, USN Reservist Dorothy, 42

Pregnancy: discharge for and policies pertaining to, 3, 229; rate of, 3; serving while, 232–234

Presidio, The, of San Francisco (California), 51

Preston, Janet Gingrich. *See* Gingrich, USA Lieutenant, Janet (Preston)

Prisoners of war (POWs), 206, 217; American POWs, 217–218; Chinese POWs, 208–209, 218; North Korean POWs, 208–209, 218; Operation Big Switch, 217–218; Operation Little Switch, 217–218; POW camp on Koje-do Island (Korea), 208–209, 223

Pritchard, USANC Lieutenant Mary, 210–211

Promotions, limits on, 24, 29

Protection of women, 1, 221–223, 228

Public Health Service (PHS), 135–136

Publicity and press coverage, 73; Alice Gritsavage suggests male nurses replace female MASH nurses, 137; ARC worker Sylvia Rock on Yokohama, Japan, 151–152; Army nurses in Korea on latrine facilities in Korea, 202; Army nurses in Korea on maintaining femininity, 196–197; Black Press, 202–203, 208–209, 237–239; Frances P. Bolton and drafting women, 62–63, 81; civil-military relations, 250; of enlisted Navy women trained as medical corpsmen and serv-ing with MSTS, 134–135; film *Never Wave at a WAC* and WAC recruiting, 230; former WWII service directors on drafting women, 70, 81; General George C. Marshall on women in the military, 244; Marguerite Higgins and reporting regardless of gender, 222–224; Marguerite Higgins on war in Korea, 66–67; Korean War Era's pro-women coverage, 140; Korean War–era vs. WWII-era women, 144; of "Lucky 13" First MASH nurses in Korea, 183–184; of Alba (Martinelli) Thompson and discharge due to motherhood, 90–91, 109, 117; of nation-wide recruiting campaign, 81–83; of Navy women reservists training as seamen apprentices, 42; of new Hattie Carnegie–designed Army uniforms, 52; of nurse shortage and discriminating against male nurses, 119; of rape in the 1950s, 235; of Anna Rosenberg and racial integration of the armed forces, 241; of Anna Rosenberg's trip to Far East, 221; of WAC barracks, 40; of WAC "Soldiers of the Month," 55; of WAF, 73–74; of WAF control tower operators in Japan, 151; of WAFs assigned to Pentagon, 166; of women in the workforce, 17–19

Public Law 36–80. *See* Army-Navy Nurse Act of 1947

Public Law 90–130 (removing rank ceilings on military women), 199; President Lyndon B. Johnson signs legislation with women service directors present, **x**

Public Law 408. *See* Army–Air Force Female Physicians Bill

Public opinion of military women, 3, 42, 64, 75, 112, 132, 248–249

Puerto Rico, 67

Pulis, USA Lieutenant Colonel Esther (Corcoran), 45, **45**

Purvis, USNR Lieutenant (jg) Marvel, 96

Pusan (Korea): airfield, 66, 209–212; Army hospitals at, 170–173, 178, 205;

Navy hospital ships at port of, 186–187, 193; perimeter, 171; port, 69, 170–171; trains at, 175; WACs arrive at, 222

Pyongyang (Korea), 188–189, 191

Pyramid Service Club (Germany), 145, **146**

Quantico (Virginia), 43

Quotas: racial, 49; set by the 1948 Women's Armed Services Integration Act, 30

Race: discrimination, 36–37, 150, 236–241; integration, 36–37, 49–52, 236–243

Ramstein Air Force Base (Germany), 113

Randolph Air Field/Air Force Base (Texas), 43, 125, 241

Rape, 235

Rasmussen, USA Lieutenant Janet, 159

Raymond, USA Lieutenant Muriel (Batcheller), 78, **78**; evacuation drills in Germany 160; required to serve out enlistment regardless of marriage, 145; serving while pregnant, 220, 232–233

Recruiting: DACOWITS involvement in, 79–80; difficulties in, 86; DOD recruitment drive, 70, 81–83, 86; Operation Independence, 75–76; role of media in, 73, 81–83; servicewomen as recruiters, 83–86, 247–248; "Women in Our Armed Services" stamp, 86

Red Cross. *See* American Red Cross (ARC)

Redfern, USN Parachute Rigger Mary, 46

Reenlistment. *See* Retention

Reese, Edward (representative), 28

Reese, Margaret Feil. *See* Feil, USANC Lieutenant Margaret (Reese)

Regan, Lucille Marquis. *See* Marquis, USA Corporal Lucille (Regan)

Regensburg (Germany), 39, 160

Reichert, Jacqueline Gates. *See* Gates, USMC Staff Sergeant Jacqueline (Reichert)

Reiner, USA Lieutenant Colonel Donald, 207

Relative rank, 22

Repose, USS (Navy hospital ship), 180, 186–187, 189–190, 203, 212

Republic of Korea (ROK), 67

Reserve call-up, 67–68, 89

Reserve: Ready, 75; Standby, 75

Reservists, call-up of, 67–68, 123

Retention: problems retaining women, 10–11, 112; surveys dealing with, 8, 85–86, 245–246

Rheinholt, USS, 170, 172, 179

Richardson, Louise Gorski. *See* Gorski, USN Petty Officer Third Class Louise (Richardson)

Ridgway, USA General Matthew: as commander of Eighth Army in Korea, 190, 197; as commander of Far East Theater, 204; replaced by General Mark Clark, 212

Riley, USAF Lieutenant Colonel Emma Jane, 104

Robb, USMC Private First Class Jerry, 78, **251**, 251–252

Roberts, Ann Zoss. *See* Zoss, Ann (Roberts)

Rock, Sylvia (ARC), 151–152

Rockabrand, USANC Lieutenant Olive, **183**, 184

Rohan, USCG Ruth (Lewis), **34**

Roe, Elizabeth Alden. *See* Alden, USAF Airman Third Class Elizabeth (Roe)

Romanoff, Gladys Hahn. *See* Hahn, US Corporal Gladys (Romanoff)

Roosevelt, Eleanor, 4, 5

Rosenberg, Anna M. (assistant secretary of defense for manpower and personnel), 65; and appointment of Mary Jo Shelly as WAF Director, 110; and assigning Women Marines overseas, 155; career of, 71, **72**, 72–74; formation of DACOWITS, 79–81; and need for more servicewomen, 76; public image of servicewomen, 83; and racial integration of the U.S. Armed Forces, 241; and recall of women medical specialists 127; trip to Korea and effect of WAC assignments in Korea, 221; and "Women in Our Armed Services" stamp, 86

Rumors, 7, 83. *See also* World War II, slander campaign

Russ, USAF Technical Sergeant Mary (Veres): gender discrimination, 234; reason for enlisting, 77, 77–78; on WAF uniforms, 54

Russell, Carole Blakeman. *See* Blakeman, Carole (Russell)

Russell, Rosalind (actress, *Never Wave at a WAC*), 230

Russian, USAFNC Lieutenant Dorothy (Horne), 78, 82, **82**

Saipan, 58

Salzburg (Austria), 159, 231

San Diego (California), 95

Sasebo (Japan), 172

Scharrer, USA Private Muriel (Wimmer): and rifle training, 41, **41**, 148; on discharge at marriage, 231; on work as a medical technician at Tokyo Army Hospital, 149, 215

Schell, Josephine DeAcetis. *See* DeAcetis, USAF Staff Sergeant Josephine (Schell)

Scholljegerdes, USNNC Commander Florence M., as Lieutenant (jg), 89, **89**

Scott, Carol Stillwell. *See* Stillwell, USCG Carol (Scott)

Scott, Kate Francis (DACOWITS), 85

Seaver, Jane (Kirk) (ARC), **223**

Secretary of Defense, Office of, 7

Seelav, USA Major Beatrice (Stecher), 158

Segregation, 4, 36–37, 151–152

Selective Service Act, 65, 67

Seoul (South Korea): airport, 210; Army hospitals at, 189, 202; assignment of WAC and WAF to, 221–222; battle to recapture, 198; falls to communist troops, 190; fighting around, 201; and Task Force Smith, 66; USO at, 225

Service Command (Japan) 146

7774th Signal Battalion (Heidelberg, Germany): WACs in highly specialized communications, 156

Sexual harassment, 234–235

Shafer, Paul (representative, Michigan), 28

Shambora, USA Major General William E., 138

SHAPE. *See* Supreme Headquarters Allied Powers Europe (SHAPE)

Shaver, Dorothy (DACOWITS), 52

Shearer, USNNC Lieutenant Commander Carolyn, 154

Shelly, USAF Colonel Mary Jo, **72, 79**; appointment as WAF Director, **110**, 110–111; outgoing report, 247, 250; as WAF Director, 108–109, 167

Sheppard Air Force Base (Texas), 165

Sheppard, Harry (representative, California), 29

Sinmak (Korea), 188–189

1600 Air Traffic Squadron Air Transport Service: WAF assigned to, 73

6101st Air Base Wing and Headquarters (Nagoya, Japan): WAF assigned to, 150

Slewitzke, USANC (Retired) Brigadier General Connie, x–xi

Smarz, USANC Lieutenant Marie, **183**, 184

Smith, USA General Bedell, 71

Smith, USA Lieutenant Colonel Charles B., 66

Smith, USANC Major Genevieve, 218

Smith, Margaret Chase (senator, Maine): on permanent place for women in the armed forced and the 1948 Women's Armed Services Integration Act, 20, 28; and public attitude toward servicewomen, 83; and support of Alba Martinelli-Thompson, 91; on women and responsibilities of citizenship, 5

Smith, Mary Teague. *See* Teague, USA Lieutenant Mary (Smith)

Snow, Carmel (editor, *Harper's Bazaar*), 52

Sorrough, Irene. *See* Michels, USA Major Irene (Sorrough)

South Korea, 65, 67–68, 144

Souza, USMC Sergeant Theresa, 100

Soviet Union, 4, 14, 28, 37

Splaine, USCG Chief Warrant Officer Betty, 33–35, **34**, 115

Squire, Dee (Army Special Services), **146**

St. Albans Naval Training Hospital (Long Island, New York), 42, 124

Stalin, Joseph, 4

Stanford, USAF Airman First Class Margaret, 151

Station Hospital: 5th, 179; 7th, 59, 160; 8th, 149, 200; 118th, 179; 155th, 151; 382nd, 152–153, 200

Stecher, Beatrice Seelav. *See* Seelav, USA Major Beatrice (Stecher)

Steele, USANC Captain Ann: as chief nurse of the 8054th MASH, 171–172; on hospital train duty, 174; on recruiting duty stateside, 122–123

Stern, Edith R. (DACOWITS), **79**

Stevenson, Adlai (1952 Democratic Presidential Candidate), 87

Steyn, Joan Heath. *See* Heath, USNNC Lieutenant Commander Joan (Steyn)

Stillwell, USCG Carol (Scott), **34**

Stock, USNNC Iris, 154

Stoneman, Camp (California), 21

Strategic Air Command (SAC), 114

Stratton, Dorothy (director of WWII Coast Guard SPARs): on drafting women, 70

Streeter, Ruth Cheney (director of WWII Marine Corps Women's Reserve): helping to recruit women, **248**, 249

Stumpe, USMC Sergeant Mildred (Kennedy), **76, 77**

Stuttgart (Germany), 231–232

Sullivan, Edith Moss. *See* Moss, USA Captain Edith (Sullivan)

Sullivan, USANC Lieutenant Faye, 184

Supreme Headquarters Allied Powers Europe (SHAPE), 45, 96, 109

Suwon (Korea), 200–202, 227

Sweden, 67

Symington, W. Stuart (secretary of the Air Force), 71, 103

Tachikawa Air Force Base (Japan), 181, 195

Taebaek Mountains (Korea), 189

Taegu (Korea): airfield at, 210; Army hospitals at, 170–171, 178, 185, 189, 197, 199; POW hospital at, 208; trains at, 211, 213; USO at, 225

Taejon (Korea): Army hospitals at, 170, 173, 213; Captain Margaret Blake's accident at, 185; orphanage in, **194**; train at, 123

Tai Tong (Korea), 174

Taylor, Elizabeth Prewitt (DACOWITS), **79**

Task Force Smith, 66, 171

Teague, USA Lieutenant Mary (Smith), 49–50

1060th Communications Group (the Pentagon, Washington, D.C.): WAF assigned to, 166

1063rd WAF Communications Squadron (Maxwell Air Force Base, Texas): new teletype network pioneered by, 166

Theilmann, USA Major Ethel M., 205

38th Parallel: cease-fire line at, 217; and the Communist Chinese counterattack, 75, 200; and the invasion of Inchon, 69–70, 182, 188; and the stalemate 136, 211; and the start of the war, 65, 169

3743rd (Colored) WAF Training Squadron (Lackland Air Force Base, Texas), 51

Thomas, Barbara Northrup. *See* Northrup, USAFNC Captain Barbara (Thomas)

Thomas, Ernestine Johnson. *See* Johnson, USAF Staff Sergeant Ernestine (Thomas)

Thompson, Alba Martinelli. *See* Martinelli, USA Major Alba (Thompson)

Thurness, USANC Captain Jane, **183**, 184

Titania, USS, 173

Tokyo (Japan): air evacuation from, 163; Army hospitals at, 199, 215; hospital trains at 180; General MacArthur's headquarters in, 67; Mitsubishi Building, **41**, 141; rifle range in, 148; WAC detachments at, 41, 141, 146, 148–149, 215; WAF assigned to, 50, 149

Tollefson, USANC Captain Margaret, 172–173

Tolman, USANC Lieutenant Donna E., **69**

Tomasik, USAF Airman Second Class Jacquelyn (Anderson): marriage during service, **233**, 233–234; overseas service, 155, 233; pregnancy and subsequent discharge from Air Force, 234; reason for enlisting, 77

Tosti, Louis, 86

Towle, USMC Colonel Katherine: on age requirement to enlist, 98; on assignment of women to nontraditional jobs, 100–101; on DACOWITS, **72**; on public image of Women Marines, 56; on public's lack of acceptance of women in the service during times of peace, 64; on registration of women, 63; with women service directors, **110**

Training: basic, Marine Corps women, 42, 98; basic, Navy women 95; basic, WAC, 40, 92; basic, WAF, 43, 103, 108; flight, 125; officer, Marine Corps women, 43, 98; officer, Navy women, 41–42, 95, 246; officer, WAF, 44, 102; officer, WAC, 39; Navy Nurses Corps, 124; Universal Military Training (UMT), 29, 72, 241; weapons, 40–41, 148

Trask, Florence, 68

Travis Air Field (California), 163, 181

Treasure Island (California), 142

Trieste (Italy), 59, 160

Tripler Army Hospital (Hawaii), 141, 163

Troy, USAF Corporal Dolores, 73

Truman, Harry S. (president): asks Congress for an extension of the draft 70; and Executive Order 9981 ending segregation in the U.S. Armed Forces, 36–37, 51, 237, 239; expanded troop strength in Europe, 144; fires General MacArthur, 75, 150, 201; and military budget cuts, 36; and the National Security Act, 24; and peace talks, 204; quoted, 4, 21; sends troops to South Korea, 68; and the "Women in Our Armed Services" stamp, 86

Turck, USA Private Dorlamae, 162

Turkey, 67

Twyman, Florence Alwyn. *See* Alwyn, USNNC Florence (Twyman)

Uijonbu (Korea), 202

Ulrey, Dorothy Crawford. *See* Crawford, USAF Corporal Dorothy (Ulrey)

Unified Recruiting Campaign, 86

Uniforms: Air Force supply problem, 80–81, 102, 108; Army Nurse Corps, 52; Army Women's Medical Specialist Corps, 52; Hattie Carnegie, 52; Major General Jeanne Holm on the relationship between military uniforms and morale, 52; Mainbocher, 54; Marine Corps, 8, 54–55; Navy, 8, 54; WAC, 8, 40, 52–53; WAF, 8, 53–54, 80–81, 102, 104, 108, 111, 113

Universal Military Training (UMT), 29, 72, 241

United Nations, 4, 67, 216; Command, 212; troops, 69–70, 94, 149, 171, 207

United Service Organizations (USO), 11, 224–226

Vance Air Force Base (Oklahoma), 181

Vandenberg, USAF General Hoyt (Air Force Chief of Staff), 103–107, 110

Vanden Oever, USA Sergeant Dorothy J. (Barron), 94

Van Fleet, USA General James A., 221

Van Hook, Constance Bennett. *See* Bennett, USA Captain Constance (Van Hook)

Van Houten, USA Lieutenant Colonel Irene (Munster): postpones marriage, 145; requests assignment with her husband, 231; service on Eisenhower's staff in Europe, 44–45, **45**; on traveling to Berlin 39;

Vaught, USAF (Retired) Brigadier General Wilma L., viii, x–xi

Veres, Mary Russ. *See* Russ, USAF Technical Sergeant Mary (Veres)

Veterans Readjustment Assistance Act of 1952 (Korean War G.I. Bill), 72

Vienna (Austria), 159

Vinson, Carl (representative, Georgia), 20, 24, 28

Vogel, USA Colonel Emma: recruiting, 60; career of 127–128, **128**

Voyles, USA Captain Martha, 222

Wake Island, 181

Walker, USA General Walton: and correspondent Marguerite Higgins, 223–224; killed, 190, 197; and Assistant Secretary of Defense Anna Rosenberg, 71

Walter Reed Army Hospital (Washington, D.C.), 68, 93, 128, 131

Walters, USN Lieutenant Commander Bernice R. (M.D.), 132, 175

Ward, USANC Captain Mary, **183**, 184

Warner, USMC Captain Nita Bob, 56

Weapons: WAF Captain Jeanne M. Holm carrying loaded pistol due to potential hostile German drivers toward Allied personnel, 156; Navy women permitted to qualify in and carry, 97; WAC Sergeant First Class Gladys Nielsen and proficiency with Army carbine, 162; WAC training, 40–41, 148; WAF not permitted train in, 103; Helen Weaver (North), member of USN and USMC women's pistol team, 155;

Weaver, USN Lieutenant (jg) Helen (North), 155

Weisbaden Air Force Base (Germany), 109

Werner, USANC Captain Alice E., **69**

Westover Air Force Base (Massachusetts), 165, 167

Whitcomb, USA General Richard, 222

White, Betty Miller. *See* Miller, USAF Lieutenant Betty (White)

White, USN Lieutenant Ruth Carolyn, 163

Wilde, USN Captain Louise, 94

Williams, USANC Lieutenant Betty E., **69**

Williams, John (representative, Mississippi), 241

Williams, USA Captain Rebecca (Burr), 231

Wilson, Charles (secretary of defense), 246

Wilson, USMC Colonel Helen A.: as a captain and platoon commander, 56; as a captain at Marine Corps Air Station Cherry Point (North Carolina), 99; on racial integration, 242

Wilson, USANC Lieutenant Katherine, 185

Wilson, USNR Lieutenant Commander Kay, 96

Wimmer, Muriel Scharrer. *See* Scharrer, USA Private Muriel (Wimmer)

Wolf, Morris (male nurse), 117, 119

Women in the Air Force (WAF): attrition, 111, 114; band, 83, 167; Cochran Report, 103–108; enlisted training, 43, 103, 108; in Europe, 47, 84, 109, 113, 155, 228; housing, 111, 114; gender integration, 49, 102; in Japan, 109, 148–151; in Korea, 221–222; number of, 32–33, 70–71, 73, 80, 102–103, 109, 114; occupations, 48, 73–74, 102, 112–113, 165–168; officer training, 44, 102; officer placement, 109; at Pentagon, 166; racial integration, 52, 241; recruiting, 73, 75, 102, 113, 247–248; retention, 85–86, 112–113; Reserve, 103; scarcity of uniforms, 80–81, 102, 108; squadrons, 109; stateside, 43, 165; uniforms, 8, 53–54, 104, 111, 113

Women's Armed Services Integration Act (1948), 2, 5, 6, 97, 121, 220, 241; Congressional debate on, 22–29; enactment of, 29, 31; limitations on servicewomen's careers, 23, 29–30; limits on the numbers of servicewomen, 30; and the Marine Corps, 99–100; nucleus concept, 250; provisions of, 29–30; termination authority, 91; women not to command men, 48

Women's Army Corps (WAC): assignments, 93–94; basic training, 40, 92; 8225th WAC Detachment, 149; in Europe, 142–143, 155–159; in Japan, 10, 141, 146–148, 151; in Korea, 221–222; Integration Act of 1946, 21; Leadership School, 49; military occupational specialty (MOS), 11, 44, 92–93; number of, 32, 70, 73, 80, 92; Officer Candidate School, 39; in Okinawa, 153; racial integration, 49–51, 238–240; recruiting, 73, 80, 86, 92; Reservists, 91–92; retention, 85–86; Soldiers of the Month, 55–56; stateside, 162; Training Center, 41, 49; WAC Detach-

Women's Army Corps (WAC) *(continued)*
ment, 3rd Armored Division (Fort
Knox, Kentucky), 94; uniforms, 8, 40,
52–53
Weapons training, 40–41, 148; World War
II WAC, 14
Women's Liberation Movement, 4
Wonju (Korea), 203
Wonson (Korea), 189, 225
Woo, USA Major Theresa T. (M.D.), 133
Wood, USMC Chief Warrant Officer
Ruth, 102
World War II, 1, 4, 5–6, 14, 16, 17, 75;
Army nurses, 122, 125; Cadet Nurse
Corps, 58, 82; China–Burma–India
Theater, 198; Coast Guard Women's
Reserve (SPARs), 14, 33; demobili-
zation following, 13–14; lessons of,
69; Merrill's Marauders, 198; nurse
draft, 6; nurse POWs, 137; recruiting
women during, 115; relative rank, 22,
128; slander campaign, 83; Women's
Army Auxiliary Corps (WAAC), 23,
25, 107; WASP, 103; WAVES, 14, 27,
94, 96 108, 110; women service directors, 20
Wright-Patterson Air Force Base (Ohio),
51

Yachwan, USMC Staff Sergeant Anna:
reason for enlisting, 78, **78**; on sexual
harassment, 234–235

Yalu River (Korea), 189, 192
Yeomen (F) of WWI, 26, 46, 247
Yetman, USA Sergeant Dawn E. (Youells
Croshaw), 142
Yokohama (Japan), 218; African Ameri-
can servicewomen stationed at, 151–
152, 203; 121st Evacuation Hospital
sails from, 184; WAC detachments at,
146, 148
Yokosuka (Japan): air raid drills at, 200;
Marine casualties sent to, 193; Naval
Hospital at, 123; Navy nurse casualties
en route to, 218; Navy sends vessels
from, 253
Yokota Air Base (Japan), 10, 179
Yongdong (Korea), 173–174, 184, 201–
202
Yonpo Air Field (Korea), 194
Yorke, USANC Captain Eleanor E., 203

Zane, USANC Captain Margaret (Flem-
ing), **183**, 184, 196
Zeller, USAFNC Colonel Verena Pet-
toruto Seberg: career of, 125, **125**; with
DACOWITS, **79**; recruiting, 124–126;
shortage of flight nurses, 58
Zinn, USANC Lieutenant Neta, 172–173
Zoschak, USANC Major Mary, 176
Zoss, Ann (Roberts) (Department of the
Air Force Civilian), 226–227, **227**
Zuverink, USAFNC Lieutenant Agnes
(Norman), 214–215